Escape

Escape

AN ANTHOLOGY

EDITED AND INTRODUCED BY

MICHAEL MASON

CHATTO & WINDUS

LONDON

First published in 1996

1 3 5 7 9 10 8 6 4 2

Selection and Introduction copyright © Michael Mason 1996

Michael Mason has asserted his right under the Copyright,
Designs and Patents Act, 1988 to be identified
as the author of this work.

First published in Great Britain in 1996 by
Chatto & Windus Limited
Random House, 20 Vauxhall Bridge Road
London SW1V 2SA

Random House Australia (Pty) Limited
20 Alfred Street, Milsons Point, Sydney
New South Wales 2061, Australia

Random House New Zealand Limited
18 Poland Road, Glenfield
Auckland 10, New Zealand

Random House South Africa (Pty) Limited
PO Box 337, Bergvlei, South Africa

Random House UK Limited Reg. No. 954009

Papers used by Random House UK Limited are natural,
recyclable products made from wood grown in sustainable forests.
The manufacturing processes conform to the environmental
regulations of the country of origin

A CIP catalogue record for this book
is available from the British Library

ISBN 0 7011 6322 4

Designed by Humphrey Stone
Typeset by Deltatype Ltd, Ellesmere Port, Cheshire
Printed in Great Britain by
Mackays of Chatham PLC, Chatham, Kent.

CONTENTS

INTRODUCTION

The pieces which follow have been chosen for their power to entertain, to stir, to remind the reader of what humans can endure and what they can inflict. They had to be concise and vivid. Where real-life escape was involved, I looked for first-person descriptions. I have been obliged to leave out some memorable passages about escape which are not self-contained or brief enough to work on their own, and some memorable escapes of which there are, frustratingly, no sufficiently exciting descriptions. I have included nothing from Stevenson's *Kidnapped*, or from James Dickey's *Deliverance*, or from Lionel Davidson's *The Night of Wenceslas*, for instance, because in each of these novels the escaping is continuous. And although the escapes by, or due to Pandora, Elizabeth Barrett and Robert Browning, and Alfie Hinds are part of our communal lore of escape, none of them (as far as I know) is reported in single, strong description.

The last fact shows something important: that escape-stories sometimes have a vitality which exceeds any written account. They can also of course be transmitted in mediums other than the purely verbal: such as opera (*Fidelio*) or, very notably in this century, cinema. I wish there were written equivalents for the escapes in *King Kong*, *La Grande Illusion*, and *The Deerhunter* (and, indeed, that the novels on which Hitchcock's *The Thirty-Nine Steps* and *The Third Man* are based were as good as the films). Escape is itself an escaper, which cannot be restrained; it will force its way out in one medium or another, and often just in casual but perennial lore.

The written record of escape is, nonetheless, extraordinarily rich. Collecting material for the anthology, I have fished in teeming waters: wherever I cast my line there was beautiful and vigorous prey. And although an anthology like this cannot do full justice to the role of escape in the Western imagination over the last 2500 years, it is faithful to the past in implying that escape has at all periods been attempted energetically, and found admirable and exciting to contemplate when performed by other people, whether real or imaginary. When I started to explore the subject I knew that escape was a very persistent theme, but I have still been surprised to discover just how unquenchable it is. I had rather foreseen that I would encounter a degree of disapproval and silence about escape before the Renaissance, especially in the Christian Middle Ages – with perhaps a climax of enthusiasm for it in the Romantic era, with its Bastilles and Fidelios. I did not at that stage know Orderic Vitalis's reluctantly admiring account of the escape of the disgraceful Ranulph Flambard in the twelfth century, or how the chroniclers were fascinated by the escape of the Empress Mathilda from Oxford (see pages 347, 17).

In crude quantitative terms there is certainly a shortage of texts concerning escape before about 1800, compared with the modern situation. But the modern discursive situation – with its scores of memoirs of Second World War escape, for example – is peculiar, part of a fantastic pullulation of the written word on every aspect of human life. One becomes sharply aware, in tracing a branch of discourse such as this, of how printed publication has come in the last two hundred years to seem a normal dimension of any moderately interesting personal experience, as opposed to being an unusual, accidental dimension of even the most bizarre, as it was in earlier times. In this perspective, what we nowadays tend to regard as urgent self-expression, as inner experience transformed into public statement under the stress of its own intensity, looks more like a demand elicited by a supply – and the medium of print as something to be classed with the physical amenities and comforts of modern life for its power to create a need by offering its satisfaction.

In the barer textual scene of earlier times, people did write quite frequently about escape. Almost invariably acts of escaping, and the escapers, emerged in a good light. My intuition that things would be otherwise, in the Middle Ages at least, was based on the thought that escape from humanly contrived restraint (though not from restraint by natural forces) is always to some extent *transgressive*, if only by the standards of the restrainer. There are, it is true, various strategies for playing down the transgressiveness of escape. Was there a changing pattern in the resort to them, over time?

Two strategies in particular occur in many passages. Escapes can be legitimated: by presenting the captivity or restraint as unjust and oppressive, and the imprisoning party as cruel, tyrannical, and so forth. Or escapers can be rendered passive: by playing down any violence they may commit, and attributing their feats to a divine or other mysterious agency. A generalisation may be ventured that there was a shift in the handling of the transgressiveness of escape, over the centuries covered by this anthology, from the second strategy to the first: the passivity of Noah (page 47) gives way to the enterprise of Bligh (page 310), while the lack of grievance of Daniel (page 304) gives way to the righteous indignation of 'Papillon' (page 42).

But one may find dozens of exceptions to this rule: violent and resourceful escapes in the Bible, the classics, and medieval lore; modern accounts in which passivity is taken to the medieval-sounding extreme of a wholly *internal* escape from one's bonds (see pages 255, 259), or even in which God is taken to be directly involved (see page 241). My impression is that the transgressiveness of escape is something of a sideshow, even if most escape stories try to cope with it clearly enough. It adds lustre to an escape if it is not disturbingly transgressive, but such is the potency of the theme that people have not absolutely required this, at any period.

A strong indicator is the rarity of bad escapers in the literature, even though some escapes are baneful in their effects. It is Satan's courageous escape from Hell at the end of Book Two of *Paradise Lost* (page 177) which above all makes it difficult for us to disapprove of him, but this is also the start of his direct attack on mankind. Conversely, complaints about the immorality of escape are hardly to be encountered. Uncle Tom declines the chance of liberty if it involves killing Simon, but recommends escape to Cassy 'if ye could go without blood-guiltiness' – and she hits on a way of doing just this (see page 125). I have included in this anthology a handful of the many hundreds of notices collected in Lathan Windley's huge compilation *Runaway Slave Advertisements* (1983). I think the reader will agree that these announcements by slaveowners strike a deeply unfamiliar note. They are shocking for what they reveal about the inhumanity of slaveholding practices, of course, but also for their utter confidence in the depravity of escape, and in the rightness of recovery of the runaway – with subsequent shackling, flogging and branding. A prison governor is represented in the anthology (see page 125), a man by profession on the side of captivity, but he falls well short of these slaveowners of Virginia, South Carolina, Maryland and Georgia in his antagonism to escape.

Perhaps we admire escape because there is a core of denial in all of us that any person, or group of persons, is entitled to restrain another person. But I doubt if this is a universal factor in our admiration, if only because it cannot be part of what excites us in stories of escape from inanimate forces. Indeed, in general, it is probably wrong to look for a single, key ingredient in the human love of escape. Escape represents several other human goods: among them release from suffering, the fulfilment of hopes, and the successful exercise of physical and mental capacities. So our delight in it is overdetermined. Different people no doubt find different satisfactions in the spectacle of escape. There were some witnesses of Houdini's feats of escape (see pages 261, 333) who were convinced that he had exercised powers of telekinesis, despite his own perfectly explicit demonstrations of how these stunts had been pulled.

Those of a non-spiritualist persuasion in the audience, it is tempting to say, enjoyed the purely physical ingenuity involved in a Houdini escape – or did they? Do we enjoy conjuring tricks because great skill is on display – or rather because we seem to be witnessing the physically impossible? At the risk of violating my own principle that there are many satisfactions in escape, with no single essence to the matter, I would like to give a primacy to whatever it was that audiences felt at a Houdini performance in the early part of this century. These stunts were, after all, a kind of distillation of escape, escape isolated in the laboratory. And it may be that the audience reaction was more homogeneous than appears, that all were moved by a quality which the spiritualists just expressed leadenly and reductively as 'psycho-plastic'.

The first escape described in the pages which follow (it is the earliest surviving account of escape by an ordinary, non-legendary individual) involves the captors' incredulity at what strikes them as a physical impossibility. The soothsayer Hegesistratus has cut off part of his own foot to get it out of its shackle. He has transcended the supposed conditions of the material. Many of the passages thereafter deal with abandoned, thwarted, semi-successful, or ambiguous escapes. But in those which celebrate unreservedly an escape wholly achieved the note of the magical, of the dissolving of physical conditions, can be heard surprisingly often.

There are other motifs, sometimes quite down-to-earth, which recur in descriptions of escape. In this anthology I have arranged the passages so that each, to some extent, picks up a motif from the one before it. Because these motifs are so persistent it has proved easy to do what is always stimulating in a collection like this, namely, to juxtapose passages which differ widely in their historical settings and in their styles. The collection is also split up into a number of sections, which are meant to give the reader additional resting-points, rather than imply any classification of the subject. Even within each section I have, I hope, managed to create a high degree of variety-cum-continuity.

[ix]

The topics which keep appearing in the literature of escape are for the most part just a reflection of practicalities: of how people can be restrained, what they are likely to experience in restraint, and the possible means of getting free from restraint. Chains, woundings, keys, concealment, tunnels, ladders, disguises, despair, thoughts about God, weapons, violence, privation, fear, and speed, are all natural concomitants of being restrained and trying to do something about it. But it is clear that writers describing escapes, and even the men and women trying to escape, have also been mindful of precedents. Orderic Vitalis thought that Ranulph Flambard was like Daedalus, as did James Joyce about his younger self fleeing his island home (pages 347, 349). Joyce's *Portrait* is, admittedly, not really autobiography, and this comparison should perhaps be thought of as a fictional touch – more like Tom's comparing of himself to Daniel in the lions' den, in *Uncle Tom's Cabin* (page 127). But Gladys Aylward's young charges did, in real life, think of themselves as being like the Israelites crossing the Red Sea (page 84). Monica Baldwin, who left a nunnery in 1941 after twenty-eight years as a nun (see page 186), was very conscious that she was a descendant of Thomas Baldwin, a celebrated escaper from the Tower in 1585. She used the resulting family motto ('Per Deum meum transilio murum') in the title of her book about her experiences, *I Leapt Over the Wall* (Thomas Baldwin's feat is a case of a well-known escape of which I could not, unfortunately, find a vivid enough account). Henry Latude, legendary escaper from the Bastille, had a system of codewords for the apparatus of his escape, and he called the secret storage-space 'Polyphemus', 'in allusion to the den in the fable' (see page 161).

So the lore of escape has not necessarily been escapist in its role. Sometimes it seems to have prompted or encouraged practical escape. I trust that a closeness to reality, to personal possibilities, will also tinge the reader's experience of the anthology. Its pleasures, unquestionably, are mainly escapist, in the best sense: the pleasures of being transported into the worlds of other men and women in strange and interesting predicaments. But I hope that every now and then there will also be a bite, an extra edge of personal engagement, a response from the blood, in the effect these passages produce. Escape is, after all, one of the great themes of Western literature (though I don't think this fact has ever been fully recognised). As with the theme of love, its enduring vitality must mean that here tradition has managed to intersect, repeatedly, with human impulse.

ONE

'It seemed incredible, and yet – '

INSTEAD OF TORTURE

Hegesistratus, an Elean, and the most renowned of the Telliads, was Mardonius's soothsayer. This man had once been taken captive by the Spartans, who, considering that he had done them many grievous injuries, laid him in bonds, with the intent to put him to death. Thereupon Hegesistratus, finding himself in so sore a case, since not only was his life in danger, but he knew that he would have to suffer torments of many kinds before his death – Hegesistratus, I say, did a deed for which no words suffice. He had been set with one foot in the stocks, which were of wood but bound with iron bands; and in this condition received from without an iron implement, wherewith he contrived to accomplish the most courageous deed upon record. Calculating how much of his foot he would be able to draw through the hole, he cut off the front portion with his own hand; and then, as he was guarded by watchmen, forced a way through the wall of his prison, and made his escape to Tegea, travelling during the night, but in the daytime stealing into the woods, and staying there. In this way, though the Lacedæmonians went out in full force to search for him, he nevertheless escaped, and arrived the third evening at Tegea. So the Spartans were amazed at the man's endurance, when they saw on the ground the piece which he had cut off his foot, and yet for all their seeking could not find him anywhere. Hegesistratus, having thus escaped the Lacedæmonians, took refuge in Tegea; for the Tegeans at that time were ill friends with the Lacedæmonians. When his wound was healed, he procured himself a wooden foot, and became an open enemy to Sparta.

Herodotus, *History*, trans. George Rawlinson, 1858

BACK FOR FIVE DAYS

RUN away from the subscriber, the 19th of March, the mulatto fellow named PETER: he is about 5 feet 6 inches high, well set, and about 25 years old. The said slave run away once before, and was out upwards of a twelvemonth, he was brought home the 14th, on which day I branded him S on the cheek, and R on the other, though very probably he will endeavour to take them out, or deface them. I likewise had his hair cut off, which is long, when grown out, and very black. His greatest resort, during the time he was out before, was Petersburg, Chesterfield, Prince George, and as far as Roanoke, near Mush Island, and James river, passing as a free man, and working on board of vessels; I therefore hereby forewarn all masters of vessels, and others, from entertaining him, or carrying him out of the country. The said slave was raised in the upper part of Prince George, by one Mr Chambliss, of whom I bought him about 6 years ago. He has a brother belonging to Mr Dunlop, near Cabin Point, who I suspect harbour him; he has also several brothers and sisters in North Carolina. Whoever conveys him to me in Amelia, shall receive a reward of FIVE POUNDS, if taken an hundred miles from home, and in proportion for a less distance, including what the law allows.

SAMUEL SHERWIN

NB As Peter had not one article of the dress he went off in before, when he came home, I think it needless to describe that particular.

Virginia Gazette, 9 May 1771

A SOUPLE JADE

But *Tam* kend what was what fu' brawlie,
There was ae winsome wench and wawlie,
That night enlisted in the core,
(Lang after kend on *Carrick* shore;
For mony a beast to dead she shot,
And perish'd mony a bony boat,
And shook baith meikle corn and bear,
And kept the country-side in fear:)
Her cutty sark, o' Paisley harn,
That while a lassie she had worn,
In longitude tho' sorely scanty,
It was her best, and she was vauntie –
Ah! little kend thy reverend grannie,
That sark she coft for her wee Nannie,
Wi' twa pund Scots, ('twas a' her riches),
Wad ever grac'd a dance of witches!

But here my Muse her wing maun cour;

Sic flights are far beyond her pow'r;
To sing how Nannie lap and flang,
(A souple jade she was, and strang),
And how *Tam* stood, like ane bewitch'd,
And thought his very een enrich'd;
Even Satan glowr'd, and fidg'd fu' fain,
And hotch'd and blew wi' might and main:
Till first ae caper, syne anither,
Tam tint his reason a' thegither,
And roars out, 'Weel done, Cutty-sark!'
And in an instant all was dark:
And scarcely had he Maggie rallied,
When out the hellish legion sallied.

As bees bizz out wi' angry fyke,
When plundering herds assail their byke;
As open pussie's mortal foes,
When, pop! she starts before their nose;
As eager runs the market-crowd,
When 'Catch the thief!' resounds aloud;
So Maggie runs, the witches follow,
Wi' mony an eldritch skreech and hollow.

Ah, *Tam*! Ah, *Tam*! thou'll get thy fairin!
In hell they'll roast thee like a herrin!
In vain thy *Kate* awaits thy comin!
Kate soon will be a woefu' woman!
Now, do thy speedy utmost, Meg,
And win the key-stane of the brig;
There at them thou thy tail may toss,
A running stream they dare na cross,
But ere the key-stane she could make,
The fient a tail she had to shake!
For Nannie, far before the rest,
Hard upon noble Maggie prest,
And flew at *Tam* wi' furious ettle;
But little wist she Maggie's mettle –
Ae spring brought off her master hale,
But left behind her ain gray tail:
The carlin claught her by the rump,
And left poor Maggie scarce a stump.

Now, wha this tale o' truth shall read,
Ilk man and mother's son, take heed:
Whene'er to drink you are inclin'd,
Or cutty-sarks run in your mind,
Think, ye may buy the joys o'er dear,
Remember Tam o' Shanter's mare.

Robert Burns, 'Tam o'Shanter', 1790

ABOMINABLE SAFETY MATCHES

After the fatigues, excitements, and terrors of the past days, and in spite
of my grief, this seat and the tranquil view and the warm sunlight were
very pleasant. I was very tired and sleepy, and soon my theorising
passed into dozing. Catching myself at that, I took my own hint, and
spreading myself out upon the turf I had a long and refreshing sleep.

I awoke a little before sunsetting. I now felt safe against being caught
napping by the Morlocks, and, stretching myself, I came on down the
hill towards the White Sphinx. I had my crowbar in one hand, and the
other hand played with the matches in my pocket.

And now came a most unexpected thing. As I approached the
pedestal of the sphinx I found the bronze valves were open. They had
slid down into grooves.

At that I stopped short before them, hesitating to enter.

Within was a small apartment, and on a raised place in the corner of
this was the Time Machine. I had the small levers in my pocket. So here,
after all my elaborate preparations for the siege of the White Sphinx,
was a meek surrender. I threw my iron bar away, almost sorry not to
use it.

A sudden thought came into my head as I stooped towards the
portal. For once, at least, I grasped the mental operations of the
Morlocks. Suppressing a strong inclination to laugh, I stepped through
the bronze frame and up to the Time Machine. I was surprised to find it
had been carefully oiled and cleaned. I have suspected since that the
Morlocks had even partially taken it to pieces while trying in their dim
way to grasp its purpose.

Now as I stood and examined it, finding a pleasure in the mere touch
of the contrivance, the thing I had expected happened. The bronze

panels suddenly slid up and struck the frame with a clang. I was in the dark – trapped. So the Morlocks thought. At that I chuckled gleefully.

I could already hear their murmuring laughter as they came towards me. Very calmly I tried to strike the match. I had only to fix on the levers and depart like a ghost. But I had overlooked one little thing. The matches were of that abominable kind that light only on the box.

You may imagine how all my calm vanished. The little brutes were close upon me. One touched me. I made a sweeping blow in the dark at them with the levers, and began to scramble into the saddle of the machine. Then came one hand upon me and then another. Then I had simply to fight against their persistent fingers for my levers, and at the same time feel for the studs over which these fitted. One, indeed, they almost got away from me. As it slipped from my hand, I had to butt in the dark with my head – I could hear the Morlock's skull ring – to recover it. It was a nearer thing than the fight in the forest, I think, this last scramble.

But at last the lever was fixed and pulled over. The clinging hands slipped from me. The darkness presently fell from my eyes. I found myself in the same grey light and tumult I have already described.

H.G. Wells, The Time Machine, 1895

SKY

Theseus first fastened one end of his coil of string to a pointed rock, and then began to look about him. The labyrinth was dark, and he slowly walked, holding the string, down the broadest path, from which others turned off to right or left. He counted his steps, and he had taken near three thousand steps when he saw the pale sky showing in a small circle cut in the rocky roof, above his head, and he saw the fading stars. Sheer walls of rock went up on either hand of him, a roof of rock was above him, but in the roof was this one open place, across which were heavy bars. Soon the daylight would come.

Theseus set the lamp down on a rock behind a corner, and he waited, thinking, at a place where a narrow dark path turned at right angles to the left. Looking carefully round he saw a heap of bones, not human bones, but skulls of oxen and sheep, hoofs of oxen, and shank bones. 'This,' he thought, 'must be the place where the food of the Minotaur is let down to him from above. They have not Athenian youths and

maidens to give him every day! Beside his feeding place I will wait.'
Saying this to himself, he rose and went round the corner of the dark
narrow path cut in the rock to the left. He made his own breakfast,
from the food that Ariadne had given him, and it occurred to his mind
that probably the Minotaur might also be thinking of breakfast time.

He sat still, and from afar away within he heard a faint sound, like
the end of the echo of a roar, and he stood up, drew his long sword, and
listened keenly. The sound came nearer and louder, a strange sound,
not deep like the roar of a bull, but more shrill and thin. Theseus
laughed silently. A monster with the head and tongue of a bull, but
with the chest of a man, could roar no better than that! The sounds
came nearer and louder, but still with the thin sharp tone in them.
Theseus now took from his bosom the phial of gold that Medea had
given him in Athens when she told him about the Minotaur. He
removed the stopper, and held his thumb over the mouth of the phial,
and grasped his long sword with his left hand, after fastening the clue of
thread to his belt.

The roars of the hungry Minotaur came nearer and nearer; now his
feet could be heard padding along the echoing floor of the labyrinth.
Theseus moved to the shadowy corner of the narrow path, where it
opened into the broad light passage, and he crouched there; his heart
was beating quickly. On came the Minotaur, up leaped Theseus, and
dashed the contents of the open phial in the eyes of the monster; a white
dust flew out, and Theseus leaped back into his hiding place. The
Minotaur uttered strange shrieks of pain; he rubbed his eyes with his
monstrous hands; he raised his head up towards the sky, bellowing and
confused; he stood tossing his head up and down; he turned round and
round about, feeling with his hands for the wall. He was quite blind.
Theseus drew his short sword, crept up, on naked feet, behind the
monster, and cut through the back sinews of his legs at the knees.
Down fell the Minotaur, with a crash and a roar, biting at the rocky
floor with his lion's teeth, and waving his hands, and clutching at the
empty air. Theseus waited for his chance, when the clutching hands
rested, and then, thrice he drove the long sharp blade of bronze through
the heart of the Minotaur. The body leaped, and lay still.

Theseus kneeled down, and thanked all the gods, and promised rich
sacrifices, and a new temple to Pallas Athene, the Guardian of Athens.
When he had finished his prayer, he drew the short sword, and hacked
off the head of the Minotaur. He sheathed both his swords, took the
head in his hand, and followed the string back out of the daylit place, to
the rock where he had left his lamp. With the lamp and the guidance of

the string he easily found his way to the door, which he unlocked. He noticed that the thick bronze plates of the door were dinted and scarred by the points of the horns of the Minotaur, trying to force his way out.

Andrew Lang, Tales of Troy and Greece, 1907

'NOT PERSONALLY. HE HAS CANINO'

'I know who you are.'

Her very blue eyes flashed so sharply that I could almost see the sweep of their glance, like the sweep of a sword. Her mouth tightened. But her voice didn't change.

'Then I'm afraid you're in a bad spot. And I hate killing.'

'And you Eddie Mars' wife? Shame on you.'

She didn't like that. She glared at me. I grinned. 'Unless you can unlock these bracelets, which I'd advise you not to do, you might spare me a little of that drink you're neglecting.'

She brought the glass over. Bubbles rose in it like false hopes. She bent over me. Her breath was as delicate as the eyes of a fawn. I gulped from the glass. She took it away from my mouth and watched some of the liquid run down my neck.

She bent over me again. Blood began to move around in me, like a prospective tenant looking over a house.

'Your face looks like a collision mat,' she said.

'Make the most of it. It won't last long even this good.'

She swung her head sharply and listened. For an instant her face was pale. The sounds were only the rain drifting against the walls. She went back across the room and stood with her side to me, bent forward a little, looking down at the floor.

'Why did you come here and stick your neck out?' she asked quietly. 'Eddie wasn't doing you any harm. You know perfectly well that if I hadn't hid out here, the police would have been certain Eddie murdered Rusty Regan.'

'He did,' I said.

She didn't move, didn't change position an inch. Her breath made a harsh quick sound. I looked around the room. Two doors, both in the same wall, one half open. A carpet of red and tan squares, blue curtains at the windows, a wallpaper with bright green pine trees on it. The furniture looked as if it had come from one of those places that advertise on bus benches. Gay, but full of resistance.

She said softly: 'Eddie didn't do anything to him. I haven't seen Rusty in months. Eddie's not that sort of man.'

'You left his bed and board. You were living alone. People at the place where you lived identified Regan's photo.'

'That's a lie,' she said coldly.

I tried to remember whether Captain Gregory had said that or not. My head was too fuzzy. I couldn't be sure.

'And it's none of your business,' she added.

'The whole thing is my business. I'm hired to find out.'

'Eddie's not that sort of man.'

'Oh, you like racketeers.'

'As long as people will gamble there will be places for them to gamble.'

'That's just protective thinking. Once outside the law you're all the way outside. You think he's just a gambler. I think he's a pornographer, a blackmailer, a hot car broker, a killer by remote control, and a suborner of crooked cops. He's whatever looks good to him, whatever has the cabbage pinned to it. Don't try to sell me on any high-souled racketeers. They don't come in that pattern.'

'He's not a killer.' Her nostrils flared.

'Not personally. He has Canino. Canino killed a man tonight, a harmless little guy who was trying to help somebody out. I almost saw him killed.'

She laughed wearily.

'All right,' I growled. 'Don't believe it. If Eddie is such a nice guy, I'd like to get to talk to him without Canino around. You know what Canino will do – beat my teeth out and then kick me in the stomach for mumbling.'

She put her head back and stood there thoughtful and withdrawn, thinking something out.

'I thought platinum hair was out of style,' I bored on, just to keep sound alive in the room, just to keep from listening.

'It's a wig, silly. While mine grows out.' She reached up and yanked it off. Her own hair was clipped short all over, like a boy's. She put the wig back on.

'Who did that to you?'

She looked surprised. 'I had it done. Why?'

'Yes. Why?'

'Why, to show Eddie I was willing to do what he wanted me to do –

[8]

hide out. That he didn't need to have me guarded. I wouldn't let him down. I love him.'

'Good grief,' I groaned. 'And you have me right here in the room with you.'

She turned a hand over and stared at it. Then abruptly she walked out of the room. She came back with a kitchen knife. She bent and sawed at my rope.

'Canino has the key to the handcuffs,' she breathed. 'I can't do anything about those.'

She stepped back, breathing rapidly. She had cut the rope at every knot.

'You're a kick,' she said. 'Kidding with every breath – the spot you're in.'

'I thought Eddie wasn't a killer.'

She turned away quickly and went back to her chair by the lamp and sat down and put her face in her hands. I swung my feet to the floor and stood up. I tottered around, stiff-legged. The nerve on the left side of my face was jumping in all its branches. I took a step. I could still walk. I could run, if I had to.

'I guess you mean me to go,' I said.

She nodded without lifting her head.

'You'd better go with me – if you want to keep on living.'

'Don't waste time. He'll be back any minute.'

'Light a cigarette for me.'

I stood beside her, touching her knees. She came to her feet with a sudden lurch. Our eyes were only inches apart.

'Hello, Silver-Wig,' I said softly.

She stepped back, around the chair, and swept a package of cigarettes up off the table. She jabbed one loose and pushed it roughly into my mouth. Her hand was shaking. She snapped a small green leather lighter and held it to the cigarette. I drew in the smoke, staring into her lake-blue eyes. While she was still close to me I said:

'A little bird named Harry Jones led me to you. A little bird that used to hop in and out of cocktail bars picking up horse bets for crumbs. Picking up information too. This little bird picked up an idea about Canino. One way and another he and his friends found out where you were. He came to me to sell the information because he knew – how he knew is a long story – that I was working for General Sternwood. I got his information, but Canino got the little bird. He's a dead little bird now, with his feathers ruffled and his neck limp and a pearl of blood on his beak. Canino killed him. But Eddie Mars wouldn't do that, would he, Silver-Wig? He never killed anybody. He just hires it done.'

'Get out,' she said harshly. 'Get out of here quick.'

Her hand clutched in midair on the green lighter. The fingers strained. The knuckles were as white as snow.

'But Canino doesn't know I know that,' I said. 'About the little bird. All he knows is I'm nosing around.'

Then she laughed. It was almost a racking laugh. It shook her as the wind shakes a tree. I thought there was puzzlement in it, not exactly surprise, but as if a new idea had been added to something already known and it didn't fit. Then I thought that was too much to get out of a laugh.

'It's very funny,' she said breathlessly. 'Very funny, because, you see – I still love him. Women –' She began to laugh again.

I listened hard, my head throbbing. Just the rain still. 'Let's go,' I said. 'Fast.'

She took two steps back and her face set hard. 'Get out, you! Get out! You can walk to Realito. You can make it – and you can keep your mouth shut – for an hour or two at least. You owe me that much.'

'Let's go,' I said. 'Got a gun, Silver-Wig?'

'You know I'm not going. You know that. Please, please get out of here quickly.'

I stepped up close to her, almost pressing against her. 'You're going to stay here after turning me loose? Wait for that killer to come back so you can say so sorry? A man who kills like swatting a fly. Not much. You're going with me, Silver-Wig.'

'No.'

'Suppose,' I said thinly, 'your handsome husband *did* kill Regan? Or suppose Canino did, without Eddie's knowing it. Just suppose. How long will *you* last, after turning me loose?'

'I'm not afraid of Canino. I'm still his boss's wife.'

'Eddie's a handful of mush,' I snarled. 'Canino would take him with a teaspoon. He'll take him the way the cat took the canary. A handful of mush. The only time a girl like you goes for a wrong gee is when he's a handful of mush.'

'Get out!' she almost spit at me.

'Okey.' I turned away from her and moved out through the half-open door into a dark hallway. Then she rushed after me and pushed past to the front door and opened it. She peered out into the wet blackness and listened. She motioned me forward.

'Good-by,' she said under her breath. 'Good luck in everything but one thing. Eddie didn't kill Rusty Regan. You'll find him alive and well somewhere, when he wants to be found.'

I leaned against her and pressed her against the wall with my body. I pushed my mouth against her face. I talked to her that way.

'There's no hurry. All this was arranged in advance, rehearsed to the last detail, timed to the split second. Just like a radio program. No hurry at all. Kiss me, Silver-Wig.'

Her face under my mouth was like ice. She put her hands up and took hold of my head and kissed me hard on the lips. Her lips were like ice, too.

I went out through the door and it closed behind me, without sound, and the rain blew in under the porch, not as cold as her lips.

Raymond Chandler, The Big Sleep, 1939

A STRANGER AT LAST

Tuesday, June 23rd

> 'Do I sleep? do I dream?
> Do I wonder and doubt?
> Are things what they seem?
> Or is visions about?'

What has happened? I can still scarcely grasp it. How incessant are the vicissitudes in this wandering life! A few days ago swimming in the water for dear life, attacked by walrus, living the savage life which I have lived for more than a year now, and sure of a long journey before us, over ice and sea, through unknown regions, before we should meet with other human beings – a journey full of the same ups and downs, the same disappointments, that we have become so accustomed to – and now living the life of a civilised European, surrounded by everything that civilisation can afford of luxury and good living, with abundance of water, soap, towels, clean, soft woollen clothes, books, and everything that we have been sighing for all these weary months.

It was past midday on June 17th when I turned out to prepare breakfast. I had been down to the edge of the ice to fetch salt water, had made up the fire, cut up the meat, and put it in the pot, and had already taken off one boot preparatory to creeping into the bag again, when I saw that the mist over the land had risen a little since the preceding day. I thought it would be as well to take the opportunity of having a look round, so I put on my boot again, and went up on to a hummock near to look at the land beyond. A gentle breeze came from the land, bearing with it a confused noise of thousands of bird-voices from the mountain there. As I listened to these sounds of life and movement, watched flocks of auks flying to and fro above my head, and as my eye followed the line of coast, stopping at the dark, naked cliffs, glancing at the cold, icy plains and glaciers in a land which I believed to be unseen by any human eye and untrodden by any human foot, reposing in arctic majesty behind its mantle of mist – a sound suddenly reached my ear, so like the barking of a dog, that I started. It was only a couple of barks, but it could not be anything else. I strained my ears, but heard no more, only the same bubbling noise of thousands of birds. I must have been mistaken, after all; it was only birds I had heard; and again my eye passed from sound to island in the west. Then the barking came again, first single barks, then full cry; there was one deep bark, and one sharper; there was no longer any room for doubt. At that moment, I remembered having heard two reports the day before, which I thought sounded like shots, but I had explained them away as noises in the ice. I now shouted to Johansen that I heard dogs farther inland. Johansen started up from the bag where he lay sleeping, and tumbled out of the tent. 'Dogs?' He could not quite take it in, but had to get up and listen with his own ears, while I got breakfast ready. He very much doubted the possibility of such a thing, yet fancied once or twice that he heard something which might be taken for the barking of dogs; but then it was drowned again in the bird-noises, and, everything considered, he thought that what I had heard was nothing more than that. I said he might believe what he liked, but I meant to set off as quickly as possible, and was impatient to get breakfast swallowed. I had emptied the last of the Indian meal into the soup, feeling sure that we should have farinaceous food enough by the evening. As we were eating we discussed who it could be, whether our countrymen or Englishmen. If it was the English expedition to Franz Josef Land which had been in contemplation when we started, what should we do? 'Oh, we'll just have to remain with them a day or two,' said Johansen, 'and then we'll have to go on to Spitzbergen, else it will be too long before we get home.' We were quite agreed on this point; but we would take care to get some good provisions for the voyage out of them. While I went on, Johansen was to stay behind and mind the kayaks, so that we should run no risk of their drifting away with the ice. I got out my snowshoes, glass, and gun, and was ready. Before starting, I went up once more to listen, and look out a road across the uneven ice to the land. But there was not a sound like the barking of dogs, only noisy auks, harsh-toned little auks, and screaming kittiwakes. Was it these, after all, that I had heard? I set off in doubt. Then in front of me I saw the fresh tracks of an animal. They could hardly have been made by a fox, for if they were, the foxes here must be bigger than any I had ever seen. But dogs? Could a dog have been no more than a few hundred paces from us in the night without barking, or without our having heard it? It seemed scarcely probable; but whatever it was, it could never have been a fox. A wolf, then? I went on, my mind full of strange thoughts, hovering between certainty and doubt. Was all our toil, were all our troubles, privations, and sufferings, to end here? It seemed incredible, and yet— Out of the shadowland of doubt, certainty was at last beginning to dawn. Again the sound of a dog yelping reached my ear, more distinctly than ever; I saw more and more tracks which could be nothing but those of a dog. Among them were foxes' tracks and how small they looked! A long time passed, and nothing was to be heard but the noise of the birds. Again arose doubt as to whether it was all an illusion. Perhaps it was only a dream. But then I remembered the dogs' tracks; they, at any rate, were no delusion. But if there were people here, we could scarcely be on Gillies Land or a new land, as we had believed all the winter. We must after all be upon the south side of Franz Josef Land, and the suspicion I had had a few days ago was correct, namely, that we had come south through an unknown sound and out between Hooker Island and Northbrook Island, and were now off the latter, in spite of the impossibility of reconciling our position with Payer's map.

It was with a strange mixture of feelings that I made my way in towards land among the numerous hummocks and inequalities. Suddenly I thought I heard a shout from a human voice, a strange voice, the first for three years. How my heart beat, and the blood rushed to my brain, as I ran up on to a hummock, and hallooed with all the strength of my lungs. Behind that one human voice in the midst of the icy desert, this one message from life, stood home and she who was waiting there; and I saw nothing else as I made my way between bergs and ice-ridges. Soon I heard another shout, and saw, too, from an ice-ridge, a dark form moving among the hummocks farther in. It was a dog; but farther off came another figure, and that was a man. Who was it? Was it Jackson or one of his companions, or was it perhaps a fellow-countryman? We approached one another quickly; I waved my hat: he did the same. I heard him speak to the dog, and I listened. It was English, and as I drew nearer I thought I recognised Mr Jackson, whom I remembered once to have seen.

I raised my hat; we extended a hand to one another, with a hearty 'How do you do?'

Fridtjof Nansen, 'Farthest North', 1897

BLACK ICE

It was after midnight when we drove out, and, the conditions being good, the drive over the sea to a point well along the Finnish coast, a distance of some forty-odd miles, was to take us between four and five hours. The sledge was of the type known as *drovny*, a wooden one, broad and low, filled with hay. The *drovny*, used mostly for farm haulage, is my favourite kind of sledge, and nestling comfortably at full length under the hay I thought of long night-drives in the interior in days gone by, when someone used to ride ahead on horseback with a torch to keep away the wolves.

In a moment we were out, flying at breakneck speed across the ice, windswept after recent storms. The half-inch of frozen snow just gave grip to the horse's hoofs. Twice, suddenly bumping into snow ridges, we capsized completely. When we got going again the runners sang just like a saw-mill. The driver noticed this too, and was alive to the danger of being heard from shore a couple of miles away; but his sturdy pony, exhilarated by the keen frosty air, was hard to restrain.

Some miles out of Petrograd there lies on an island in the Finnish Gulf the famous fortress of Cronstadt, one of the most impregnable in the world. Searchlights from the fortress played from time to time across the belt of ice, separating the fortress from the northern shore. The passage through this narrow belt was the crucial point in our journey. Once past Cronstadt we should be in Finnish waters and safe.

To avoid danger from the searchlights, the Finn drove within a mile of the mainland, the runners hissing and singing like saws. As we entered the narrows a dazzling beam of light swept the horizon from the fortress, catching us momentarily in its track; but we were sufficiently near the shore not to appear as a black speck adrift on the ice.

Too near, perhaps? The dark line of the woods seemed but a stone's throw away! You could almost see the individual trees. Hell! what a noise our sledge-runners made!

'Can't you keep the horse back a bit, man?'

'Yes, but this is the spot we've *got* to drive past quickly!'

We were crossing the line of Lissy Nos, a jutting point on the coast marking the narrowest part of the strait. Again a beam of light shot out from the fortress, and the wooden pier and huts of Lissy Nos were lit as by a flash of lightning. But we had passed the point already. It was rapidly receding into the darkness as we regained the open sea.

Sitting upright on the heap of hay, I kept my eyes riveted on the receding promontory. We were nearly a mile away now, and you could no longer distinguish objects clearly. But my eyes were still riveted on the rocky promontory.

Were those rocks – moving? I tried to pierce the darkness, my eyes rooted to the black point!

Rocks? Trees? Or – or—

I sprang to my feet and shook the Finn by the shoulders with all my force.

'Damn it, man! Drive like hell – we're being pursued!'

Riding out from Lissy Nos was a group of horsemen, five or six in number. My driver gave a moan, lashed his horse, the sledge leapt forward, and the chase began in earnest.

'Ten thousand marks if we escape!' I yelled in the Finn's ear.

For a time we kept a good lead, but in the darkness it was impossible to see whether we were gaining or losing. My driver was making low moaning cries, he appeared to be pulling hard on the reins, and the sledge jerked so that I could scarcely stand.

Then I saw that the pursuers were gaining – and gaining rapidly! The moving dots grew into figures galloping at full speed. Suddenly there was a flash and a crack, then another, and another. They were firing with carbines, against which a pistol was useless. I threatened the driver with my revolver if he did not pull ahead, but dropped like a stone into the hay as a bullet whizzed close to my ear.

At that moment the sledge suddenly swung round. The driver had clearly had difficulty with his reins, which appeared to have got caught in the shaft, and before I realised what was happening the horse fell, the sledge whirled round and came to a sudden stop.

At such moments one has to think rapidly. What would the pursuing Red guards go for first, a fugitive? Not if there was possible loot. And what more likely than that the sledge contained loot?

Eel-like, I slithered over the side and made in the direction of the shore. Progress was difficult, for there were big patches of ice, coal-black in colour, which were completely windswept and as slippery as glass. Stumbling along, I drew from my pocket a packet, wrapped in dark brown paper, containing maps and documents which were sufficient, if discovered, to assure my being shot without further ado, and held it ready to hurl away across the ice.

If seized, I would plead smuggling. It seemed impossible that I should escape! Looking backward I saw the group round the sledge. The Reds, dismounted, were examining the driver; in a moment they would renew the pursuit, and I should be spotted at once, running over the ice.

Then an idea occurred.

The ice, where completely windswept, formed great patches as black as ink. My clothes were dark. I ran into the middle of a big patch and looked at my boots. I could not see them!

To get to the shore was impossible, anyway, so this was the only chance. Jerking the packet a few yards from me where I might easily find it, I dropped flat on the black ice and lay motionless, praying that I should be invisible.

It was not long before I heard the sound of hoofs and voices approaching. The search for me had begun. But the riders avoided the slippery windswept places as studiously as I had done in running, and, thank heaven! just there much of the ice was windswept. As they rode round and about, I felt that someone was bound to ride just over me! Yet they didn't, after all.

It seemed hours and days of night and darkness before the riders retreated to the sledge and rode off with it, returning whence they had come. But time is measured not by degrees of hope or despair, but by fleeting seconds and minutes, and by my luminous watch I detected that it was only half-past one. Prosaic half-past one!

Was the sombre expanse of frozen sea really deserted? Cronstadt loomed dimly on the horizon, the dark line of woods lay behind me, and all was still as death – except for the sea below, groaning and gurgling as if the great ice-burden were too heavy to bear.

Slowly and imperceptibly I rose, first on all fours, then kneeling, and finally standing upright. The riders and the sledge were gone, and I was alone. Only the stars twinkled, as much as to say: 'It's all over! 'Twas a narrow squeak, wasn't it? but a miss is as good as a mile!'

Paul Dukes, *Red Dusk and the Morrow*, 1922

The Countess of Anjou, always betraying a fierce and inflexible temper, though she had been much shaken and almost worn to death by the retreat from Winchester, no sooner found herself in safety and recovered her strength, than, with a strong body of troops, she moved to Oxford, which was well affected to her cause. Encouraging and supporting her friends in opposition to the king, she sent out several troops of horse to scour the country, she stirred up those who owed her fealty, both by her letters and messengers, to furnish all possible aid, and she strengthened the castles by all the means in her power, some to control the royalists with more effect, others more thoroughly to protect her own dependents. One of these, at Woodstock, was the favourite seat of privacy and retirement of King Henry; another was at the village of Radcot? surrounded by marshes, and inaccessible on account of the waters; a third was at Cirencester close to the abbey of monks, like another Dagon near the ark of the Lord; a fourth was in the village of Benton in the church tower, an ancient structure of admirable design, and of massive and most skilful architecture; with some others which in various parts of England she permitted her adherents to fortify. In these were planted the seeds of the grievous oppression of the people, of the universal devastation of the kingdom, and of the wars and insurrections which sprung up on all sides.

King Stephen becoming aware of this, and, as it were, roused from sleep and waking to life and new activity, summoned his adherents, with whom were joined a strong band of his standing army, and came suddenly to Cirencester. Finding the castle deserted, for the guards had dispersed and concealed themselves, he set it on fire, and razing the wall and outworks to the ground, continued his march to Benton, taking the one by storm, the other by voluntary surrender. Like Cæsar, he 'thought nothing done while aught was left undone,' and he therefore proceeded from thence to Oxford boldly to try issues with the Countess of Anjou. Oxford is a place strongly fortified, and almost inaccessible from the deep waters which flow round it; on one side it is narrowly guarded by a wall and ditch, on the other by an impregnable castle with a lofty keep of great strength and stateliness.

Here the countess had established herself with a gallant body of men-at-arms in false security, relying on her possessing the castle and all the neighbouring country, and on the strength of the position which adds to an enemy's glory, when the king with a numerous body of veteran soldiers suddenly took his ground on the opposite side of the river. Seeing the enemy running in crowds from the city to observe him, some assailing him and his people with abuse across the river, and others, shaking their arrows out of their quivers, sharply annoying them over the water, he crossed the river by an ancient and very deep ford which was pointed out to him. He boldly plunged into the stream himself at the head of his troops, and, swimming rather than wading across, they charged the enemy with impetuosity, driving them back to the city gates after a sharp engagement. The rest of his troops had now crossed the river, and, being formed in one column, the whole advanced against the enemy, who, flying through the open gates into the city, and the royalists being mingled with them, found themselves within the walls without opposition, and, throwing firebrands among the houses, obtained a signal success. None escaped suffering the consequences of this severe disaster; those who resisted either fell by the sword or were fettered and reserved for ransom; some had again to hide themselves in the coverts which had lately sheltered them; and others, with their lady, in all haste shut themselves up in the castle.

After this success, the king pressed the siege of the countess and her followers in the castle with the utmost vigour; perceiving clearly that the civil wars would be brought to a close, if he were able to subdue her with whom they originated. He therefore posted vigilant guards from place to place round the castle, with orders to keep a strict watch on all the avenues by day and by night. Three months he was detained before it with a large force, and the garrison were reduced to great extremities by famine. But blind man is unconscious of what the providence of God determines; for the design which the king was bent on manfully accomplishing, the Almighty frustrated. It was the king's purpose to press the siege until the countess became his prisoner; but notwithstanding the host of the besiegers, and the sentries carefully posted round the castle, and watching in the dead of the night, she escaped out of it uninjured in an extraordinary way. For provisions and the means of subsistence beginning to fail in the garrison, and the king exhausting every effort to reduce it by violent assaults and by his military engines, she became much straightened, and despairing of any relief coming from without, she issued forth one night, attended only by three knights chosen for their wary prudence. The ground was white with snow, which lay deep over the whole country, the rivers were frozen hard, and for six miles she and her companions had to make their toilsome way, on foot, over snow and ice. What was very remarkable, and indeed truly miraculous, she crossed dry-shod, and without wetting her garments, the very waters into which the king and his troops had plunged up to the neck on their advance to attack the city; she passed too through the royal posts, while the silence of night was broken all around, by the clang of trumpets and the cries of the guard, without losing a single man of her escort, and observed only by one man of the king's troops who had been wrought with to favour her escape. Having thus got out of the castle undiscovered and unmolested, she reached Wallingford in the course of the night, after a very toilsome journey. I know not whether it was for her future elevation to the highest honour, or whether, by the judgment of God, to aggravate the distress of the kingdom, but certainly I have never heard of any woman having such marvellous escapes from so many enemies threatening her life, and from such exceeding perils.

The Acts of Stephen, trans. Thomas Forester, 1853

At this time king Stephen, hearing that the empress was at Oxford Castle with a small retinue, collected a numerous army, and, marching thither after Michaelmas, besieged that fortress until Advent. The empress, seeing that for so long a time none of her friends came to her assistance, played off a woman's trick upon king Stephen, and escaped by night over the river Thames, which was frozen, dressed in white, and attended by a few companions, and so escaped, for the enemy could not see her, on account of the dazzling of the snow, and the similarity of colour between it and her clothes.

Roger of Wendover's Flowers of History, trans. J.A. Giles, 1849

2,305 MILES

The new year, 1846, had come, and I was resolved to accomplish my purpose in the winter, since I had twice failed in the summer. I had learned that a great fair was held annually at Irbit (in the Perm gubernium) during February, and that the immense traffic on the roads thither quite prevented any official supervision of travellers. I resolved to go to this fair, and taking the shortest of the five roads at my disposal, proceed thence to Archangel.

A periodical, entitled *La Russie Pittoresque*, had some time previously been commenced at St Petersburg. It embraced a geographical, archæological, and statistical description of the empire, on the plan of *La France Pittoresque*. Fortunately the Archangel gubernium was given in the first part, accompanied by a map. I obtained this, and learnt that not less than 4,000 or 5,000 merchant vessels, nearly all from foreign countries, visit this great northern port every year. I trusted that once in Archangel, I could easily secure a passage in one of these, and my difficulties would be overcome. There were, however, 2,305 miles between me and the port. February came, and Shrove-tide was early that year; those feasted and made merry in its honour who would. I had quite other matters to occupy me. The nearer the moment of my deliverance came, the more resolutely I kept guard over myself; even in the presence of my dearest friends, I refrained from any expressions of discontent, until they all thought Siberia was far more endurable to me than it once had been.

As my baldness was especially noted down in my signalement, I determined to manufacture a wig. I succeeded in producing one, and of a true Siberian type. It was made of an undressed goatskin, and the tangled hair very well represented unkempt human locks, and would be very comfortable against the cold.

Having at length secured, with no little difficulty and patience, all the requisites for my journey, I resolved on the evening of the second day from Shrove Tuesday to bid adieu to the place of my long sojourn. I cannot describe the feelings which possessed my mind up to the final moment, nor could they be understood by any one who has not been placed in a similar position.

The evening had far advanced as I completed my preparations. I put on three Siberian shirts – the outer one coloured – a waistcoat of coarse blue cloth, two pairs of drawers, wide cloth trowsers, a short sheep-skin wrapper reaching to the knee and well seasoned with tallow, an armiak, a great sheep-skin cloak, two pairs of woollen stockings bound fast with cloth bands, and a long black, red and white striped scarf round my waist; I donned my wig, and as it exhibited a tendency to slip aside, tied it fast with a handkerchief, which at the same time protected my ears; above it came a round velvet cap, bordered with fur, such as Siberian peasants wear on festivals. I turned up the collar of my great cloak and secured that also with a handkerchief to keep the cold from my cheeks. Thus accoutred, I packed up a pair of new lighter boots, a shirt, a pair of Russian blue summer trowsers, my blue pocket-book which accompanied me from France, and a supply of bread and fish. I stuffed my trowsers well into my boots, Russian fashion, and concealed the clasp-knife in the same receptacle, so that I might have it always in readiness in case of danger. I had 190 paper notes of five and ten roubles. My hands were well protected with stout fur gloves, and I added a thick stick to complete my costume. It would have been scarcely possible for anyone to recognise me in this disguise, especially as I had never been seen in a dress of the kind. I commended myself to God's protection, prayed for strength and endurance, and about ten o'clock at night on the 6th or 8th of February, 1846, turned my back on the place where for seventeen months I had endured such unutterable weariness.

My heart throbbed fast with hope and fear, not for my life, but for the success of my plan. It was intensely cold; the winter was a harder one than had been known, even in Siberia, for many years, and the snow lay unusually deep. The moonlight fell bright and pale on the great snow-fields and silvered all the frozen atoms of the air. I passed the Irtisch, my rubicon, on the ice, and hurried on the road towards Tara as fast as my heavy garments permitted. Siberian winter nights are very long, there was no chance of pursuit until the morning, and in this lay my chief reliance, for I could certainly get over a great deal of ground before daylight. What the end would be I could not know; but God had given me no craven's heart, and come what might I was prepared.

Let the worst happen, I thought, if it must be so; it can be but the worst, and so I hastened on to Tara, about nine miles distant. I had not gone far when I heard a sledge approaching from behind, and in another moment it had drawn up close to me, and the driver cried, without further preface:

'Where are you going?'

'To Tara.'

'And where do you come from?'

'From Zalivina' (this was a village not far from the distillery).

'I'll take you to Tara for sixty kopeks.'

'I'll give you fifty.'

'That'll do, jump in!'

And on we rushed as though the horses were pursued by wolves. In half an hour we had reached Tara. I got down, paid my fare, and pursued my way to the first house I could see; and, according to the custom of the country, shouted under the windows, 'Any horses here?'

'Where to?'

'To Irbit – for the great fair.'

'How many?'

'A pair – and how much the verst?'

'Eight kopeks.'

'Too much. I'll give six.'

'All right.'

In a few minutes the horses were harnessed to a sledge, and we were ready to start. My driver asked:

'Where may you come from?'

'From Tomsk. My master has gone on ahead; I've been detained by all sorts of business, so I must make up for the lost time, or it will be the worse for me, as I have to go back with him; if you look sharp you shall have a glass of brandy into the bargain.'

Rufin Piotrowski, *Escape from Siberia*, trans. 'E.S.', 1863

GASSING AGAIN

Toad eagerly scrambled into the seat vacated by the driver, took the steering-wheel in his hands, listened with affected humility to the instructions given him, and set the car in motion, but very slowly and carefully at first, for he was determined to be prudent.

The gentlemen behind clapped their hands and applauded, and Toad heard them saying, 'How well she does it! Fancy a washerwoman driving a car as well as that, the first time!'

Toad went a little faster; then faster still, and faster.

He heard the gentlemen call out warningly, 'Be careful, washerwoman!' And this annoyed him, and he began to lose his head.

The driver tried to interfere, but he pinned him down in his seat with one elbow, and put on full speed. The rush of air in his face, the hum of the engine, and the light jump of the car beneath him intoxicated his weak brain. 'Washerwoman, indeed!' he shouted recklessly. 'Ho, ho! I am the Toad, the motor-car snatcher, the prison-breaker, the Toad who always escapes! Sit still and you shall know what driving really is, for you are in the hands of the famous, the skilful, the entirely fearless Toad!'

With a cry of horror the whole party rose and flung themselves on him. 'Seize him!' they cried, 'seize the Toad, the wicked animal who stole our motor-car! Bind him, chain him, drag him to the nearest police-station. Down with the desperate and dangerous Toad!'

Alas! they should have thought, they ought to have been more prudent, they should have remembered to stop the motor-car somehow before playing any pranks of that sort. With a half-turn of the wheel the Toad sent the car crashing through the low hedge that ran along the roadside. One mighty bound, a violent shock, and the wheels of the car were churning up the thick mud of a horse-pond.

Toad found himself flying through the air with the strong upward rush and delicate curve of a swallow. He liked the motion, and was just beginning to wonder whether it would go on until he developed wings and turned into a Toad-bird, when he landed on his back with a thump, in the soft, rich grass of a meadow. Sitting up, he could just see the motor-car in the pond, nearly submerged; the gentlemen and the driver, encumbered by their long coats, were floundering helplessly in the water.

He picked himself up rapidly, and set off running across country as hard as he could, scrambling through hedges, jumping ditches, pounding across fields, till he was breathless and weary, and had to settle down into an easy walk. When he had recovered his breath somewhat, and was able to think calmly, he began to giggle, and from giggling he took to laughing, and he laughed till he had to sit down under a hedge. 'Ho, ho!' he cried, in ecstasies of self-admiration, 'Toad, again! Toad, as usual comes out on the top! Who was it got them to give him a lift! Who managed to get on the front seat for the sake of fresh air? Who persuaded them into letting him see if he could drive? Who landed them all in a horse-pond? Who escaped, flying gaily and unscathed through the air, leaving the narrow-minded, grudging, timid excursionists in the mud where they should rightly be? Why, Toad, of course; clever Toad, great Toad, *good* Toad!'

Then he burst into song again, and chanted with uplifted voice:

'The motor-car went Poop-poop-poop,
    As it raced along the road.
Who was it steered it into a pond?
    Ingenious Mr Toad!

O, how clever I am! How clever, how clever how very clev—'

A slight noise at a distance behind him made him turn his head and look. O horror! O misery! O despair!

About two fields off, a chauffeur in his leather gaiters and two large rural policemen were visible, running towards him as hard as they could go!

Poor Toad sprang to his feet and pelted away again, his heart in his mouth. 'O my!' he gasped, as he panted along, 'what an *ass* I am! What a *conceited* and heedless ass! Swaggering again! Shouting and singing songs again! Sitting still and gassing again. O my! O my! O my!'

He glanced back, and saw to his dismay that they were gaining on him. On he ran desperately, but kept looking back and saw that they still gained steadily. He did his best, but he was a fat animal, and his legs were short, and still they gained. He could hear them close behind him now. Ceasing to heed where he was going, he struggled on blindly and wildly, looking back over his shoulder at the now triumphant enemy, when suddenly the earth failed under his feet, he grasped at the air, and, splash! he found himself head over ears in deep water, rapid water, water that bore him along with a force he could not contend with; and he knew that in his blind panic he had run straight into the river!

He rose to the surface and tried to grasp the reeds and the rushes that grew along the water's edge close under the bank, but the stream was so strong that it tore them out of his hands. 'O my!' gasped poor Toad, 'if ever I steal a motor-car again! If ever I sing another conceited song' – then down he went, and came up breathless and spluttering. Presently he saw that he was approaching a big dark hole in the bank, just above his head, and as the stream bore him past he reached up with a paw and caught hold of the edge and held on. Then slowly and with difficulty he drew himself up out of the water, till at last he was able to rest his elbows on the edge of the hole. There he remained for some minutes, puffing and panting, for he was quite exhausted.

As he sighed and blew and stared before him into the dark hole, some bright small thing shone and twinkled in its depths, moving towards him. As it approached a face grew up gradually around it, and it was a familiar face!

Brown and small, with whiskers.

Grave and round, with neat ears and silky hair.

It was the Water Rat!

Kenneth Grahame, *The Wind in the Willows*, 1908

In a miserable bar, which I had entered to fortify myself, I was only able to get warm stout and one piece of cake. Everything else had been consumed, and when the bar closed I was again on the street. I turned into an aristocratic lane where beautiful mansions were surrounded by carefully tended gardens. I was hardly able to stand on my feet, and at the first favourable moment I jumped with quick decision over one of the garden fences and hid myself in a thick box hedge, only a foot away from the pavement. It is difficult to describe my state of mind. My pulses were hammering, and thoughts raced wildly through my tired brain. Wrapped in my mackintosh, I lay in my hiding-place, stealthily – like a thief.

If anyone had found me here in this dreadful situation – me, a German officer! I felt like a criminal, and in my heart I was firmly resolved never to disclose to anyone the details of my despicable adventure. Oh, had I known then where I should soon have to hang about at night, and even find nothing odd in it, I should have felt my position less keenly!

After I had lain for about an hour in my refuge, the French window of the house, leading to a beautiful veranda, opened, and several ladies and gentlemen in evening dress came out to enjoy the coolness of the night. I could see them and hear every word. Soon the sounds of a piano mingled with those of a splendid soprano voice, and the most wonderful songs of Schubert overwhelmed my soul with longing.

At last total exhaustion prevailed, and I slept heavily, seeing in my mind the most beautiful pictures of the future.

Next morning I was awakened by the regular heavy tread of a policeman who marched up and down the street, quite close to where I lay, with the bright, warm rays of the sun shining down upon me.

So after all I had overslept – it behoved me to be careful. The policeman ambled idiotically up and down without dreaming of departure. At last fortune favoured me. An enchanting little lady's maid opened the door, and hey presto! the policeman was at her side, playfully conversing with the pretty dear.

Without being seen by either, with a quick motion I vaulted over the fence into the street. It was already six o'clock, and Hyde Park was just being opened. As the Underground was not yet running, I went into the Park and dropped full length on a bench, near to other vagabonds who had made themselves comfortable there. I then pulled my hat over my face and slept profoundly until nine o'clock.

With fresh strength and courage I entered the Underground, and was carried to the harbour area. In the Strand huge, yellow posters attracted my attention, and who can describe my astonishment when I read on them, printed in big, fat letters, that:

(1) Mr Trefftz had been recaptured the evening before; (2) Mr Plüschow was still at large; but that (3) the police were already on his track.

The first and the third items were news; but I knew all about the second. I promptly bought a newspaper, went into a tea-shop, where I read with great interest the following notice:

Extra Late War Edition
HUNT FOR ESCAPED GERMAN
High-pitched Voice as a Clue

Scotland Yard last night issued the following amended description of Gunther Plüschow, one of the German prisoners who escaped from Donington Hall, Leicestershire, on Monday:

Height, 5 feet 5½ inches; weight, 135 lb.; complexion, fair; hair, blond; eyes, blue; and tattoo marks: Chinese dragon on left arm.

As already stated in the *Daily Chronicle*, Plüschow's companion, Trefftz, was recaptured on Monday evening at Millwall Docks. Both men are naval officers. An earlier description stated that Plüschow is twenty-nine years old. His voice is high-pitched.

He is particularly smart and dapper in appearance, has very good teeth, which he shows somewhat prominently when talking or smiling, is 'very English in manner', and knows this country well. He also knows Japan well. He is quick and alert, both mentally and physically, and speaks French and English fluently and accurately. He was dressed in a grey lounge suit or grey-and-yellow mixture suit.

Poor Trefftz! So they had got him! I was clear in my mind as to what I was going to do, and the warrant gave me some valuable points. First, I had to get rid of my mackintosh. I therefore went to Blackfriars Station and left my overcoat in the cloakroom. As I handed the garment over, the clerk suddenly asked me: 'What is your name, sir?' This question absolutely bowled me over, as I was quite unprepared for it. With shaking knees I asked: 'Meinen?' (mine), answering in German as I naturally presumed that the man had guessed my identity.

'Oh, I see, Mr Mine – M-i-n-e,' and he handed me a receipt in the name of Mr Mine. It was a miracle that this official had not noticed my terror, and I felt particularly uncomfortable when I had to pass the two policemen who stood on guard at the station, and who scrutinised me sharply.

I had escaped in a dark blue suit which had been made in Shanghai and worn in quick succession by Messrs Brown and Scott, by the millionaire MacGarvin and then by the locksmith, Ernst Suse, then again falling on better days when donned by a German naval officer, and now concluding its existence on the body of the dock labourer, George Mine. Under the coat I wore a blue sailor's jersey which a naval prisoner had given to me at Donington Hall. In my pocket I carried a tattered old sports cap, a knife, a small looking-glass, a shaving-set, a bit of string and two rags which represented handkerchiefs. In addition, I was the proud possessor of a fortune of 120 shillings which I had partly saved and partly borrowed; but never, either then or later, did I possess papers or passports of any kind.

I now sought a quiet, solitary spot. My beautiful soft hat fell accidentally into the river from London Bridge; collar and tie followed suit from another spot; a beautiful gilt stud held my green shirt together. After that a mixture of vaseline, bootblack and coal dust turned my blond hair black and greasy; my hands soon looked as if they had never made acquaintance with water; and at last I wallowed in a coal heap until I had turned into a perfect prototype of the dock labourer on strike – George Mine.

Gunther Plüschow, *My Escape from Donington Hall*, trans. Pauline de Chary, 1922

FIENDISH GLEE

'They talk,' said he, 'about identifying me! Why I could dodge any bobby living! I have dodged all the detectives in London many a time. I have walked past them, looked them straight in the face; and they have thought I was a mulatto.'

Then he asked us if we knew how he did it; and said 'Just turn your faces away a minute, and I'll show you.'

We turned our heads away, and when we looked again we found he had completely altered the expression of his countenance, and so entirely distorted and disfigured it – save the mark! – that he did not look like the same man.

He threw out his under jaw, contracted the upper portion of his face, and appeared to be able so to force the blood up into his head as to give himself the appearance of a mulatto.

Then he laughed heartily at his cleverness; went through pantomimic gestures that would have done credit to 'Quilp', and again boasted of the many times he had 'put on that face', and walked past the cute detectives in London and elsewhere.

We then made allusion to the clever way in which he dodged the police and got away from Sheffield on the night of the murder; and he at once went off into a long story of his escape, telling it with almost fiendish glee, and occasionally laughing joyously at his exploits. He said:

'After that affair at Bannercross I went straight over the field opposite, and through Endcliffe Wood to Crookes, and round by Sandygate. Then I doubled and came down to Broomhill, and there I took a cab and was driven down to the bottom of Church-street.

'I got out and walked into Spring-street, to the house of an old pal. There I doffed my own clothes and disguised myself. I stopped there a short time, and then I went boldly through the streets to the railway station, and took train for Rotherham. I walked from that station down to Masbro', where I took a ticket for Beverley.

'On reaching Normanton I left the train, retaining my ticket, and took a ticket for York, where I put up that night. The next morning I went to Beverley, and then walked on to Hull.

'I got in an eating house near the docks, where I stopped a considerable time, and did a 'bit of work' – (meaning, of course, committed a few robberies).

'Then I went to Leeds, and from Leeds to Bradford; and from Bradford I went to Manchester. I was there a short time and then I went to Nottingham; and in a lodging house there I picked up Mrs Thompson.

'Whilst we were together one night, an inspector, who had heard I was there and suspected I was a "fence", came and said to the landlady – "You have got a lodger here – have you not?" She said, "Yes, he is upstairs."

'He said he wanted to see me, and upstairs he came into our bedroom. When I saw him I said "Hullo!" He answered, "Where do you come from?" and I told him from Tunbridge Wells. "What is your name?" he asked. "John Ward," said I. "Well," he said, "what trade are you?"

'At that I let out and said, "What's that to you what trade I am? What do you want to know for?"

'He told me he wanted an answer. "Then," said I, "if you do I'll give you one – I am a hawker!" "Oh," said he, "a hawker. Have you got any stock?"

'I told him my stock and licence were downstairs, and if he would step down my wife and I would come and show him all. He was as soft as barm and went down.

'I said to Mrs Thompson, "I must hook it," and, hastily dressing myself, I bolted through the window and dropped into a yard, where I encountered a man, who was surprised to see me. I told him there was a screw loose, and the bobbies were after me with a warrant for neglecting my wife and family. I asked him not to say I had gone that way. He promised he would not.

'To leave the yard I had to go through the passage of a public-house, and at the door stood the landlady. She was frightened to see me without stockings or boots on; but when I told her the same tale as I had told the man in the yard she said it was all right, and I passed on.

'I took refuge in a house not forty yards from that I had left, and in a short time I got the woman who kept it to go for my boots, and she brought them.'

Charles Peace; or, The Adventures of a Notorious Burglar, 1879

A POLICEMAN'S FOOT

Some of my escapes were from police cells. I was small enough up to the age of fourteen to squeeze through the small hatches in the cell doors. I made a habit of banging the door and shouting when they locked me in the cells, so that they just ignored me. This then allowed me to bang the closed hatch to make the catch jump outwards whilst at the same time I placed the flat of my hand against the hatch and pulled down. The jump of the catch and the downward pull would eventually coincide and the hatch would slide down. I would then get through and find the hatch leading into the air-shaft, which was only about a foot square, and squeeze through this to the top out on to the roof. The narrowness of the shaft was quite frightening at first, I was afraid of becoming wedged and not being able to return. But I stifled my sense of claustrophobia and continued. I escaped four or five times from Old Street Police Station, once from Hackney, once from Victoria, and once from one which I think was Rochester Row.

The police believed at one time that I had a secret passage leading from the block of houses that ours was in, for they had many times surrounded the block before approaching the house and seen me leave via roofs at the back of the house. Yet they were still unable to catch me once I was loose in the block. The answer was very simple although they never found it. There were several factories at the end of the road and the trapdoor on the roof was left unlocked. I used to get inside and shoot the bolt. When the police arrived on this roof after methodically searching the others, they would try the trapdoor and find it locked. They would remark, 'He can't be in there, it's locked', and off they would go. On one occasion I surfaced too soon and, as I looked over the parapet wall, I was spotted on this same roof, so up they came again, tried the trapdoor and, finding it locked, made a similar remark and went off again.

I was twice chased, at different times, and trapped in a block which was completely surrounded, and yet still escaped. On the first of these occasions I got under a tarpaulin sheet that had been lain on a roof that was being retiled. Policemen clambered all over the roof and one actually trod on me without realising it. I waited until two o'clock in the morning and left the block in a swirl of fog. On the other occasion I had unsuccessfully tried to get up a chimney after being chased over rooftops, back and forth, from one end of this block to the other. Eventually I decided to bluff it out, and walked through someone's back door, through the passage and out through the front door. There were police all round the block. They stared at me curiously and uncertainly as I boldly emerged from the house and shut the door firmly behind me. My casual manner completely threw them. They were obviously deeply suspicious because of my soot-covered appearance, but I was not acting like a fugitive. It was not until I had got outside of the cordon that one of the policemen emerged from the block and recognised me, but by that time I was haring down the road and they had little chance of catching me. My fleetness of foot was something that perpetually dismayed the police.

Walter Probyn, Angel Face, 1977

FRIGHT AND FLIGHT

ONE THOUSAND DOLLARS REWARD

June 10, 1780

RAN away, on the 8th day of May last, from the subscriber, living on the south side of Severn river, near Rawlings's tavern, and within 9 miles of Annapolis, in Maryland, a country born Negro man, named PHIL, 21 years of age, about 5 feet 7 inches high, is a likely straight made fellow, has had the small-pox when young, and is pitted about the nose, has a scar about an inch long on one of his temples, is very scary when attacked with any thing, and will make his escape if possible, has a very smiling countenance when in good humour, was whipped on his backside the day he ran away, and very likely may have some scars there, is a vile rogue and one of the worst of liars: Had on, when he went away, a straw hat bound with tow, a tow linen shirt, a short under jacket, with sleeves made of woollen cloth wove kersey, but not filled, old breeches; stockings, and shoes; he is a very cunning artful fellow, and very likely may pass as a free man, and may endeavour to inlist himself in the service, or enter on board some vessel, or make to the new settlements out back, or to the southward after the army, and no doubt has changed his cloaths and name. Whoever takes up the said Negro, shall receive, if ten miles from home, 200 Dollars Reward; if twenty miles, 400 Dollars; if forty miles, 600 Dollars; and if out of the state the above Reward, and reasonable charges when brought home, paid by

VACHEL and ELIZABETH WORTHINGTON

NB All masters of vessels are forbid carrying him off at their peril.

Baltimore, *Maryland Journal and Baltimore Advertiser*, 12 June 1780

IN A MEADOW

Though I was never taken, I often had such narrow escapes that I have since seen that it did not please our Lord to make use of me in any way but that in which I was engaged. I will briefly relate one or two cases.

When the holy Father Roger Filcock was taken, with whom, as I have said before, I sailed from Spain to Calais in France, he got to know a few days before his martyrdom that a certain great spy, who knew both him and me very well, had purposely taken a room in the street in which he suspected that I lived. In this he was not far wrong, for the house to which I usually resorted when I came to London, was directly opposite that in which he had taken a room from which to spy me out. Good Father Roger managed to have me warned of the danger. After I had had the warning, I neither went in nor out of that house except at night, and by other doors, one of which opened on another street, and another on the river Thames, and even this with the greatest caution. I let my beard grow so long as to change my appearance very much; and in this way I spent some months. During this time he met me more than once, but did not know me sufficiently well to induce him to take me. This I afterwards knew from himself, and in the following manner.

One day I was in company with some Catholic lords and knights, who were well known in London to be such. As I left the house with some of them, the spy I was speaking of was in the street, and as he knew very well that the gentlemen with whom I was were Catholics, he looked more attentively at me than he had done before, and yet he could not altogether make up his mind that I was the man of whom he was in search. He waited until I bade them good-bye, and then remained in a passage down which I had passed in order to reach a meadow, a way I had taken in order to get free from the houses. I had passed him where he stood without thinking of him, or of meeting any other molestation in that quiet place, when I heard somebody salute me in Spanish with these words, 'Guarda Dios a Vuestra Merced.' At once I turned my head to see who had spoken, when who should I see coming quickly towards me but the spy. He knew that I understood Spanish, and seeing me turn my head, he felt sure that I was the man he was looking for. At that moment I perceived that it was the spy whom I was trying to avoid. I waited where I was with more courage in my face than in my heart; indeed I went towards him, and taking him by the hand I congratulated myself on having met him after so long a time that I had not seen him. I entertained him with good words until I had led him aside to some little distance from the public footpath in that meadow. It then occurred to him that he was without help, and that I had led him on purpose to that solitary place; so he began to try to make me understand that he wished me no harm, but that certain other spies (and he named them to me) had begged of him to help them to take me, and that therefore I must be on the look out. I told him plainly what I had heard of him, and bade him leave such evil designs and reconcile himself anew to God and His holy Church, promising him my help. And further I promised that if I were satisfied with his proceedings I would provide him a master with whom he could live like a Catholic.

He made a show of hearing all this with content and pleasure, and bringing him to a place where I had nothing more to fear from him, I got away from him for that time, to the great surprise of those who knew how long and with what pains he had been trying to take me.

Oswald Tesimond, *Autobiography* (events of 1606), trans. John Morris, 1872

TWO

'Where was my friend?'

Messrs Emmett, Tone, and Dowling had called on me the day I expected to have been brought before the privy council, and it was determined I should tell the whole of the transaction without concealment, except of names of individuals. I mentioned to them my plan of escape, which I had commenced, after Jackson's arrest, in the Fives Court, with Mr Dowell, jun. the under jailer. I told him that I had been pressed for money, and had sold a small estate, which was to have been paid for long since, but the purchaser, or rather the attorney, had started an objection, on account of my signing the deeds while in prison, by which my heirs might hereafter contest the sale; but the attorney had said also, that by an additional expense of about £50 or £100 the risk might be evaded; that I looked upon this as a mere cheatery of the attorney; that I would rather give twice the sum to any person, and that I would consult Mr Dowling.

The next day was the 1st of May, I told Mr Dowell that it had been suggested to me, that he might easily assist me, if he would take me out of the prison just so long as to enable the witnesses to attest the signature being made out of the precincts of the jail; and I declared that if he could contrive that, I should rejoice to give him the £100 instead of the attorney. He said he would ask the head jailer, and perhaps he would consent to it. I objected to this by saying that the head jailer might think, that during the course of my imprisonment he might take the same liberty at other times, and therefore he had better not make the application. Shortly after, he asked me whether he might not tell his father; to which I immediately consented; and it was agreed that he should give me an answer. A little before dinner-hour he came and desired me to be ready at *twelve o'clock*. This I immediately communicated to my friend Dowling, who proposed to meet me at that hour on horseback at the end of Sackville-street. We had a Swiss butler who had lived with us some years, to whom I laid open this part of the plan, and I directed a table to be laid out above stairs, with wine, &c. &c. in a front two-pair-of-stair room, the door of which commanded a view of the staircase. He was instructed, when we came to the door, to show us up stairs, and say the gentlemen had called, but they would shortly return.

About twelve o'clock Mr Dowell appeared in the prison, with his sabre and pistols in his girdle, and thence accompanied me to my own house. On our arrival there, the servant did as he was instructed. I then sat down with Mr Dowell to take some refreshment; in the mean time I had prepared the purse with the 100 guineas, which I threw across the table to him, saying I was much better pleased with his having it than *Six-and-eightpenny*. And here I must record that he put the purse back to me, saying he did not do it for gain; but I remonstrated, and he relented. At this moment I accused myself of my insincerity; but, as Godwin describes in Caleb Williams, under somewhat similar circumstances, I was not prepared to 'maintain my sincerity at the expence of a speedy close to my existence.'

I then said as we could not remain long absent, if he had no objection, I would step into the back room opposite, where my wife and eldest boy slept. To this he immediately consented; and I desired I might be called when the gentlemen returned. I entered, changed my clothes for those of my herd, who had opportunely come to town that day with a cow for the children. I then descended from the window by a knotted rope, which was made fast to the bed-post and reached down to the garden. I went to the stable, took my horse, and rode to the head of Sackville-street, where Mat Dowling had appointed to meet me. Here I was obliged to wait nearly half an hour before Dowling appeared. His delay was occasioned by some friends having called on him to supper; Mat never being the first to break up company, was obliged to remain until the party separated of themselves, lest he should be suspected of being concerned in my escape. Some of my friends advised my taking my pistols with me, but I had made up my mind not to be taken alive, so I only put a razor in my pocket. At last Dowling came up, and we set out for the house of Mr Sweetman, who was a friend of his, and lived on the sea-side at Sutton, near Baldoyle, by whom, and his then wife, I was received with the utmost kindness; and in a short time afterwards Dowling returned home.

Archibald Hamilton Rowan, *Autobiography*, 1840

TOOTHACHE

Mr John More *to Sir* Ralph Winwood

Right honourable my very good Lord,   *8th June* 1611
   The first of thys Moneth (by the Ordinary of *Middleburg*) I sent your Lordship some Advertisements of small Importance, and that which now I send is for the most Part of no better Stuff. The quick-winged and

various Fame of my Lady *Arabella*'s and Mr *Seimour*'s Flight will farre outstrippe the Passage of this Letter; yet in the certaine manner of their Escape it may perhaps in some Points clear the obscuritie of forerunning Bruites. On *Monday* last in the Afternoone my Lady *Arabella* lying at Mr *Coniers*'s House near *Highgate*, having induced her keepers and Attendants into Securitie by the fayre Shew of Conformitye and Willingness to goe on her Journey towards *Durham*, (which the next Day she must have don,) and in the mean tyme *disguising her selfe by drawing a pair of great French-fashioned Hose over her Petticotes, putting on a Man's Doublet, a man-lyke Perruque with long Locks over her Hair, a blacke Hat, black Cloake, russet Bootes with red Tops, and a Rapier by her Syde*, walked forth between three and four of the Clock with Mr *Markham*. After they had gon a foot a Myle and halfe to a sorry Inne, where *Crompton* attended with their Horses, she grew very sicke and fainte, so as the Ostler that held the Styrrop, said *that Gentleman would hardly hold out to* London. Yet being set on a good Gelding *astryde* in an unwonted Fashion, the stirring of the Horse brought Blood enough into her face, and so she rid on towards *Blackwall*; where arryving about six a Clock, finding there in a Readiness two Men, a Gentlewoman and a Chambermaid, with one Boate full of Mr *Seimour*'s and her Trunks, and another Boate for their Persons, they hasted from thence towards *Woolwich*. Being come so farre they bade the Watermen row on to *Gravesend*, There the Watermen were desirous to land, but for a double Fraight were contented to go on to *Lee*: Yet being almost tyred by the way, they were faine to lye still at *Tilbury* whilst the Oares went a land to refreshe themselves. Then they proceeded to *Lee*, and by that tyme the Day appeared, and they discovered a Shippe at Anchor a Myle beyond them, which was the *French Barque* that wayted for them. Here the *Lady* would have lyen at Anchor expecting Mr *Seimour*, but through the Importunitye of her Followers they forthwith hoisted Saile to Seawarde. In the meane while Mr *Seimour* with *a Perruque and Beard of blacke Hair and in a tauny Cloth Suit*, walked alone *without Suspition* from his Lodging out at the Great Weste Doore of the *Tower, following a Cart that had brought him Billets*. From thence he walked along by the *Tower Warfe* by the *Warders* of the south Gate, and so to the *Iron Gate*, where *Rodney* was ready with Oares for to receive him. When they came to *Lee* and fownd that the *French* Ship was gon, the Billows rising high, they hyred a *Fisherman* for twenty Shillings to set them aboard a certain Ship that they saw under Saile. That Ship they found not to be it they looked for, so they made forwards to the next under

Saile, which was a Shippe of *Newcastle*. This, with much ado they hyred for 40*l*. to carry them to *Calais*: But whither the *Collier* did perfourm his Bargaine or no, is not as yet here known. On *Tewsday* in the Afternoone my *Lord Treasurer* being advertized that the Lady *Arabella* had made an Escape, sent forthwith to the *Leiutenant* of the *Tower* to set straight Guard over Mr *Seimour*; which he, after his *yare manner*, would *throughly do, that he would*: But coming to the Prisonner's Lodgings he fownd (to his great Amazement) that he was gonne from thence one whole Day before.

I may not omitt in this Relation to inserte the simple Parte of two silly Persons; the one called *Tom. Barber* Servant to Mr *Seimour*, who (believing his Master spake *bonâ fide*,) did according to his Instructions tell every one that came to enquire for his Master, *that he was newly betaken to his rest being much troubled with the Tooth-ach*; and when the Matter was dicovered, did seriously persist to perswade Mr *Leiutenant* that *he was gon but to lye a Night with his Wife, and would surely return thither of himself again*. The other, a Minister's Wife attending *the Lady*; who seeing her Mistress disguise her selfe and slippe away, was trewly perswaded that she intended but to make *a private Visit to her Husband*, and did duly attend her Returne at the Tyme appointed.

Sir Ralph Winwood, *Memorials of Affairs of State*, ed. Edmund Sawyer, 1725

BOTH VERY SENSIBLE

TWENTY POUNDS REWARD

RUN away from the Subscriber in King William, CAESAR and KATE, very likely Virginia born Negroes. Caesar is about forty Years old, of middle Stature, well made, strong and active, has a remarkable Scar on one of his Heels, which was nearly cut off when a Youth, some Scars, or Indian Marks, on one of his Arms near the Shoulders, and an R on each of his Cheeks, with which he was branded by the Sheriff of Dinwiddie; but as it is many Years since, it may now be scarcely visible. Kate is pretty tall, near forty Years of Age, and both she and her Husband, Caesar, have dark Complexions, their Teeth somewhat worn with Pipes, are smooth tongued, and very sensible. They had Variety of Clothes, and Articles for House keeping not very portable; hence it is imagined they will attempt to get a Distance by Water, and then probably endeavour to pass as free Persons. Whoever will bring the said Slaves to me shall have the above Reward, if taken out of the Colony, or TEN POUNDS for either; if within fifty Miles from home, FIVE POUNDS for each; and FIFTY SHILLINGS for each, if under that Distance.

ROBERT RUFFIN

Virginia Gazette, 24 September 1772

GUNS 'N' ROSES

Right after the 5.30 count, I signed out with my floor officer and told her I was going to the laundry room. This was consistent with my routine. I carried my sweaty tennis shoes with me.

There was a window in the laundry that was not secured. Who knows why? Maybe they'd painted it and forgotten to put the stays back on. But there it was, calling out to me like one of the sirens.

It was not as small as the newspapers reported the next day. I think the prison exaggerated the smallness of the window to minimise their fault, and implied I had somehow wriggled through a hole about six inches square. Actually, it was about two feet by two feet. It was high off the ground, but I was in wonderful shape because I'd been running five miles every day and doing aerobics four nights a week, not to mention my tennis matches.

There I was, pushing myself through the window, on my way Out.

I can honestly say I've never been so scared in my entire life. My heart was pounding so hard it was like drums beating in my ears.

Security vans patrolled the grounds, but they, too, had their routines. Through simple observation I'd learned when they had deliveries to make and other things to do.

I was afraid of them, of course.

I was also afraid of the screwy inmates. Someone could easily have spotted me. Of course, anyone with half a brain wouldn't have said anything, but prisons are full of the other kind, too – people who will blurt out anything that comes into their heads. 'Hey, everybody! I just saw somebody!' They would! There are people so bored they have nothing to do but look out the window. You have to anticipate that.

There was an apple orchard behind the housing unit, and I knew the cameras couldn't see past it. If I could only get into the woods past the orchard, I'd be safe. Well, maybe not safe, but cool . . .

In the first few seconds after I got out I paused in the woods behind the Housing Unit to catch my breath and make sure no one had seen me. There is a large stone grotto with a statue of the Virgin Mary. So much for separation of Church and State.

I wore a leather jacket, to protect me from branches in the woods, so I got through the woods without a scratch. I'd never been in those woods before, and it was scary. Woods at night are always creepy, and when you're in a hurry, even more so. I didn't want to lose an eye to a low-hanging branch; nor did I want to fall into a hidden ravine and break a leg. I didn't know whether there were any ravines. The woods sloped generally uphill from the housing unit to the highway beyond. To freedom.

I was still within the perimeter of the fence.

It was hot, and very dark in the woods. I sweated profusely; I had the hood of my sweatshirt over my head. My heart was pounding. I was afraid I would hyperventilate because I was panting like a horse. The air seemed thick and rank. I just wanted to get through those woods!

I went up, and farther up, and eventually I could see light at the end of the woods, I was running toward the light, scrambling over fallen trees, crossing one small ravine on a deadfall bridge, like a balance beam, but I just went, driving myself, trying not to panic, trying to keep going.

I reached the fence. It was tall, maybe nine or ten feet, with barbed wire at the top. I wrapped my belt around the barbed wire and I pulled it taut, and no sooner had I done so than I heard a car coming.

I didn't know if it was Nick, but I couldn't risk being seen at the top of the fence, so I jumped down, ran for cover and waited. It could be a prison van doing a perimeter check.

When the truck had passed, I tried again.

This time I became hooked on the barbed wire. It snagged my pants, and I felt it tear into my leg. I yanked at it, and the barbs raked my leg, but I freed myself.

I left half my pant leg on the wire. Talk about fibre evidence!

Later, I saw three or four big gashes in my leg. It looked as though I'd been attacked by a mountain lion – four big claw marks in the flesh. I worried about infection, but it healed eventually.

I was out!

I had to run for cover.

The truck that had passed hadn't been Nick after all. We two amateurs had got the timing down pat. Nick showed up right on time.

A witness at his trial later swore he'd seen Nick parked near the fence where he picked me up. It still amazes me what lies people will tell, just to get into the papers or on television. Nick *never* parked anywhere – we had worked that out ahead of time. Drive up and down twenty times if you must, I'd warned him, but don't ever stop, it will only attract attention. He'd agreed, and did as I suggested.

He pulled up, I jumped in, and we sped off. To freedom!

I'd made it! It was an amazing feeling. My heart was still going. My adrenaline levels must have been off the charts! Ecstasy mingled with fear.

I scrunched down and started peeling layers of clothes off to cool myself. I took my leather jacket off, then my sweatshirt, down to a tank top. Hand in hand, with Guns 'n' Roses blasting on the tape player, we just drove straight through to Canada. It took us all night.

. . . It was mid-morning by the time we got to Canada. There were some things in our favor. I was in good shape and I was suntanned, so I didn't look like the stereotypical jailbird. We were sitting there holding hands like an ordinary couple.

'What's your business in Canada?' the border officer asked.

Could I have told them an earful! Refuge, I wanted to say.

'We're on honeymoon,' I said.

'Okay then, have a nice time,' she said, smiling and waving us off.

Freedom! I rolled down the window and let the breeze speed through my hair. The sun beat furiously over the tops of the pine trees. The sky was a brilliant blue.

I looked over at Nick and said, 'Well, maybe there is a God.' Me, an unwavering atheist for so many years!

Lawrencia Bembenek, *Woman on Trial*, 1992

THE LITTLE BAG

I had flour sack trousers cut off at the knee, a woollen sweater and a good knife in my belt. I also had a waterproof bag that I was going to hang round my neck – it held cigarettes and a tinder lighter. Salvidia had made a waterproof knapsack full of manioc flour that he had soaked in oil and sugar. About seven pounds, he told me. It was late. I sat there on my bed waiting for my friend. My heart was thumping hard. In a few minutes the break was going to begin. May good luck and almighty God be on my side, so that I may escape from the road down the drain and leave it for good and all!

It was strange, but my thoughts only touched on the past but faintly, glancing towards my father and my family. Not a single picture of the assizes, the jury or the prosecuting counsel. But just as the door opened, in spite of myself I once more had a vision of Matthieu standing there, carried along the surface of the sea by the sharks.

'Papi, let's go!' I followed him. Quickly he closed the door and hid the key in a corner of the passage. 'Quick, quick.' We reached the dispensary: the door was open. Getting the empty barrel out was child's play. He slung the ropes over his shoulder and I took the wire and the knapsack with flour in it. In the pitch dark night I started rolling my barrel down towards the sea. He came behind, with the oil barrel. Fortunately he was very strong and it was quite easy for him to keep it from plunging down the steep descent.

'Slowly, slowly, take care it doesn't run away with you.' I waited for him, in case he should lose his hold on the barrel – if he did, I could block its run with mine. I went down backwards, me in front and my barrel behind. We reached the bottom of the path without any sort of difficulty. There was a little path in the direction of the sea, but after that it was very hard going over the rocks.

'Empty the barrel: we'll never get across with it full.' There was a stiff wind blowing and the waves were crashing furiously against the rocks. Fine, the barrel was empty. 'Ram the bung in hard. Wait a minute: put this bit of tin over it.' The holes were already made. 'Drive the nails right home.' The hammering would never be heard over the roaring of the wind and sea.

We lashed the two barrels tight together; but carrying them over the rocks was very difficult. Each of them was made to hold fifty gallons; they took up a lot of space and they were very awkward to handle. The place my friend had chosen for the launching made things no easier, either. 'Shove, for God's sake! Up a bit. Look out for the wave!' Both of us and the two barrels were picked up and flung hard back on to the rock. 'Take care. They'll smash, to say nothing of us breaking an arm or a leg!'

'Take it easy, Salvidia. Either go in front, towards the sea, or stand here behind. That's right. Heave the moment I give a shout. I'll shove at the same second and then we'll certainly get free of the rocks. But to do

[43]

it, we've just got to hold tight and stay where we are, even if the sea breaks right over us.'

I shouted these orders to my friend in the midst of the thunder of the wind and the waves, and I think he heard them: a big wave swept completely over us as we clung to the barrels. At this moment I shoved madly on the raft with all my strength. And he must certainly have done the same, because all at once there we were afloat, away from the rocks. He was up on the barrels before me, but just as I hauled myself on, a huge breaker heaved up beneath us and tossed us like a feather on to a pointed rock farther out at sea. The impact was so shattering that the barrels smashed open, scattering in fragments. When the wave drew back it swept me more than twenty yards from the rock. I swam and let myself be carried in by the next wave that ran straight for the shore. I landed in a sitting position between two rocks. I just had time to cling on before being swept away. Bruised all over, I managed to scramble out; but when I reached dry land, I realised that I'd been carried more than a hundred yards from the place where we'd launched the raft.

Taking no sort of care I shouted, 'Salvidia! Romeo! Where are you?' There was no answer. Quite overwhelmed I lay down on the path: I took off my sweater and my trousers, and there I was again, naked, wearing just my slippers. Christ, where was my friend? And once again I shouted with all my strength, 'Where are you?' Only the wind, the sea and the waves replied. I stayed there I don't know how long, numbed, completely shattered, mentally and physically. Then, weeping with fury, I threw away the litle bag I had round my neck for my tobacco and lighter – a mark of my friend's real affection, for he himself was no smoker.

Standing there facing the wind and the huge waves that had swept everything away, I raised my clenched fist and insulted God. 'You swine, You filthy bugger, aren't You ashamed of persecuting me like this? You're supposed to be a good God, aren't You? You're a disgusting brute, that's all. A sadist, a bloody sadist! A perverted sod! I'll never utter Your name again. You don't deserve it.'

Henri Charrière, *Papillon*, trans. Patrick O'Brian, 1970

We seemed to be riding safely when an immense sea struck the lifeboat like a thunderbolt, and before any of us could realise what had happened she was completely overturned, and a few of us were grasping ropes and the sides of the boat and the thwarts – anything that drowning men could grip.

That awful sea which struck the lifeboat and capsized her swept some of the men to an instant and merciful death. She was just picked up and turned upside-down.

It is no use for any man to say that he can clearly remember what happens at such a time. All I know is that we were upset, and that in an instant some of my comrades had perished.

A few of the men were clinging to the outside of the boat, and I and a few more were made prisoners underneath her, in the bitter water and pitch darkness, hurled and tossed by every wave that broke on the sands where the barque had struck.

There we were, a handful of us, up to the neck in water, and forced to live on the air which found its way between the bottom of the upturned boat and ourselves.

We were just like rats in a trap, and there did not seem to be the shadow of a chance of escape for any one of us. People wonder how the air got in. I will tell you. In the bottom of the lifeboat were a number of holes with valves at their tops. When she was afloat these valves were kept closed by the pressure of the water from below, but when the boat shipped a heavy sea the weight of the water above depressed the valves and made its escape, and so cleared the craft.

As you will see, the valves were naturally forced upward when the boat capsized, and allowed the air to come in and keep us alive.

It is a merciful thing that even when there seems to be no possibility of escape from an awful death, hope is still left to us. I, at any rate, believed that one or two of us might escape with our lives, and I trusted that when the tide turned we should be carried back towards the sandy beach and be able to get ashore.

It was a forlorn hope, I admit, because there was still a strong chance that even if we did get to the beach the heavy boat, weighing several tons, would fall upon us and crush us to death.

When that big sea capsized us, several men, as I have told you, perished instantly. During the time we were held prisoners two or three men died of exhaustion. They were frozen to death.

As for those of us who lived, we cheered each other as best we could, declaring that if we could only hold out long enough we should be safe; yet I believe that most of them never supposed they would see another day break.

I heard a voice in the darkness say, 'I don't think she'll ever right. I think we shall all be drowned.' Henry Robinson answered, 'I think so, too.'

About that time Robinson was leaning heavily on my arm; but a heavy sea came and carried him away.

Two or three of us managed to crawl outside the boat and hang on, but it was worse there than inside, where there was shelter from the piercing wind and breaking seas.

The water was terribly cold, but not so hard to bear underneath the boat as it was in the open night. It always seems so difficult to make people understand what it means to be in icy water for such a long time; but just think what it would mean to keep in an ordinary cold bath in winter for even an hour, not to say several hours in a sea which hammers and hurls you about all the time. Even a man of iron constitution can scarcely stand it, and more than one of my comrades dropped away from his hold and sank.

I knew from the feel of the boat that she was dragging at her anchor. Her short length of cable prevented her from being carried too violently towards the shore when the tide turned and she began to go with it.

Several times she tried to right herself, but never did so. I suppose this was because she was held down by the anchor, and, of course, she would be affected by the weight of the men who were clinging to her. But there was no real chance of her getting clear of the anchor, and never a man dared to let go his hold. That would have meant instant death. His only hope lay in holding hard and fast.

For two long hours the lifeboat drifted shoreward in that strange fashion, with her keel turned up to the black sky, and the few of us who still lived holding on and being kept in place by our cork jackets and the lifelines.

The people ashore had not the least idea that the lifeboat had capsized, and it was not until she was actually cast on to the beach by a big roller that the accident was known.

It was about three o'clock in the morning when the *Eliza Fearnley* was thrown up on the sands, about three miles west of Southport.

By that time I was almost dead. I had no feeling whatever in my body, and my hands clung mechanically to a lifeline. I knew, however, that we were almost ashore, because when the boat dipped in the trough of the sea I had touched the sand. I was instantly filled with hope that even now I should be saved, yet I realised how perilous it would be to get away from the boat and crawl up the beach.

To this day I really cannot tell exactly what happened, but I do know that when the boat struck the beach the handful of us who were still underneath were thrown out. Two or three of the poor fellows were drowned or killed instantly.

Three of us got on to the sands – myself, Henry Robinson, and John Ball. Not one of us was able to do more than try to save his own life. John Ball was found about an hour later standing knee-deep in water. He was put into a cab and taken at once to the infirmary; but he had only a flicker of life left in him, and died soon after he reached the hospital.

Under the boat, entangled with the lifelines, cable, oars, and gear, Peter Jackson, Peter Wright, and Timothy Rigby, three fine fellows, were found dead. Another comrade, Ralph Peters, came ashore with the boat, but only a spark of life was left in him, and he very soon died.

John Jackson's narrative in Survivors' Tales of Famous Shipwrecks,
ed. Walter Wood, 1932

ON BOARD FOR ONE YEAR, TEN DAYS

12 And God looked upon the earth, and behold, it was corrupt; for all flesh had corrupted his way upon the earth.

13 And God said unto Noah, The end of all flesh is come before me; for the earth is filled with violence through them; and, behold, I will destroy them with the earth.

14 ¶ Make thee an ark of gopher wood; rooms shalt thou make in the ark, and shalt pitch it within and without with pitch.

15 And this *is the fashion* which thou shalt make it *of*: The length of the ark *shall be* three hundred cubits, the breadth of it fifty cubits, and the height of it thirty cubits.

16 A window shalt thou make to the ark, and in a cubit shalt thou finish it above; and the door of the ark shalt thou set in the side thereof; *with* lower, second, and third *stories* shalt thou make it.

17 And, behold, I, even I, do bring a flood of waters upon the earth, to destroy all flesh, wherein *is* the breath of life, from under heaven; *and* every thing that *is* in the earth shall die.

18 But with thee will I establish my covenant; and thou shalt come into the ark, thou, and thy sons, and thy wife, and thy sons' wives with thee.

19 And of every living thing of all flesh, two of every *sort* shalt thou bring into the ark, to keep *them* alive with thee; they shall be male and female.

20 Of fowls after their kind, and of cattle after their kind, of every creeping thing of the earth after its kind, two of every *sort* shall come unto thee, to keep *them* alive.

21 And take thou unto thee of all food that is eaten, and thou shalt gather *it* to thee; and it shall be for food for thee, and for them.

22 Thus did Noah; according to all that God commanded him, so did he.

CHAPTER 7

And the LORD said unto Noah, Come thou and all thy house into the ark; for thee have I seen righteous before me in this generation.

2 Of every clean beast thou shalt take to thee by sevens, the male and his female; and of beasts that *are* not clean by two, the male and his female.

3 Of fowls also of the air by sevens, the male and the female; to keep seed alive upon the face of all the earth.

4 For yet seven days, and I will cause it to rain upon the earth forty days and forty nights; and every living substance that I have made will I destroy from off the face of the earth.

5 And Noah did according unto all that the LORD commanded him.

6 And Noah *was* six hundred years old when the flood of waters was upon the earth.

7 ¶ And Noah went in, and his sons, and his wife, and his sons' wives with him, into the ark, because of the waters of the flood.

8 Of clean beasts, and of beasts that *are* not clean, and of fowls, and of every thing that creepeth upon the earth.

9 There went in two and two unto Noah into the ark, the male and the female, as God had commanded Noah.

10 And it came to pass after seven days, that the waters of the flood were upon the earth.

11 ¶ In the six hundredth year of Noah's life, in the second month, the seventeenth day of the month, the same day were all the fountains of the great deep broken up, and the windows of heaven were opened.

12 And the rain was upon the earth forty days and forty nights.

13 In the selfsame day entered Noah, and Shem, and Ham, and Japheth, the sons of Noah, and Noah's wife, and the three wives of his sons with them, into the ark;

14 They, and every beast after his kind, and all the cattle after their kind, and every creeping thing that creepeth upon the earth after his kind, and every fowl after his kind, every bird of every sort.

15 And they went in unto Noah into the ark, two and two of all flesh, wherein *is* the breath of life.

16 And they that went in, went in male and female of all flesh, as God had commanded him: and the Lord shut him in.

17 And the flood was forty days upon the earth; and the waters increased, and bare up the ark, and it was lift up above the earth.

18 And the waters prevailed, and were increased greatly upon the earth; and the ark went upon the face of the waters.

19 And the waters prevailed exceedingly upon the earth; and all the high hills, that *were* under the whole heaven, were covered.

20 Fifteen cubits upward did the waters prevail; and the mountains were covered.

21 And all flesh died that moved upon the earth, both of fowl, and of cattle, and of beast, and of every creeping thing that creepeth upon the earth, and every man:

22 All in whose nostrils *was* the breath of life, of all that *was* in the dry *land*, died.

23 And every living substance was destroyed which was upon the face of the ground, both man, and cattle, and the creeping things, and the fowl of the heaven; and they were destroyed from the earth: and Noah only remained *alive*, and they that *were* with him in the ark.

24 And the waters prevailed upon the earth an hundred and fifty days.

CHAPTER 8

And God remembered Noah, and every living thing, and all the cattle that *was* with him in the ark: and God made a wind to pass over the earth, and the waters asswaged;

2 The fountains also of the deep and the windows of heaven were stopped, and the rain from heaven was restrained;

3 And the waters returned from off the earth continually: and after the end of the hundred and fifty days the waters were abated.

4 And the ark rested in the seventh month, on the seventeenth day of the month, upon the mountains of Ararat.

5 And the waters decreased continually until the tenth month: in the tenth *month*, on the first *day* of the month, were the tops of the mountains seen.

6 ¶ And it came to pass at the end of forty days, that Noah opened the window of the ark which he had made:

7 And he sent forth a raven, which went forth to and fro, until the waters were dried up from off the earth.

8 Also he sent forth a dove from him, to see if the waters were abated from off the face of the ground;

9 But the dove found no rest for the sole of her foot, and she returned unto him into the ark, for the waters *were* on the face of the whole earth: then he put forth his hand, and took her, and pulled her in unto him into the ark.

10 And he stayed yet other seven days; and again he sent forth the dove out of the ark;

11 And the dove came in to him in the evening; and, lo, in her mouth *was* an olive leaf pluckt off: so Noah knew that the waters were abated from off the earth.

12 And he stayed yet other seven days; and sent forth the dove; which returned not again unto him any more.

13 ¶ And it came to pass in the six hundredth and first year, in the first *month*, the first *day* of the month, the waters were dried up from off the earth: and Noah removed the covering of the ark, and looked, and, behold the face of the ground was dry.

14 And in the second month, on the seven and twentieth day of the month, was the earth dried.

Genesis 6:12–8:14

TRITON'S HORN

Neptune himself smites the earth with his trident. She trembles, and at the stroke flings open wide a way for the waters. The rivers overleap all bounds and flood the open plains. And not alone orchards, crops and herds, men and dwellings, but shrines as well and their sacred contents do they sweep away. If any house has stood firm, and has been able to resist that huge misfortune undestroyed, still do the over-topping waves cover its roof, and its towers lie hid beneath the flood. And now the sea and land have no distinction. All is sea, but a sea without a shore.

Here one man seeks a hill-top in his flight; another sits in his curved skiff, plying the oars where lately he has plowed; one sails over his fields of grain or the roof of his buried farmhouse, and one takes fish caught in the elm-tree's top. And sometimes it chanced that an anchor was embedded in a grassy meadow, or the curving keels brushed over the vineyard tops. And where but now the slender goats had browsed, the ugly sea-calves rested. The Nereids are amazed to see beneath the waters groves and cities and the haunts of men. The dolphins invade the woods, brushing against the high branches, and shake the oak-trees as they knock against them in their course. The wolf swims among the sheep, while tawny lions and tigers are borne along by the waves. Neither does the power of his lightning stroke avail the boar, nor his swift limbs the stag, since both are alike swept away by the flood; and the wandering bird, after long searching for a place to alight, falls with weary wings into the sea. The sea in unchecked liberty has now buried all the hills, and strange waves now beat upon the mountain-peaks. Most living things are drowned outright. Those who have escaped the water slow starvation at last o'ercomes through lack of food.

The land of Phocis separates the Boeotian from the Oetean fields, a fertile land, while still it was a land. But at that time it was but a part of the sea, a broad expanse of sudden waters. There Mount Parnasus lifts its two peaks skyward, high and steep, piercing the clouds. When here Deucalion and his wife, borne in a little skiff, had come to land – for the sea had covered all things else – they first worshipped the Corycian nymphs and the mountain deities, and the goddess, fate-revealing Themis, who in those days kept the oracles. There was no better man than he, none more scrupulous of right, nor than she was any woman more reverent of the gods. When now Jove saw that the world was all one stagnant pool, and that only one man was left from those who were but now so many thousands, and that but one woman too was left, both innocent and both worshippers of God, he rent the clouds asunder, and when these had been swept away by the North-wind he showed the land once more to the sky, and the heavens to the land. Then too the anger of the sea subsides, when the sea's great ruler lays by his three-pronged spear and calms the waves; and, calling sea-hued Triton, showing forth above the deep, his shoulders thick o'ergrown with shell-fish, he bids him blow into his loud-resounding conch, and by that signal to recall the floods and streams. He lifts his hollow, twisted shell, which grows from the least and lowest to a broad-swelling whorl – the shell which, when in mid-sea it has received the Triton's breath, fills with its notes the shores that lie beneath the rising and the setting sun. So then, when it had touched the sea-god's lips wet with his dripping beard, and sounded forth the retreat which had been ordered, 'twas heard by all the waters both of land and sea; and all the waters by which 'twas heard it held in check. Now the sea has shores, the rivers, bank full, keep within their channels; the floods subside, and hill-tops spring into view; land rises up, the ground increasing as the waves decrease; and now at length, after long burial, the trees show their uncovered tops, whose leaves still hold the slime which the flood has left.

The world was indeed restored. But when Deucalion saw that it was an empty world, and that deep silence filled the desolated lands, he burst into tears and thus addressed his wife: 'O sister, O my wife, O only woman left on earth, you whom the ties of common race and family, whom the marriage couch has joined to me, and whom now our very perils join: of all the lands which the rising and the setting sun behold, we two are the throng. The sea holds all the rest. And even this hold which we have upon our life is not as yet sufficiently secure. Even yet the clouds strike terror to my heart. What would be your feelings, now, poor soul, if the fates had willed that you be rescued all alone? How would you bear your fear, alone? who would console your grief? For be assured that if the sea held you also, I would follow you, my wife, and the sea should hold me also. Oh, would that by my father's arts I might restore the nations, and breathe, as did he, the breath of life into the moulded clay. But as it is, on us two only depends the human race. Such is the will of Heaven: and we remain sole samples of mankind.'

Ovid, *Metamorphoses*, trans. Frank Justus Miller, 1951

A SMALL PIECE OF DRY PAPER

It rained and it rained and it rained. Piglet told himself that never in all his life, and *he* was goodness knows *how* old – three, was it, or four? – never had he seen so much rain. Days and days and days.

'If only,' he thought, as he looked out of the window, 'I had been in Pooh's house, or Christopher Robin's house, or Rabbit's house when it began to rain, then I should have had Company all this time, instead of being here all alone, with nothing to do except wonder when it will stop.' And he imagined himself with Pooh, saying, 'Did you ever see such rain, Pooh?' and Pooh saying, 'Isn't it *awful*, Piglet?' and Piglet saying, 'I wonder how it is over Christopher Robin's way,' and Pooh saying, 'I should think poor old Rabbit is about flooded out by this time.' It would have been jolly to talk like this, and really, it wasn't much good having anything exciting like floods, if you couldn't share them with somebody.

For it was rather exciting. The little dry ditches in which Piglet had nosed about so often had become streams, the little streams across which he had splashed were rivers, and the river, between whose steep banks they had played so happily, had sprawled out of its own bed and was taking up so much room everywhere, that Piglet was beginning to wonder whether it would be coming into *his* bed soon.

'It's a little Anxious,' he said to himself, 'to be a Very Small Animal Entirely Surrounded by Water. Christopher Robin and Pooh could escape by Climbing Trees, and Kanga could escape by Jumping, and Rabbit could escape by Burrowing, and Owl could escape by Flying, and Eeyore could escape by – by Making a Loud Noise Until Rescued, and here am I, surrounded by water and I can't do *anything*.'

It went on raining, and every day the water got a little higher, until now it was nearly up to Piglet's window . . . and still he hadn't done anything.

'There's Pooh,' he thought to himself. 'Pooh hasn't much Brain, but he never comes to any harm. He does silly things and they turn out right. There's Owl. Owl hasn't exactly got Brain, but he Knows Things. He would know the Right Thing to Do when Surrounded by Water. There's Rabbit. He hasn't Learnt in Books, but he can always Think of a Clever Plan. There's Kanga. She isn't Clever, Kanga isn't, but she would be so anxious about Roo that she would do a Good Thing to Do without thinking about it. And then there's Eeyore. And Eeyore is so miserable anyhow that he wouldn't mind about this. But I wonder what Christopher Robin would do?'

Then suddenly he remembered a story which Christopher Robin had told him about a man on a desert island who had written something in a bottle and thrown it into the sea; and Piglet thought that if he wrote something in a bottle and threw it in the water, perhaps somebody would come and rescue *him*!

He left the window and began to search his house, all of it that wasn't under water, and at last he found a pencil and a small piece of dry paper, and a bottle with a cork to it. And he wrote on one side of the paper:

HELP!
PIGLIT (ME)

and on the other side:

IT'S ME PIGLIT, HELP HELP!

Then he put the paper in the bottle, and he corked the bottle up as tightly as he could, and leant out of his window as far as he could lean without falling in, and he threw the bottle as far as he could throw – *splash!* – and in a little while it bobbed up again on the water; and he watched it floating slowly away in the distance, until his eyes ached with looking, and sometimes he thought it was the bottle, and sometimes he thought it was just a ripple on the water which he was following, and then suddenly he knew that he would never see it again and that he had done all that he could do to save himself.

'So now,' he thought, 'somebody else will have to do something, and I hope they will do it soon, because if they don't I shall have to swim, which I can't, so I hope they do it soon.' And then he gave a very long sigh and said, 'I wish Pooh were here. It's so much more friendly with two.'

A. A. Milne, *Winnie-the-Pooh*, 1926

READING THE TAPESTRY

As soon as Philomela was safely embarked upon the painted ship and the sea was churned beneath the oars and the land was left behind, Tereus exclaimed: 'I have won! in my ship I carry the fulfilment of my prayers!' The barbarous fellow triumphs, he can scarce postpone his joys, and never turns his eyes from her, as when the ravenous bird of Jove has dropped in his high eyrie some hare caught in his hooked talons; the captive has no chance to escape, the captor gloats over his prize.

And now they were at the end of their journey, now, leaving the travel-worn ship, they had landed on their own shores; when the king dragged off Pandion's daughter to a hut deep hidden in the ancient woods: and there, pale and trembling and all fear, begging with tears to know where her sister was, he shut her up. Then, openly confessing his horrid purpose, he violated her, just a weak girl and all alone, vainly calling, often on her father, often on her sister, but most of all upon the great gods. She trembled like a frightened lamb, which, torn and cast aside by a grey wolf, cannot yet believe that it is safe; and like a dove which, with its own blood all smeared over its plumage, still palpitates with fright, still fears those greedy claws that have pierced it. Soon, when her senses came back, she dragged at her loosened hair, and like one in mourning, beating and tearing her arms, with outstretched hands she cried: 'Oh, what a horrible thing you have done, barbarous, cruel wretch! Do you care nothing for my father's injunctions, his affectionate tears, my sister's love, my own virginity, the bonds of wedlock? You have confused all natural relations: I have become a concubine, my sister's rival; you, a husband to both. Now Procne must be my enemy. Why do you not take my life, that no crime may be left undone, you traitor? Aye, would that you had killed me before you wronged me so. Then would my shade have been innocent and clean. If those who dwell on high see these things, nay, if there are any gods at all, if all things have not perished with me, sooner or later you shall pay dearly for this deed. I will myself cast shame aside and proclaim what you have done. If I should have the chance, I would go where people throng and tell it; if I am kept shut up in these woods, I will fill the woods with my story and move the very rocks to pity. The air of heaven shall hear it, and, if there is any god in heaven, he shall hear it too.'

The savage tyrant's wrath was aroused by these words, and his fear no less. Pricked on by both these spurs, he drew his sword which was hanging by his side in its sheath, caught her by the hair, and twisting her arms behind her back, he bound them fast. At sight of the sword Philomela gladly offered her throat to the stroke, filled with the eager hope of death. But he seized her tongue with pincers, as it protested against the outrage, calling ever on the name of her father and struggling to speak, and cut it off with his merciless blade. The mangled root quivers, while the severed tongue lies palpitating on the dark earth, faintly murmuring; and, as the severed tail of a mangled snake is wont to writhe, it twitches convulsively, and with its last dying movement it seeks its mistress's feet. Even after this horrid deed – one would scarce believe it – the monarch is said to have worked his lustful will again and again upon the poor mangled form.

With such crimes upon his soul he had the face to return to Procne's presence. She on seeing him at once asked where her sister was. He groaned in pretended grief and told a made-up story of death; his tears gave credence to the tale. Then Procne tore from her shoulders the robe gleaming with a broad golden border and put on black weeds; she built also a cenotaph in honour of her sister, brought pious offerings to her imagined spirit, and mourned her sister's fate, not meet so to be mourned.

Now through the twelve signs, a whole year's journey, has the sun-god passed. And what shall Philomela do? A guard prevents her flight; stout walls of solid stone fence in the hut; speechless lips can give no token of her wrongs. But grief has sharp wits, and in trouble cunning comes. She hangs a Thracian web on her loom, and skilfully weaving purple signs on a white background, she thus tells the story of her wrongs. This web, when completed, she gives to her one attendant and begs her with gestures to carry it to the queen. The old woman, as she was bid, takes the web to Procne, not knowing what she bears in it. The savage tyrant's wife unrolls the cloth, reads the pitiable tale of her misfortune, and (a miracle that she could!) says not a word. Grief chokes the words that rise to her lips, and her questing tongue can find no words strong enough to express her outraged feelings. Here is no room for tears, but she hurries on to confound right and wrong, her whole soul bent on the thought of vengeance.

It was the time when the Thracian matrons were wont to celebrate the biennial festival of Bacchus. Night was in their secret; by night Mount Rhodope would resound with the shrill clash of brazen cymbals; so by night the queen goes forth from her house, equips herself for the rites of the god and dons the array of frenzy; her head was wreathed with trailing vines, a deer-skin hung from her left side, a light spear rested on her shoulder. Swift she goes through the woods with an attendant throng of her companions, and driven on by the madness of grief, Procne, terrific in her rage, mimics thy madness, O Bacchus! She comes to the secluded lodge at last, shrieks aloud and cries 'Euhoe!' breaks down the doors, seizes her sister, arrays her in the trappings of a Bacchante, hides her face with ivy-leaves, and, dragging her along in amazement, leads her within her own walls.

Ovid, *Metamorphoses*, trans. Frank Justus Miller, 1951

HELMER (*keeping his composure with difficulty*). Are you clear and certain on this point too?

NORA. Yes, quite. That is why I won't stay here any longer.

HELMER. And can you also make clear to me, how I have forfeited your love?

NORA. Yes, I can. It was this evening when the miracle did not happen. For then I saw you were not the man I had taken you for.

HELMER. Explain yourself more clearly; I don't understand.

NORA. I have waited so patiently all these eight years; for of course, I saw clearly enough that miracles do not happen every day. When this crushing blow threatened me, I said to myself confidently, 'Now comes the miracle.' When Krogstad's letter lay in the box, it never occurred to me that you would think of submitting to that man's conditions. I was convinced that you would say to him, 'Make it known to all the world,' and that then—

HELMER. Well? When I had given my own wife's name up to disgrace and shame—?

NORA. Then I firmly believed that you would come forward, take everything upon yourself, and say, 'I am the guilty one.'

HELMER. Nora!

NORA. You mean I would never have accepted such a sacrifice? No, certainly not. But what would my assertions have been worth in opposition to yours. That was the miracle that I hoped for and dreaded. And it was to hinder that that I wanted to die.

HELMER. I would gladly work for you day and night, Nora – bear sorrow and want for your sake – but no man sacrifices his honour, even for one he loves.

NORA. Millions of women have done so.

HELMER. Oh you think and talk like a silly child.

NORA. Very likely. But you neither think nor talk like the man I could share my life with. When your terror was over – not for me, but for yourself – when there was nothing more to fear – then it was to you as though nothing had happened. I was your lark again, your doll – whom you would take twice as much care of in future, because she was so weak and fragile. (*Stands up*). Torvald, in that moment it burst upon me, that I had been living here these eight years with a strange man, and had borne him three children – Oh! I can't bear to think of it – I could tear myself to pieces!

HELMER (*sadly*). I see it, I see it; an abyss has opened between us – But, Nora, can it never be filled up?

NORA. As I now am, I am no wife for you.

HELMER. I have strength to become another man.

NORA. Perhaps – when your doll is taken away from you.

HELMER. To part – to part from you! No, Nora, no; I can't grasp the thought.

NORA (*going into the room, right*.) The more reason for the thing to happen.

[*She comes back with outdoor things and a small travelling bag, which she puts on a chair.*]

HELMER. Nora, Nora, not now! Wait till tomorrow.

NORA (*putting on cloak*). I can't spend the night in a strange man's house.

HELMER. But can't we live here as brother and sister?

NORA (*fastening her hat*). You know very well that would not last long. Goodbye, Torvald. No, I won't go to the children. I know they are in better hands than mine. As I now am, I can be nothing to them.

HELMER. But sometime, Nora – sometime—

NORA. How can I tell? I have no idea what will become of me.

HELMER. But you are my wife now and always!

NORA. Listen, Torvald – when a wife leaves her husband's house, as I am doing, I have heard that in the eyes of the law he is free from all duties towards her. At any rate I release you from all duties. You must not feel yourself bound any more than I shall. There must be perfect freedom on both sides. There, there is your ring back. Give me mine.

HELMER. That too?

NORA. That too.

HELMER. Here it is.

NORA. Very well. Now it is all over. Here are the keys. The servants know about everything in the house, better than I do. Tomorrow when I have started, Christina will come to pack up my things. I will have them sent after me.

HELMER. All over! All over! Nora, will you never think of me again.

NORA. Oh I shall often think of you, and the children – and this house.

HELMER. May I write to you, Nora?

NORA. No, never. You must not.

HELMER. But I must send you—

NORA. Nothing, nothing.

HELMER. I must help you if you need it.

NORA. No, I say. I take nothing from strangers.

HELMER. Nora, can I never be more than a stranger to you?

NORA (*taking her travelling bag*). Oh, Torvald, then the miracle of miracles would have to happen.

HELMER. What is the miracle of miracles?

NORA. Both of us would have to change so that – Oh, Torvald, I no longer believe in miracles.

HELMER. But I will believe. We must so change that—?

NORA. That communion between us shall be a marriage. Goodbye.

[*She goes out.*]

HELMER (*sinks in a chair by the door with his face in his hands.*) Nora! Nora! (*He looks round and stands up.*) Empty. She's gone! (*A hope inspires him.*) Ah! The miracle of miracles—?!

[*From below is heard the reverberation of a heavy door closing.*]

Henrik Ibsen, A Doll's House, trans. William Archer, 1889

'WE HAVE KILLED YOU IN KILLING HIM'

We all stood up close together in a corner of the hut; each of us took up one of the logs of wood that lay on the ground, as some means of defence. I did not know if my husband had his gun, as it was too dark in the hut to see even our faces. The sepoys then began to pull off the roof: the cowardly wretches dared not come in, as they thought we had weapons. When they had unroofed the hut, they fired in upon us. At the first shot we dropped our pieces of wood, and my husband said, 'We will not die here, let us go outside.' We all rushed out; and Mrs Blake, Mrs Raikes, and I clasped our hands and cried, 'Mut maro, mut maro' (do not kill us). The sepoys said, 'We will not kill the memsahibs, only the sahib.' We were surrounded by a crowd of them, and as soon as they distinguished my husband, they fired at him. Instantly they dragged Mrs Blake, Mrs Raikes, and me back; but not into the bearer's hut; the mehter's was good enough for us, they said. I saw no more; but volley after volley soon told me that all was over.

Here we again lay crouched on the ground; and the stillness was such, that a little mouse crept out and looked at us with its bright eyes, and was not afraid. Mrs Campbell came rushing in with her hair hanging about; she wore a native's dress, her own having been torn off her: she had been left alone the whole night. Then poor Mrs Kirke, with her little boy, joined us: she had that instant seen her husband shot before her eyes; and on her crying 'Kill me too!' they answered, 'No, we have killed you in killing him.' Her arms were bruised and swollen; they had torn off her bracelets so roughly: even her wedding ring was gone. They spared her little boy; saying; 'Don't kill the butcha; it is a missie baba.' Poor child! his long curls and girlish face saved his life! He was only four years of age.

I was very thankful to see Mrs Campbell, after the frightful report we had heard; for till then we had thought her to be safe under Major Macpherson's protection. The sepoys soon returned, and crowded in to stare at us. They made the most insulting remarks, and then said, 'Let us carry them to our lines;' whereupon they seized our hands, and dragged us along very fast. It was a beautiful morning, and the birds were singing. Oh! how could the bright sun and clear blue sky look on such a scene of cruelty! It seemed as if God had forgotten us, and that hell reigned on earth. No words can describe the hellish looks of these human fiends, or picture their horrid appearance: they had rifled all the stores, and drank brandy and beer to excess, besides being intoxicated with bhang. They were all armed, and dressed in their fatigue uniform. I noticed the number on them; it was the 4th – that dreaded regiment. Some were evidently the prisoners who had been let out from the gaol the night before; and they were, if possible, more furious than the rest. Several mounted sowars (the same, I believe, whom I had seen ride in the day before) were riding about the roads and keeping guard, and wished to fire at us, but the infantry would not let them. The road was crowded with sepoys laden with plunder, some of which I recognised as our own.

After they had dragged us to their lines, they took us from house to house, and at last placed us on a charpoy under some trees. Mrs Gilbert and her child now arrived, and poor Mrs Proctor; the latter in a dreadful state, having just seen her husband killed. All our horses and carriages were drawn up in a line under some trees, and I saw a beautiful Arab of Mrs Raikes' lying shot. Hundreds of sepoys now came to stare at us, and thronged round us so densely we could scarcely breathe. They mocked and laughed at us, and reviled us with the most bitter language, saying: 'Why don't you go home to your houses? Don't you think it is very hot here? Would you like to see your sahibs *now*?' We said we wished to go to Agra; they replied, 'Oh! Agra is burnt to the ground, and all the Feringhis are killed.' They then struck the native gong. I think it was about eight o'clock.

After keeping us for some time, as a spectacle on which to wreak their contempt, when they had tired themselves with using insulting language, they said we might go where we liked; but when we asked how? they demurred at giving us one of the carriages, till some, more merciful than the rest, at last said we might have one. They gave us Mrs Blake's – a large landau. The horses were very spirited and plunged a good deal: the morning before, they had broken the traces. How we all got in I can't say: there were Mrs Blake, Mrs Raikes, her baby and ayah, Mrs Kirke and her little boy, Mrs Campbell and myself; and some sergeants' wives clung to the carriage: how they hung on I don't know. The sepoys threw into the carriage one or two bottles of beer, and a bottle of camphor-water. The first thing the horses did, was to run down a bank and across a small nullah.

Muza drove; and a syce went with us a little way, but soon grew tired, and fell back. When we got a little way from the station, we came up with some more sergeants' wives and children; some of them nearly naked, and in great distress, having seen their husbands shot, and dragged about, and others not knowing the fate of their husbands. Poor things, their distress was very pitiable; their feelings being less under control than ours.

R. M. Coopland, *A Lady's Escape from Gwalior*, 1859

THE PASSIONATE SWORD

They say it happened that as a young girl in her earliest years, scarce yet marriageable, but warm with the love of Christ, she bravely withstood godless commands, refusing to make herself over to idols and desert her holy faith. For though she was first assailed with many arts, now with seductive words from a smooth-tongued judge, and again with threats of cruel torture, she stood firm with strength indomitable, and even offered her body for the sore torment, not refusing to die. Then said the savage persecutor: 'If it is easy for her to overcome the pains and bear the suffering and she scorns life as of little worth, still the purity of her dedicated maidenhood is dear to her. I am resolved to thrust her into a public brothel unless she lays her head on the altar and now asks pardon of Minerva, the virgin whom she, a virgin too, persists in slighting. All the young men will rush in to seek the new slave of their sport.' 'Nay,' says Agnes, 'Christ is not so forgetful of his own as to let our precious chastity be lost and abandon us. He stands by the chaste and does not suffer the gift of holy purity to be defiled. You may stain your sword with my blood if you will, but you will not pollute my body with lust.' When she had thus spoken he gave order to place the maid publicly at a corner of the square; but while she stood there the crowd avoided her in sorrow, turning their faces away lest any look too rudely on her modesty. One, as it chanced, did aim an impudent gaze at the girl, not fearing to look on her sacred figure with a lustful eye; when behold, a fire came flying like a thunderbolt and with its quivering blaze struck his eyes, and he fell blinded by the gleaming flash and lay convulsed in the dust of the square. His companions lifted him from the ground between life and death and bewailed him with words of lamentation for the departed. But the maiden passed in triumph, singing of God the Father and Christ in holy song because, when an unholy peril fell on her, her virginity won the day, finding the brothel chaste and pure. Some have told that being asked she poured forth prayers to Christ that He would restore sight to the prostrate sinner, and that then the breath of life was renewed in the young man and his vision made perfect.

But this was only the first step that Agnes took towards the court of heaven; then she was granted a second ascent. For frenzy was working up her blood-thirsty enemy's wrath. 'I am losing the battle,' he complained. 'Go draw the sword, soldier, and give effect to our lord the emperor's sovereign commands.' When Agnes saw the grim figure standing there with his naked sword her gladness increased and she said: 'I rejoice that there comes a man like this, a savage, cruel, wild man-at-arms, rather than a listless, soft, womanish youth bathed in perfume, coming to destroy me with the death of my honour. This lover, this one at last, I confess it, pleases me. I shall meet his eager steps half-way and not put off his hot desires. I shall welcome the whole length of his blade into my bosom, drawing the sword-blow to the depths of my breast; and so as Christ's bride I shall o'erleap all the darkness of the sky and rise higher than the ether. O eternal ruler, open the gates of heaven which formerly were barred against the children of earth, and call, O Christ, a soul that follows Thee, a virgin's soul and a sacrifice to the Father.' So saying she bowed her head and humbly worshipped Christ, so that her bending neck should be readier to suffer the impending blow; and the executioner's hand fulfilled her great hope, for at one stroke he cut off her head and swift death forestalled the sense of pain. Now the disembodied spirit springs forth and leaps in freedom into the air, and angels are round her as she passes along the shining path. She marvels at the world that lies beneath her feet; as she mounts on high she looks at the darkness below and laughs at the circling of the sun's orb, the turning and intertwining of all the universe, the life that is lived in the black whirlwind of circumstance, the vanities that the inconstant world seizes on, kings, despots, power and rank, the pomp of dignitaries swollen with foolish pride, the masses of silver and gold which all seek after with a furious thirst by every wicked means, the gorgeously built dwellings, the empty vanities of fancily embroidered garments, anger, fear, desires, hazards, the alternations of long sadness and short-lived joy, the smoking brands of black spite that darken men's hopes and honour, and the foulest of all their ills, the filthy clouds of paganism.

Prudentius, *Crowns of Martyrdom*, trans. H.J. Thomson, 1961

MANY SCARS

Run away, about the 15th of December last, a small yellow Negro wench named HANNAH, about 35 years of age; had on when she went away a green plains petticoat, and sundry other clothes, but what sort I do not know, as she stole many from the other Negroes. She has remarkable long hair, or wool, is much scarified under the throat from one ear to the other, and has many scars on her back, occasioned by whipping. She pretends much to the religion the Negroes of late have practised, and may probably endeavour to pass for a free woman, as I understand she intended when she went away, by the Negroes in the neighbourhood. She is supposed to have made for Carolina. Whoever takes up the said slave, and secures her so that I get her again, shall be rewarded according to their trouble, by

STEPHEN DENCE

Virginia Gazette, 26 March 1767

THREE

'It didn't matter what these men had done'

May, 1944. Day and night the transports kept coming from Hungary. Ninety-five per cent of the new arrivals were sent directly from the cattle trucks to the gas chambers. The crematoria blazed away without a stop, their chimneys belching flames. The camp was enveloped in a thick black smoke. The stench of the burning bodies was suffocating. 'Operation Hoess' had reached its peak. The crematoria could no longer accommodate the accelerated tempo of the transports. The victims were standing around for hours, waiting their 'turn' for the 'bath'. We were not allowed to get near them. We could not cry out to them that they were being deceived, that they were going to their deaths. And even if we could what good would it have done? They were surrounded by SS men, armed to their teeth.

Mala's barracks was located very close to the barbed wire fence where the nearby path led to the crematoria. Through the walls she could hear the conversations of the waiting victims, the wailing of the children, the shouting of the SS and their barking dogs, the screams of the beaten and, frequently, the shooting. She could endure it no longer. She decided to escape and alarm the world – tell the world what was happening. We believed that if only the world knew . . .

Escape? But how? Some Poles had tried, those who came from the region, and had friends and relatives there. And they had not succeeded. How would a Jew? And even if she succeeded in escaping, where would she go? Who would help her? But the thought gave her no rest.

One day Mala told me of the escape plan of a Pole named Edek Galinski. He had been in camp since 1940. He had come with the first transport and had worked on the construction of the camp. His number was 531. He was familiar with every part of the giant complex Auschwitz-Birkenau. As a mechanic he came into contact with civilians who did various jobs in the camp that the Germans did not entrust to prisoners for fear of sabotage. It was through them that he got in touch with people in the outside world. His work frequently took him to the women's camp and that was how he got to know Mala.

This was Edek's plan: He would get an SS uniform and, disguised as an SS officer, would lead a friend, a fellow prisoner, out of the camp, presumably for outside work. For this he needed a Passierschein (a special permit). Mala was in a position to steal such a permit from the guardhouse to which she had access. She agreed to do it and proposed to Edek that he should take her along. Edek's friend was against it. He was afraid to escape with a woman, especially a Jewish woman. Edek then decided to escape with Mala. He too wanted to arouse the world.

They decided to leave on a Saturday. On Saturday at noon some of the SS men went off duty and the guard was somewhat lighter than usual. Mala was to wear a man's uniform. As a prisoner-functionary she was allowed to let her hair grow. That was an advantage on the outside. But disguised as a man she would have to tuck her hair well under her cap and carry a washbowl on her head to hide her face.

Mala confided her plan to me and to her closest friends, the three 'runners' with whom she worked and who lived in the same barracks. They promised to help.

Everything was ready for the appointed date – June 24, 1944. On that day Mala put on an abdominal belt in which was hidden a stripeless dress. (On the backs of all prisoners' clothing a thick stripe or cross was painted in red, a telltale mark that made escape difficult.) We said goodbye to each other. Mala was calm. We all marvelled at her and envied her courage.

The camp was ringed with two *Posten-Kette* (chains of guard posts). The first was an electrified wire fence that surrounded all parts of the camp, with a watchtower at every fifty metres manned by SS with machine-guns. If Edek and Mala succeeded in getting past the guardhouse they would find themselves in the second *Posten-Kette*, which ringed all the camps of the Auschwitz-Birkenau complex, in the middle of armed SS and the dogs that guarded the prisoners working outside the camp.

As Mala approached the gate of Camp A her three friends, the 'runners', were already standing at the *Blockführerstube* (the guardhouse). They were always there ready to carry out the commands of the SS, but this time they were there as lookouts to warn Mala if anyone should suddenly appear.

It was midday. The SS sentry, now off duty, emerged from the guardhouse and rode away on his motor-cycle. Mala and one of the 'runners' entered the guardhouse. Only one woman SS overseer was there. They knew her well. She liked to drink. Mala had a present for her, a bottle of vodka. The overseer thanked her and poured herself a drink. The 'runner' engaged her in conversation while Mala left the room and went to the washroom where Edek had hidden the uniform and the washbowl.

From a distance I could see Mala leaving the guardhouse, bent under the weight of the washbowl on her head, her face almost completely hidden by it. Outside, Edek was waiting. He had concealed himself in a potato bunker (a kind of cellar) not far from the guardhouse and, at a sign from his friends, emerged from the bunker unnoticed.

Edek let Mala go first and followed a few paces behind her. This was the procedure for an SS man leading a prisoner and Edek was well acquainted with the rules. This was how he himself was frequently led to work outside the camp.

Now they were both heading in the direction of Camp Budy. They knew that on the way they would probably run into some sentries, but they took comfort in the fact that these were new arrivals from the front 'for a spell in Auschwitz', who were not yet familiar with the guard personnel of the camp, numbering around 3,000 SS men.

The plan was that if Edek and Mala passed Camp Budy without a mishap Mala would discard the heavy wash-bowl somewhere in a cornfield and take off her uniform. Edek would remain dressed in his and give the appearance of an SS man out for a good time with his girlfriend.

One day a rumour spread throughout the camp that Mala and Edek had been caught – that they were already in Auschwitz I, in Block 11, where prisoners were tortured to death during interrogations and shot by the hundreds at the Black Wall.

Mala and Edek in the Bunker? We could not believe it. We did not want to believe it. After two weeks? How was it possible? But the rumour turned out to be true. Mala managed to send us a message, smuggled out from her Bunker: 'I know what is awaiting me. I am prepared for the worst. Be brave and remember everything.'

Various fantastic versions of their capture were circulated in camp but nobody knew exactly how they were caught. In the men's camp a barber working for the SS said he had heard that Mala and Edek were caught in a restaurant for SS men. Edek was still in his uniform and he was recognised by an Auschwitz guard. The girls working in the Political Department had another version: The two were caught at the border as they were about to cross into Czechoslovakia.

Boger himself conducted the interrogation. Known as 'the devil of Auschwitz', he would extract all the information he wanted from his victims with his horrible tortures. In this case he wanted to know who had helped Mala and Edek to escape. Despite the tortures Mala and Edek maintained their silence. Weeks passed and no one else was called to the Political Department; no one else was interrogated.

It was the evening of August 22, nearly two months since her attempted escape. Once again the orchestra played as the slaves returned from work. This time nobody was missing at the *Appell*. All were accounted for. Even Mala was there, standing at the gate. Why had they brought her to Birkenau? What was the verdict? There were no gallows in sight so we consoled ourselves with the thought that she would probably be flogged publicly and then sent to a punitive Kommando.

After the roll-call a command was shouted: 'All Jews must gather in camp B.' When we got there I remained standing in the first row. We wanted Mala to see us and we wanted her to know that we wanted to see her. We wondered what would happen next.

Mala came walking proudly, head high. Behind her walked Riters, head of work details. He ordered her to stop a few paces away from us. Mala stared at us but I had the feeling that she did not see us. Her glance was vague and distant. The camp commander, Frau Mandel, appeared. She read something from a paper but I did not hear a word. I kept looking at Mala. She was smoothing down her hair. Suddenly Mala began to cut her wrist with a razor. We were petrified with horror. We bit our lips to keep from screaming and remained glued to the spot.

Riters probably noticed the expression on our faces and suspected that something was happening. He looked at Mala – then grabbed her arm. Mala slapped his face with her bloody hand. Riters pulled her arms behind her and shouted: 'You want to be a heroine! You want to kill yourself! That's what we are here for. That's our job!'

'Murderers!' Mala cried out. 'You will soon pay for our sufferings! Don't be afraid, girls! Their end is near. I am certain of this. I know. I was free!'

Riters struck Mala on the head with his revolver and pushed her in the direction of the hospital. The camp kapo blew her whistle and ordered the prisoners to disband and return to the barracks. Two nurses came running out of the hospital carrying a stretcher, but Frau Mandel shouted: 'No! Take it back! This one belongs to the crematorium. This one must be burned alive!' She ordered that a handcart be brought.

Meanwhile Mala was dragged into hospital barracks Number 4. There they tied her arm tightly so that she would not bleed to death and beat her. The girls returned with the handcart and put Mala into it. She noticed the tears in their eyes. 'Do not cry,' she pleaded in a weak voice. 'The day of reckoning is near. You hear me? Remember everything they did to us.'

'Shut your mouth, you swine!' an SS man shouted.

'For two years I had to keep silent. Now I can say what I please,' Mala said, with all the strength she could muster.

The SS man taped her mouth with adhesive. 'Now she'll be quiet,' he said to Frau Mandel. He accompanied the cart to the crematorium compound.

Giza Weisblaum, 'The Escape and Death of the "Runner" Mala Zimetbaum', in *They Fought Back*, ed. Yuri Suhl, 1968

'VERY BLACK'

RAN AWAY from the subscriber, in Chesterfield County, near Osborne's, on the 1st of May, 1781, when the British troops were there, the following NEGROES, viz. Daniel, a low well-made fellow, about 21 or 22 years old, has on his sides and back several large bumps like warts, occasioned by whipping. Dinah, a lusty made young wench, about 19 or 20 years old, full round face, and very large breasts. The above Negroes much given to singing hymns. Tom, about 16 or 17 years old, and has been badly burnt from his knees up to his breast, occasioned by his cloaths catching fire. Lewis, about 14 or 15 years old, spare made, and is left handed. All the above Negroes are very black. Whoever will bring the above Negroes to me, shall receive TEN POUNDS for each so brought; and if any person will give me intelligence so that I may recover them, shall receive FIVE POUNDS for each so recovered.

SAMUEL HATCHER
June 14, 1782

Virginia Gazette or American Advertiser, 22 June 1782

CHILD LEFT BEHIND

Annapolis, June 4, 1780

RAN away last night from the subscriber a dark mulatto woman named PLEASANT; twenty-seven years of age, about five feet high, sharp visage, very artful and talkative, especially when she get a little liquor, which she is very fond of, speaks a little in the negro accent, may change her name, though well known by the name of Adams's Pleasant in this neighbourhood and over South river, where it is supposed she is gone and may be harboured by the negroes. She left a sucking child behind her, which may be easily perceived on examining her breasts. She had on and took with her a country made striped petticoat, and three osnabrig shirts, two of which are new, but may have other cloaths. Whoever takes up and secures the above wench so that her master may get her again, shall be paid fifty dollars continental currency, if taken in this neighbourhood, or over South river, and if at a greater distance one hundred dollars, and all reasonable charges if brought home.

HENRY SEWALL

Annapolis, *Maryland Gazette*, 9 June 1780

TRUTHFUL MASTERS

Let us try this public opinion by another test, which is important in three points of view: first, as showing how desperately timid of the public opinion slave-owners are, in their delicate descriptions of fugitive slaves in widely circulated newspapers; secondly, as showing how perfectly contented the slaves are, and how very seldom they run away; thirdly, as exhibiting their entire freedom from scar, or blemish, or any mark of cruel infliction, as their pictures are drawn, not by lying abolitionists, but by their own truthful masters.

The following are a few specimens of the advertisements in the public papers. It is only four years since the oldest among them appeared; and others of the same nature continue to be published every day, in shoals . . .

'Ran away, the Mulatto wench Mary. Has a cut on the left arm, a scar on the left shoulder, and two upper teeth missing.'

I should say, perhaps, in explanation of this latter piece of description, that among the other blessings which public opinion secures to the negroes, is the common practice of violently punching out their teeth. To make them wear iron collars by day and night, and to worry them with dogs, are practices almost too ordinary to deserve mention.

'Ran away, my man Fountain. Has holes in his ears, a scar on the right side of his forehead, has been shot in the hind parts of his legs, and is marked on the back with the whip.'

'Two hundred and fifty dollars reward for my negro man Jim. He is much marked with shot in his right thigh. The shot entered on the outside, halfway between the hip and knee joints.'

'Brought to jail, John. Left ear cropt.'

'Taken up, a negro man. Is very much scarred about the face and body, and has the left ear bit off.'

'Ran away, a black girl, named Mary. Has a scar on her cheek, and the end of one of her toes cut off.'

'Ran away, my Mulatto woman, Judy. She has had her right arm broke.'

'Ran away, my negro man, Levi. His left hand has been burnt, and I think the end of his forefinger is off.'

'Ran away, a negro man, NAMED WASHINGTON. Has lost a part of his middle finger, and the end of his little finger.'

'Twenty-five dollars reward for my man John. The tip of his nose is bit off.'

'Twenty-five dollars reward for the negro slave, Sally. Walks *as though* crippled in the back.'

'Ran away, Joe Dennis. Has a small notch in one of his ears.'

'Ran away, negro boy, Jack. Has a small crop out of his left ear.'

'Ran away, a negro man, named Ivory. Has a small piece cut out of the top of each ear.'

While upon the subject of ears, I may observe that a distinguished abolitionist in New York once received a negro's ear, which had been cut off close to the head, in a general post letter. It was forwarded by the free and independent gentleman who had caused it to be amputated, with a polite request that he would place the specimen in his 'collection.'

Charles Dickens, American Notes, 1842

MODERATE CORRECTION

RUN from the Subscriber's plantation in Albemarle county, a tall slim Negro fellow, named GEORGE; he is marked in the face as the Gold Coast slaves generally are, had the usual clothing of labouring Negroes, and is supposed to be harboured at some of the plantations on Cary's creek, in Goochland county. Also run away from the subscriber's quarter called Westham, in Henrico county, another

Negro fellow, named ROBIN: he is very tall, slim and of a thin visage, having lost some of his teeth; he formerly belonged to Col. Benjamin Harrison of Berkeley, and is supposed to be gone in the neighbourhood of his plantation on Nottoway river, where he formerly lived. Whoever will convey the former Negro to Mr Lucas Powell in Albemarle, and the latter to William Walker at Westham, shall receive FORTY SHILLINGS for each of them, besides what is allowed by law. As I have been always tender of my slaves, and particularly attentive to the good usage of them, I hope wherever these fellows may be apprehended that they will receive such moderate correction as will deter them from running away for the future; and wherever any of my Negroes are taken up as runaways, I desire the favour of the magistrate, who may be applied to for a certificate, to order them back to their respective overseers, instead of sending them to me in this city,

RO. C. NICHOLAS

Virginia Gazette, 15 January 1767

TOO MUCH INDULGED

FREDERICKSBURG,
March 11, 1772

FIFTEEN POUNDS Reward for taking up, and delivering to me, my Man CHRISTMAS. He is a lusty, well made, genteel Fellow, has waited on me from my Infancy, can shave and dress extremely well, and is about thirty Years of Age; his Complexion is rather light (his Father being a light Mulatto) very pleasant, and well featured. He has been innoculated for the Smallpox, but has no Marks except the Scar of the Incision on one Arm, and at present a large Cut on his Shin, the Effect of a late Night Revel; he can read, is very fluent of Speech, speaks with great Propriety, and is so artful that he can invent a plausible Tale at a Moment's Warning, which makes me suspect that he will now pass unmolested, under some Pretence or other, as a Freeman, which I presume will be most desirable to him; though he has lived little short of it with me, having been too much indulged, and being very idle during my present Indisposition, he has grown wanton in Licentiousness, and several gross Acts of ill Behaviour this Week past, are now completed by an Elopement last Monday Night. It will be in vain to

[73]

describe his Dress, as he has already changed his Livery, and it seems has taken a brown Kersey Waistcoat belonging to my cook, which I presume he will retain as Part of his Dress. The above Reward will be proportioned, and paid according to the Distance he may be taken up and brought home, namely, FIVE POUNDS if above twenty and under fifty Miles, TEN POUNDS is [SIC] above fifty and under a Hundred Miles, and FIFTEEN POUNDS for any Distance above a Hundred Miles in this Colony; but if he is taken out of the Colony, I will give TWENTY POUNDS.

JAMES MERCER

Virginia Gazette, 19 March 1772

RESERVATIONS

Eric Williams made me realise that there was an unendurable agony in being pinned behind barbed wire and he could understand the emotional upset of the convict who realised that it was his own fault, either because of his crime or because he was careless enough to be found out, that he was inside a prison.

Whatever else he might think about it, Williams thought the imprisoning of men was a loathsome business and he doubted if it achieved the end aimed at. It was a punishment that befouled the souls of those it punished and degraded those who had to enforce it.

I am not going to develop Williams' very controversial point of discussion, although any intelligent man would be inclined to agree with him, with reservations. But Williams is not only an intelligent man, he is a sensitive man and I want to quote his experience some time ago to illustrate a point about prisoners who escape.

Eric Williams lives on the edge of Dartmoor. From his lovely cliff home looking obliquely at Start Point you climb through Totnes to the grimmer prospect of the Moor.

Recently Williams heard on the wireless that two prisoners had escaped from Dartmoor. That night a heavy mist clung to the Moor. Rain beat against the window-panes and wind played a dirge through the trees.

'When I heard the words . . . escaped from Dartmoor . . . I felt the thrill of the old days again,' he said, 'and almost instinctively I put myself in the sodden uniforms and mud-caked boots of the convicts and joined them in the run. Before I realised it I had got down an ordnance survey map and was discussing with myself the route I would have taken if I had been one of the convicts. You see, by now it didn't matter what these men had done or why they were in prison. They were now two hunted men and I had been a hunted man myself once.'

Without the same vivid memories he must have felt, I have often wondered when I was Governor there which way I would have struck if I had tried to escape from Dartmoor.

Williams would have struck north. He would have avoided Prince-town and the south because of the possibility of encountering civilians trained by custom to respond to the emergency machinery of a prison escape. It is like a reflex action with these people.

'The only free way was north of the prison across the rough farmlands, which give roadways for some distance, so that as many miles as possible could be put between myself and the pursuers.

'My first aim would be to break into the first habitation far enough away, to steal food, clothing and money. I would need all three badly. And then I would lay up for the hours of daylight.'

Now this is interesting because it shows the mind of the intelligent escapee. Many of the prison escapees just escape and hope for the best. They revel in their moments of freedom and usually they are recaptured in a few hours suffering from the discomforts of the hunt.

Captain Gerold Fancourt Clayton, The Wall is Strong:
The Life of a Prison Governor, 1958

CROSS-ROADS

I am free! *Free*! Out of the welter of events which have packed themselves into the last thirty-six hours, that is the one great fact that emerges. My prearranged plans have been turned topsyturvy; I am footsore and weary and perhaps heading for all manner of trouble; but none the less, as I write this, prison life is behind me and I am a free man again!

Already it requires an effort to recall exactly how this came about, but the essential factor was that we were moved, as expected, from our camp near Boulogne and taken in the direction of Belgium. We travelled in open lorries, and at first were amply guarded by an NCO in the front of each vehicle and a squad of men, all fully armed, at the back. We had a long run under these conditions, which, with one halt, brought us to Lille. There were depressing sights to be seen en route – as for instance British lorries, which the former owners had for some reason failed to destroy, doing service for the German forces. In some cases the German drivers had amused themselves by decorating these vehicles with war trophies. It was not uncommon to see a British or French helmet hung from the radiator cap, while a very popular device was to fix a British gas-mask over each of the headlamps, the face-piece in each case looking like a ghastly death's head. With a little imagination one could visualise the driver as a Borneo headhunter, unaccountably dressed in the green German uniform, returning from a successful mechanised raid upon the adjoining tribe!

It was depressing to enter Lille again under these conditions, for many of us had recollections of the town in the days before the invasion of Belgium, when it was a favourite resort of the British troops stationed in the neighbourhood. 'Let's go into Lille and have a bath and some dinner' had been a popular suggestion then in many a mess after the usual day's training was over. Now we were taken to a building on the far side of the town, where it appeared that some thousands of prisoners were housed. We were at first told to remain in the yard, which was surrounded by high railings, and here we became an object of attention for whole bevies of pretty French girls from the town. They came not just to stare but to bring us little gifts of chocolate or biscuits, and in some cases to hand in a letter (for the German guards were good-natured enough to turn a blind eye to this), which they hoped that we might be able to deliver to some prisoner relative or friend. In a way this touch of femininity was pleasant; but personally I would have preferred to have been spared it. Pretty girls in Lille were altogether too reminiscent of the carefree evenings and the cheery company which most of us could not hope to experience again until perhaps many a dreary year had passed.

We spent about an hour in this yard, and then it appeared that, through some miscalculation, the Germans could not find the necessary accommodation for us; they would have to transfer us, with a few other officer prisoners, to a nearby prison camp in Belgium. (Lille is, of course, close to the French-Belgian frontier.) Another lorry was therefore brought up and we were packed into the back of it. A couple of Germans got into the front seat, but it seemed there were no men available to travel in the back with us; perhaps it was thought that, the projected journey being so short and the intention being to make a non-stop run of it, there was no real need for this precaution; or perhaps, our former guards having dispersed, they could not immediately be reassembled. At any rate, after a little discussion the gates opened and the lorry moved off.

The possibilities of the situation struck me at once, and I lost no time in pointing out to H. that we were no longer under close surveillance. He, however, did not seem to be impressed; the lorry, to be sure, was soon travelling at a fast and steady speed, while the road was positively crowded with other German transport of every description. I myself did not dare to feel too optimistic; but a chance is a chance – and I quickly rummaged through my kit, found the two tins of 'bully', crammed them into my pockets, and then forced my way into a position on the lorry's tail-board. I was determined at least to be ready for a quick move.

There followed a nerve-racking twenty minutes of alternate hope and despondency. Sometimes I would look out behind, waiting for a moment when there should be no other German vehicle in sight – only to find that on such occasions our speed was far too high to make it possible for me to jump. At other times I would stand up to get a forward view, watching for some contingency of traffic which would force our driver to slow down; but at such times it always seemed that a German car or motor-truck would be close on our tail, the occupants viewing my antics with suspicious, penetrating eyes!

Finally it seemed that my last hope had gone, for we were already on the outskirts of Tournai, and when the lorry at last came to a stop, it was outside a building which, by its grim appearance and the sentries on patrol outside it, proclaimed itself to be a prison. I had already resigned myself to the inevitable when there came a temporary reprieve. The building was indeed a prison, but not the particular prison to which we were consigned; the latter was apparently a little further on, and we had to skirt round the town for some distance to reach it.

We set off again – and even at this eleventh hour I would not entirely abandon hope. True, one could hardly imagine a worse place for making an escape than the outskirts of a town midway between two German prisons. On the other hand, being now in Belgium, it seemed evident that we were en route for Germany; thus it looked like being a case of 'now or never', since an escape from German territory would obviously present enormously increased difficulties.

At this last moment as it happened, the luck turned in my favour. Our lorry drove on for a quarter of a mile and then slowed down at a cross-roads where, by a happy chance, the only individuals in sight were Belgians. The driver, coming almost to a standstill, called out to one of these, presumably to ask the way.

This, for me, was the crucial moment. With more agility than I knew myself to possess, I slipped over the tail-board of the lorry and took up a position in the roadway just behind it, invisible both to the driver and to the other German in the cab. For a period of, I suppose, a few seconds only, the debate as to the route continued (to me it seemed endless, for there was imminent danger of other troops coming into view). Then the lorry moved on, leaving me standing alone.

The Earl of Cardigan, *I Walked Alone*, 1950

AUDACITY

Absented himself from the Subscriber, the 4th of this Instant, a NEGRO Man, named LIMUS; he is of a yellow Complexion, and has the Ends of three of his Fingers cut off his left Hand; he is well known in Charles-Town from his saucy and impudent Tongue, of which I have had many Complaints; therefore, I hereby give free Liberty, and will be also much obliged to any Person to flog him (so as not take his Life) in such Manner as they shall think proper, whenever he is found out of my Habitation without a Ticket; for though he is my Property, he has the audacity to tell me, he will be free, that he will serve no Man, and that he will be conquered or governed by no Man. I forwarn Masters of Vessels from carrying him off the Province, and all Persons from harbouring him in their Houses or Plantations.

JOSHUA EDEN

South-Carolina Gazette, 7 November 1775

FOUR

'They were on their own'

We walked in a long procession split up by all the ox-carts. I watched over Somaly all the time to make sure that she didn't get separated from the main column. Da and Lay were as good as their word and took good care of Panita. Sometimes, Lay carried Panita on his shoulders and sometimes Da gave her a piggyback or held her hand while walking along in the dark. From time to time, Lay lifted Panita up and put her in an ox-cart in spite of the protests from the driver, who feared that the extra weight might break the axle. This gave me an idea and I walked close to an ox-Cart with Somaly. I told her to put her hand on to the back of the cart and to hold on tight. This had the effect of dragging her forward. Every two hours or so, Yom let us stop to get about 20 minutes' rest. A half-moon came out and helped us to see our way. It also cast eerie shadows in front of us and made the journey more terrifying as we imagined the Khmer Rouge lying in ambush for us.

At about 9 p.m. Yom's men came down the line and told everyone to stop and not to move. Talking was strictly forbidden and babies were put at their mothers' breasts to prevent them from crying. Silence descended over our group like a blanket and we began to hear the sounds of the jungle which had been previously masked by the noise of the column. From far away, the wind brought us the long drawn-out cry of a wild animal. We had no idea what was going on, but were frozen in fear. Someone whispered that it was a Khmer Rouge recognition signal. This meant that we had been heard and a Khmer Rouge patrol was trying to check our identity. We were in trouble and I wondered how far we could all run before the Khmer Rouge would catch up with us and begin shooting. I imagined bullets ripping into my flesh and into my children's bodies.

Now the man who had recognised the Khmer Rouge signal approached Yom and said: 'I used to work closely with the Khmer Rouge and I know all of the different recognition signals that they use in the forest. If you like, I can give them the correct reply.' Yom immediately answered: 'Make the signal. You're our only hope of avoiding an ambush.' The man then cupped his hands together and emitted a strange cry. The Khmer Rouge call came once more and again the villager replied. We held our breath in suspense and our hearts beat faster. Would it work? There was silence now from the Khmer Rouge and we waited quietly to see what would happen. Our own eyes tried to pierce the gloom of the forest and our ears strained to hear any movements coming towards us. The slightest noise would have started a panic and we would have fled in all directions. However, after some time there was still no sound from the direction of the cry and we began to have hope that the ploy had succeeded. Yom thanked the villager and we set off once more towards the border . . .

Somaly was very tired and lay on the ground where she had collapsed when we had all stopped. Panita was still sitting on the cart, but she was in tears and very frightened that she might get separated from us. She was also afraid that the cart driver might throw her off his cart. Da stayed close to comfort her. Somaly said that she could not go on any further and that she was going to sleep. She dozed off immediately and I let her sleep. Soon after, everyone started to get up and leave again. No one had said anything, but I guessed that they had finally worked out where we were. I shook Somaly to wake her up. She curled up tighter and mumbled that she was too tired and that she just wanted to sleep. It was time for some shock tactics. I told her that she could sleep, but she would have to stay alone. It was cruel but effective. She scrambled up immediately and we continued on our journey. There was no trail now and we had to force our way through bushes and thick undergrowth. Branches snatched at our faces and at our clothes, and left red weals down our cheeks. The trees soared above us and blocked out any light from the stars and the moon. The soles of our feet became scratched and torn and it was acutely painful to walk.

The ground was very uneven and, on a couple of occasions, we came to a deep depression. The men searched around in the forest to find bamboo, which they cut down and tied together to make a bridge for the ox-carts. Time seemed to drag on forever. Would we ever find our way out of this forest? I was very tired and my mind started to play tricks on me. The trees looked like men. The branches were AK47 rifles and B40 rocket launchers. Would the night ever end?

At some point in the journey, an elderly woman died and the column stopped. We were towards the back and didn't know what was going on. A few people screamed. Most of us were too tired to react and we remained where we were. Some ran towards the screams. There was no time to bury the old lady, even though we knew that her body would be eaten by wild animals if we left her. Her family had an ox-cart. They took their possessions off it and gently laid the body of the woman on top of it. This was her coffin and funeral pyre although we could not set fire to it for fear of attracting the Khmer Rouge. The column moved on with the family weeping quietly. My heart went out to the family and I felt for them. While we all knew of the possibility of death on the escape, this was the first one. I wondered how many more would die before we could reach safety.

We knew that we were getting closer to the border and we walked in single file. Yom ordered us not to stray from the path because of land-mines. We came across a cleared area, which was covered with bamboo spikes. They had been dug into the ground by the Khmer Rouge and were specifically designed to prevent people from escaping. They were angled towards us and each one had been sharpened. The Khmer Rouge had painted the tip of each spike with a poison made from boiling a concoction of roots together so that any wound caused by it would fester. The spikes were intended to prevent people from running in the event of their being chased by the Khmer Rouge. At regular intervals there were also holes dug in the ground covered with dried grass and, as I was told, lined with bamboo spikes at the bottom. These were intended to snare the unwary, who would have been impaled on the spikes if they had fallen into the holes. Land-mines had also been planted indiscriminately.

Fortunately, the Khmer Rouge didn't have enough men to patrol all the time, so if we could get through these obstacles safely, we might yet survive. There was ample evidence of those who had tried unsuccess-fully to escape before us. As dawn broke, I could see skeletons from afar. Over the whole place of horror lay the smell of rotting flesh. We could not see the decomposing corpses but they were there somewhere – perhaps caught in one of the spiked holes. I shuddered and kept a tight grip on Somaly as we went forward.

On the far side of the area with the bamboo spikes, Yom turned around and announced to everyone that we had just crossed the border out of Cambodia into Thailand. It was about 5 a.m. on Sunday, March 11th, 1979. Relief washed through us all and there was a feeling of joy in the air. We had made it. I hugged Somaly and went to find Panita and Da to give them hugs as well. I thanked Lay and Da for their help with Panita. Without them, my joy would have been empty.

There was no time for a party and we had to get away from the border as soon as possible. We could hear the sound of dogs barking and cocks crowing in the distance. It was a familiar sound to us who had lived in villages for so many years. Then, it had meant the start of another day of slavery under the Khmer Rouge. Now, it signified that we were near a Thai village and freedom.

Var Hong Ashe, From Phnom Penh to Paradise, 1975

And here it were fit to leave this point, touching the concurrence of military virtue and learning; (for what example would come with any grace after those two of Alexander and Cæsar?) were it not in regard of the rareness of circumstances that I find in one other particular, as that which did so suddenly pass from extreme scorn to extreme wonder; and it is of Xenophon the philosopher, who went from Socrates' school into Asia, in the expedition of Cyrus the younger, against King Artaxerxes. This Xenophon at that time was very young, and never had seen the wars before; neither had any command in the army, but only followed the war as a voluntary, for the love and conversation of Proxenus his friend. He was present when Phalynus came in message from the great king to the Grecians, after that Cyrus was slain the field, and they a handful of men left to themselves in the midst of the king's territories, cut off from their country by many navigable rivers, and many hundred miles. The message imported, that they should deliver up their arms, and submit themselves to the king's mercy. To which message before answer was made, divers of the army conferred familiarly with Phalynus, and amongst the rest Xenophon happened to say, *Why, Phalynus, we have now but these two things left, our arms and our virtue; and if we yield up our arms, how shall we make use of our virtue?* Whereto Phalynus smiling on him, said, *If I be not deceived, young gentleman, you are an Athenian: and, I believe you study philosophy, and it is pretty that you say: but you are much abused, if you think your virtue can withstand the king's power.* Here was the scorn; the wonder followed: which was, that this young scholar or philosopher, after all the captains were murdered in parley by treason, conducted those ten thousand foot through the heart of all the king's high countries from Babylon to Græcia in safety, in despite of all the king's forces, to the astonishment of the world, and the encouragement of the Grecians in time succeeding to make invasion upon the kings of Persia: as was after purposed by Jason the Thessalian, attempted by Agesilaus the Spartan, and achieved by Alexander the Macedonian, all upon the ground of the act of that young scholar.

Francis Bacon, The Advancement of Learning, 1605

We walked to the military headquarters where I asked the captain, 'Are there any boats going across the river today?'

'The river is closed. There will be no boats going across because they are all at the other side.'

'But what about the ferry?'

'That is closed too. We can do nothing. The Japanese are expected any hour now.'

I went down on my knees and begged for food for my children, but they would give me none. I went to another military post and begged again. They would hardly believe that what I told them was true.

'Where have you come from?'

'We have walked from Yangcheng over the mountains. It has been a terrible journey.'

'We will give you a little food, but we have only enough for the smallest children. We cannot possibly feed you all.'

I was almost in despair. All night I worried and prayed, prayed and worried. I was at the end of my tether.

If only I wasn't saddled with all these children, I thought bitterly. *Nobody else bothered about them, why did I have to get myself and them into this mess?*

Then a voice said, 'I died for these children. I loved every one of them. I gave them to you to look after, for My sake.'

So the hours went by until the dawn broke. A girl of thirteen, called Sualan, stood beside me. 'Ai-weh-deh, do you remember when God called Moses that he took the children of Israel through the Red Sea on dry land and every one of them got safely across?'

I nodded. Sualan smiled sweetly at me as she asked, 'Do you believe it?'

'Of course, I do!' I replied immediately. 'I would not teach you anything I did not believe.'

'Then why don't *we* go across?' she asked simply.

That shook me. 'But I am not Moses,' I gasped.

'Of course you are not, but Jehovah is still God!'

That was like a physical blow. All the years I had been preaching had I really believed that Moses did take the children of Israel through the Red Sea? Did I believe that the waters rolled back, and stood up on either side while they crossed dry-shod? I had staked my life on God's mighty power. Why did I doubt now?

I turned to Sualan. 'We will go across,' I said, and truly I believed it. Sualan called some of the older ones together and we knelt in prayer. Sualan prayed simply, 'Here we are, Lord, just waiting for You to open the Yellow River for us.'

For myself, I bowed in silence, but in my heart said, 'O God, I am finished. I can do nothing more. I am at the end. I am nothing. It is only You, Lord, now – You above! O God, don't let us down. Save us – prove Yourself.'

Some of the little boys ran up and pulled my skirt. 'Get up, get up!' they shouted. 'There is a big man here!'

I was trembling all over when I stood up. A Chinese officer stood watching me.

'Are you in charge of these children?' he asked.

'Yes.'

'How many are here?'

'A hundred.'

'What are you doing here?'

'Waiting to cross the river.'

'But who are you?'

'I am Ai-weh-deh of the mission hall in Yangcheng.'

'Are you crazy? Do you not realise that we expect a Japanese infantry attack at any moment? Don't you know that Japanese aircraft are patrolling all the time? If they spot these children they will machine-gun them. Who are these children, anyway?'

'We are refugees trying to reach Sian.'

'Refugees! Then why did you not cross the river long ago?'

'We could not get a boat.'

'You did not expect us to leave boats for the Japanese, did you? But I will signal for one now.'

He made a long, low whistle, like a seabird, 'Oo – oo – oo!' and raised his arm.

'The boat will be across at once. There is a village on the other side where you can get food.'

'Oh, thank you!'

'Are you looking after these children alone?'

'Yes.'

'But surely you are a foreigner?'

'Yes.'

'You have chosen a strange occupation.'

He had hardly finished speaking when the children cried out

excitedly that the boat was coming. The first lot got in, and the boat went backward and forward until all were safely over.

The people of the town took the children into their homes and fed them until they could eat no more. Then the children talked, telling of their terrible journey over the mountains.

'All of us bigger ones helped to carry the little ones,' they boasted. 'And Ai-weh-deh was always carrying one or two of the sick ones. And when we got to the river we waited and waited for a boat. We prayed for the river to be opened so that we could walk across like the children of Israel did, across the Red Sea, but God knew we were so tired of walking so He sent a boat, and that was far better.'

Gladys Aylward: Her Personal Story as Told to Christine Hunter, 1970

DEATH IN THE WILDERNESS

17 ¶ And it came to pass, when Pharaoh had let the people go, that God led them not *through* the way of the land of the Philistines, although that *was* near; for God said, Lest peradventure the people repent when they see war, and they return to Egypt:

18 But God led the people about, *through* the way of the wilderness of the Red sea: and the children of Israel went up harnessed out of the land of Egypt.

19 And Moses took the bones of Joseph with him: for he had straitly sworn the children of Israel, saying, God will surely visit you; and ye shall carry up my bones away hence with you.

20 ¶ And they took their journey from Succoth, and encamped in Etham, in the edge of the wilderness.

21 And the LORD went before them by day in a pillar of a cloud, to lead them the way; and by night in a pillar of fire, to give them light; to go by day and night:

22 He took not away the pillar of the cloud by day, nor the pillar of fire by night, *from* before the people.

CHAPTER 14

And the LORD spake unto Moses, saying,

2 Speak unto the children of Israel, that they turn and encamp before Pi-hahiroth, between Migdol and the sea, over against Baal-zephon: before it shall ye encamp by the sea.

3 For Pharaoh will say of the children of Israel. They *are* entangled in the land, the wilderness hath shut them in.

4 And I will harden Pharaoh's heart, that he shall follow after them; and I will be honoured upon Pharaoh, and upon all his host; that the Egyptians may know that I *am* the LORD. And they did so.

5 ¶ And it was told the king of Egypt that the people fled: and the heart of Pharaoh and of his servants was turned against the people, and they said, Why have we done this, that we have let Israel go from serving us?

6 And he made ready his chariot, and took his people with him:

7 And he took six hundred chosen chariots, and all the chariots of Egypt, and captains over every one of them.

8 And the LORD hardened the heart of Pharaoh king of Egypt, and he pursued after the children of Israel: and the children of Israel went out with an high hand.

9 But the Egyptians pursued after them, all the horses *and* chariots of Pharaoh, and his horsemen, and his army, and overtook them encamping by the sea, beside Pi-hahiroth, before Baal-zephon.

10 ¶ And when Pharoah drew nigh, the children of Israel lifted up their eyes, and, behold, the Egyptians marched after them; and they were sore afraid; and the children of Israel cried out unto the LORD.

11 And they said unto Moses, Because *there were* no graves in Egypt, hast thou taken us away to die in the wilderness? wherefore hast thou dealt thus with us, to carry us forth out of Egypt?

12 *Is* not this the word that we did tell thee in Egypt, saying, Let us alone, that we may serve the Egyptians? For *it had been* better for us to serve the Egyptians, than that we should die in the wilderness.

13 ¶ And Moses said unto the people, Fear ye not, stand still, and see the salvation of the LORD, which he will shew to you to day: for the Egyptians whom ye have seen to day, ye shall see them again no more for ever.

14 The LORD shall fight for you, and ye shall hold your peace.

15 ¶ And the LORD said unto Moses, Wherefore criest thou unto me? speak unto the children of Israel, that they go forward:

16 But lift thou up thy rod, and stretch out thine hand over the sea, and divide it: and the children of Israel shall go on dry *ground* through the midst of the sea.

17 And I, behold, I will harden the hearts of the Egyptians, and they shall follow them: and I will get me honour upon Pharaoh, and upon all his host, upon his chariots, and upon his horsemen.

18 And the Egyptians shall know that I *am* the Lord, when I have gotten me honour upon Pharaoh, upon his chariots, and upon his horsemen.

19 ¶ And the angel of God, which went before the camp of Israel, removed and went behind them; and the pillar of the cloud went from before their face, and stood behind them:

20 And it came between the camp of the Egyptians and the camp of Israel; and it was a cloud and darkness *to them*, but it gave light by night *to these*: so that the one came not near the other all the night.

21 And Moses stretched out his hand over the sea; and the Lord caused the sea to go *back* by a strong east wind all that night, and made the sea dry *land*, and the waters were divided.

22 And the children of Israel went into the midst of the sea upon the dry *ground*: and the waters *were* a wall unto them on their right hand, and on their left.

23 ¶ And the Egyptians pursued, and went in after them to the midst of the sea, *even* all Pharaoh's horses, his chariots, and his horsemen.

24 And it came to pass, that in the morning watch the Lord looked unto the host of the Egyptians through the pillar of fire and of the cloud, and troubled the host of the Egyptians,

25 And took off their chariot wheels, that they drave them heavily; so that the Egyptians said, Let us flee from the face of Israel; for the Lord fighteth for them against the Egyptians.

26 ¶ And the Lord said unto Moses, Stretch out thine hand over the sea, that the waters may come again upon the Egyptians, upon their chariots, and upon their horsemen.

27 And Moses stretched forth his hand over the sea, and the sea returned to his strength when the morning appeared; and the Egyptians fled against it; and the Lord overthrew the Egyptians in the midst of the sea.

28 And the waters returned, and covered the chariots, and the horemen, *and* all the host of Pharaoh that came into the sea after them; there remained not so much as one of them.

29 But the children of Israel walked upon dry *land* in the midst of the sea; and the waters *were* a wall unto them on their right hand, and on their left.

30 Thus the Lord saved Israel that day out of the hand of the Egyptians; and Israel saw the Egyptians dead upon the sea shore.

Exodus 13:20–14:30

OCTOBER 11:

In the morning we suddenly heard horrible screams and shooting from automatic rifles. Soon thereafter came a command that no one was to leave the workshops. The Camp I gates were shut. The number of guards was increased everywhere. The screaming and the shooting were heard more frequently.

'What do you think happened?' Shloime asked. 'It seems to me that the shooting comes from the Nord-Camp. Maybe the fellows there couldn't control themselves and escaped.'

'No, it's not from there. The shooting comes from closer by, somewhere in Camp II. I hear women screaming. A new transport has probably arrived. But why the shooting?'

It lasted for some time. Then it grew quiet. It was not until five in the evening that we learned what had happened. A new transport had arrived. When the people were already undressed, they realised where they were being taken and began to run, naked. But where was there to run? They were already in camp and fenced in on all sides. So they ran towards the barbed wire fence. There they were met by a hail of bullets from the automatic rifles. Many fell dead on the spot. The rest were led away to the gas chambers.

This time the fires crackled until late into the night. The flames shot fiercely upwards to the black fall sky. The terrifying blaze lighted up the entire camp and cast its awesome reflection on the distant outlying areas. Dumb with horror we looked at the fires where our tortured sisters' and brothers' bodies burned.

OCTOBER 12:

I shall never forget that day. Eighteen of our camp inmates had been sick for several days. In the morning a group of Germans, led by Franz, barged into the barracks. Franz ordered the sick to rise at once. It was clear they were being taken to their death. One of the eighteen was a young man from Holland. He could hardly stand on his feet. His wife found out where they were taking her husband.

She threw herself at the Germans, screaming, 'Murderers! I know where you're taking my husband. Take me with him. I will not, you hear, I will not live without him. Murderers! Scum!' She took her husband's arm, supporting him, and marched off with the others to her death.

At lunchtime I arranged with Shloime that we call a meeting with a small group of people for nine o'clock that evening. The meeting was held at the cabinetmakers' shop at which Baruch, Shloime, Janek, the head of the cabinetmakers' brigade; Juzef, the head of the tailors' brigade; the shoemaker, Jakub; Manny, myself, and two others were present.

In the yard and at the gate of Camp I lookouts were posted to warn us in case we had to scatter.

First I gave a report of my talk with Brzecki and asked the comrades to express themselves on whether he should be taken into our group. The general opinion was that it could and should be done. Manny left and returned soon with Brzecki.

'Brzecki,' I said, 'we have decided to invite you to our meeting. I think you are aware of the responsibility you are taking upon yourself by coming here. If we fail, you will be among the first to be killed.'

'I understand,' Brzecki replied. 'You needn't worry.'

'So, comrades,' I said, 'my plan is as follows: First we must do away with the officer group that administers the camp. Naturally, one by one, and without the slightest sound . . .'

I worked in a section of the cabinetmakers' shop. Through the windows one could see the entire yard of Camp I. In the nearby barracks worked Shloime and a specially selected group of twenty men. They had made the dugouts. It was arranged beforehand that at four o'clock Unterscharführer Berg would come to the tailor's shop for a fitting for the uniform which he had ordered. At a quarter past four the chief of the camp guards would come there for the same purpose. The chief of Camp III, Goettinger, and Oberscharführer Greischutzuere to come at four o'clock to the shoemakers' shop. And Franz was to come to my barracks to look over the closets. At that very time Unterscharführer Friedrich Haulstich was to examine Shloime's work. Baruch was responsible for getting four officers into Camp II. The rest were to be invited to workshops on one pretext or another.

All the men who had to carry out the assassinations worked with Shloime that day. He sent them individually to me and I gave each of them his assignment. Kalimali was the first to arrive. His real name, as I have already said, was Shubayev. In 1940 he graduated from the University of Rostova as a transport engineer. He was a tall, slender fellow of about twenty-five, with black, curly hair. Not very talkative, simple and strong, he was a good comrade.

'With you I don't have to waste any words,' I said to him. 'You and Benny will go to the tailor shop. Take along a plane, a chisel, and a hatchet. Remember, it has to be done in such a way that he doesn't utter a sound.'

'That's clear.'

'Well, go. I wish you success.'

We shook hands silently and he left. I asked him to send in Tsibulsky.

Tsibulsky hailed from Donbas. He was a drayman, a big strong man of about thirty-five, a good-natured, jolly fellow but something of a blabbermouth. We had to keep many things from him, but whatever he undertook to do he carried through.

'Boris,' I said to him, 'you and I did time together in the cellar. I know you better than anyone else. You are getting the most difficult assignment. Benny and Michael will accompany you. Brzecki will come for you and take you to Camp II to Baruch. Take along the hatchets. Keep in mind, Boris, that yours will be the first blow. It'll have to give courage to all the others. If anyone of the other fellows going with you gets scared, put another one in his place. No one should be compelled to do this.'

'You can be at ease, Sasha; all are awaiting the signal.'

'And don't forget to remove the pistols from the dead. Go, do it right.'

'It has to be done right.'

Unterscharführer Ernst Berg rode up to the tailors' shop, as was arranged beforehand, dismounted from his horse and left it standing there with its reins hanging down. From what I learned later this is what happened inside: When the Unterscharführer entered everybody rose as usual. Shubayev (Kalimali) walked over to the edge of the table. In the corner, near one of the table's legs, lay a hatchet wrapped in a shirt. The Unterscharführer removed his belt together with his holster and pistol and laid them on the table. Then he took off his jacket. Juzef, the tailor, immediately came over with the uniform and began to take the fitting. Senie moved up to the table to be able, if necessary, to grab the pistol. Juzef turned the German around with his back to Shubayev, explaining that he did so in order to get a better light on the uniform. At that moment Shubayev clouted the Hitlerite on the head with the flat side of the hatchet. He let out a frightful scream. Outside, the horse quivered and pricked up its ears. The second blow silenced the Hitlerite for good. The body was shoved under the bed and covered up. The bloodstains on the floor were also wiped away and covered.

Soon afterwards Shubayev came running into my barracks. 'Here, take it,' he said, handing me the German's pistol.

'Now, even if anyone would want to turn back it would be impossible for him to do so. Thank you, Kalimali.'

We embraced and kissed. He was in a hurry. Another 'client' was to arrive soon in the shop.

'Run, run back,' I said to him. 'How did the others do?'

'Splendidly.'

Shubayev hurried back. Ten minutes later the chief of the guards, Oberscharführer Erbert Helm, entered the tailor shop. He never came out again. He was waylaid by Senie as soon as he crossed the threshold.

At exactly four o'clock, as was arranged beforehand, Oberscharführer Goettinger, chief of Camp III, entered the shoemakers' shop. Arkady Vaispapir was repairing a stool. Grisha was standing near the door. The chief executioner was in a happy mood. 'The sun is shining, it's warm, good,' he babbled on. 'Are my boots ready?'

'Here, please,' Jakub said, handing him the boots, 'try them on.'

'Hey, you, Jakub,' the Oberscharführer went on, 'five days from now I'll be going to Germany. You must make a pair of slippers for my wife. Remember that.'

'I hope your wife will be satisfied,' Jakub replied.

At this moment Arkady brought the hatchet down on his head. The corpse was dragged away by his feet to a corner and covered with rags. The blood, too, was hurriedly covered with sand. Oberscharführer Greischutz was already on his way to the shop for the uniform he had ordered.

At a quarter to five Tsibulsky returned from Camp II. He was excited but not confused. 'We finished off all four,' he announced. 'The telephone connection too is cut where it should be. No one is allowed to leave Camp II. Baruch is in charge there. He asks to be notified in time when to lead the people out.'

'Where are the pistols?'

'Two remained there. One I have and one Michael has.'

'Everything is in order. You, in the meantime, go into Shloime's barracks.'

At four o'clock Luka arrived. I had called her out. 'Luka,' I said, 'in half an hour from now we are escaping. Change into men's clothes. In the woods you'll be both cold and uncomfortable in a dress.'

'Who's escaping? How? What are you talking about? Sasha!'

'Luka, dear, don't waste time on unnecessary questions. We've already killed nearly all of the camp's officers. To waver now is impossible.'

'Yes, yes, I understand, Sasha, but I'm afraid. For such a long time only death was always before me. Don't listen to me. Do what has to be done.' . . .

At four thirty Brzecki and his group returned from the Nord-Camp.

Just then Unterscharführer Haulstich appeared in the yard. Shloime ran up to him. 'Unterscharführer,' he said, 'I don't know how to continue with the dugouts. I must have your instructions. The people are standing around, doing nothing.'

The Unterscharführer started walking towards the barracks. The kapo, Schmidt, followed behind him. As soon as I noticed this I ran over to Brzecki. 'Take Schmidt away from here. He must not enter the barracks.'

Brzecki took Schmidt by the arm. 'Don't go in there,' he said to him. 'Why? What happened?'

'If you want to come out alive, don't mix into this. Nearly all the officers have already been killed. Every move of yours is being watched. Don't mix in, I'm telling you.'

Schmidt was shocked by what he heard. His lips quivered. He was speechless.

In the meantime the Unterscharführer was taken care of inside. Shloime himself had finished him off. Skinny little Schloime clouted him once on the back of the neck with the sharp side of the hatchet and that was sufficient. He didn't have to do it again.

It was time to give the signal but Franz was still alive. He was in no hurry to come and inspect the closets which, according to prior arrangement, he was supposed to do. A while ago he was in the yard but did not come into the shop. The head of the camp administration was still intact.

Presently our tinsmiths arrived carrying tin pipes. In these pipes were concealed six rifles with cartridges. One girl brought cartridges for the pistols. She took them from the quarters of the dead officers. We heard that Engel, a locksmith from Lodz, had killed the Unterscharführer Walter Ryba in the garage where he was working that day. The German had entered the garage armed with an automatic. Engel was suspicious and finished him off right on the doorstep. It was clear that this incident at the garage would become known very soon. We couldn't wait any longer. But what about Franz?

'The devil take him,' Shloime said. 'Sooner or later he'll get the bullet he deserves. Time to get away from here. Every minute is precious.'

We stood there listening for a moment. A deadly silence had descended on the camp. I ordered Brzecki to give the signal. The silence was shattered by a piercing whistle. Shloime dispatched someone to Camp II to inform them that we were marching out.

People came streaming from all sides.

Beforehand we had selected seventy men, nearly all of them Soviet prisoners of war, whose task it was to attack the arsenal. That was why they were in the forefront of the column. But all the others who had only suspected that something was being arranged but didn't know when and how, now found out at the last minute. They began to push and jostle forward, fearing they might be left behind. In this disorderly fashion we reached the gate of Camp I.

The commander of the watchtower, a German from Near-Volga, approached us. 'Hey, you sons-of-bitches,' he shouted, 'didn't you hear the whistle? So why are you pushing like a bunch of cattle? Get in line, three in a row!'

As though in response to a command several hatchets suddenly appeared from under coats and came down on his head.

At that moment the column from Camp II was advancing towards us. Several women, shaken by the unexpected scene, began to scream. One prisoner was on the verge of fainting. Another began to run blindly, without any direction. It was clear that under these circumstances it would be impossible to line up the people in an orderly column.

'Comrades, forward!' I called out loud.

'Forward!' Someone on my right picked up the slogans.

'For our Fatherland, forward!'

The slogans reverberated like thunder in the death camp, and united Jews from Russia, Poland, Holland, France, Czechoslovakia, and Germany, six hundred pain-racked, tormented people surged forward with a wild 'hurrah' to life and freedom.

The attack on the arsenal did not succeed. A barrage of automatic fire cut us off. The majority of the people made a rush for the central exit. Trampling the guards, firing from the several rifles in their possession, hurling stones at the Fascists they met and blinding them with sand, they pushed through the gate and made for the woods.

One group bore left. I saw them hacking their way through the barbed wire. Farther on they had to pass a mine field about fifteen yards wide. There many most certainly perished. I and some others ran to the officers' house and made a passageway through the wire fence. My assumption that the field behind the officers' house was not mined was justified. Three were felled not far from the fence, but it is possible that they were killed, not by mines but by bullets, because we were shot at intermittently from all sides.

And there we were, on the other side of the fence! On the other side of the mine field! Already we had run a hundred yards! Another hundred! . . . And running faster, faster, through the barren strip of land, bodies so nakedly exposed to the eyes of the pursuers, so unprotected from bullets! Faster, faster, and into the woods, among the trees, under cover. And there I was – in their shadow.

I stopped a while to catch my breath and to glance back. Men and women, falling behind, continued running in a crouched position, getting closer to the woods. Where was Luka? Where was Shloime?

Alexander Pechersky, 'Revolt in Sobibor, in *They Fought Back*, ed. Yuri Suhl, 1968

PER SEDEM LATRINE

Most men escaped singly or in little groups through their own initiative, as they have been doing ever since. One early story of an individual escape is worth repeating for its peculiarity. About 1225 a man who had already escaped from Oxford prison was rearrested and imprisoned at Northampton. While at Northampton he had an attack of claustrophobia which induced the hallucination that the devil had appeared to him in the form of a monk. To defend himself from the devil, as he said, he began to pull stones out of the prison wall and this appears to have led him to break down a substantial piece of the wall itself. At the eventual inquiry it was reported that he made three breaches from which he severally extracted a cart-load, a barrow-load, and a bowlful of stones and through one of these breaches he made his exit. No accomplices are mentioned and it is extraordinary that the man could have demolished so much unaided and undetected.

It is very easy to find examples of collective or multiple escapes. In the two years 1229–31 no fewer than thirty-one thieves escaped from Winchester prison. In the next century, about 1356, some clerks convict imprisoned in the archbishop of Dublin's prison at Swords dug an underground passage and escaped through it. A few years before, in 1347, twelve prisoners in Old Salisbury castle had dug a pit 4 feet deep under the wall of the gaol and would have left the castle by that means had they not been disturbed by the keepers. Ten years later some men got out of one of the gaols in the castle of Newcastle upon Tyne *per sedem latrine*. At a much later date (1455) certain felons released themselves from York city gaol by breaking through the floor above the chamber or vault in which they were confined. Another daring escape was staged in Winchester gaol about 1441. When the gaoler's servant was leaning over the stocks to search several of the prisoners, his keys were seized by those whom he was searching. With them the prisoners undid the fastenings of the stocks and their fetters and chains. They then beat the servant and, opening the prison doors, got easily away.

Newgate, as the chief criminal prison and the place of custody of the worst type of offender, was naturally the scene of many escapes. In 1275 nineteen persons broke out. Ten years later four men and a woman broke from custody, climbed on the roof, and held the prison officers at bay *a mane* until prime. In 1325 three events occurred in Newgate in such rapid succession that they look like parts of a concerted operation. In June the prison gate-keeper was killed by an escaped prisoner in the 'high street' of Farringdon Within, whither he had gone in pursuit of his murderer and three other fugitives. In September six approvers and four others cut a hole in the prison wall and escaped through it, and in November a woman was detected in the act of supplying prisoners with 'iron instruments' and otherwise abetting escapes. A riot occurred during the Cade revolt which resulted in much damage to the fabric and the dismissal of the gaoler. It is not quite certain whether on this occasion escapes actually occurred, but when another riot was staged in 1456, the prisoners actually broke custody, ascended to the leads, and threw down stones and other missiles. The sheriffs and their officers could not withstand the rioters unsupported and only induced their antagonists to surrender by calling upon the generality of the citizens for aid. This riot seems to have been set off by the escape of Lord Egremont and his brother Sir Richard Percy, but it is not clear how near in time to one another the two incidents were. According to one account the riot followed immediately upon the escape, according to another within the same month. Other London prisons were also troubled by such incidents, for in 1504–5 many or most of the prisoners in the Marshalsea broke out. The disturbance, however, seems to have been successfully quelled.

Ralph B. Pugh, *Imprisonment in Medieval England*, 1968

PRISON OFFICERS FIGHTING

At 3.25 p.m., nearly an hour after the take-over had begun, the kitchen lorry, driven by an officer, accompanied by an orderly, arrived at H Block 7. It had been expected at 3 p.m. and the twenty-five-minute hold-up was to prove problematic when the escapers got as far as the main gate. The driver and orderly were hastily grabbed and the driver ordered to take the lorry back along the route to the main gate. To ensure he concentrated on the task, his left foot was tied to the vehicle's clutch, his door lock was jammed and he was told that a cord beneath his seat was attached to a hand grenade – though in reality it was tied to the frame of the seat.

As prisoner Gerry Kelly lay on the floor of the cab with his gun trained on the driver, thirty-seven others climbed into the back of the lorry. The shutter was lowered and the driver set off for the gate. Back in H Block 7 a rearguard party of prisoners, armed with chisels and screwdrivers from the block workshops, were left to make sure staff did not raise the alarm until the escapers had got away.

When the lorry reached the first gate, the driver and orderly were recognised by the officer on duty and allowed through without question. At the next gate the same thing happened. There was now only the main gate left to negotiate – and that was where difficulties created by the twenty-five-minute delay were going to happen.

The escape had been timed to get the men to the gate when there would only be five prison officers on duty in the lodge. Now it was all happening at the same time as staff changed shifts and instead of there being just five staff there were many more, coming off and arriving for duty. But a lorry load of prisoners all intent on escape was not going to turn back now – nine prisoners dressed in officers' uniforms jumped out of the lorry and held up the five staff on duty in the lodge. As others checked in their passes, they too were taken captive by the armed prisoners.

Confusion and chaos reigned as prison officers were held up by what appeared to be other prison officers wielding guns. At first some thought it was an exercise by the army, until the reality of the situation dawned. One officer managed to reach an alarm, which brought a telephone check from the emergency control room to the lodge. Disaster for the jailbreakers was averted when another officer with a gun pointed at his head took the call and reported that alarm had been pressed by mistake and all was in order. He tried to hint that this was not really so, but the hint was not picked up.

As the number of officers arriving at the lodge from their afternoon break increased, it was becoming more difficult for the prisoners to maintain control. Suddenly an officer, James Ferris, ran out of the building, shouting to a colleague to raise the alarm. He was chased by a prisoner and stabbed in the chest. The forty-three-year-old officer died soon afterwards.

In what was fast developing into a full-scale melee, one of the captive officers managed to contact the emergency control room and tell what was happening. It would later emerge that staff there had just received a call from a soldier in a watchtower, who reported seeing what he thought was prison officers fighting. He had been told that everything was all right. This time the control room took the call seriously and the alarm was raised. It was 4.12 p.m. and, in the midst of the fighting and confusion at the lodge, an officer with a gun pointed at his head had just opened the gate.

Prison officers ran for the gate as the escapers raced for freedom, a freedom that many could not legally have expected to see this side of the twenty-first century. There was shouting, screaming and swearing – and as dogs barked, bullets flew and warders fought with prisoners, three more officers fell with stab wounds, allegedly caused by the man who had killed James Ferris.

Outside the main gate the men had to negotiate the perimeter wire, stretched out in rolls across the ground. Some became caught up in it and were quickly recaptured. Others got clear and took to their heels. It had been hoped to drive the lorry right out of the prison, but this part of the plan had been aborted in the confusion at the gate and the vehicle had been abandoned. A prison officer's car was taken but soon crashed and the men inside ran across neighbouring fields, chased by officers and soldiers. One officer was shot in the thigh and the man who fired the shot was himself brought down by a soldier firing from the tower post by the main gate . . .

By the Monday morning, seventeen of the thirty-eight men who had got out of the gate were back in custody. Some got no further than the wire, others were picked up on foot, in cars as they tried to make their way out of the area, even out of the River Lagan as they tried to hide among reeds. An IRA back-up unit had waited a distance from the prison, but with the abandoning of the lorry, the escapers had no means of reaching their intended rescuers. When the unit, listening closely to the radio heard what was happening, it was decided that nothing could be done for the escapers; they were on their own.

The twenty-one men who got away were:

Hugh Corey, aged 27, serving life for the murder of a part-time Ulster Defence Regiment man;
Kevin Barry Artt, 24, life for the murder of an Assistant Governor at the Maze;

Kieran Fleming, 23, detained at the Secretary of State's pleasure for the murder of a policewoman;

Brendan McFarlane, 31, life for his part in a gun and bomb attack on a Shankhill Road bar, in which five people died;

Seamus McElwaine, 22, life for the murder of a UDR officer and reserve constable;

Gerard Fryers, 24, twenty years for a sniper attack on an army base;

Robert Russell, 25, twenty years for the attempted murder of a policeman;

Gerard Kelly, 30, life for his part in a bomb attack at the Old Bailey;

Paul Brennan, 30, sixteen years for possession of explosives;

Dermot McNally, 26, life for causing explosions;

Seamus Campbell, 26, fourteen years for possession of 1,000 bombs in a lorry in County Tyrone;

Patrick McKearney, 29, fourteen years for possession of a loaded sten-gun;

Dermot Finucane, 22, eighteen years for possessing firearms and ammunition;

Patrick McIntyre, 25, fifteen years for attempted murder of a UDR man;

James Smyth, 28, twenty years for the attempted murder of a prison officer;

Anthony Kelly, 22, detained at the Secretary of State's pleasure for the murder of a reserve constable;

James Clarke, 27, eighteen years for attempted murder;

Terence Kirby, 27, life for murder of a garage owner;

Anthony McAllister, 25, life for murder of a soldier;

Gerard McDonnell, 32, sixteen years for possession of bomb-making equipment;

Seamus Clarke, 27, life for murder of five people in a Shankhill Road bar.

J. P. Bean, *Over the Wall*, 1994

WIZARD, OR ASTROLOGER?

As our numbers diminished every day, whilst those of the enemy increased, as also did the fury of their attacks, at the same time as we from our wounds were less able to make resistance; our powder being almost exhausted, our provisions and water intercepted, our friend the good Montezuma dead, and our proposals for peace rejected, the bridges by which we were to retreat broken down, and in fine, death before our eyes in every direction, it was determined by Cortes and all of the officers and soldiers, to quit the city during the night, as we hoped at that time to find the enemy less alert. In order to put them the more off their guard, we sent a message by a chief priest, informing them that if we were permitted to quit the city unmolested within the space of eight days, we would surrender all the gold which was in our possession.

There was with us a soldier named Botello, of respectable demeanour, who spoke latin, had been at Rome, and was said to be a necromancer; some said he had a familiar, and others called him an astrologer. This Botello had discovered by his figures and astrologies, and had predicted four days before, that if we did not quit Mexico on this night, not one of us should ever go out of it alive. He had also foretold that Cortes should undergo great revolutions of fortune, be deprived of his property, and honours, and afterwards rise to a greater state than ever, with many other things of this kind.

Orders were now given to make a portable bridge of very strong timber, to be thrown over the canals where the enemy had broken down the bridges, and for conveying, guarding, and placing this, were assigned, one hundred and fifty of our soldiers and four hundred of the allies. The advanced guard was composed of Sandoval, Alzevido el Pulido, F. de Lugo, D. de Ordas, A. de Tapia, and eight more captains of those who came with Narvaez, having under them one hundred picked soldiers, of the youngest and most active. The rear guard was composed of one hundred soldiers, mostly those of Narvaez, and many cavalry, under the command of Alvarado and Velasquez de Leon. The prisoners, with Donna Marina and Donna Luisa, were put under the care of thirty soldiers and three hundred Tlascalans; and Cortes, with A. de Avila, C. de Oli, Bernardino Vasquez de Tapia and other officers, with fifty soldiers, composed a reserve, to act wherever occasion should require.

By the time that all this was arranged night drew on. Cortes then ordered all the gold which was in his apartment to be brought to the great saloon, which being done, he desired the officers of His Majesty, A. de Avila and Gonzalo Mexia, to take His Majesty's due in their charge, assigning to them for the conveyance of it eight lame or wounded horses, and upwards of eighty Tlascalans. Upon these were loaded as much as they could carry of the gold which had been run into large bars, and much more remained heaped up in the saloon. Cortes then called to his secretary Hernandez and other royal notaries and said, 'Bear witness that I can no longer be responsible for this gold; here is to the value of above six hundred thousand crowns, I can secure no more than what is already packed; let every soldier take what he will, better so than that it should remain for those dogs of Mexicans.' As soon as he had said this, many soldiers of those of Narvaez, and also some of ours fell to work, and loaded themselves with treasure. I never was avaricious, and now thought more of saving my life which was in much danger; however when the opportunity thus offered, I did not omit seizing out of a casket, four calchihuis, those precious stones so highly esteemed amongst the Indians; and although Cortes ordered the casket and its contents to be taken care of by his major domo, I luckily secured these jewels in time, and afterwards found them of infinite advantage as a resource against famine.

A little before midnight the detachment which took charge of the portable bridge set out upon its march, and arriving at the first canal or aperture of water, it was thrown across. The night was dark and misty, and it began to rain. The bridge being fixed, the baggage, artillery, and some of the cavalry passed over it, as also the Tlascalans with the gold. Sandoval and those with him passed, also Cortes and his party after the first, and many other soldiers. At this moment the trumpets and shouts of the enemy were heard, and the alarm was given by them, crying out, 'Taltelulco, Taltelulco, out with your canoes! the Teules are going, attack them at the bridges.' In an instant the enemy were upon us by land, and the lake and canals were covered with canoes. They immediately flew to the bridges, and fell on us there, so that they intirely intercepted our line of march. As misfortunes do not come single, it also rained so heavily that some of the horses were terrifyed, and growing restive fell into the water, and the bridge was broken in at the same time. The enemy attacked us here now with redoubled fury, and our soldiers making a stout resistance, the aperture of water was soon filled with the dead and dying men, and horses, and those who were struggling to escape, all heaped together, with artillery, packs, and bales of baggage, and those who carried them. Many were drowned here, and many put into the canoes and carried off for sacrifice. It was dreadful to hear the cries of the unfortunate sufferers, calling for assistance and invoking the Holy Virgin or St Jago, while others who escaped by swimming, or by clambering upon the chests, bales of baggage, and dead bodies, earnestly begged for help to get up to the causeway. Many who on their reaching the ground thought themselves safe, were there seized or knocked in the head with clubs.

Away went whatever regularity had been in the march at first; for Cortes and the captains and soldiers who were mounted clapt spurs to their horses and gallopped off, along the causeway; nor can I blame them, for the cavalry could do nothing against the enemy, of any effect; for when they attacked them, the latter drew themselves into the water on each side the causeway, and others from the houses with arrows, or on the ground with large lances, killed the horses. It is evident we could make no battle with them in the water, and without powder, and in the night, what else could we do than what we did; which was, to join in bodies of thirty or forty soldiers, and when the Indians closed upon us, to drive them off with a few cuts and thrusts of our swords, and then hurry on, to get over the causeway as soon as we could. As to waiting for one another, that would have lost us all; and had it happened in the day time, things would have been worse with us. The escape of such as were fortunate enough to effect it, was owing to Gods mercy, who gave us force to do so; for the very sight of the number of the enemy who surrounded us, and carried off our companions in their canoes to sacrifice, was terrible.

Bernal Diaz del Castillo, *The True History of the Conquest of Mexico*,
trans. Maurice Keatinge 1809

IN THE TROJAN SIDESTREETS

Thereat I again gird on my sword, and fitting my left arm into the clasps of the shield, strode forth of the palace. And lo! my wife clung round my feet on the threshold, and held little Iülus up to his father's sight. 'If thou goest to die, let us too hurry with thee to the end. But if thou knowest any hope to place in arms, be this household thy first defence. To what is little Iülus and thy father, to what am I left who once was called thy wife?'

So she shrieked, and filled all the house with her weeping; when a sign arises sudden and marvellous to tell. For, between the hands and before the faces of his sorrowing parents, lo! above Iülus's head there seemed to stream a light luminous cone, and a flame whose touch hurt not to flicker in his soft hair and play round his brows. We in a flutter of affright shook out the blazing hair and quenched the holy fires with spring water. But lord Anchises joyfully upraised his eyes; and stretching his hands to heaven: 'Jupiter omnipotent,' he cries, 'if thou dost relent at any prayers, look on us this once alone; and if our goodness deserve it, give thine aid hereafter, O lord, and confirm this thine omen.'

Scarcely had the aged man spoken thus, when with sudden crash it thundered on the left, and a star gliding through the dusk shot from heaven drawing a bright trail of light. We watch it slide over the palace roof, leaving the mark of its pathway, and bury its brilliance in the wood of Ida; the long drawn track shines, and the region all about fumes with sulphur. Then conquered indeed my father rises to address the gods and worship the holy star. 'Now, now delay is done with: I follow, and where you lead, I come. Gods of my fathers, save my house, save my grandchild. Yours is this omen, and in your deity Troy stands. I yield, O my son, and refuse not to go in thy company.'

He ended; and now more loudly the fire roars along the city, and the burning tides roll nearer. 'Up then, beloved father, and lean on my neck; these shoulders of mine will sustain thee, nor will so dear a burden weigh me down. Howsoever fortune fall, one and undivided shall be our peril, one the escape of us twain. Little Iülus shall go along with me, and my wife follow our steps afar. You of my household, give heed to what I say. As you leave the city there is a mound and ancient temple of Ceres lonely on it, and hard by an aged cypress, guarded many years in ancestral awe: to this resting-place let us gather from diverse quarters. Thou, O father, take the sacred things and the household gods of our ancestors in thine hand. For me, just parted from the desperate battle, with slaughter fresh upon me, to handle them were guilt, until I wash away in a living stream the soilure . . .' So spoke I, and spread over my neck and broad shoulders a tawny lion-skin for covering, and stoop to my burden. Little Iülus, with his hand fast in mine, keeps uneven pace after his father. Behind my wife follows. We pass on in the shadows. And I, lately moved by no weapons launched against me, nor by the thronging bands of my Grecian foes, am now terrified at every breath, startled by every noise, thrilling with fear alike for my companion and my burden.

And now I was nearing the gates, and thought I had outsped all the way; when suddenly the crowded trampling of feet came to our ears, and my father, looking forth into the darkness, cries: 'My son, my son, fly; they draw near. I espy the gleaming shields and the flicker of brass.' At this, in my flurry and confusion, some hostile god bereft me of my senses. For while I plunge down byways, and swerve from where the familiar streets ran, Creüsa, alas! whether, torn by fate from her unhappy husband, she stood still, or did she mistake the way, or sink down outwearied? I know not; and never again was she given back to our eyes; nor did I turn to look for my lost one, or cast back a thought, ere we were come to ancient Ceres' mound and hallowed seat; here at last, when all gathered, one was missing, vanished from her child's and her husband's company. What man or god did I spare in frantic reproaches? or what crueller sight met me in our city's overthrow? I charge my comrades with Ascanius and lord Anchises, and the gods of Teucria, hiding them in the winding vale. Myself I regain the city, girding on my shining armour; fixed to renew every danger, to retrace my way throughout Troy, and fling myself again on its perils. First of all I regain the walls and the dim gateway whence my steps had issued; I scan and follow back my footprints with searching gaze in the night. Everywhere my spirit shudders, dismayed at the very silence. Thence I pass on home, if haply her feet (if haply!) had led her thither. The Grecians had poured in, and filled the palace. The devouring fire goes rolling before the wind high as the roof; the flames tower over it, and the heat surges up into the air. I move on, and revisit the citadel and Priam's dwelling; where now in the spacious porticoes of Juno's sanctuary, Phoenix and accursed Ulysses, chosen sentries, were guarding the spoil. Hither from all quarters is flung in masses the treasure of Troy torn from burning shrines, tables of the gods, bowls of solid gold, and raiment of the captives. Boys and cowering mothers in long file stand round. . . . Yes, and I dared to cry abroad through the darkness; I filled the streets with calling, and again and yet again with vain reiterance cried piteously on Creüsa. As I stormed and sought her endlessly among the houses of the town, there rose before mine eyes a melancholy phantom, the ghost of very Creüsa, in likeness larger than her wont. I was motionless; my hair stood up, and the accents faltered on my tongue. Then she thus addressed me, and with this speech allayed my distresses: 'What help is there in this mad passion of grief, sweet my husband? not without divine influence does this come to pass: nor may it be, nor does the high lord of Olympus allow, that thou shouldest carry Creüsa hence in thy company. Long shall be thine exile, and weary spaces of sea must thou furrow through; and thou shalt come to the land Hesperia, where Lydian Tiber flows with soft current through rich and populous fields. There prosperity awaits thee, and a kingdom, and a king's daughter for thy wife. Dispel these tears for thy beloved Creüsa. Never will I look on the proud homes of the Myrmidons or Dolopians, or go to be the slave of Greek matrons, I a daughter of Dardania, a daughter-in-law of Venus the goddess. . . . But the mighty mother of the gods keeps me in these her borders. And now farewell, and still love thy child and mine.' This speech uttered, while I wept and would have said many a thing, she left me and retreated into thin air. Thrice there was I fain to lay mine arms round her neck; thrice the vision I vainly clasped fled out of my hands, even as the light breezes, or most like to fluttering sleep. So at last, when night is spent, I revisit my comrades.

Vergil, Aeneid, trans. J. W. Mackail, 1885

MAN AND WIFE

Rock-Creek, Montgomery County,
Maryland, Jan. 31.

FOUR THOUSAND DOLLARS REWARD

RAN away, from the subscriber, on the 22nd of January instant, a white Mulatto Slave, named LEONARD, 31 years of age, about six feet high, well made, a strong healthy fellow, has a scar on his under lip and chin, which were split by sawing at the whipsaw, another under his chin, caused by a swelling; he wears his hair hanging short behind, and is much sunburnt: had on when he went away, a short blue cloth coat and waistcoat, leather breeches, white yarn stockings, and took several pair of shoes, &c. with him. He is a carpenter by trade, and took with him some carpenters and joiners tools. He was persuaded off by a white woman, who calls herself Rachel Dorsey, and says that, about 8 or 9 years ago, she left Pennsylvania. It appears that she had two children by the above slave, both boys, the eldest named Samuel, about five years of age; the other named Basil, two years of age. It is supposed they will pass for man and wife, and make for Pennsylvania, or the Eastern Shore.

WHOEVER takes up the said SLAVE, and secures him in gaol, so that I get him again, shall receive Two Thousand Dollars; and if brought home, the above Reward, paid by

BARBARA WILLIAMS

Baltimore Maryland Journal and Baltimore Advertiser, 6 February 1781

FIVE

'Wouldn't you like your liberty?'

In the meantime, the preparations for concealing the Prince's person, by assuming a workman's dress, continued; of which Thélin gives the following account: – 'The Prince put on his usual dress, grey pantaloons and boots; then he drew over his waistcoat, a coarse linen shirt, cut off at the waist, a blue cotton handkerchief, and a blouse, not merely clean, but somewhat elegant in its cut; and, finally, he drew on a pair of large trousers of coarse blue linen, which had been worn and were very dirty. Under these he concealed the lower part of the first blouse, as much worn and dirty as the pantaloons. The rest of his costume consisted of an old blue linen apron, a long black-haired wig, and a bad cap. Being thus apparelled, and his hands and face painted with red and black, the moment of action being at hand, all emotion had ceased; and the Prince breakfasted as usual with a cup of coffee, put on his sabots, took a common clay pipe in his mouth, hoisted a board upon his shoulders, and was in readiness to set out!'

At a quarter before seven, Thélin called to him all the workmen who were engaged on the stairs, and invited them to go into the dining-room, to take their morning dram, telling Laplace, his man-of-all-work, to pour out the liquor for them to drink. In this manner they got rid also of the latter. Immediately after he came to give notice to the Prince, that the decisive moment had come; and descended the staircase at the bottom of which the two keepers, Dupin and Issali, were posted by order of the commander, and where, besides, there was a workman occupied in repairing the baluster. Thélin exchanged a few words with the keepers, who bid him good morning, and seeing that Thélin had his overcoat on his arm, and was prepared to set out, they wished him a good journey. Thélin then pretended to have something to say to Issali, drew him aside from the wicket, and so placed himself that Issali, in order to hear, must have his back towards the Prince.

At the very moment at which the Prince quitted his chamber, some of the workmen were already coming from the dining-room, situated at the other end of the corridor; but Conneau was there to turn away their attention, and none of them observed the Prince, who was slowly passing down the stairs. When he came within a few steps of the bottom, he found himself face to face with Dupin, the keeper, who drew back in order to avoid the plank, which placed horizontally on the shoulder, prevented the profile of the face from being seen, and could not, therefore, observe the Prince's face. The Prince then passed through the two wicket-gates, going behind Issali, whom Thélin kept in close conversation. He then entered the courtyard, where a workman, who came down the stairs immediately after, followed him very close, and appeared as about to speak to him. This was a locksmith's boy, whom Thélin immediately called to him, and formed some pretext for sending him back again up stairs.

On passing before the first sentinel, the pipe dropped from the Prince's mouth, and fell at the soldier's feet; he stopped to pick it up; the soldier looked at him mechanically, and continued his monotonous pace. At the top of the canteen, the Prince passed very near the Officer of the Guard, who was reading a letter. The Officer of Engineers and Contractor for the Works, were at a distance of some paces further, the officer busily occupied in examining some papers. The Prince continued his way, and passed through the middle of a score of soldiers, who were basking in the sun in front of the guard-house. The drummer looked at the man with the plank with an insulting glance, but the sentinel paid no attention to him whatever. The gate-keeper was at the door of his lodge, but he merely looked at Thélin, who kept a few yards behind, and, in order more surely to draw attention to himself, led the Prince's dog in a leash. The sergeant, who was standing by the side of the wicket, looked steadily at the Prince, but his examination was interrupted by a movement of the plank, which obliged the soldier who held the bolt to withdraw himself.

He immediately opened the gates, and turning round, the Prince went out – the door was closed behind him. Thélin afterwards wished the gate-keeper 'good day', and passed out in his turn.

Between the drawbridges the Prince met two workmen, coming straight towards him on the side on which his figure was not concealed by the plank. They looked at him with great eagerness from the distance at which they still were, and, in a loud voice, expressed their surprise at not knowing him. On his part, the Prince, pretending to be tired of carrying the plank on his right shoulder, moved it to the left; the men, however, appeared so curious that the Prince thought for a moment he should not be able to escape them, and when at last he was near them, and they appeared as if approaching to speak to him, he had the satisfaction of hearing one of them exclaim: 'Oh! it's Bertou.'

F.T. Briffault, *The Prisoner of Ham: Authentic Details of the Captivity and Escape of Prince Napoleon Louis*, Eng. trans. 1846

SEX CHANGE

The first English camp I was taken to as a German prisoner of war in July 1917 was Colsterdale, near Masham, up north in Yorkshire, and I hope it will be taken in good part when I say that I didn't want to stay there. I tried several times to get through the barbed wire and I also took part in one of the tunneling schemes which was, however, discovered by the British just before the tunnel was completed. Then one fine day I hit upon the idea of just walking out through the gate disguised as our English canteen manager, who was about my size and figure – his name was Mr Budd – I wonder if, by chance, he may read these words and if he still remembers it all. So evening after evening I started observing closely his every movement on leaving the camp, and noticed to my satisfaction that the sentries never asked him for the password. Everybody knew Mr Budd too well for that. This was also, of course, rather a drawback; but my idea was to do the thing in the evening after dark.

I'd been informed – I think quite wrongly – that every male passenger in those war days was supposed to produce a pass or other document when booking a railway ticket, particularly when travelling to London, and as I didn't feel like walking the whole way there I decided to travel as a woman.

We had private codes between the camps and our people at home so I sent a message to my mother asking her to send me every conceivable thing which I should need for this disguise. After some time I received news that a wig was arriving camouflaged as tobacco; that all sorts of fake jewellery, a compass and similar handy things had been sent off in marmalade jars, or baked in a cake – and, last but not least, that I would soon receive a large quilt with a skirt, petticoat, veil, some sort of a hat, silk stockings and a nice silk coat all sewn up in it. I had asked for everything in black, even the necklace and brooches, as I wanted to look like a poor widow so that people on the trains wouldn't speak to me as freely as if I were dressed as a giddy young girl.

Then I heard rumours of Mr Budd being transferred to some other camp, so I couldn't afford to wait for the arrival of these mysterious packages and began collecting an outfit in the camp. My skirt was made out of an old blanket and the hat and muff were mostly composed of parts of fur waistcoats. We had plenty of fancy costumes in the camp, beautiful wigs, hats, and so on, but they were all under 'word of honour' not to be used except for theatrical purposes, and so of course I couldn't use them.

Then the great day arrived and I put on all the clothes, man and woman's mixed together, so that I was able to change from one to the other with a few slight manipulations.

I approached the gate disguised as Mr Budd with a false moustache and a pair of spectacles, worn exactly the way Mr Budd wore them. My cap, mackintosh and bag were also exact replicas of the ones with which Mr Budd used to leave the camp every evening. Even the most pessimistic of my friends thought I really was Mr Budd when they saw me.

Mr Budd was in the habit of leaving the camp about 8 p.m. and I had timed my attempt for about ten minutes to eight. Meanwhile a few friends of mine would keep the real Mr Budd busy in the canteen until shortly *after* eight, and as the sentries were usually changed at 8 o'clock sharp I was sure that the new sentry would not be surprised to see the second and real Mr Budd leaving camp. So off I went straight to the gate gaily smoking my pipe as if after a good day's work at the canteen. A few yards from it I shouted 'Guard', as this was the way Mr Budd used to announce himself day by day. The sentry called out, 'Who's there?' 'Budd,' I answered. 'Right,' he said and opened the big door.

I walked slowly down the street from the camp towards Masham station. I had about a two-hours' walk before me; but I hadn't gone more than fifty yards when I espied our Commandant coming towards me. Within a fraction of a second I had torn off the moustache and spectacles as, of course, I didn't want the Colonel to address the false Mr Budd. As I passed him I just said 'Good evening,' and so did he.

A little further on I decided to change into a woman. This was only a matter of a few seconds. I exchanged Mr Budd's cap with the woman's hat and veil which I carried in my bag, and took off my mackintosh, which covered a navy-blue civilian jacket, trimmed with all sorts of lace and bows. My skirt was hitched up with a leather belt round my hips so I had only to undo the belt to release the skirt. Luckily for me skirts in those days reached down to the ground, so my leggings were completely covered by the skirt and couldn't be seen in the dark.

I met some Tommies on the road, and they all behaved very decently; they all bade me 'good evening', and none of them insisted on starting a conversation with the very reserved woman who did not even reply to their 'good evening'.

Only once I was a bit troubled, by a shepherd's dog, but he soon withdrew when the strange woman took something out of her muff and sprinkled it on the road. It is very important for an escaper always to carry a box of pepper to defend himself against dogs.

I'd been walking now for quite some time, making good progress

towards the station of Masham, when I noticed three soldiers
following me and overtaking me. One of them was equipped with a
rifle with fixed bayonet and I knew that this must surely be a sentry
from the camp as there were no other military in the neighbourhood. I
at once thought of throwing away my bag which might so easily give
me away, but anything of that sort would immediately have aroused
suspicion. The soldiers came steadily closer and closer until finally they
overtook me. They then stopped and said 'Good evening, miss. Have
you by any chance seen a man with a bag like yours? A prisoner of war
has escaped and we are out looking for him.' Well, I tried for a time,
really only for a very short time, to speak in a high voice, telling them
please not to bother a decent young girl by starting a conversation with
her, but all they said was might they have a look at the bag I carried. I
refused, of course, but it was only a matter of another few seconds
before I realised that it was all over with me. I was found out.

Heinz H.E. Justus, 'An Unconducted Tour of England', in *Escapers All*,
ed. J.R. Ackerley, 1932

WOLF-WHISTLES

I now loathed the Wülzburg and began to dream of escape.

Escape I must! But not talk about it. 'PGs' apart – I did not really
worry about them – the merest hint of escape talk was pounced on by
appeasing voices (as in the ghetto business) that said: 'It's selfish. The
Germans will cut down the privileges of the rest of us.'

The germ of a plan survived from the time, more than a year earlier,
of my abortive conversation with the called-up Bavarian. Now I knew,
as then I had not, that Wülzburg prisoners whose homes were in
Germany were allowed to be visited by their families; that visits took
place every Thursday; that visitors came in through the main gate and
went out through it; that consequently there was, almost every
Thursday, a dribbling in-and-out traffic of pedestrian civilians.

The very great majority of them were women. That might not
matter. The Wülzburg amateur theatricals were well-established, and I
had played a saucy servant in *Twelfth Night* and an American girl in an
adaptation of a novel by P.G. Wodehouse. Moreover, Wülzburgians,
owing to the links that some had with outside German life, had been
able to send for stocks of actual clothes, and the *Kommandantur* had

allowed these to be brought in. There were high-heeled shoes, silk stockings, handbags, dresses in styles commonly used, sets of ordinary make-up.

I thought. I had a friend, John Ford. He had volunteered to fight for Finland, had reached that country when the war with Russia was over, and while retracing his steps had entered Oslo in time to be picked up by the Germans as they entered it. He (with four others in identical plight) had then been posted to the Wülzburg. He was a person of versatile talent and also of character. If I had to trust anybody I would trust him; I had to trust somebody.

John was a star of the Wülzburg football field whose nets had been woven by seamen from the string of Red Cross parcels. I, an inglorious spectator, hung about, while enthusiasts stamped on the touchline. Whistle blew. 'Out to your wing, man!' 'Pay attention to that wing, Frankie!' The Prefect, alongside two TocHers, strained vociferous. I nursed my scheme.

The match over, I told John my plan which hinged on the fact that Frau Scharre's canteen-shop was bisected by a ground-level corridor of which one entrance was in the prisoners' enclosure, the other in the outer *Kommandantur* area. Departing visitors emerged into this outer area through a guarded gate in a continuous fence. All things being helpful, the same effect could be achieved by someone who came out through Frau Scharre's corridor.

With John I noted habits of the guards and office-soldiers of the outer area and of visitors as they walked away. Often a departing visitor turned her head to wave to a high window.

It was early September. In the hot weather theatrical varieties were given in the grounds; a goal canopied with blankets made a backcloth, in its shade a tiny piano, drum and percussion-set. The producer, a slight, nervy, brow-mopping man, invariably compered turns with apologetic references to 'very trying conditions' and 'exceedingly difficult circumstances'. The French contributed a trick-cyclist, the Egyptians a team of acrobats and a Strong Man with a prodigious stomach whom the compere always introduced by regretting that 'exceedingly trying conditions' made it impossible for him to perform his principal act, which consisted of allowing a car to run over him, any horsepower. There was a West Indian, Jeff Luis, who sang the Wülzburg signature-tune 'The Castle could hardly be called a Hotel'. Jeff also had charge of all costume and make-up and the time had come to broach my plan to him.

Jeff, who was enthusiastic, concluded after many things had been tried on that the disguise ought to suggest the character of a young, respectable married woman. That meant that I could not wear a richly-curled barmaid-blonde wig, pride of the wardrobe, and so would need to hide my hair, especially at the back of the neck, with a converted scarf. There were no coats. Jeff said he would make one. But out of what? I had a camel-hair blanket, teddy-bear colour, a present from home. With this Jeff made in less than a week a superb coat with a belt and large, disc-shaped woolly buttons.

The business of dressing-up had next to be co-ordinated with that of getting from the prisoners' quarters into Frau Scharre's door. I could not trip downstairs and cross the grounds in full costume, nor could the whole change be done in the exposed doorway. The main change – stockings, frock, basic make-up – could be made upstairs in the empty theatre provided that there was a screening escort from there to the shop. John chose three people besides himself and Jeff. In the doorway finishing touches – shoes, coat, lipstick, cowled scarf – would need less than half a minute and would be screened.

A date was fixed. Intervening days went like dreams. There was an outdoor concert party. Everyone was merry, everything seemed funny. The producer-compere, dripping with success, mounted a shaky stool to announce that the party would close with English community-singing 'if our Dutch, French, and Egyptian friends will bear with us for just a very few minutes'. 'Roll out the Barrel', 'Nellie Dean', 'If You Were the Only . . .' The singing was thin. The little man, perilously asway, made inhibited, frantic conducting movements crying 'Come on, now, sing it as though you meant it!' with the result, truly English, that the singing died altogether.

What was extraordinary was that everything worked as hoped. The din of Dutch clogs roared round on the stone stairs as I descended semi-transformed, huddling, unseeing. At the shop-door hands flashed. In the passage a little white dog, not reckoned with, yapped. Feeling suddenly the sun-white gravel of the *Kommandantur* area I turned my head right and up and did not cease agitating a tiny handkerchief until cool shade intimated that I was in the vaulted tunnel leading to the main gate. I faced a vast blank door in whose wall-like front there was a small wicket-door. I turned a handle. The wicket opened outward and revealed a sentry. I hesitated. The sentry sprang forward, opened the wicket wide and stood back, holding it open.

I was on the drawbridge. The morning was golden. The air was heavenly. The warm stone parapet wanted to be leaned on. The basking moat begged for a lingering look.

The track-like road whorled down. In the rough, pine-needles glinted like pins. Now I stepped confidently. Another bend. Whistles! My heart seemed to stop. Ahead, almost blocking the track, stood uniformed men. I drew level, they stood watching, waiting, unmistakably waiting to detain me. I was in the thick of them, as in among a herd of cattle when they, just like cattle, barged reluctantly outwards. Growls of voices, then aimed whistles hit my moving back. Suddenly, suddenly I understood. Those whistles – they were wolf-whistles! Those uniformed men – loutish *Luftwaffe* youths looking for a pick-up and very likely knowing that on Thursdays women had to walk down this hill. *Women!* In the joy of freedom I had utterly forgotten my revised exterior. Young respectable married woman – what a test! – what a triumph! Not the kind that she would care for, she would be feeling indignant now, at least looking it. I looked indignant.

Giles Romilly, *The Privileged Nightmare*, 1954

BODY SEARCH

There he remained all day, and at night sailed for Loch Boysdale, which is about 30 miles south of Loch Karnon, and belongs to the MacDonalds. There he arrived safe, and stayed 8 days upon a rock, making a tent of the sail of the boat, and lived upon fish and fowl of his own killing.

There he found himself in the most terrible situation, for having intelligence on June 18th that Captain Caroline Scott had landed at Killbride within less than two miles of them, he was obliged to dismiss the boat's crew, and taking only O'Neil with him, he went to the mountains, where he remained all night, and soon after was informed that General Campbell was at Barnare (an island lying between North Uist and Harris), being about two miles long and one broad. It belongs to the MacLeods. So that now he had forces not far from him on both sides, and was absolutely at a loss to know which way to move, having forces on both the land sides of him, and the sea on the other, without any vessel to venture into securely.

In this perplexity Captain O'Neil accidentally met with Miss Funivella or Flora MacDonald, to whom he proposed assisting the Prince to make his escape, which she at last consented to, on condition the Prince would put on women's cloaths, which he complied with. She

[115]

then desired they would goe to the mountain of Corradale and stay there till they heard from her, which should be soon.

There they arrived, and accordingly remained two days in great distress, and then hearing nothing from the young lady, the Prince concluded she would not keep her word. But about 5 o'clock in the evening a message came from her desiring to meet her at Rushness, being afraid to pass the Ford, which was the shortest passage, because of the militia. They luckily found a boat which carried them to the other side Uia, where they remained part of the day afraid of being seen of the country people.

In the evening they set out in the same boat for Rushness, and arrived there at 12 o'clock at night, but not finding the young lady, and being alarmed by a boat full of militia they were obliged to return back two miles, where the Prince remained on a muir till O'Neil went to the young lady, and brought her with him to the place appointed about sunset next evening.

About an hour after they had got to the Prince they got an account of General Campbell's arrival at Benbecula, which obliged them to move to another part of the island, where, as the day broke, they discovered four vessels full of armed men close on the shore. They having seen the fire on the land, made directly up to the place where they were, so that there was nothing left for them to do but to throw themselves among the heath, by which means they escaped being found.

When the wherries were gone they resolved to go to Clanranold's house. But when they were within a mile of it they heard that General Campbell was there, which obliged them to retreat again to Rushness; from whence they set out in a little yawl or boat for the isle of Sky about the end of June, and were at sea all night. The next day as they were passing the point of Watternish, in the west corner of Sky, the wind being contrary, and the female frighted at turning back, they thought to have landed there, but found it possess'd by a body of forces; which obliged them immediately to put to sea again after having received several shots from the land.

From hence they went and landed at Killbride, in Troternish in Sky, about twelve miles north from the above mentioned point. There they also found a body of troops within less than two miles of them, whose commanding officer rode as far as Moystod or Mougestot, not far from Sir Alexander MacDonald's seat, near which place they landed. He there enquired of Miss Flora MacDonald who she was, and who was with her, which she answered as she thought proper. The officer, however, would not be satisfied until he had searched the boat. In the mean time the Prince was hid on shore, so near as to hear what passed.

Immediately after this scene was over the Prince parted with his female guide, and took to the hills, and travelled without rest 15 long miles south south-east in women's cloaths till he came to Mr MacDonald of Kingsburgh's house, where his female guide met him again, having gone a nearer way. There the Prince got his first refreshment, and stayed till next day, towards the evening; when he set out from Kingsburgh's house, but would not, on any account, let the consequence be what it would, consent to put on women's cloaths again, having found them so cumbersome the day before. He went 15 long miles to a place called Portree or Purtry, where again he met his female preserver, who had gone a different route, and which was the last time they saw each other ...

Mrs MacDonald said that she behoved to employ her daughter as handmaid to the Prince for putting on his womens cloaths, 'For,' said she, 'the deel a preen he could put in.' When Miss MacDonald was a dressing of him, he was like to fall over with laughing. After the peeness, gown, hood, mantle, etc., were put on, he said, 'O, Miss, you have forgot my apron. Where is my apron? Pray get me my apron here, for that is a principal part of my dress.'

Kingsburgh and his lady both declared that the Prince behaved not like one that was in danger, but as chearfully and merrily as if he had been putting on women's cloathes merely for a piece of diversion.

Agreeable to Kingsburgh's advice they met at the edge of the wood, where the Prince laid aside his female rags, which were deposited in the heart of a bush till a proper opportunity should offer of taking them up; for these that were present resolved to preserve them all as valuable tokens of distress ...

In the Journal taken from the mouths of the Laird of MacKinnon, Malcolm MacLeod, etc., Miss MacDonald has omitted several things which she particularly mentioned to those who conversed with her when she was lying in the Road of Leith on board the *Eltham* and the *Bridgewater* ships of war. She told that when the Prince put on women's cloaths he proposed carrying a pistol under one of his petticoats for making some small defence in case of an attack. But Miss declared against it, alleging that if any person should happen to search them the pistol would only serve to make a discovery. To which the Prince replied merrily: 'Indeed, Miss, if we shall happen to meet with any that will go so narrowly to work in searching as what you mean they will certainly discover me at any rate.' But Miss would not hear of any arms at all, and therefore the Prince was obliged to content himself with only a short heavy cudgel, with which he design'd to do his best to knock down any single person that should attack him.

She us'd likewise to tell that in their passage to the Isle of Sky a heavy rain fell upon them, which with former fatigues distressed her much. To divert her the Prince sung several pretty songs. She fell asleep, and to keep her so, the Prince still continued to sing. Happening to awake with some little bustle in the boat she found the Prince leaning over her with his hands spread about her head. She asked what was the matter? The Prince told her that one of the rowers being obliged to do somewhat about the sail behoved to step over her body (the boat was so small), and lest he should have done her hurt either by stumbling or trampling upon her in the dark (for it was night) he had been doing his best to preserve his guardian from harm.

The Lyon in Mourning or a Collection of Speeches Letters Journals etc.
Relative to the Affairs of Prince Charles Edward Stuart
by the Rev. Robert Forbes, ed. Henry Paton, *1895*

ENVISAGING ESCAPE

But I was going to escape; I was determined. I knew that success depended upon my self-control. The problem before me was very simple, but the least error might prove fatal. It was necessary to act with mathematical precision. I paced my cell up and down, rehearsing under my breath: 'I have to remove the board noiselessly, and crawl through without making a sound. I have to do all this before the guard has time to turn his face to me. Then I have to walk ten steps in a straight line, and turn to the right. I must walk slowly.' But deep down in my heart there was a creeping sensation, and a stealthy thought, '*Will* you do it? will you have the courage to put your head at the very feet of the sentry?' lurked in my mind. And I had a feeling as if somebody were trying to choke me . . .

Thus passing from hope to despair I spent Thursday and Friday. The evening roll-call was over, and I was locked up for the night. Only at night I was alone, in the daytime a guard was always with me. Oh, how I loved the night! At night I felt free. I did not see the dreary walls or the guards. In my dreams I soared into space, I dwelt in the skies, I performed miracles. The walls of the prison crumbled under my touch, bullets did not strike me, and I could defeat all the czar's legions. But the first glimmer of day scattered my dreams, and I, chained, was again in the hands of my enemies.

It was midnight. Everything was asleep and quiet, only the measured steps of the sentry under my window could be heard. Quietly, without rising from my cot, I ripped my pillow open and took out my masculine garb. I was afraid to move, because the soldier peeped into my window every minute. With trembling hands I cut my long tresses. I put a kerchief on my head, and on the top of my masculine attire I donned the prisoner's grey coat. And thus, fully dressed, I lay. I could not sleep, and I did not want to sleep. There were only a few hours left for me to live, I thought, and I was willing to fall from the soldier's bullet outside the prison wall rather than go back to Akatúi. At six o'clock I got up. The sun was rising over my window, bright and smiling as ever, but in my heart there was no response to its smiles, no reflection of its rays – only darkness and uncertainty were there. Minutes and hours passed. My heart was growing cold, and at times almost ceased beating. When I came out into the yard for my last walk the regular strokes of a hammer reached my ear. Through crevices in the wall I could see two prisoners at work; they were building a staircase to the watchman's tower. They were guarded by a soldier. All grew dark before me. There was no more hope. Another soldier at the gate!

The clock struck ten. I stood near the wall where the sounds came from, and it seemed to me that with every stroke of the hammer they nailed down the cover of my coffin. But a sudden thought flashed through my mind. I asked the guard who watched me to fetch my book in the cell, and he went on this errand. I knocked on the wall. The strokes of the hammer ceased.

'Brother, hello, brother!'

'What do ye want?' asked a gruff voice.

'Where is the soldier that is watching you?'

'He went away for a minute. He isn't afraid of us – we shan't run away. We have got only three days more to serve.'

My heart fairly leaped with joy. With one jump I was near the gate. I threw down my prisoner's coat. I removed the board from under the gate without making the slightest sound, and crawled through. I rose from the ground, and at that moment the soldier on guard, having come to the end of his beat, turned his face to me. I saw the carriage standing on the corner. I knew that I had to make just ten steps. But seconds seemed eternities to me, and the short distance between me and the carriage turned into interminable space. It seemed to me that I was not moving at all, but standing as if chained to the spot by the bewildered look of the sentry. Suddenly a shot rang out, and the bullet whizzed over my head. But before the smoke had cleared away I was already in the carriage. Bullets were falling about us in a shower. I shot aimlessly into the air, to scare off our pursuers. Soon we were lost from the view of the pursuing soldiers in a thoroughfare of Irkutsk. A feeling of utter happiness, the happiness of freedom, filled my whole being. I inhaled the dusty air of the street, and it seemed to me to be permeated with the odor of roses and violets.

Marie Sukloff, *The Life-story of a Russian Exile*, trans. Gregory Yarros, 1914

TWO MINUTES

Dinner was at last brought up. Just as we were going to sit down to table, an old nurse of ours, Madame Dutoit, who had accompanied Josephine, came in very ill. Madame de Lavallette had left her in the registering-room, intending to send her after me when I should be gone; but the heat of the German stove and her emotion had made her so ill, and she had so long insisted on seeing me once more, that the turnkey let her in without the permission of the jailer. Far from being useful to us, the poor woman only added to our confusion. She might lose her presence of mind at the sight of my disguise; but what was to be done? The first object was to make her cease her moanings, and Emilie said to her in a low but firm voice, 'No childishness. Sit down to table, but do not eat; hold your tongue, and keep this smelling-bottle to your nose. In less than an hour you will be in the open air.'

This meal, which to all appearance was to be the last of my life, was terrible. The bits stopped in our throats; not a word was uttered by any of us, and in that situation we were to pass almost an hour. Six and three-quarters struck at last. 'I only want five minutes, but I must speak to Bonneville,' said Madame de Lavallette. She pulled the bell, and the valet-de-chambre came in; she took him aside, whispered a few words to him, and added aloud, 'Take care that the chairmen be at their posts, for I am coming. – Now,' she said to me, 'it is time to dress.'

A part of my room was divided off by a screen, and formed a sort of dressing-closet. We stepped behind the screen, and, while she was dressing me with charming presence of mind and expedition, she said to me, 'Do not forget to stoop when you go through the doors; walk slowly through the registering-room, like a person exhausted with fatigue.' In less than three minutes my toilet was complete. We went back to the room, and Emilie said to her daughter, 'What do you think of your father?' A smile of surprise and incredulity escaped the poor girl: 'I am serious, my dear, what do you think of him?' I then turned round, and advanced a few steps: 'He looks very well,' she answered; and her head fell again, oppressed, on her bosom. We all advanced in silence towards the door. I said to Emilie, 'The jailer comes in every evening after you are gone. Place yourself behind the screen, and make a little noise, as if you were moving some piece of furniture. He will think it is I, and will go out again. By that means I shall gain a few minutes, which are absolutely necessary for me to get away.' She understood me, and I pulled the bell. 'Adieu!' she said, raising her eyes to Heaven. I pressed her arm with my trembling hand, and we exchanged a look. If we had embraced, we had been ruined. The turnkey was heard; Emilie flew behind the screen; the door opened; I passed first, then my daughter, and lastly Madame Dutoit. After having crossed the passage, I arrived at the door of the registering-room. I was obliged, at the same time, to raise my foot and to stoop lest the feathers of my bonnet should catch at the top of the door. I succeeded; but, on raising myself again, I found myself in the large apartment, in the presence of five turnkeys, sitting, standing, and coming in my way. I put my handkerchief to my face, and was waiting for my daughter to place herself on my left hand. The child, however, took my right hand; and the jailer, coming down the stairs of his apartment, which was on the left hand, came up to me without hindrance, and, putting his hand on my arm, said to me, 'You are going away early, Madame.' He appeared much affected, and undoubtedly thought my wife had taken an everlasting leave of her husband. It has been said, that my daughter and I sobbed aloud: the fact is, we scarcely dared to sigh. I at last reached the end of the room. A turnkey sits there day and night, in a large arm-chair, and in a space so narow, that he can keep his hands on the keys of two doors, one of iron bars, and the other towards the outer part, and which is called the first wicket. This man looked at me without opening his doors. I passed my right hand between the bars, to show him I wished to go out. He turned, at last, his two keys, and we got out. There my daughter did not mistake again, but took my right arm. We had a few steps to ascend to come to the yard; but, at the bottom of the staircase there is a guard-house of gendarmes. About twenty soldiers, headed by their officer, had placed themselves a few paces from me to see Madame de Lavallette pass. At last, I slowly reached the last step, and went into the chair that stood a yard or two distant. But no chairman, no servant was there. My daughter and the old woman remained standing next to the vehicle, with a sentry at six paces from them, immoveable, and his eyes fixed on me. A violent degree of agitation began to mingle with my astonishment. My looks were directed towards the sentry's musket, like those of a serpent towards its prey. It almost seemed to me that I held that musket in my grasp. At the first motion, at the first noise, I was resolved to seize it. I felt as if I possessed the strength of ten men; and I would most certainly have killed whoever had attempted to lay hands on me. This terrible situation lasted about two minutes; but they seemed to me as long as a whole night. At last I heard Bonneville's voice saying to me, 'One of the chairmen was not punctual, but I have found another.'

Memoirs of Count Lavalette, Eng. trans. 1831

A SOLDIER AND HIS WOMAN

The unorganised condition of the prisoners in the Murder Wing helped us to plan an escape. There was nothing tangible for the enemy to thrust at; we had slowly won over most of the day guards by adjusting them to ourselves. Our morale, through increasing control of our part of the gaol, was good. The police were slack; they were soldiers first, and soldiers make bad gaolers. Sallow-face alone, of the officers, was more watchful; his face and manner made a warden of him. The real danger would come from anyone amongst the prisoners who might be watching Moran or Teeling, from a slip made by our soldier, who was as intense as we now were, or from the betrayal of our purpose through our close-knit comradeship. I had no intention of being hanged. I was going to escape, dead or alive.

A small bottle of drugged whisky was sent in. If we could give it mixed with more drink to the night guards I could get quicker to Teeling's cell, but how to get on proper terms with them was a problem. Some of them would ask for cigarettes after lights out; I often pushed some through the peep hole. I would hear 'Thank ye, mate,' and an awkward silence as the man continued to stand against the door.

A man in plain clothes came into my cell. He looked like a pleasant official from the RIC depot; there was an air of protective humanity when he spoke.

'Bernard,' he began, 'I'm your friend, now don't forget that. They have made up their minds to hang you for the Macroom ambush.'

'But I wasn't at Macroom, and they know it right well.'

'They will hang you unless you give your mother's address. Think of what she is suffering, she doesn't even know where you are. I can tell her you're safe, can't I?'

'But they will burn her house, that's what I'm afraid of.'

'Bernard,' he said, soothingly, 'don't be afraid, remember I'm your friend, I don't approve of what some of them do.'

'I know that.'

'Well, Bernard, think it over. I'll be back again in a few days, and that will be your last chance, and they'll hang you for Macroom if you don't give your mother's address.' He placed his hand on my shoulder, 'It's not much to ask. Remember, Bernard, I'm your friend.'

'I know you are, thanks very much.'

He had kept me back from another identification parade. As I hurried down the identification yard I wondered if there was any connection between his visit and my possible selection through the slits.

That evening Teeling came into my cell after tea; his eyes were beating up and down with light. He grabbed my arms.

'Come on, quick. It's all right, the bolt's cut.' He rubbed his hands.

'When? You don't . . .'

'Just now, the soldier and I. Like this,' he snapped his teeth. We held our hands crossways and gripped hard. We both laughed.

'We'll get Paddy and take Doyle and the boys from the First Battalion,' I said.

Paddy Moran was writing a letter. 'Come on, Paddy, Teeling's cut the bolt.' He stood up. 'God, that's great, but . . . I'm not going.'

'You must. You're with us, you were willing enough the other night.'

'No, I'm not going. I won't let down the witnesses who gave evidence for me.'

'To hell with the witnesses,' I said, 'come on.'

'O, come on, Paddy,' said Teeling, 'come on.' Moran shook his head slowly, smiling.

'I'm your senior in rank, but what's the sense in giving an order. You talk to him, Teeling, I'll get Doyle and the others.' The First Battalion boys were not in their cells. That morning they had told sallow-face what they thought of him; he had sent them to punishment cells on a lower landing. I could not find our soldier; there was no chance of getting a key. I went to Simon Donnelly's cell.

'Hop it, Simon, we're escaping – now.'

He smiled. 'Is that all?'

'I'm serious, Simon, come on. You know the neighbourhood.'

'Good,' he said, as he followed me.

Teeling's face was strained. 'It's no use, he won't come.'

'Someone has to die for this, Paddy,' I said. 'Maybe Teeling or myself, but they'll hang you for certain if we get through.'

'God keep you now,' said Paddy Moran, as he held our shoulders. 'I'll start a concert to keep the police busy, you'll not be missed until lock up.'

We were sad as we left the cell. On the passage towards the stairs I went into Desmond Fitzgerald's cell. He had been Director of Publicity.

'Any atrocities, Desmond?'

'No, but I saw Mabel today; she was asking for you.'

'Desmond, could you please lend me sixpence for tram fare?'

He smiled. 'I can give you five shillings.'

'No. Sixpence will do. I'm tired of this place.'

He laughed at my joke as he handed me the silver. 'For tram fare, young shaver.'

We opened one half of the gate, it was heavy to move; then we closed it. I was first with the .38 in my hand. I saw figures in the darkness close to the wall; one had a peaked cap, but they had not heard me. I touched Teeling with my hand: 'Soldiers, there's something wrong; an outside patrol, I think. I'll stick them up and if I have to shoot, you two make a dash for it.' They halted whilst I went forward. A soldier was holding a woman tight in his arms. I went back to tell the others. We moved on under the wall passing other soldiers and girls locked together.

The wind was cold, it blew clean and sweet in our faces. Gas lamps beamed out of the blackness; front porches shone on to small evergreen shrubs in tiny gardens and the stars winked at us in a friendly way. 'You'd better hide the gun somewhere,' said Simon, 'you're never sure of a hold-up in the streets.' It was fine on top of a tram. We felt inclined to sing and shout; instead we pinched each other with delight. There was so much colour, dun brick shining, people walking along the South Circular, and talk coming up from the street. We held our faces into the wind.

Ernie O'Malley, *On Another Man's Wound*, 1936

Stung to madness and despair by the crushing agonies of a life, Cassy had often resolved in her soul an hour of retribution, when her hand should avenge on her oppressor all the injustice and cruelty to which she had been witness, or which *she* had in her own person suffered.

One night, after all in Tom's cabin were sunk in sleep, he was suddenly aroused by seeing her face at the hole between the logs, that served for a window. She made a silent gesture for him to come out.

Tom came out the door. It was between one and two o'clock at night – broad, calm, still moonlight. Tom remarked, as the light of the moon fell upon Cassy's large, black eyes, that there was a wild and peculiar glare in them, unlike their wonted fixed despair.

'Come here, Father Tom,' she said, laying her small hand on his wrist, and drawing him forward with a force as if the hand were of steel; 'come here – I've news for you.'

'What, Misse Cassy?' said Tom, anxiously.

'Tom, wouldn't you like your liberty?'

'I shall have it, Misse, in God's time,' said Tom.

'Ay, but you may have it tonight,' said Cassy, with a flash of sudden energy. 'Come on.'

Tom hesitated.

'Come!' said she, in a whisper, fixing her black eyes on him. 'Come along! He's asleep – sound. I put enough into his brandy to keep him so. I wish I'd had more – I shouldn't have wanted you. But come, the back door is unlocked; there's an axe there, I put it there – his room door is open; I'll show you the way. I'd a done it myself, only my arms are so weak. Come along!'

'Not for ten thousand worlds, Misse!' said Tom, firmly, stopping and holding her back, as she was pressing forward.

'But think of all these poor creatures,' said Cassy. 'We might set them all free, and go somewhere in the swamps, and find an island, and live by ourselves; I've heard of its being done. Any life is better than this.'

'No!' said Tom, firmly. 'No! good never comes of wickedness. I'd sooner chop my right hand off!'

'Then *I* shall do it,' said Cassy, turning.

'O, Misse Cassy!' said Tom, throwing himself before her, 'for the dear Lord's sake that died for ye, don't sell your precious soul to the devil, that way! Nothing but evil will come of it. The Lord hasn't called us to wrath. We must suffer, and wait his time.'

'Wait!' said Cassy. 'Haven't I waited? – waited till my head is dizzy and my heart sick? What has he made me suffer? What has he made hundreds of poor creatures suffer? Isn't he wringing the life-blood out of you? I'm called on; they call me! His time's come, and I'll have his heart's blood!'

'No, no, no!' said Tom, holding her small hands, which were clenched with spasmodic violence. 'No, ye poor, lost soul, that ye mustn't do. The dear, blessed Lord never shed no blood but his own, and that he poured out for us when we was enemies. Lord, help us to follow his steps, and love our enemies.'

'Love!' said Cassy, with a fierce glare; 'love *such* enemies! It isn't in flesh and blood.'

'No, Misse, it isn't,' said Tom, looking up; 'but *He* gives it to us, and that's the victory. When we can love and pray over all and through all, the battle's past, and the victory's come – glory be to God!' And, with streaming eyes and choking voice, the black man looked up to heaven.

And this, oh Africa! latest called of nations – called to the crown of thorns, the scourge, the bloody sweat, the cross of agony – this is to be *thy* victory; by this shalt thou reign with Christ when his kingdom shall come on earth.

The deep fervor of Tom's feelings, the softness of his voice, his tears, fell like dew on the wild, unsettled spirit of the poor woman. A softness gathered over the lurid fires of her eye; she looked down, and Tom could feel the relaxing muscles of her hands, as she said,

'Didn't I tell you that evil spirits followed me? O! Father Tom, I can't pray – I wish I could. I never have prayed since my children were sold! What you say must be right, I know it must; but when I try to pray, I can only hate and curse. I can't pray!'

'Poor soul!' said Tom, compassionately. 'Satan desires to have ye, and sift ye as wheat. I pray the Lord for ye. O! Misse Cassy, turn to the dear Lord Jesus. He came to bind up the broken-hearted, and comfort all that mourn.'

Cassy stood silent, while large, heavy tears dropped from her downcast eyes.

'Misse Cassy,' said Tom, in a hesitating tone, after surveying her in silence, 'if ye only could get away from here – if the thing was possible – I'd 'vise ye and Emmeline to do it; that is, if ye could go without blood-guiltiness – not otherwise.'

'Would you try it with us, Father Tom?'

'No,' said Tom; 'time was when I would; but the Lord's given me a work among these yer poor souls, and I'll stay with 'em and bear my

cross with 'em till the end. It's different with you; it's a snare to you –
it's more'n you can stand – and you'd better go, if you can.'

'I know no way but through the grave,' said Cassy. 'There's no beast
or bird but can find a home somewhere; even the snakes and the
alligators have their places to lie down and be quiet; but there's no
place for us. Down in the darkest swamps, their dogs will hunt us out,
and find us. Everybody and everything is against us; even the very
beasts side against us – and where shall we go?'

Tom stood silent; at length he said,

'Him that saved Daniel in the den of lions – that saves the children in
the fiery furnace – Him that walked on the sea, and bade the winds be
still – He's alive yet; and I've faith to believe he can deliver you. Try it,
and I'll pray, with all my might, for you.'

By what strange law of mind is it that an idea long overlooked, and
trodden under foot as a useless stone, suddenly sparkles out in new
light, as a discovered diamond?

Cassy had often revolved, for hours, all possible or probable schemes
of escape, and dismissed them all, as hopeless and impracticable; but at
this moment there flashed through her mind a plan, so simple and
feasible in all its details, as to awaken an instant hope.

'Father Tom, I'll try it!' she said, suddenly.

'Amen!' said Tom; 'the Lord help ye!'

Harriet Beecher Stowe, Uncle Tom's Cabin, 1852

'LORD! WHAT SHALL I DO NOW?'

At nine in the morning, the two men upon deck went to pumping. Then
I turned out from the sail, where the boy and I then lay, and pulled off
my coat that I might be the more nimble in the action: and having but
little hair, I hauled off my cap, that if they had the fortune to knock me
in the head, they might kill me with it.

Having fitted myself for the action, I went up the Gun Room scuttle
into the Steerage, to see what posture they were in; and being satisfied
therein, I leapt down the scuttle and went to the boy: who seeing me
resolved upon the action, with an earnest entreaty to him to join with
me; he, at last, did consent.

Then the boy coming to me, I leapt up the Gun Room scuttle, and said, 'Lord! be with us, and strengthen us in the action!'; and then I told the boy that the drive-bolt was by the scuttle in the Steerage.

Then I went softly aft into the Cabin, and put my back against the bulk head, and took the iron crow (it was lying without the Cabin door), and held it with both my hands in the middle of it, and put my legs abroad to shorten myself, because the Cabin was very low.

But he that lay nighest to me, hearing me, opened his eyes; and perceiving my intent, and upon what account I was coming, endeavoured to rise, to make resistance against me: but I prevented him, by a blow upon his forehead, which mortally wounded him. And the other man, which lay with his back to the dying man's side, hearing the blow, turned about and faced me; very fiercely endeavouring to come against me. I struck at him, but he let himself fall from his left arm, and held his arm for a guard; whereby he did keep off a great part of the blow: but still his head received a great part of the blow.

The Master lying in his Cabin on my right hand, hearing the two blows, rose, and sat in his cabin; and seeing what I had done, he called me *Boogra!* and *Footra!* But I having my eyes every way, I pushed at his ear betwixt the turnpins with the claws of the crow: but he falling back for fear thereof. It seemed, afterwards, that I struck the claws of the crow into his cheek, which blow made him lie still as if he had been dead.

While I struck at the Master, the fellow that fended off the blow with his arm, rose upon his legs, and ran towards me, with his head low (I suppose he intended to run his head against my breast to overset me): but I pushed the point at his head, and stuck it an inch and a half into his forehead (as it appeared since by the chirurgeon that searched the wound); and as he was falling down, I took hold of him by the back, and turned him into the Steerage.

I heard the boy strike the man at the helm, two blows; after I knocked down the first man: which two blows made him lie very still.

As soon as I turned the man out of the Cabin, I struck one blow more at him that I struck first, thinking to leave no man alive aft of myself.

The Master all this while did not stir: which made me conclude that I had struck him under the ear, and had killed him with the blow.

Then I went out to attack the two men that were at the pump; where they continued pumping, without hearing or knowing what I had done.

As I was going to them, I saw that man that I had turned out of the Cabin into the Steerage, crawling out upon his hands and knees upon the deck; beating his hands upon the deck to make a noise, that the men at the pump might hear: for he could not cry out or speak.

And when they heard him, seeing the blood running out of the hole in his forehead, they came running aft to me, grinding their teeth as they would have eaten me.

But I met them as they came with the Steerage door, and struck at them: but the Steerage being not about four foot high, I could not have a full blow at them. Whereupon they fended off the blow, and took hold of the crow with both their hands close to mine, striving to haul it from me.

Then the boy might have knocked them down with much ease, while they were contending with me; but that his heart failed him, so that he stood like a stake at a distance on their left side.

Two feets' length of the crow being behind their hands, on their left side, I called to the boy to 'take hold of it, and haul as they did, and I would let it go all at once!' Which the boy accordingly did. I pushed the crow towards them, and let it go: and was taking out my knife to traverse amongst them: but they seeing me put my right hand into my pocket, fearing what would follow, both let go the crow to the boy, and took hold of my right arm with both their hands, grinding their teeth at me.

The Master, that I thought I had killed in his Cabin, coming to himself; and hearing that they had hold of me, came out his Cabin and also took hold of me, with both his hands round my middle.

Then one of the men that had hold of my right arm, let go; and put his back to my breast, and took hold of my left hand and arm, and held it close to his breast, and strove to cant me upon his back.

And the Master let go from my middle, and took hold of my right arm, and he, with the other that had hold of my right arm, did strive to turn me over from the other back: thinking to get me off my legs. But I knowing that I should not be long in one piece if they got me down, I put my left foot against the ship's side on the deck for a supporter, and, with the assistance of God I kept upon my feet; when they three, and one more (for the man that the boy knocked down at the helm, rose up and put his hands about my middle, and strove to haul me down) did strive to throw me down.

The boy seeing that man rise, and take hold of me, cried out! fearing then that I should be overcome by them; but did not come to help me, nor did strike one blow at any of them: neither did they touch him all the time.

When I heard the boy cry out, I said, 'Do you cry! you villain! now I am in such a condition! Come quickly, and knock this man on the head that hath hold on my left arm!'

The boy perceiving that my heart did not fail me; he took some courage from thence, and endeavoured to give that man a blow on his head with the drive-bolt: but struck so faintly, that he missed his blow; which greatly enraged me against him.

And I feeling the Frenchman which hung about my middle hang very heavy, said to the boy, 'Do you miss your blow! and I in such a condition! Go round the binnacle, and knock down that man that hangeth upon my back;' which was the same man the boy knocked down at the helm.

So the boy did strike him one blow upon the head, which made him fall, but he rose up immediately; but being incapable of making any further resistance, he went out upon deck staggering to and fro, without any further molestation from the boy.

Then I looked about the beams for a marlin-speck, or anything else to strike them withal: but seeing nothing, I said, 'Lord! what shall I do?'

Then casting up my eye upon my left side, and seeing a marlin-speck hanging with a strap to a nail on the larboard side, I jerked my right arm forth and back, which cleared the two men's hands from my right arm, and took hold of the marlin-speck, and struck the point four times, about a quarter of an inch deep, into the skull of that man that had hold of my left arm, before they took hold of my right arm again. I also struck the marlin-speck into his head three times after they had hold of me, which caused him to screech out: but they having hold of me, took off much of the force of the three last blows; and he being a strong-hearted man, he would not let go his hold of me.

The two men finding that my right arm was stronger than their four arms were, and observing the strap of the marlin-speck to fall up and down upon the back of my hand so that it struck him that had his hands nearest to my right one: he let go his right hand and took hold of the strap, and hauled the marlin-speck out of my hand. And I, fearing what in all likelihood would follow, put my right hand before my head for a guard, although three hands had hold of that arm: for I concluded he would knock me on the head with it, or else throw it at my head.

But, through God's wonderful providence! it either fell out of his hand, or else he threw it down! for it did fall so close to the ship's side that he could not reach it again, without letting go his other hand from mine. So he did not attempt the reaching of it; but took hold of my arm with his other hand again.

At this time, the Almighty God gave me strength enough to take one man in one hand, and throw at the other's head: and looking about again to see for anything to strike them withal, but seeing nothing I said, 'Lord! what shall I do now?'

And then it pleased God to put me in mind of my knife in my pocket. And although two of the men had hold of my right arm, yet God Almighty strengthened me so, that I put my right hand into my right pocket, and took out my knife and sheath, holding it behind my hand that they should not see it. But I could not draw it out of the sheath with my left hand, because the man that I struck in the head with the marlin-speck had still hold of it, with his back to my breast.

So I put it between my legs, and drew it out; and then cut that man's throat with it, that had his back to my breast: and he immediately dropped down, and scarce ever stirred after.

Then with my left arm, I gave both the men a push from me; and hauled my right arm, with a jerk, to me; and so cleared it of them: and fetching a stroke with an intent to cut both their throats at once, they immediately apprehending the danger they were in, both put their hands together, and held them up crying, '*Corte! Corte! Monsieur! moy allay pur Angleterre si vou plea.*'

Robert Lyde, *A True and Exact Account of the Retaking of a Ship, Called the* Friends' Adventure, *of Topsham from the French,* 1693

UNDER THE STAIRS

The first streaks of dawn were just appearing when, as if by magic, an absolute silence fell. We did not dare believe our ears and listened with our heads glued to the wall.

The Doctor declared that he was going to see what was happening outside. Everyone protested, for even to push the door a little way open would have been enough to expose him to a volley from a tommy-gun. But he shrugged his shoulders.

'Death's inevitable now and I'd rather be killed by a bullet than be burnt alive by a flame-thrower.'

He walked over to the door, turned the handle and went out. Trembling all over, I stuffed my fingers into my ears but the shots I was expecting with such terror did not occur. A few moments later, the Doctor's voice rang out through the silence.

'Hi, all of you in there! You can come out now – they've gone. Everyone's left the house!'

A frantic joy took possession of us. We burst out into shrieks and exclamations. The lawyer hopped about on one leg, yelling at the top of his voice:

'The Germans have gone! We're saved!'

It was he who rejoiced the most at this meagre hope of life: this man who was already eighty . . .

Mr Radnai's lips were still blue with fear but already he was affirming in a confident voice:

'I knew for certain that they were going to leave. You know, I have presentiments about that kind of thing.'

But no one paid any attention to him.

We staggered out into the courtyard. It was beginning to be daylight and somewhere over in the east the sun was climbing towards the edge of the horizon to bathe the ruined city of Budapest in its rays.

The courtyard was full of machine-guns and arms of various kinds and littered with ammunition and empty cartridge-cases. In front of the street door lay a German soldier's cap and two cases of unused shells yawned open beside the deserted little cannon.

In this strange, murky glimmer, things no longer had any real existence: the courtyard, the street, the whole town, all blurred in a light that seemed to belong to another world, looked like a landscape on the moon. Everywhere there lay abandoned weapons. Opposite us, a house had collapsed on its inhabitants. Death had overtaken them in the course of the hideous struggle against suffocation. Over there, on the right, was the fragment of a fourth storey where a piano only stayed in place, thanks to a few bricks; of the neighbouring room, which must have been a bathroom, nothing remained but a wall with a towel-rail.

Everywhere, as far as the eye could see, ruins, ruins, and still more ruins.

In front of the confectioner's on the corner, lay the corpses of the three horses we had brought out from under the staircase. The sweetish smell of putrefaction assaulted our nostrils from all sides. We did not then know that the atmosphere of the town would be impregnated with this loathsome stench for many long weeks to come.

But wherever had the Germans gone to? One might have thought that they had evacuated the street . . . But that was surely impossible . . . Why was there this silence? Terror came over us. The silence became more and more oppressive. The banker's widow was of the opinion that the Russians must be here already because they had been holding the neighbouring quarter for the past three months. But where were they, then?

This uncertainty was appalling! We had the impression of watchful presences behind the walls, behind the ruins, even behind the corpses of the horses. The Russians must be very close, perhaps even in the next building. Or did they think the Germans were still in our house and were they preparing a fresh assault?

A panic fear made us beat a retreat, first under the porch and then into the rooms on the ground floor.

After a quarter of an hour of anguished waiting, Ilus ran up, gasping for breath, and announced that they had just found a wounded German under the stairs. We rushed to the place. And there, indeed, in the space behind the great marble staircase, where in the old days, they used to keep the children's prams, a young soldier lay prone in a pool of blood.

'It only needed this,' exclaimed Mr Radnai. 'If the Russians find us here, we shall all be executed.'

In a few moments, we were all standing round the wounded man who was losing quantities of blood.

'We ought to do something for him,' suggested Ilus in a hesitating voice. 'I'll go and get something to make a bandage with.'

'Don't be in such a hurry,' replied Mr Radnai. 'This man would have had no scruples about letting us die like dogs in our cellar. And, if the Russians find out that we've given medical aid to a German, heaven help us!'

The lawyer had arrived on the scene, leaning on his wife.

'Gentlemen, we must dress this soldier's wounds. The Russians themselves would not act otherwise. First-aid to the wounded is a duty according to all the international conventions.'

The Doctor shrugged his shoulders and mumbled:

'The old man's talking through his hat. Where is any international convention respected these days? What's our beautiful city been turned into? A heap of stinking filth, with thousands of corpses left to rot.'

The banker's widow exclaimed impatiently:

'For goodness' sake, make up your minds one way or the other! The Russians may be here any moment now and you do nothing but argue. Personally, I'm getting out of this – I've seen nothing and I've heard nothing!'

The soldier had laboriously raised himself on his elbow and kept turning his eyes, dim with weakness and pain, towards whichever person was speaking. His gaze fastened on our lips, as if he had been deaf: he did not understand a word of Hungarian and fever made the trend of our discussion even more impossible to grasp. Nevertheless, he knew that it was being decided whether he should live or die.

His gaze became so embarrassing that soon we relapsed into complete silence – a silence that was like a thick fog muffling all sense of reality.

I no longer had the will-power to avert my eyes from that blood which seeped faster and faster through the torn uniform.

Suddenly, I had the impression that the ruins above our heads vanished and that, from the height of heaven, God was watching us to see how we were going to pass through this perilous ordeal, almost like death itself. In such an extremity, were we going to be capable of seeing nothing but a uniform and of letting a human life ooze away, drop by drop, under our very eyes? I was convinced that God was looking down at us with pity and that it was the impact of His look that made the Doctor shake himself abruptly.

'I'll go and get some bandages,' he said in a hoarse voice.

He came back a few moments later and applied dressing and bandages with quick, expert movements.

'He's severely wounded on the hip,' he told us. 'He won't last long. He must be in atrocious pain.'

Christine Arnothy, I Am Fifteen and I Do Not Want to Die,
trans. Antonia White, 1956

A FRENCH FARMYARD

The story of Embry's adventures and contacts as he walked through France does not differ greatly from that of many other evaders. He seems to have passed through a country infested with Germans with little difficulty, and it was an ill chance that landed him once more in the hands of the enemy. He had just swum the Somme and was crossing a field when, in the dark, he ran straight into a number of German soldiers. He was instantly collared and beaten up, and finally, after a most unpleasant and painful experience, was taken before a German officer to whom he told his usual – and now familiar – tale. The German made the following answer.

'I don't believe a word of what you say. I think you are a British officer trying to escape. You are in civilian clothes so that, if you are what I think you are, you will be shot as a spy tomorrow.'

After these discouraging remarks, Embry was led away to a large farmhouse which proved to be a German HQ. This farm was of the normal type to be found everywhere in northern France. The building formed three sides of a square and the fourth side consisted of a wall in which was the main gate. In the middle of the courtyard was an enormous manure heap on which ducks, chickens and pigs roamed at will. About midday, Embry was deposited in a small room, normally used for storage purposes. A sentry was placed over the door and a second sentry stood in the courtyard outside the only exit.

After carefully considering his position, Embry came to the conclusion that his chances of being shot the following morning were distinctly promising; for the possibility of passing successfully through an interrogation made by a competent man who spoke French well, was almost nil. His story would be exposed as a lie, and with the German suspicions aroused, he could think of no other story likely to hold water. He could talk no other language but English sufficiently well to pass as a native. He had been caught in the German lines dressed in civilian clothes, so he could see no good reason why he should not be shot as a spy. (In actual fact, the Geneva Convention lays down that the question of whether a man is a spy or not is a question of fact which must be proved against a prisoner before he can be legitimately shot.) Many airmen have baled out over German occupied territory in this war, have changed into civilian clothes and have subsequently been caught by the Germans; but none, as far as I know, have been shot as a spy merely for being in civilian clothes. However, the Germans were often in doubt on this matter, and from time to time posted up notices threatening to shoot all combatants found out of uniform, but never carried out this threat. In acting thus, I have always thought that the Germans behaved with a leniency and moderation which is frankly surprising, considering the depths to which they descended in shooting and torturing the unfortunate natives who gave assistance to our evaders. All this Embry could not have known at the time, but I am inclined to agree with his view that in his particular circumstances he was unlikely to receive the benefit of any doubt.

Having come to the conclusion that his position was really desperate, Embry was the last man to take it lying down.

He asked his sentry for a glass of water and when he returned with it, hit him as hard as he could on the point of the jaw. He took the rifle and having made sure that this sentry was 'out' in a satisfactory manner, he advanced cautiously down the passage. Just outside the exit into the courtyard was a second sentry with his back towards him. As Embry came out, the man turned and at that moment Embry hit him with his full force on the side of the head with the butt of the rifle. His head caved in, and Embry rushed along the side of the building towards the gate, clutching the rifle. There was no one about in the courtyard. Just as he came to a passage between the two buildings, a German soldier came round the corner carrying two buckets of water, and stood for a second, a look of intense astonishment on his face. Embry hit him, too, in the same manner and with the same result, and then, there being nothing else for it, dived into the manure heap and dug a passage for himself through the straw and well into the muck. It was not long before the hue and cry started, but no one thought of the manure heap – perhaps no one thought it possible that a man could live in it.

A.J. Evans, *Escape and Liberation 1940–1945*, 1945

NOT HUMAN

At last, at ten o'clock in the morning on the 3rd September, my chance came. The cart was loading up at its first port of call, and the sentry left it for a few minutes. I leaped out of my uniform and got ready; and although there were several Germans in the neighbourhood nobody saw me.

I found a lot of cut grass in the cart, and wrapped it about my head and shoulders as well as I could, so as to protect myself from the garbage. The two Poles who were loading the cart covered me up conscientiously, and little by little the pile of cinders, stones, broken china and other rubbish rose above me in a reassuring but nauseating fashion. I managed to keep an air-hole open, so that while my legs were crushed under an ever-increasing weight my head was fairly free and I could breathe a bit. At last the work was finished, the cart loaded, and ready to drive away as soon as the horses were brought back and harnessed to.

Alas for the best-laid plan of this man! For the very first time the horses were not immediately forthcoming. The Poles and the sentry went away. Then I heard nothing, except the footsteps of some of my fellow-prisoners strolling about the court, all unaware of my presence.

The horses must be in use elsewhere, but for how long? I must hang on as long as possible, but the position was not an agreeable one.

An hour passed, bearable but unpleasant. But little by little the crushing weight on my legs became unbearable. Lieutenant Blehaut, who had been with me since Strasburg and was the only man I had taken into my confidence, strolled by from time to time to ask me if I was still all right. Towards noon, I had to tell him to fetch an orderly we could trust, and ask him to climb up on the cart as though he were working there and try to ease my position for me. A soldier, David, agreed to do this, although he risked a long term of imprisonment if he should be caught trying to help me. But he saw immediately that he could not do anything for me without at least partially emptying the cart. He nevertheless tried his best to shift the weight off me a little, but the result was not what I had hoped, for when the released blood began to circulate again through my crushed legs the pain was so great that I was afraid I should faint if I had to stay there. I told David to fetch two or three friends and openly unload the cart, without trying to conceal their activities. If any German questioned them they were to say that they had lost some money in the garbage and were looking for it.

I only took this decision when it became quite obvious that I could not stay in the cart much longer without being suffocated, and that all that was left to do was to try to get out of it without being seen. I was anxious to do this not to avoid a few days in the cells – I was well hardened to that, having already passed one hundred and four days there – but in order to save my civilian clothing, my maps and money, and so be in a position to have another try for it at the first opportunity. But it seemed nearly impossible that such a delicate operation could be carried out unnoticed in the middle of a crowded courtyard. And indeed it was not possible, for no sooner had the three orderlies set to work to unbury me than a German came up and asked them what they were doing. David answered as I had told him, and the man accepted his explanation and went away.

As for myself, it was high time that I was disinterred, for the pain had become so intense that I was afraid of betraying myself by crying out. My rescuers worked as fast as they could, but there was a thickness of over a yard of debris over me, and it took time to move it all.

A second German soldier came and demanded explanations. He was not so easily satisfied as the first, but in the end he went away. Then the camp gatekeeper himself came up, and reprimanded the orderlies sharply, but they kept their heads and repeated their little story for the third time. But this time the tailboard of the cart had been taken out, and the German came to have a look inside. The whole upper part of my body and my head had already been dug out, and were in consequence perfectly visible. I kept rigidly still, waiting to see what would happen, and sure that I was discovered. I could see the German, and he could see me perfectly well, but I was so thoroughly camouflaged with garbage that he did not identify me as being a human being.

Paul L. Richard, 'The Prince of Escapers', in *On the Run*,
ed. H.C. Armstrong, 1934

SIX

'Anything was better than further suspense'

She took the rope that Ma handed her, took a turn around her waist
with it. Bellying down on the ground, she got her legs over the edge of
the pit and squirmed slowly backwards. She paused there, half-
suspended in space, breathing very rapidly. Then she looked up and
gave Ma the nod to lower her.

'Got somethin' on your mind.' Ma held her where she was for the
moment. 'Maybe you better unload it while you can.'

'I – nothing, I guess. I was just going to ask about the sleeping pills. I
mean, why you and Doc seem to take it for granted that we'll need
them.'

'Why?' Ma frowned incredulously. 'Hey, you ain't been around
much, have you, honey?'

'Well – I used to think so.'

'Uh-huh,' Ma said. 'Mmm-hmm. Well, I'll tell you somethin' about
them pills. Don't you doubt that you'll need 'em. An' don't wait to take
'em until you do. You gulp you down some right to begin with, an'
when them wears off . . .'

She tugged upward on the rope, then slacked off on it. Carol swung
off the brink, and moved slowly down towards the water.

'Yes?' she called, shivering as her feet touched the water. 'When they
begin to wear off?'

'Take some more,' Ma said.

The hole lay on a slant, and for its first two or three feet it was largely
filled with water, making it all but impossible to breathe until one had
navigated it.

Carol came through it at a frantic scramble; continued to scramble
forwards with eyes closed, breath held, until her head butted against
the rock at the end of the hole. And then gratefully, gasping in the air,
she let herself go prone.

Strangely, it was not absolutely dark. Wherever the faint seepage of
air came from, there was an equally faint seepage of light, if only the
relative light of the night outside, to relieve the blackness of this hidden
cave.

It was like being in a coffin, she thought. A dimly lit, well-ventilated
coffin. It wasn't uncomfortable; not yet at least. Merely confining. As
long as one was content to remain in it, and did not try to get out . . .

Abruptly, she cut off her thought.

Fumbling in the dimness, running her hands up to the end of the hole, she encountered the oval canvas-covered surface of a water canteen. She shook it, felt the swish and swing of the liquid inside. She laid it down again and continued to fumble until she found a small tightly capped bottle. She got the cap off and sniffed the contents. Taking out one of the capsules, she pinched it and touched her tongue to it.

Mildly bitter; a faintly salty taste. She dropped it back into the bottle and screwed the lid back on.

She didn't need that stuff. She wasn't going to take anything that made her any more helpless than she was already. Ma had told her, in so many words, that she had nothing to fear. She and Doc were both under Ma's protection, until they struck out on their own again. But just the same, she wasn't knocking herself out with goof balls. Ma might be absolutely on the square. She might be. But Doc could outsmart someone like her, without even halfway trying. And if he decided to have things his own way, and if he thought it was safe – well, never mind. But no sleeping pills for her.

If they *were* sleeping pills.

Her mind moved around and around the subject, moving with a kind of fuzzy firmness. With no coherent thought process, she arrived at a conviction – a habit with the basically insecure; an insecurity whose seeds are invariably planted earlier, in under- or overprotectiveness, in a distrust of parental authority which becomes all authority. It can later, with maturity – a flexible concept – be laughed away, dispelled by determined clear thinking. Or it can be encouraged by self-abusive resentment and brooding self-pity. It can grow ever greater, until the original authority becomes intolerable, and a change becomes imperative. Not to a radical one in thinking; that would be too troublesome, too painful. The change is simply to authority in another guise which, in time, and under any great stress, must be distrusted and resented even more than the first.

Thrashing it – and herself – Carol wondered why she feared Doc as she did – how she could fear him and be unable to trust him. And yet love him as she could never love another.

Even now, despite her fear and distrust, she would have given anything to have him with her.

He was always, or virtually always, so calm and self-assured. He always knew just what to do, and how to do it. He could be breaking

[141]

apart inside and you'd never know it from the way he acted. He'd be just as pleasant and polite as if he didn't have a care in the world. You had to be careful with someone like that. You could never know what he was thinking. But . . .

She sighed uxoriously, squirming a little. Doc McCoy – one hell of a guy, Ma had called him. And that seemed to say it all.

There just wasn't anyone else in the world like Doc, and there never would be.

She toyed with the bottle of pills. Then, turning on her side, she tapped on the wall with it. He couldn't be too far away from her, just a few feet through this coldly sweating rock. If she could make him hear her, and if he would reply to it – well, it would be nice. Each would be comforted, she persuaded herself, to know that the other was all right.

She tapped and listened. Tapped and listened. She frowned, with a kind of angry nervousness. Then, brightening, she turned and tapped on the opposite wall. Perhaps he was there, on that side. After all, he just about had to be, didn't he? He had to be on one side or the other.

She tapped and listened. Tapped and listened.

The silence between tappings pressed in around her. It became an aching thing, a void crying to be filled. It was unbearable, and since the unbearable cannot be borne, her imagination, that friendly enemy, stepped in.

Quite clearly, she heard Doc's answering taps. Well, not clearly perhaps – the imagination does have its limitations – but she did hear them.

She tapped and he – it – tapped. The signals went back and forth. A great relief spread through her; and then, on its heels, overlaying it, an increasing restlessness and irritation.

What was the point in just tapping, in just making a meaningless noise? Now, if she could send him a message. Ask him, tell him to – to . . .

But maybe he'd already thought of that. And thought it was impossible. And maybe it was.

She pushed herself back against the wall, then measured the space to the opposite wall. There seemed to be enough room for two people, that is. It could get to be a tight squeeze, of course; you couldn't continue it indefinitely. But just for a little while, an hour or so, it would be fine.

The overhead space? Well. She placed her palms against the roof of the hole, gave a start at its nearness to her. In the dimness it had seemed much farther away. She pushed on it, not realising that she was pushing. And suddenly she pounded on it with her fists.

She stopped that very quickly, and lay very still for a few minutes until the wild pounding of her heart had stopped. Then, pushing herself with heels and elbows, she began to scoot towards the entrance.

Water touched her feet. She jerked them away from it. She let them slide into it again, and remain there for a moment. And then with resentful resignation she withdrew them. For obviously she couldn't leave this place, go back out into the pit. Someone might see her. For all she knew, the place might be swarming with cops by this time. At any rate, the water was very deep – bottomless, Ma had said – and she could swim very little. If she should be unable to find the hole Doc was in, or if she was unable to get into it or get back into this one . . .

Perhaps *they* had planned it that way. *They* hoped and expected that she would try to leave, knowing that she would drown if she did.

But, anyway, leaving was out of the question. She had to stay here until she was got out, as – her pendulum mind swinging back again – she assured herself she would be. Doc would get her out. After all, she was his wife and they'd been through a lot together, and she'd done a lot for him. And – and – if he'd really wanted to get rid of her, he'd had plenty of chances before this.

He'd get her out all right, as soon as it was safe.

Ma would make him.

It was just a little roomier, down here near the entrance to the hole. The roof was just a little higher. She measured the distance with her upstretched palms, thinking that there was almost room enough to sit up. And no sooner had the thought entered her mind than she knew she must sit up.

She had to. She could not remain prone, or lie half-propped up on her elbows another minute.

Tucking her chin against her chest, she raised herself experimentally. Six inches, a foot, a foot and a half, a – the stone pressed against her head. She shoved against it stubbornly, then with a suppressed 'Ouch!' she dropped back to the floor.

She rested for a moment, then tried again. A kind of sideways try this time, with her knees pulled upward. That got her up a little farther, though not nearly far enough. But it did – or seemed to – show her how the trick could be done.

She was very lithe and limber, more so now than ever after the arduous thinning-down of their cross-country journey. So she sucked

[143]

her stomach in, drew her knees flat against it, and pressed her chin down against them. And thus, in a kind of flat ball, she flung herself upward and forward.

Her head struck the roof with a stunning bump, then skidded along it gratingly, leaving a thin trail of hair and scalp. She would have stopped with the first painful impact, but the momentum of her body arced her onwards. And then at last she was sitting up. Or rather, sitting. Bent forward as she was, it would have been far from accurate to say that she was sitting *up*.

The roof pressed upon her neck and shoulders. Her head was forced downward. Her widespread legs were flattened against the floor and, to support herself, she had her hands placed between them. She raised one of them to brush at her face, but the strain was so intolerable that she hastily put it back in use as a brace.

She rested, breathing heavily, finding it difficult to breathe at all in that constricting position; thinking, Well, at least I know I can do it now. I can sit up if I want to. Then, as the awkward pose became agonising, she tried to lie down again. And was held almost motionless exactly as she was.

She couldn't accept the fact. It was too terrible. Now, surely, she thought, if I got into this I can get out of it. If I can sit up, then I can – I can lie down again.

'Of course I can,' she spoke, grunted, aloud. 'Why not, anyway?'

There was, of course, every reason why not. It was impossible to draw her legs up, as she had in the first instance. Almost impossible to move them at all. As for balling herself up – well, she already was; even more than she had been originally. But now there was no give in the ball. Her body was like an overburdened spring, so heavily laden that it can only go down farther and never up.

'No,' she said quietly. 'No.'

Then, on an ascending note, 'No, no, n-no!'

She waited, panting, the blood running to her head and her hair tumbled over her eyes. Her wrists throbbed, and her elbows ached with sugary pain. And suddenly they doubled under her and her torso lurched downward, and a tortured scream burbled from her lips.

Sobbing painfully, she braced herself again. Tears ran down her face, and she could not brush them away. And in her agony and growing hysteria, that seemed the most unbearable thing of all.

'C-can't – can't even raise a finger,' she wept. 'Can't even r-raise a . . .'

Then, so softly that she could hardly be heard, 'Ma said tomorrow night. Tomorrow night, prob'ly.'

The words trickled off into silence. Her panting grew more laboured. She wheezed and coughed, groaned with the jerking of her body, and her tears ran harder.

'I – can't – stand – it!' she gasped. 'You hear me? *I can't stand it!* Can't stand it, can't stand it, *c-caa-an't stand eet, can't stand ee-yaahhhhhh . . .'*

She screamed and the pain of the exertion caused her to scream even louder, and that scream wrung still another from her throat. She writhed and screamed, gripped in a frenzy of pain and fury. Her head pounded against the roof and her heels dug and kicked into the floor, and her elbows churned and banged and scraped against the imprisoning sides of the hole.

Blood mingled with tears on her face. It streamed down her back, over her arms and legs and thighs. From a hundred tiny cuts and scratches and bruises it came, coating her body; warm red blood – combining slippery with the dust of the cave.

She never knew when she broke free. Or how. Or that she had. She was still struggling, still screaming, when she got the cap off the pill bottle and upended it into her mouth . . .

Peevishly, she came up out of the pleasant blackness. Something was gripping her ankle, and she tried to jerk away from it. But the thing held tight. It yanked, skidded her down the hole, peeling more hide from her body. She cried out in protest, and the cry was choked off suddenly as water closed over her.

Choking and kicking, she slid out of the hole and into the pit. It was night again – or night still? And in the moonlight, she looked blurrily into the flattest eyes she had ever seen.

'I'm Earl,' he grinned, showing twisted teeth. 'Just hold tight now, an' I'll getcha . . .'

'Leggo!' She flung herself frantically backwards. 'Just leave me alone! I don't want to go anywhere! P-please, please, don't make me! Just let me s-stay where . . .'

She made a grab for the bushes, tried to pull herself back into the hole. Treading water, Earl gave her a hard slap in the face.

'Son of a gun,' he mumbled, getting a rope around her waist, signalling to Ma and Doc. 'Wasn't forty-eight hours enough for yuh?'

Jim Thompson, *The Getaway*, 1972

After going below the floor on the night of the 26th February, we prepared to make ourselves as comfortable as the surroundings would permit. We decided to sleep in the compartment which I have described elsewhere, next to the ventilators underneath the verandah, as here the atmosphere was not quite so close as in the other chambers. We only possessed one blanket apiece, not daring to take more below with us for fear of arousing suspicion, since a person who was believed to have got clear away would hardly take all his bedding with him. The ground made a very hard couch, and this, added to the lack of fresh air and the excitement of the adventure, caused sleeping to be very difficult.

At length, after a night of continual turning over and over, trying to find a softer spot, we saw by the faint light which filtered through the ventilators that another day had come. This day, we thought, meant for us either discovery and imprisonment or non-discovery and escape. But escape was farther off than we supposed. Ere we shook the dust of Pretoria from off our feet, we had to undergo what it makes one shudder to recall.

It was now 5.30 a.m., and stealthy footsteps were audible overhead. It was the commandant going his morning rounds, and counting his charges as they lay asleep. A surprise was in store for him. Suddenly his footsteps ceased. In imagination we pictured what was occurring. He had reached one of the vacant beds; he was looking at it in amazement. No dummy figure had been deemed necessary this time. His tread was heard again, and twice more it ceased as two more blanks were seen. Then came a sound of voices. He was inquiring from some drowsy mortal where the usual occupants of the vacant beds were. The conversation was of the briefest; what reply he got I do not know, so I cannot give it here; and perhaps it is as well, for the hour was early and the inquirer had no claim to popularity among us. Whatever was its nature, the sounds of his retreating footsteps were soon heard as he left the room. We knew and were satisfied that our absence was at least suspected.

The hours rolled slowly on. At 8 a.m. a roll-call took place. Our absence passed from the region of doubt to certainty. What would happen next?

At 9.45 I heard the voice of Colonel Bullock bidding all go outside the building. A search was about to be made. An exciting moment was drawing near, yet we felt reasonably confident that our hiding-place would be overlooked. Soon the tramp of many feet, 'of armèd men the hum', resounds from the tiles of the passage. Nearer and nearer it comes; our hearts begin to beat a little faster. The door is reached, barred by the arm of no fair brave scion of the house of Douglas. In they throng, a posse of detectives and armed police, with but an inch of deal between them and their prey. We hold our breath as they approach the roof of our humble dwelling. The room above does not offer many hiding-places – no secret panel or priest's hole – nought but four bare walls, ten beds, a cupboard. Soon they leave. All the talent of the Vidocqs and Le Coqs (with apologies for the comparison) of Pretoria has failed to scent our lair. We breathe freely again.

The anxiety of our faithful comrades who remained outside was great, and their relief when they heard we had not been discovered greater still. After leaving our room the crowd of searchers hunted through the other rooms, and finding nothing of us, they repaired to the roof. Here our rude trap-door was immediately seen, and near it, left there by accident, lay my saw. This was pounced on by Dr Gunning for the Museum, an interesting account of which appeared in the *Strand Magazine* of April. The break in the electric wire was also noticed. By 10.45 the search was over, and the usual occupants of the building were crowding in. Not satisfied with searching the school, several houses in the neighbourhood also were honoured with a domiciliary visit, and the same precautions to prevent our escape were taken as already described in Churchill's case. The conclusion arrived at by the authorities was that we had made our way out during the darkness of the previous night, and had gone to Mafeking.

The following day an account of our evasion appeared in the local paper, the *Volkstem*. It said that a Kaffir had found the remains of a roast fowl and a hat, some few miles on the Mafeking road, where we were supposed to have bivouacked, and thither the inspector of police and his myrmidons rode in hot haste. I hope some day I may find and reward that imaginative Zulu . . .

The most trying part of the under-floor life, next to the lack of fresh air, was the constrained position in which we constantly had to remain. To move about we had to creep on hands and knees. I don't know what a 'housemaid's knee' may be, but we all developed very delicate knees, after a few days, from creeping on the rough ground. Our heads, too, suffered a good deal from bumping against the beams and hitting hard walls in the dark. Lack of any kind of exercise, if one is not weak and ill, is more intolerable that might be supposed.

Coughing, sneezing, or talking above a whisper was absolutely forbidden, for 'love, a cough, and smoke will not remain secret'. After a day or two we broke through the cross-wall and got under the next room. This made our dwelling a little more airy, and was otherwise advisable. How we passed our time will not take long to tell. We generally tried to make our night last till 10 a.m., then had a little food, played patience; lunch at 1 p.m. over, we read or slept; food again at seven, cocoa, and bed. Not an exciting way of passing the twenty-four hours, but the only way.

Unfortunately we had no means of washing, and to get a bucket of water through the trap-door was too unsafe. We had therefore to join the brigade of the 'great unwashed' till better times. The noise of the occupants of the rooms above tramping up and down was very trying, and I suffered much from headaches, aggravated by walking into cross-beams. Such was the damp that our boots, money-belts, and anything of leather, turned green in a night, and burning candles did not help much in drying the atmosphere.

Six uneventful days passed. Though at first great hopes were held out of a move, they grew less and less as day succeeded day. We thought at first that a week would be about as much of this kind of life as we could endure. Now we hardened ourselves to hold out for a fortnight. We fully recognised that each day that passed would give us a longer start when the time to emerge from the school came; for the officials had no idea that we were in Pretoria, and our having escaped was becoming ancient history. This was the sole consolation we could draw from the situation.

Captain Aylmer Haldane, *How We Escaped from Pretoria*, 1900

LATIN GIBBERISH

The State Model Schools stand in the midst of a quadrangle, and are surrounded on two sides by an iron grille and on two by a corrugated iron fence about 10 ft. high. These boundaries offered little obstacle to anyone who possessed the activity of youth, but the fact that they were guarded on the inside by sentries, fifty yards apart, armed with rifle and revolver, made them a well-nigh insuperable barrier. No walls are so hard to pierce as living walls. I thought of the penetrating power of gold, and the sentries were sounded. They were incorruptible. I seek not to deprive them of the credit, but the truth is that the bribery market in the Transvaal has been spoiled by the millionaires. I could not afford with my slender resources to insult them heavily enough. So nothing remained but to break out in spite of them. With another officer who may for the present – since he is still a prisoner – remain nameless, I formed a scheme.

After anxious reflection and continual watching, it was discovered that when the sentries near the offices walked about on their beats they were at certain moments unable to see the top of a few yards of the wall. The electric lights in the middle of the quadrangle brilliantly lighted the whole place but cut off the sentries beyond them from looking at the eastern wall, for from behind the lights all seemed darkness by contrast. The first thing was therefore to pass the two sentries near the offices. It was necessary to hit off the exact moment when both their backs should be turned together. After the wall was scaled we should be in the garden of the villa next door. There our plan came to an end. Everything after this was vague and uncertain. How to get out of the garden, how to pass unnoticed through the streets, how to evade the patrols that surrounded the town, and above all how to cover the two hundred and eighty miles to the Portuguese frontiers, were questions which would arise at a later stage. All attempts to communicate with friends outside had failed. We cherished the hope that with chocolate, a little Kaffir knowledge, and a great deal of luck, we might march the distance in a fortnight, buying mealies at the native kraals and lying hidden by day. But it did not look a very promising prospect.

We determined to try on the night of the 11th of December, making up our minds quite suddenly in the morning, for these things are best done on the spur of the moment. I passed the afternoon in positive terror. Nothing, since my schooldays, has ever disturbed me so much as this. There is something appalling in the idea of stealing secretly off in the night like a guilty thief. The fear of detection has a pang of its own. Besides, we knew quite well that on occasion, even on excuse, the sentries would fire. Fifteen yards is a short range. And beyond the immediate danger lay a prospect of severe hardship and suffering, only faint hopes of success, and the probability at the best of five months in Pretoria Gaol.

The afternoon dragged tediously away. I tried to read Mr Lecky's *History of England*, but for the first time in my life that wise writer wearied me. I played chess and was hopelessly beaten. At last it grew dark. At seven o'clock the bell for dinner rang and the officers trooped off. Now was the time. But the sentries gave us no chance. They did not walk about. One of them stood exactly opposite the only practicable part of the wall. We waited for two hours, but the attempt was plainly impossible, and so with a most unsatisfactory feeling of relief to bed.

Tuesday, the 12th! Another day of fear, but fear crystallising more and more into desperation. Anything was better than further suspense. Night came again. Again the dinner bell sounded. Choosing my opportunity I strolled across the quadrangle and secreted myself in one of the offices. Through a chink I watched the sentries. For half an hour they remained stolid and obstructive. Then all of a sudden one turned and walked up to his comrade and they began to talk. Their backs were turned. Now or never. I darted out of my hiding place and ran to the wall, seized the top with my hands and drew myself up. Twice I let myself down again in sickly hesitation, and then with a third resolve scrambled up. The top was flat. Lying on it I had one parting glimpse of the sentries, still talking, still with their backs turned; but, I repeat, fifteen yards away. Then I lowered myself silently down into the adjoining garden and crouched among the shrubs. I was free. The first step had been taken, and it was irrevocable.

It now remained to await the arrival of my comrade. The bushes of the garden gave a good deal of cover, and in the moonlight their shadows lay black on the ground. Twenty yards away was the house, and I had not been five minutes in hiding before I perceived that it was full of people; the windows revealed brightly lighted rooms, and within I could see figures moving about. This was a fresh complication. We had always thought the house unoccupied. Presently – how long afterwards I do not know, for the ordinary measures of time, hours, minutes, and seconds are quite meaningless on such occasions – a man came out of the door and walked across the garden in my direction. Scarcely ten yards away he stopped and stood still, looking steadily towards me. I cannot describe the surge of panic which nearly overwhelmed me. I must be discovered. I dared not stir an inch. My heart beat so violently that I felt sick. But amid a tumult of emotion, reason, seated firmly on her throne, whispered, 'Trust to the dark background.' I remained absolutely motionless. For a long time the man and I remained opposite each other, and every instant I expected him to spring forward. A vague idea crossed my mind that I might silence him. 'Hush, I am a detective. We expect that an officer will break out here tonight. I am waiting to catch him.' Reason – scornful this time – replied: 'Surely a Transvaal detective would speak Dutch. Trust to the shadow.' So I trusted, and after a spell another man came out of the house, lighted a cigar, and both he and the other walked off together. No sooner had they turned than a cat pursued by a dog rushed into the bushes and collided with me. The startled animal uttered a 'miaul' of alarm and darted back again, making a horrible rustling. Both men stopped at once. But it was only the cat, as they doubtless observed, and they passed out of the garden gate into the town.

I looked at my watch. An hour had passed since I climbed the wall. Where was my comrade? Suddenly I heard a voice from within the quadrangle say, quite loud, 'All up.' I crawled back to the wall. Two officers were walking up and down the other side jabbering Latin words, laughing and talking all manner of nonsense – amid which I caught my name. I risked a cough. One of the officers immediately began to chatter alone. The other said slowly and clearly, '. . . cannot get out. The sentry suspects. It's all up. Can you get back again?' But now all my fears fell from me at once. To go back was impossible. I could not hope to climb the wall unnoticed. Fate pointed onwards. Besides, I said to myself, 'Of course, I shall be recaptured, but I will at least have a run for my money.' I said to the officers, 'I shall go on alone.'

Now I was in the right mood for these undertakings – that is to say that, thinking failure almost certain, no odds against success affected me. All risks were less than the certainty. A glance at the plan will show that the gate which led into the road was only a few yards from another sentry. I said to myself, 'Toujours de l'audace:' put my hat on my head, strode into the middle of the garden, walked past the windows of the house without any attempt at concealment, and so went through the gate and turned to the left. I passed the sentry at less than five yards. Most of them knew me by sight. Whether he looked at me or not I do not know, for I never turned my head. But after walking a hundred yards and hearing no challenge, I knew that the second obstacle had been surmounted. I was at large in Pretoria.

Winston Churchill, *London to Ladysmith, via Pretoria*, 1900

THE SOUND OF SHOE-LEATHER

I climbed back into the car. Blake's voice was still blaring from the radio, now close to panic.

'*Fox Michael! You MUST throw the ladder now, you simply* must!

There is no more time! Throw it now, Fox Michael! Throw it! Are you still there? Come in please!'

I already had the radio in my hand. I let him finish and then pressed the transmitting-button.

'Fox Michael to Baker Charlie. The ladder is coming over now. No matter what the consequences, the ladder is coming over now. Over.' I spoke slowly, deliberately.

'All right, Fox Michael, all right. But you must hurry! There is no more time! I expect to be taken at any moment. Throw it now! This is the last chance. Over.'

'It is coming over now,' I repeated. 'Just watch the wall. Over and out.'

I got out of the car, went round to the boot and very carefully took the rope ladder out of the paper bag, gripping it in the manner I had so painstakingly practised. I shut the boot quietly. The ladder had twenty rungs; they would hang down on the inside. The other half, my half, consisted of the two uprights wound together to make one thick rope, terminating in a loop. At the twentieth rung, the one that would be nearest the top of the wall on the inside, I had wound two large knots of rope, one around each upright. These would keep the ladder a couple of inches out from the wall as it hung down and so make it easier for Blake to grip the rungs.

I put my left arm through the loop, gripping the thick rope with my left hand; I held the folded rungs in my right. I looked up at the wall and started to swing. Then I hesitated. That wall seemed a lot higher when you stood directly underneath it. I wanted the ladder to go over first time, one clean throw. I doubted if I could do it.

I looked at the car; it was only inches from the wall. The numberplate was on the middle of the boot, and above it the numberplate light was contained in a protective metal housing that projected outwards a couple of inches. I placed my left foot on this projection and sprang forwards and upwards onto the roof of the car. I glanced quickly towards Du Cane Road. This, then, was the showdown. A car turning into Artillery Road now would catch me full in its headlights, standing on the roof of my car swinging a rope ladder. Now *I* had reached the point of no return.

I looked up at the wall. The combined height of the car and my own body had brought the stone coping at the top very much nearer. I swung the folded ladder three times and threw it. I was *too* careful: it went several feet higher than necessary, but dropped neatly down on the inside. I jumped down off the car and jerked the ladder a couple of yards to the right. I did not want Blake to land on the car; he would probably go through the roof. At the same time I pulled the ladder towards me till I could feel the resistance of those two knots touching the coping. That meant that the twentieth rung was now near the top of the wall and so the first one would be actually on the ground. The loop was still wound round my left arm, and now I held firmly onto the thick rope with both hands. I would not have to take all of Blake's weight; because of the sharp angle, the wall would take most of it.

I stood very close to the wall to make this angle as acute as possible. My forehead was actually touching the brickwork as I waited to feel the strain on the rope. At first nothing happened, and I wondered if Blake had been caught. It seemed ages since I had thrown the ladder. 'Come on, come on, come on!' I hissed through my teeth, and I was beating my forehead painfully against the brick wall. There had been no more cars for several minutes, but this luck could not last. My own car shielded me from view, since it was between me and the main road, but it could not conceal the upper half of the rope. Blake himself, the moment he appeared, would be exposed, and there was now no means of giving any further warning.

I kicked the wall. 'For God's sake, man, hurry up!' I said, almost shouting. The rain was pouring down my face and neck and my clothes were saturated right down to my underwear. Then I heard the wall being kicked directly in front of me and low down, near the ground. Then another kick, a little higher up, and then another. Somebody was climbing the ladder, but I could feel hardly any strain. The wall was taking more of the weight than I had expected. But was it Blake who was climbing? Or a screw?

The regular impacts of stout shoe-leather against solid brickwork were now occurring half-way up the wall. Who was it? Was I helping Blake? Or was I at this moment playing an active role in my own destruction? I looked up at the wall, keeping my eyes fixed firmly on the spot where the rope disappeared over the coping. If the wrong face appeared there I would let go.

The kicking against the brickwork was now very high up. Any moment, I thought, any moment. Then a pair of hands slapped loudly over the stone coping, fingers wide apart and desperately rigid. A moment later a face appeared. It was Blake.

Seán Bourke, *The Springing of George Blake*, 1970

I crept out first; Balbi followed me. Soradaci, who had accompanied us to the roof, was ordered to pull the sheet of lead down again and then to go and pray to his saint. Crawling on my knees on all fours, I clutched my crowbar firmly, and, stretching as far as I could, I slipped it obliquely between the points of the sheets; then, grasping the edge of the sheet I had turned up, I dragged myself up to the ridge of the roof. The friar, to follow me, inserted the fingers of his right hand into the belt of my breeches. Thus I had the double task of a beast which drags and carries both at once, and that on a steep roof, made slippery by a dense fog. Half-way up this dreadful climb Balbi bid me stop, for one of his parcels had fallen, and he hoped it might not have gone further than the gutter. My first impulse was to give him a kick and send him after his bundle; but, God be praised, I had enough self-command not to do this, for the punishment would have been too severe for both of us, since I alone could never have escaped. I asked him whether it was the packet of ropes, but as he replied that it was only his bundle, in which he had a manuscript he had found in the loft, and which he had hoped would make his fortune, I told him he must take patience, for that a step backwards would be fatal. The poor monk sighed, and, clinging still to my waistband, we climbed on again.

After having got over fifteen or sixteen sheets of lead with immense difficulty, we reached the ridge, on which I perched myself astride, and Balbi did the same. We had our backs to the island of San Giorgio Maggiore, and two hundred yards in front of us we saw the numerous cupolas of the church of Saint Mark, which is in fact part of the Ducal Palace; for the church of Saint Mark is, properly speaking, no more than the Doge's chapel, and certainly no sovereign can boast of a finer one. I began by relieving myself of my load, and desired my companion to follow my example. He tucked his bundle of ropes under him as best he might, but, wanting to take off his hat which inconvenienced him, he managed so badly that it rolled from ledge to ledge, and went to join the bundle of clothes in the canal. My poor comrade was in despair.

'A bad omen!' he exclaimed. 'Here I am at once without a shirt, without a hat, and bereft of a precious manuscript containing a most curious and unknown history of the festivals at the Ducal Palace.'

I, less disposed to be fierce than I had been when I was climbing, calmly assured him that these two little accidents had nothing so extraordinary about them as that a superstitious spirit should regard them as ominous; that I did not think them so, and that they did not in the least discourage me.

'They should serve you, my good fellow,' said I, 'as a warning to be prudent and wise, and to suggest to you that God certainly protects us; for if your hat, instead of tumbling to the right, had slipped off to the left, we should have been lost. It would have fallen into the courtyard, where the guards must have found it, and it would of course have told them that there must be some one on the roof. We should have been recaptured at once.'

After sitting for some minutes looking about me, I desired the monk to remain motionless till I should return, and I made my way forward, shuffling along astride on the roof without any difficulty, my bolt in my hand. I spent above an hour going about the roof, examining and observing every corner, but in vain; nowhere did I see anything to which I could attach a cord. I was in the greatest perplexity. I could not for a moment think of the canal, nor of the palace courtyard, and among the many cupolas of the church I saw nothing but precipitous walls leading to no open space. To get beyond the church to the Canonica I should have had to surmount such steep slopes that I had no hope of achieving it, and it was natural that I should reject as impossible everything that did not seem feasible. The situation in which I found myself required daring, but absolutely no rashness. It was such a dilemma as I imagine can have no parallel for difficulty in any moral question.

However, I had to come to some conclusion; I must either get away or return to my cell, never probably to leave it again; or, again, throw myself into the canal. In this predicament a great deal must be left to chance, and I must begin somewhere. I fixed my eyes on a dormer window on the side towards the canal, and about two-thirds of the way down. It was far enough from the spot we had started from to make me think that the loft it lighted was not connected with the prison I had broken out of. It could light only an attic, inhabited or vacant, over some room in the palace, where, when day should dawn, the doors no doubt would be opened. I was morally certain that the attendants in the palace, even those of the Doge himself, who should happen to see us, would be eager to favour our escape rather than place us in the hands of justice, even if they had recognised us as the greatest of state criminals, so horrible was the Inquisition in their eyes.

With this idea I decided on inspecting that window, so, letting myself slip gently down, I soon was astride on the little roof. Then, resting my hands on the edge, I stretched my head out and succeeded in seeing and touching a little barred grating, behind which there was a window glazed with small panes set in lead. The window did not trouble me, but the grating, slight as it was, seemed to me an insurmountable difficulty, for without a file I could not get through the bars, and I only had my crowbar. I was checked, and began to lose heart, when a perfectly simple and natural incident revived my spirit.

Philosophical reader, if you will for an instant imagine yourself in my place, and picture to yourself the misery I had endured for fifteen months; if you will consider the perils to which I was exposed on a leaden roof where the least rash movement would have cost me my life; if, again, you reflect that I had but a few hours in which to surmount all the difficulties which might multiply at every step, and that in case of failure I might rely on double severity on the part of an iniquitous tribunal, the confession I am about to make with the candour of truth will not lower me in your eyes; above all, if you remember that the nature of man when in anxiety and distress is not to be half so cool as when he is at ease and calm.

It was the clock of Saint Mark's at this moment striking midnight which roused my spirit, and by a sudden shock brought me out of the perplexed frame of mind in which I found myself. That clock reminded me that the morning about to dawn was that of All Saints' Day; that, consequently of my saint's day – if indeed I had a patron saint – and my Jesuit confessor's prophecy recurred to my mind. But I own that what tended most to restore my courage, and really increased my physical powers, was the profaner oracle of my beloved Ariosto:

'Fra il fin d'Ottobre, e il capo di Novembre.'

If a great misfortune sometimes makes a small mind devout, it is almost impossible that superstition should not have some share in the matter. The sound of the clock seemed to me a spoken charm which bid me act and promised me success. Lying flat on the roof, with my head over the edge, I pushed my bar in above the frame which held the grating, determined to dislodge it bodily. In a quarter of an hour I had succeeded; the grating was in my hands unbroken, and having laid it by the side of the dormer I had no difficulty in breaking in the window, though the blood was flowing from a wound I had made in my left hand.

By the help of my bar I got back to the ridge of the roof in the same way as before, and made my way back to where I had left my companion. I found him desperate and raging; he abused me foully for having left him there so long. He declared he was only waiting for seven to strike to go back to prison.

'What did you think had become of me?'

'I thought you had fallen down some roof or wall.'

'And you have no better way of expressing your joy at my return than by abusing me?'

'What have you been doing all this time?'

'Come with me and you will see.'

Having gathered up my bundles, I made my way back to the window. When we were just over it I explained to Balbi exactly what I had done, and consulted him as to how we were to get into the loft through the window. The thing was quite easy for one of us; the other could let him down. But I did not see how the second man was to follow him, as there was no way of fixing the rope above the window. By going in and letting myself drop I might break my legs and arms, for I did not know the height of the window above the floor. To this wise argument, spoken with perfect friendliness, the brute replied in these words:

'Let me down, at any rate, and when I am in there you will have plenty of time to find out how you can follow me.'

I confess that in my first impulse of indignation I was ready to stab him with my crowbar. A good genius saved me from doing so, and I did not even utter one word of reproach for his selfishness and baseness. On the contrary, I at once unrolled my bundle of rope, and fastening it firmly under his armpits I made him lie flat on his face, his feet outwards, and then let him down on to the roof of the dormer. When he was there, I made him go over the edge and into the window as far as his hips, leaving his arms on the sill. I next slipped down to the little roof, as I had done before, lay down on my stomach, and holding the rope firmly, told the monk to let himself go without fear. When he had landed on the floor of the attic he undid the rope and I, pulling it up, found that the height was above fifty feet. To jump this was too great a risk. As for the monk, now he was safe, after nearly two hours of anguish on a roof, where, I must own, his situation was far from comfortable, he called out to me to throw in the ropes, and he would take care of them. I, as may be supposed, took good care not to follow this absurd injunction.

Not knowing what to do, and awaiting some inspiration, I clambered once more to the ridge, and my eye falling on a spot near a cupola, which I had not yet examined, I made my way thither. I saw a little terrace or platform covered with lead, close to a large window closed with shutters. There was here a tub full of wet mortar with a trowel, and by the side a ladder, which I thought would be long enough to enable me to get down into the attic where my comrade was. This settled the question. I slipped my rope through the top rung, and dragged this awkward load as far as the window. I then had to get the clumsy mass into the window; it was above twelve yards long. The difficulty I had in doing it made me repent of having deprived myself of Balbi's assistance. I pushed the ladder along till one end was on the level of the dormer and the other projected by a third beyond the gutter. Then I slid down on to the dormer roof; I drew the ladder close to my side and fastened the rope to the eighth rung, after which I again allowed it to slip till it was parallel with the window. Then I did all I could to make it slip into the window, but I could not get it beyond the fifth rung because the end caught against the inner roof of the dormer, and no power on earth could get it any further without breaking either the ladder or the roof. There was nothing for it but to tilt the outer end, then the slope would allow it to slide in by its own weight. I might have placed the ladder across the window and have fastened the rope to it to let myself down, without any risk; but the ladder would have remained there, and next morning would have guided the archers and Lorenzo to the spot where we might still be hiding.

I would not run the risk of losing by such an act of imprudence the fruit of so much labour and peril, and to conceal all our traces the ladder must be got entirely into the window. Having no one to help me, I decided on getting down to the gutter to tilt it, and attain my end. This in fact I did, but at so great a risk that but for a sort of miracle I should have paid for my daring with my life. I ventured to leave go of the cord that was attached to the ladder without any fear of its falling into the canal, because it was caught on the gutter by the third rung. Then, with my crowbar in my hand, I cautiously let myself slide down to the gutter by the side of the ladder; the marble ledge was against my toes, for I let myself down with my face to the roof. In this attitude I found strength enough to lift the ladder a few inches, and I had the satisfaction of seeing it go a foot further in. As the reader will understand, this diminished its weight very perceptibly. What I now wanted was to get it two feet further in, by lifting it enough; for after that I felt sure that, by climbing up to the roof of the dormer once more, I could, with the help of the rope, get it all the way in. To achieve this, I raised myself from my knees; but the force I was obliged to use to succeed made me slip, so that I suddenly found myself over the edge of the roof as far as my chest, supported only by my elbows.

It was an awful moment, which to this day I shudder to think of, and which it is perhaps impossible to conceive of in all its horror. The natural instinct of self-preservation made me almost unconsciously lean with all my might, supporting myself on my ribs, and I succeeded – miraculously, I felt inclined to say. Taking care not to relax my hold, I managed to raise myself with all the strength of my wrists, leaning at the same time on my stomach. Happily there was nothing to fear for the ladder, for the lucky – or rather the unlucky push which had cost me so dear, had sent it in more than three feet, which fixed it firmly.

Finding myself resting on the gutter literally on my wrists and my groin, I found that by moving my right side I could raise first one knee and then the other on to the parapet. Then I should be safe. However, my troubles were not yet over, for the strain I was obliged to exert in order to succeed gave me such a nervous spasm that a violent attack of painful cramp seemed to cripple me completely. I did not lose my head, and remained perfectly still till the spasm was over, knowing that perfect stillness is the best cure for nervous cramps – I had often found it so. It was a frightful moment. A few minutes after, I gradually renewed my efforts. I succeeded in getting my knees against the gutter, and as soon as I had recovered my breath I carefully raised the ladder, and at last got it to the angle where it was parallel with the window. Knowing enough of the laws of equilibrium and the lever, I now picked up my crowbar, and climbing in my old fashion, I hauled myself up to the roof and easily succeeded in tilting in the ladder, which the monk below received in his arms: I then flung in my clothes, the ropes and the broken pieces, and got down into the attic, where Balbi received me very heartily and took care to remove the ladder.

Arm in arm, we surveyed the dark room in which we found ourselves; it was thirty paces long by about twenty wide.

At one end we felt a double door formed of iron bars. This was unpromising, but laying my hand on the latch in the middle it yielded to pressure, and the door opened. We first felt our way round this fresh room, and then, trying to cross it, ran up against a table with armchairs and stools round it. We returned to the side where we had felt windows, and having opened one, by the dim starlight we could see nothing but steep roofs between domes. I did not for an instant think of escaping by the window; I must know where I was going, and I did not recognise the spot where we were. So I closed the window, and we went back to the first room, where we had left our baggage. Quite worn out, I let myself drop on to the floor, and putting a bundle of rope under my head, utterly bereft of all power of body or of mind, I fell into a sweet sleep. I gave myself up to it so passively, that even if I had known that death must be the end of it I could not have resisted it; and I remember distinctly that the pleasure of that sleep was perfectly delicious.

Casanova's Imprisonment and Escape, trans. Clara Bell, 1892

POLYPHEMUS AGAIN

We held a conference the whole day, and the moment we had supped we wrenched an iron hinge from our table, and with it we took out a pane of the wainscot, and began to take away the mortar: in six hours we had penetrated the first ceiling, and to our great satisfaction we found there was another at three feet distance. From this moment we looked upon our escape as certain; we replaced the pane in the wainscot so as not to appear to have been taken out. The next day I broke our steel and converted it into a little pen or common knife, and with this instrument we made handles to the two hinges of our table: we gave each of them an edge: afterwards we unthreaded two of our shirts, that is after having ripped and unhemmed them, we drew out one thread after another; we tied these threads together and made of them several balls, each containing an equal and determined quantity: all these being finished, we divided them into two, and they became two great cushions. There were about fifty threads to each of sixty feet long; we then plaited them, and they made us a cord of about fifty-five feet long; and with the wood which was brought us for our fire we made twenty rounds, with which and the cord we made a ladder of twenty feet long. We afterwards took in hand the most difficult part of our work, which was to take the iron bars out of the chimney: for this purpose we attached our rope ladder with a weight to one end of the bars, it easily twisted about them, and by means of the rounds we supported ourselves in the air whilst we were at work. In less than six months we had taken all the bars out, and we restored each of them to its place in such a manner as to be able to take it instantly away in case of need. This work was very painful; my God! we never came out of the chimney without our hands covered with blood; and our bodies were in such a position when we were at work as to make it impossible for us to continue for more than an hour at a time.

This done, we wanted a wooden ladder of twenty feet long to ascend from the fosse to the parapet, where the guards are posted, and afterwards to get into the garden of the government-house. Several pieces of wood were every day given to us to make our fire; they were from eighteen to twenty inches long. We now wanted pulleys and several other things; our hinges were unfit for this work, and still more so for sawing of wood. In less than six hours, I made with an iron candlestick and the other half of the steel, an excellent saw, with which I could, in less than a quarter of an hour, have cut in two a log of wood as thick as my thigh. With the knife, the hinge, and the saw, we chipped and smoothed the logs, and made at the ends mortisses and tenons that they might be inserted one within the other, with two holes, one of which received a round and the other a peg which prevented them from loosening; and as soon as we had finished a part of our ladder we hid it between the two ceilings.

With these tools we made a compass, a square, a divider, rounds, &c. &c.

As in the day time the officers and turnkeys frequently entered our chamber when we least expected them, it was necessary to hide, not only our utensils, but the least chip or shaving which we made, as the least of them would have betrayed us. We had therefore given a new name to all these things: for instance, we called the saw, *Faune*; the divider, *Anubis*; the iron hinges, *Tubalkain*; the tambour, *Polipheme*, in allusion to the den in the fable; the wooden ladder, *Jacob*; the rounds, *counters*; a cord, *a pigeon*, &c. &c. and when any body entered, the farthestoff said, Tubalkain, Faune, Anubis, pigeon, &c. and the other, who understood what these meant, threw over the utensil in question his handkerchief, or a napkin: in short, he put out of sight that which it was necessary to hide, and we were incessantly on our guard.

The wooden ladder which we made had but one pole, and twenty feet in length, in which was inserted twenty rounds of fifteen inches long, which consequently projected six inches on each side of the pole; to each part of this pole we had attached its round, pegged and tied, so that it was not possible to make a mistake in putting it together in the night. When this ladder was finished and tried, we hid it in Polipheme, that is between the two ceilings; afterwards we made ropes for the great ladder which was to be a hundred and twenty feet long. We unthreaded our shirts, napkins, under-stockings, drawers, and silk stockings; in short, they all were applied to this use. As soon as we had made a clew of a certain length, we hid it in Polipheme; and when we had finished a sufficient number, we twisted this fine rope in one single night; it was as white as snow, and I may venture to say, that a rope-maker could not have twisted better.

Memoirs of Henry Masers de Latude, During a Confinement of
Thirty-five Years in the State Prisons of France, English trans. 1787

I went to work upon this Boat, the most like a Fool, that ever Man did, who had any of his Senses awake. I pleas'd my self with the Design, without determining whether I was ever able to undertake it; not but that the Difficulty of launching my Boat came often into my Head; but I put a stop to my own Enquiries into it, by this foolish Answer which I gave my self, *Let's first make it, I'll warrant I'll find some Way or other to get it along, when 'tis done.*

This was a most preposterous Method; but the Eagerness of my Fancy prevail'd, and to work I went. I fell'd a Cedar Tree: I question much whether *Solomon* ever had such a One for the Building of the Temple at *Jerusalem*. It was five Foot ten Inches Diameter at the lower Part next the Stump, and four Foot eleven Inches Diameter at the End of twenty two Foot, after which it lessen'd for a while, and then parted into Branches: It was not without infinite Labour that I fell'd this Tree: I was twenty Days hacking and hewing at it at the Bottom. I was fourteen more getting the Branches and Limbs, and the vast spreading Head of it cut off, which I hack'd and hew'd through with Axe and Hatchet, and inexpressible Labour: After this, it cost me a Month to shape it, and dub it to a Proportion, and to something like the Bottom of a Boat, that it might swim upright as it ought to do. It cost me near three Months more to clear the In-side, and work it out so, as to make an exact Boat of it: This I did indeed without Fire, by meer Malett and Chissel, and by the dint of hard Labour, till I had brought it to be a very handsome *Periagua*, and big enough to have carry'd six and twenty Men, and consequently big enough to have carry'd me and all my Cargo.

When I had gone through this Work, I was extremely delighted with it. The Boat was really much bigger than I ever saw a Canoe, or Periagua, that was made of one Tree, in my Life. Many a weary Stroke it had cost, you may be sure; and there remain'd nothing but to get it into the Water; and had I gotten it into the Water, I make no question but I should have began the maddest Voyage, and the most unlikely to be perform'd, that ever was undertaken.

But all my Devices to get it into the Water fail'd me; tho' they cost me infinite Labour too. It lay about one hundred Yards from the Water, and not more: But the first Inconvenience was, it was up Hill towards the Creek; well, to take away this Discouragement, I resolv'd to dig into the Surface of the Earth, and so make a Declivity: This I begun, and it cost me a prodigious deal of Pains; but who grutches Pains, that have their Deliverance in View: But when this was work'd through, and this Difficulty manag'd, it was still much at one; for I could no more stir the Canoe, than I could the other Boat.

Then I measur'd the Distance of Ground, and resolv'd to cut a Dock, or Canal, to bring the Water up to the Canoe, seeing I could not bring the Canoe down to the Water: Well, I began this Work, and when I began to enter into it, and calculate how deep it was to be dug, how broad, how the Stuff to be thrown out, I found, That by the Number of Hands I had, being none but my own, it must have been ten or twelve Years before I should have gone through with it; for the Shore lay high, so that at the upper End, it must have been at least twenty Foot Deep; so at length, tho' with great Reluctancy, I gave this Attempt over also.

This griev'd me heartily, and now I saw, tho' too late, the Folly of beginning a Work before we count the Cost; and before we judge rightly of our own Strength to go through with it.

In the middle of this Work, I finish'd my fourth Year in this Place, and kept my Anniversary with the same Devotion, and with as much Comfort as ever before; for by a constant Study, and serious Application of the Word of God, and by the Assistance of his Grace, I gain'd a different Knowledge from what I had before. I entertain'd different Notions of Things. I look'd now upon the World as a Thing remote, which I had nothing to do with, no Expectation from, and indeed no Desires about: In a Word, I had nothing indeed to do with it, nor was ever like to have; so I thought it look'd as we may perhaps look upon it hereafter, *viz.* as a Place I had liv'd in, but was come out of it.

Daniel Defoe, *Robinson Crusoe*, 1719–20

UNLIKELY WONDERS

Richard. I have been studying how I may compare
This prison where I live unto the world:
And for because the world is populous,
And here is not a creature but myself,
I cannot do it. Yet I'll hammer it out:
My brain I'll prove the female to my soul,
My soul the father, and these two beget

A generation of still-breeding thoughts;
And these same thoughts people this little world,
In humors like the people of this world,
For no thought is contented. The better sort,
As thoughts of things divine are intermixed
With scruples, and do set the word itself
Against the word; as thus: 'Come, little ones';
And then again,
'It is as hard to come as for a camel
To thread the postern of a small needle's eye.'
Thoughts tending to ambition, they do plot
Unlikely wonders: how these vain weak nails
May tear a passage thorough the flinty ribs
Of this hard world, my ragged prison walls;
And, for they cannot, die in their own pride.
Thoughts tending to content flatter themselves
That they are not the first of fortune's slaves,
Nor shall not be the last, like seely beggars
Who sitting in the stocks refuge their shame,
That many have, and others must, sit there;
And in this thought they find a kind of ease,
Bearing their own misfortunes on the back
Of such as have before endured the like.
Thus play I in one person many people,
And none contented; sometimes am I king,
Then treasons make me wish myself a beggar,
And so I am. Then crushing penury
Persuades me I was better when a king.
Then am I kinged again and, by and by,
Think that I am unkinged by Bolingbroke,
And straight am nothing. But whate'er I be,
Nor I, nor any man that but man is,
With nothing shall be pleased, till he be eased
With being nothing.

William Shakespeare, *Richard II*, Act V, sc. v. 1–41, *c.* 1595

SEVEN

'Not so much for myself'

February 28. – Being becalmed several miles north of Porto Ferrajo, I went on shore in a boat of Captain Adye's, at 10 a.m., in order to ascertain if Napoleon was still there, and then transmit whatever information I could collect to His Majesty's Minister at Florence, acting afterwards according to circumstances. We agreed that the ship should not enter the harbour, and that if I did not return in two hours it would be a sure proof of my detention; in which case Captain Adye would immediately despatch an express from Piombino to Lord Burghersh with this information and all he could obtain otherwise of the state of affairs.

Upon entering the harbour I immediately perceived, from the appearance of the National Guards as sentries on the fortifications, that the French Guards were no longer there; and, on proceeding alongside of the health-office, was informed, in answer to my inquiries after General Bertrand, that he had gone to Palmayola.

Expecting to be detained, I thought to push off immediately, but, after a moment's deliberation, considered that this would not be sufficiently satisfactory to others, although it might be so to myself, and therefore resolved upon the risk (or rather sacrifice more probably), as Captain Adye would be able to transmit the information required.

Accordingly I landed, and, proceeding towards General Bertrand's house, was met by Mr Grattan, an English gentleman, who had been conveyed to the island by Captain Adye on the 24th inst. He informed me that, about 3p.m. on the 26th, there was a sudden bustle among the troops and inhabitants, and a parade of the Corsican battalion took place. Soon afterwards the gates were shut. His servant, who had a brother a lieutenant in the Corsican battalion, told him that the Emperor and the whole of the troops were about to embark for Italy. Some spoke of Naples and Milan, others of Antibes and France. He applied several times to see General Bertrand, but could not obtain access to him under various pretexts.

At 7p.m. the troops marched out of the fortifications without music or noise, and embarked at the health-office in feluccas and boats which were alongside, a part of them being transported to the brig which lay in the harbour. At 9p.m. Napoleon with General Bertrand passed out in the Princess Pauline's small carriage drawn by four horses, embarked at the health-office in a boat, and went on board of the brig

L'Inconstant. Immediately afterwards the whole flotilla got under weigh with sweeps and boats, the soldiers crying out 'Vive l'Empereur!'

Mr Grattan says that his curiosity tempted him to hire a boat to go alongside of the brig, as he could scarcely believe his eyes and senses. There he saw Napoleon in his grey surtout and round hat pacing the quarter-deck of the brig, which, as well as all the other vessels, was crowded with troops. One of his boatmen called out that there was an Englishman on board; upon which he was questioned by an officer from the poop in English, what was his business there, and who he was? He told who he was, said that he had come merely to see the Emperor; upon which he was ordered to go away. This he immediately complied with, for he expected every moment to be fired at or seized.

Major-General Sir Neil Campbell, *Napoleon at Fontainebleau and Elba
Being a Journal of Occurrences in 1814–1815*, 1869

KEYS IN THE LAKE

Sir William Douglas, the Laird of Lochleven, owner of the castle where Mary was imprisoned, was a half-brother by the mother's side of the Regent Murray. This baron discharged with severe fidelity the task of Mary's jailer; but his youngest brother, George Douglas, became more sensible to the Queen's distress, and perhaps to her beauty, than to the interests of the Regent, or of his own family. A plot laid by him for the Queen's deliverance was discovered, and he was expelled from the island in consequence. But he kept up a correspondence with a kinsman of his own, called Little Douglas, a boy of fifteen or sixteen, who had remained in the castle. On Sunday, the 2nd May, 1568, this little William Douglas contrived to steal the keys of the castle while the family were at supper. He let Mary and her attendant out of the tower when all had gone to rest – locked the gates of the castle to prevent pursuit – placed the Queen and her waiting-woman in a little skiff, and rowed them to the shore, throwing the keys of the castle into the lake in the course of their passage. Just when they were about to set out on this adventurous voyage, the youthful pilot had made a signal, by a light in a particular window visible at the upper end of the lake, to intimate that all was safe. Lord Seaton and a party of the Hamiltons were waiting at the landing-place. The Queen instantly mounted, and hurried off to Niddry, in West Lothian, from which place she went next day to Hamilton. The news flew like lightning throughout the country, and spread enthusiasm every where. The people remembered Mary's gentleness, grace, and beauty – they remembered her misfortunes also – and if they reflected on her errors, they thought they had been punished with sufficient severity. On Sunday, Mary was a sad and helpless captive in a lonely tower. On the Saturday following, she was at the head of a powerful confederacy, by which nine earls, nine bishops, eighteen lords, and many gentlemen of high rank, engaged to defend her person and restore her power.

From Tales of a Grandfather by Walter Scott, 1828–30

PATTING A DOG

Later that afternoon, my tutors and the four members of the *Kashag* left the palace hidden under a tarpaulin in the back of a lorry; in the evening, my mother, Tenzin Choegyal and Tsering Dolma went out, disguised, on the pretext of going to a nunnery on the south side of the Kyichu river. I then summoned the popular leaders and told them of my plan, stressing the need not only for maximum co-operation (which I knew was assured), but also for absolute secrecy. I was certain that the Chinese would have spies amongst the crowd. When these men had gone, I wrote them a letter explaining my reasons for leaving and begging them not to open fire except in self-defence, trusting that they would relay this message to the people. It was to be delivered next day.

At nightfall, I went for the last time to the shrine dedicated to Mahakala, my personal protector divinity. As I entered the room through its heavy, creaking door, I paused for a moment to take in what I saw before me. A number of monks sat chanting prayers at the base of a large statue of the Protector. There was no electric light in the room, only the glow of dozens of votive butter lamps set in rows of golden and silver dishes. Numerous frescoes covered the walls. A small offering of *tsampa* sat on a plate on the altar. A server, his face half in shadow, was bending over a large urn from which he was ladling out butter for the lamps. No one looked up, although I knew that my presence must have been noticed. To my right, one of the monks took up his cymbals, whilst another put a horn to his lips and blew a long, mournful note. The cymbals clashed together and were held, vibrating. Its sound was comforting.

I went forward and presented a *kata*, a length of white silk, to the divinity. This is the traditional Tibetan gesture on departure and signifies not only propitiation, but also implies the intention of return. For a moment I lingered in silent prayer. The monks would now suspect that I was going, but I was assured of their silence. Before leaving the room, I sat down for a few minutes and read from the Buddha's *sutras*, stopping at the one which talks of the need to 'develop confidence and courage'.

On leaving, I instructed someone to dim the lights throughout the remainder of the building before going downstairs, where I found one of my dogs. I patted it and was glad that it had never been very friendly with me. Our parting was not too difficult. I was much more sad to be leaving behind my bodyguards and sweepers. I then went outside into the chill March air. At the main entrance to the building was a landing with steps running off either side down to the ground. I walked round it, pausing on the far side to visualise reaching India safely. On coming back to the door, I visualised returning to Tibet.

At a few minutes before ten o'clock, now wearing unfamiliar trousers and a long, black coat, I threw a rifle over my right shoulder and, rolled up, an old *thangka* that had belonged to the Second Dalai Lama over my left. Then, slipping my glasses into my pocket, I stepped outside. I was frightened. I was joined by two soldiers, who silently escorted me to the gate in the inner wall, where I was met by the *Kusun Depon*. With them, I groped my way across the park, hardly able to see a thing. On reaching the outer wall, we joined up with *Chikyab Kenpo*, who, I could just make out, was armed with a sword. He spoke to me in a low, reassuring voice. I was to keep by him at all costs. Going through the gate, he announced boldly to the people gathered there that he was undertaking a routine tour of inspection. With that, we were allowed to pass through. No further words were spoken.

I could sense the presence of a great mass of humanity as I stumbled on, but they did not take any notice of us and, after a few minutes' walk, we were once more alone. We had successfully negotiated our way through the crowd, but now there were the Chinese to deal with. The thought of being captured terrified me. For the first time in my life I was truly afraid – not so much for myself but for the millions of people who put their faith in me. If I was caught, all would be lost. There was also some danger that we could be mistaken for Chinese soldiers by freedom fighters unaware of what was happening.

Our first obstacle was the tributary of the Kyichu river that I used to visit as a small child, until forbidden to do so by Tathag Rinpoché. To cross it, we had to use stepping-stones, which I found extremely difficult to negotiate without my glasses. More than once I almost lost my balance. We then made our way to the banks of the Kyichu itself. Just before reaching it, we came across a large group of people. The Lord Chamberlain spoke briefly with their leaders and then we passed on to the river-bank. Several coracles were waiting for us, together with a small party of ferry-men.

The crossing went smoothly, although I was certain that every splash of oars would draw down machine-gun fire on to us. There were many tens of thousands of PLA stationed in and around Lhasa at that time and it was inconceivable that they would not have patrols out. On the other side, we met up with a party of freedom fighters who were waiting with some ponies. Here we were also joined by my mother, my brother and sister and my tutors. We then paused to wait for my senior officials, who were following, to join us. Whilst we did so, we took the opportunity to exchange, in highly charged whispers, remarks about the iniquitous behaviour of the Chinese which had driven us to this pass. I also put my glasses back on – I could bear sightlessness no longer – but then almost wished I hadn't as I could now make out the torchlight of PLA sentries guarding the garrison that lay only a few hundred yards from where we stood. Fortunately, the moon was obscured by low cloud and visibility was poor.

As soon as the others arrived, we set off towards the hill and the mountain pass, called Che-La, that separates the Lhasa valley from the Tsangpo valley. At around three o'clock in the morning, we stopped at a simple farm house, the first of many to provide us with shelter over the next few weeks. But we did not remain long and after only a little while left to continue the trek up to the pass, which we reached at around eight o'clock. Not long before we reached it, the first light of day dawned and we saw to our amusement the result of our haste. There had been a mix-up with the ponies, their harnesses and their riders. Because the monastery that had provided the animals had had almost no warning, and because of the dark, the best of them had been fitted with the worst saddles and given to the wrong people, whereas some of the oldest and shaggiest mules wore the finest harnesses and were being ridden by the most senior officials!

At the top of the 16,000-foot pass – Che-La means Sandy Pass – the groom who was leading my pony stopped and turned it round, telling me that this was the last opportunity on the journey for a look at Lhasa.

The ancient city looked serene as ever as it lay spread out far below. I prayed for a few minutes before dismounting and running on foot down the sandy slopes that gave the place its name.

Freedom in Exile: The Autobiography of His Holiness
the Dalai Lama of Tibet, 1990

SELFLESS

Both sides of the movement were in action – and the leader was behind prison bars. One can imagine his feelings and understand his eager attempts to find a way of escape. The responsibility would one day lie on his shoulders – and here he was powerless to aid or interfere. One thing he was able to do in jail. He planned for the future. Once free he decided to go to America as the representative leader of the Irish people, both to raise money for a National Loan and voice the Irish cause, and, if possible, through the medium of American politics to influence American statesmen on behalf of Ireland's claims. He hoped, in other words, to bring Ireland for the first time into the arena of international politics, and who will deny that it was at least a marvellous gamble?

It was not, then, of himself he was thinking as one morning he fingered the keys of the prison chaplain, where he saw them lying on a press in the sacristy. There was, the prisoners knew, a peculiar gate in one of the walls of the prison which seemed to give egress to the world outside. Perhaps one of these keys would fit that gate to freedom! It was the work of a few moments as he lit the candles for Mass to collect in his palm some of the warm wax and to press the key into it. Now the problem was to get the impression out and a *facsimile* key in. Sean Milroy, who happened to be in Lincoln with De Valera, drew a humorous postcard headed *Christmas 1917–Christmas 1918*, showing on one side a drunken man trying to find the key-hole of his hall door, and on the other a prisoner struggling with an enormous key at a prison gate; the happy drunk was muttering, 'I can't get in,' and the unhappy prisoner was wailing, 'I can't get out.' This card they boldly sent out under the eyes of the Governor, who merely smiled at the joke it contained. After several vicissitudes it finally found its way to Michael Collins, and after two unsuccessful attempts had been made with keys smuggled into the jail, a third key, this time unfinished, was baked in a cake with a file, and safely reached the imprisoned men. With these Alderman De Loughrey, another of the prisoners, fashioned a skeleton key, and almost two months after the original plan had been mooted a night was fixed for the escape. For almost six weeks before Frank Kelly, sent by Michael Collins, had been laying plans in Lincoln, spying out the ground and making certain that the gate in question did actually open on a free world. On the chosen night Kelly, Collins, Harry Boland, and Pat O'Donoghue, of Manchester, were ready waiting in Lincoln with a car. Leaving O'Donoghue, the other three stole across the fields at the rear of the prison as soon as dark was fallen, and, lying within sight of the prison windows, waited for the appointed hour. At the stroke of the hour they flashed with a torch, and high up in the jail a faint light flickered in response. Rising, they raced swiftly to the gate, then actually seen at close quarters for the first time, only to find that it was a double gate. Collins had a duplicate key, and thrust it in the lock. He turned it. It held firm. He struggled with it, and to his horror it snapped off short, one piece remaining in his fist, the other clogging the keyhole.

At the same moment De Valera, with two comrades, Sean McGarry and Sean Milroy, stole down the corridor from their cell and across the prison yards to the gate. The skeleton key fitted, and De Valera swung open the inner door. Parted by the outer gate, the free men and the prisoners looked at one another, Collins's bulky shape outlined against the sky, De Valera's lanky form against the prison buildings. 'I've broken a key in the lock, Dev,' Collins almost sobbed. De Valera, with a cry, thrust his own key in from the opposite side, and, by one of those chances of fortune that do not always favour the brave, he managed to eject the stub of Collins's key. Again the skeleton worked. The outer gate swung open. They were free!

The remainder of Collins's arrangement worked like clockwork. Their hearts leaped once again when they came on a party of soldiers in the fields, but Boland's salutation disarmed suspicion, and they reached the waiting car in safety. At once they set off by a relay of cars to cross England before the hue-and-cry should be on their track. From Lincoln to Newark, Newark to Sheffield, Sheffield to Manchester they sped on, while the dawn rose behind them in the sky. And once in Manchester De Valera was fairly safe. Collins had perfected a system of transport for arms and men between Liverpool and Dublin, mainly through an IRB man in the Cunard Company, and when the time came, a few weeks later, it was a comparatively easy matter to smuggle De Valera to Ireland.

The excitement caused in Ireland by De Valera's escape cannot be described. A huge Sinn Fein demonstration in the Mansion House clamoured for news of him, and of course there was no message. De Valera is just the kind of man who would not think of anything so spectacular. Boland and Collins were back, and present at the meeting, and while the audience howled for a message, they looked at one another in dismay. 'Good God!' said Harry Boland, 'what shall we do?' The next minute Collins emerged from an ante-room and held a letter aloft in his hand. It was to become an historic message. 'I have escaped from Lincoln Prison to do the country's work, and I am doing it. – Eamon De Valera.' The audience yelled and cheered with delight and demanded the paper, but Collins slipped it to a girl secretary. He had written it himself!

Seán Ó Faoláin, *The Life Story of Eamon De Valera*, 1933

GROCERIES

We thought first of the simplest way of procuring a key – namely, by stealing one, but this, we had to conclude, was out of the question. The exact number of keys available for the warders was well known, and each warder always carried his key about with him. We therefore resorted to an interesting ruse.

Our Red Cross food parcels generally contained delicacies which were greatly prized at that time in Germany, and we used to invite a friendly warder into our cell for a few moments during the day and offer him biscuits, or the like, which could not then be obtained in Germany. While he was enjoying these, one of us who spoke German would engage him in conversation. Usually, while the warder talked he played with the key in his hand, and the rest made careful mental notes of the size and shape of the key and its wards. After the warder had left the cell, notes were compared and a sketch drawn giving a flat view of the key.

This procedure was repeated from time to time until we had a fairly accurate reproduction of the key on paper. During the dinner hour, when the warder had shut himself in his little room, next door to ours on the corridor, two of us would stand as sentries at each end of the corridor, while one, furnished with a smooth-cut piece of Lifebuoy soap, stood in front of the door. When the signal was given that the corridor was clear, he firmly pressed the piece of soap against the keyhole, and thus obtained an impression of the end view of the key, which only needed to be slightly reduced in size to give an exact replica. As far as rough designs were concerned, we had all that we wanted.

The most suitable materials for making the key then presented the next problem, as we had lived too innocently in pre-war days to be able to make expert use of a skeleton key. We felt that nothing except an exact duplicate of the warder's key would meet our case. To Bob Chalmers belongs the credit of actually making the key, which he did as follows:

With a penknife he first shaped a rough wooden model. An English prisoner on the top floor, who had been in the prison for a very long time, had been granted permission to do fretwork and to make simple plaster of Paris casts in his cell. From him, on some pretext or other, we borrowed a certain amount of plaster of Paris. The wooden model was greased with sardine oil, and with the help of the plaster of Paris quite a neat mould of the dummy key was made. Examination of an ordinary biscuit tin will reveal that the upper edge is usually reinforced by a strong piece of wire about an eighth of an inch thick, over which the sheet tin is bent. We took out this wire, Chalmers bent a piece of it into the shape of a suitable handle, and bent the other end at right angles so as to give the skeleton shape of the key.

As I have said, our hearts were set upon an exact replica of the real thing. A skeleton key was no use to us, because even if the man to whose lot it fell to open the door knew how to use one, he would have precious little time to spare in the open corridor, and we needed something which would enable him to unlock the door in the shortest possible time. How were we to clothe the skeleton with flesh – in this case, with metal? Through an oversight on the part of the prison authorities, no mechanics' shop had been placed at our disposal. Our only tools were a pocket-knife, a small file, a screw-driver given to me by a grateful Pole, and last but not least, a spirit lamp with a small quantity of spirit.

Days were spent in search of bits of metal with a low melting point. We paid visits to the cells of other prisoners in the hope of finding something suitable, and often debated whether we could safely cut lead from some water pipe. We even collected all the tin-foil we could lay hands on from packets of cigarettes and chocolates. At last I was visited by a most excellent brain wave. Prison friends of mine of many nationalities had on one occasion presented me with a beer mug, a false rumour having been spread that I was to be released from the prison and sent back to camp. They were kind enough to feel sorry, clubbed together, induced a warder to buy the mug in Berlin, and had their signature engraved on the lid by a fellow-prisoner, whose skill in sketching fortresses had given us the questionable pleasure of his company.

Now the lid of that beer mug was of *pewter* and pewter has a most accommodating melting-point.

I loved that mug. I hesitated a little, and then decided to toss up for it. Heads it goes; tails I keep it. We spun the coin. Heads it was, and the fate of the pewter lid with its many engraven signatures was settled. We broke it up late one night in our cell, and placed the pieces in our crucible – a small empty Oxo cube tin.

Chalmers, who had carefully thought out his plans well ahead, knew that he would require the soft metal on all sides of the wire skeleton key if it were to have the necessary strength. He effected this by making very tiny supports or bridges out of sheet tin. These supports he placed in the plaster of Paris mould, and then laid the skeleton of the key on them. The scraps of pewter were melted in the Oxo cube tin, the molten pewter was poured into the mould very carefully, and, to our intense delight, settled all round the strong reinforcing wire. Those were delicious moments. Time was given for the metal to cool, and then we lifted out of the mould a rough – very rough – replica of the warder's key.

Wallace Ellison, *Escapes and Adventures*, 1928

AN HONEST MAN

The lockpickers or keys marked XX and X were taken from a French murderer whose speciality was robbing churches.

He was a daring criminal and was caught by the merest accident. He had laid plans for a cool and premeditated murder of one of the Geldbrief Träger in Berlin, which class of postmen carry only money sent by mail and sometimes are entrusted with large sums.

This man, Olschansky, sent through the mail to himself 100 marks, having previously hired a small room in a street where the house was almost empty of lodgers.

The room was on the top floor, and when the postman arrived Monday morning, he found Olschansky awaiting him, and to all intents and purposes, Olschansky was just seated at his morning lunch (which all Germany partakes of about 10 o'clock) consisting of bottled beer and sandwiches.

Olschansky offered the postman a bottle of beer, but gave him no glass. He was then compelled to drink out of the bottle, and as the bottle was raised to his lips, Olschansky raised a heavy board and drove the bottle down the postman's throat, stifling him, and then immediately struck him over the temple and kept on hitting the stunned man until he had beaten the life out of his body.

He took all the money from the leather bag carried by the postman, locked the door, and left the building.

But he forgot to pay the beer man, and instead of going about his business, he went to pay his bill, as he was an honest man. This man noticed blood stains on Olschansky's shirt cuff.

Olschansky paid him with a 20-mark gold piece, and this was his undoing.

In the afternoon the murdered postman was discovered, and the beer man, Gastschenkwirth, reported to the police that 20 marks were paid to him by the man who had not enough money the day before to pay for his food and drink and had asked for credit.

A search was at once instituted for Olschansky, and with the system of registering each lodger with the police by all hotel and boarding house keepers, Olschansky was found, and in his possession were the two keys herewith illustrated.

I happened to be at the Police Presidium next morning and spoke to Olschansky, who looked more like a caged wolf than a man and had very little to say.

But two weeks later, when found guilty, he had plenty to say and informed the police of the various churches he had robbed, how he obtained keys for the doors, and showed he was a far more dangerous criminal than was at first suspected.

After he had been executed, I asked for the keys that had been found in his possession and obtained them. I have found that they will open almost every church door in Germany where they do not use padlocks, and the key marked X seems to be a kind of master key to the spurious Bramah locks.

Houdini on Magic, ed. Walter B. Gibson and Morris N. Young, 1953

She finished, and the subtle fiend his lore
Soon learned, now milder, and thus answered smooth.
Dear Daughter, since thou claim'st me for thy sire,
And my fair son here show'st me, the dear pledge
Of dalliance had with thee in heaven, and joys
Then sweet, now sad to mention, through dire change
Befallen us unforeseen, unthought of, know
I come no enemy, but to set free
From out this dark and dismal house of pain,
Both him and thee, and all the heavenly host
Of spirits that in our just pretences armed
Fell with us from on high: from them I go
This uncouth errand sole, and one for all
My self expose, with lonely steps to tread
The unfounded deep, and through the void immense
To search with wandering quest a place foretold
Should be, and, by concurring signs, ere now
Created vast and round, a place of bliss
In the purlieus of heaven, and therein placed
A race of upstart creatures, to supply
Perhaps our vacant room, though more removed,
Lest heaven surcharged with potent multitude
Might hap to move new broils: be this or aught
Than this more secret now designed, I haste
To know, and this once known, shall soon return,
And bring ye to the place where thou and Death
Shall dwell at ease, and up and down unseen
Wing silently the buxom air, embalmed
With odours; there ye shall be fed and filled
Immeasurably, all things shall be your prey.
He ceased, for both seemed highly pleased, and Death
Grinned horrible a ghastly smile, to hear
His famine should be filled, and blessed his maw
Destined to that good hour: no less rejoiced
His mother bad, and thus bespake her sire.
    The key of this infernal pit by due,
And by command of heaven's all-powerful king

I keep, by him forbidden to unlock
These adamantine gates; against all force
Death ready stands to interpose his dart,
Fearless to be o'ermatched by living might.
But what owe I to his commands above
Who hates me, and hath hither thrust me down
Into this gloom of Tartarus profound,
To sit in hateful office here confined,
Inhabitant of heaven, and heavenly-born,
Here in perpetual agony and pain,
With terrors and with clamours compassed round
Of mine own brood, that on my bowels feed:
Thou art my father, thou my author, thou
My being gavest me; whom should I obey
But thee, whom follow? Thou wilt bring me soon
To that new world of light and bliss, among
The gods who live at ease, where I shall reign
At thy right hand voluptuous, as beseems
Thy daughter and thy darling, without end.
  Thus saying, from her side the fatal key,
Sad instrument of all our woe, she took;
And towards the gate rolling her bestial train,
Forthwith the huge portcullis high updrew,
Which but her self, not all the Stygian powers
Could once have moved; then in the key-hole turns
The intricate wards, and every bolt and bar
Of massy iron or solid rock with ease
Unfastens: on a sudden open fly
With impetuous recoil and jarring sound
The infernal doors, and on their hinges grate
Harsh thunder, that the lowest bottom shook
Of Erebus. She opened, but to shut
Excelled her power; the gates wide open stood,
That with extended wings a bannered host
Under spread ensigns marching might pass through
With horse and chariots ranked in loose array;
So wide they stood, and like a furnace mouth
Cast forth redounding smoke and ruddy flame.

John Milton, *Paradise Lost* 1. 815–89, 1667

And there came two angels to Sodom at even; and Lot sat in the gate of Sodom: and Lot seeing *them* rose up to meet them; and he bowed himself with his face toward the ground;

2 And he said, Behold now, my lords, turn in, I pray you, into your servant's house, and tarry all night, and wash your feet, and ye shall rise up early, and go on your ways. And they said, Nay; but we will abide in the street all night.

3 And he pressed upon them greatly; and they turned in unto him, and entered into his house; and he made them a feast, and did bake unleavened bread, and they did eat.

4 ¶ But before they lay down, the men of the city, *even* the men of Sodom, compassed the house round, both old and young, all the people from every quarter:

5 And they called unto Lot, and said unto him, Where *are* the men which came in to thee this night? bring them out unto us, that we may know them.

6 And Lot went out at the door unto them, and shut the door after him,

7 And said, I pray you, brethren, do not so wickedly.

8 Behold now, I have two daughters which have not known man; let me, I pray you, bring them out unto you, and do ye to them as *is* good in your eyes: only unto these men do nothing; for therefore came they under the shadow of my roof.

9 And they said, Stand back. And they said *again*, This one *fellow* came in to sojourn, and he will needs be a judge: now will we deal worse with thee, than with them. And they pressed sore upon the man, *even* Lot, and came near to break the door.

10 But the men put forth their hand, and pulled Lot into the house to them, and shut to the door.

11 And they smote the men that *were* at the door of the house with blindness, both small and great: so that they wearied themselves to find the door.

12 ¶ And the men said unto Lot, Hast thou here any besides? son in law, and thy sons, and thy daughters, and whatsoever thou hast in the city, bring *them* out of this place:

13 For we will destroy this place, because the cry of them is waxen great before the face of the LORD; and the LORD hath sent us to destroy it.

14 And Lot went out, and spake unto his sons in law, which married his daughters, and said, Up, get you out of this place; for the LORD will destroy this city. But he seemed as one that mocked unto his sons in law.

15 ¶ And when the morning arose, then the angels hastened Lot, saying, Arise, take thy wife, and thy two daughters, which are here; lest thou be consumed in the iniquity of the city.

16 And while he lingered, the men laid hold upon his hand, and upon the hand of his wife, and upon the hand of his two daughters; the LORD being merciful unto him: and they brought him forth, and set him without the city.

17 ¶ And it came to pass, when they had brought them forth abroad, that he said, Escape for thy life; look not behind thee, neither stay thou in all the plain; escape to the mountain, lest thou be consumed.

18 And Lot said unto them, Oh, not so, my Lord:

19 Behold now, thy servant hath found grace in thy sight, and thou hast magnified thy mercy, which thou hast shewed unto me in saving my life; and I cannot escape to the mountain, lest some evil take me, and I die:

20 Behold now, this city *is* near to flee unto, and it *is* a little one: Oh, let me escape thither, (*is* it not a little one?) and my soul shall live.

21 And he said unto him, See, I have accepted thee concerning this thing also, that I will not overthrow this city, for the which thou hast spoken.

22 Haste thee, escape thither; for I cannot do any thing till thou be come thither. Therefore the name of the city, was called Zoar.

23 ¶ The sun was risen upon the earth when Lot entered into Zoar.

24 Then the LORD rained upon Sodom and upon Gomorrah brimstone and fire from the LORD out of heaven;

25 And he overthrew those cities, and all the plain, and all the inhabitants of the cities, and that which grew upon the ground.

26 ¶ But his wife looked back from behind him, and she became a pillar of salt.

27 ¶ And Abraham gat up early in the morning to the place where he stood before the LORD:

28 And he looked toward Sodom and Gomorrah, and toward all the land of the plain, and beheld, and, lo, the smoke of the country went up as the smoke of a furnace.

29 ¶ And it came to pass, when God destroyed the cities of the

plain, that God remembered Abraham, and sent Lot out of the midst of the overthrow, when he overthrew the cities in the which Lot dwelt.

30 ¶ And Lot went up out of Zoar, and dwelt in the mountain, and his two daughters with him; for he feared to dwell in Zoar: and he dwelt in a cave, he and his two daughters.

31 And the firstborn said unto the younger, Our father *is* old, and *there is* not a man in the earth to come in unto us after the manner of all the earth:

32 Come, let us make our father drink wine, and we will lie with him, that we may preserve seed of our father.

33 And they made their father drink wine that night: and the firstborn went in, and lay with her father; and he perceived not when she lay down, nor when she arose.

34 And it came to pass on the morrow, that the firstborn said unto the younger, Behold, I lay yesternight with my father: let us make him drink wine this night also; and go thou in, *and* lie with him, that we may preserve seed of our father.

35 And they made their father drink wine that night also: and the younger arose, and lay with him; and he perceived not when she lay down, nor when she arose.

36 Thus were both the daughters of Lot with child by their father.

Genesis 19: 1–36

'HITHER WE ALL MAKE OUR WAY'

The outcome of the wedding was worse than the beginning; for while the bride was strolling through the grass with a group of naiads in attendance, she fell dead, smitten in the ankle by a serpent's tooth. When the bard of Rhodope had mourned her to the full in the upper world, that he might try the shades as well he dared to go down to the Stygian world through the gate of Taenarus. And through the unsubstantial throngs and the ghosts who had received burial, he came to Persephone and him who rules those unlovely realms, lord of the shades. Then, singing to the music of his lyre, he said: 'O ye divinities who rule the world which lies beneath the earth, to which we all fall back who are born mortal, if it is lawful and you permit me to lay aside all false and doubtful speech and tell the simple truth: I have not come down hither to see dark Tartarus, nor yet to bind the three necks of

Medusa's monstrous offspring, rough with serpents. The cause of my journey is my wife, into whose body a trodden serpent shot his poison and so snatched away her budding years. I have desired strength to endure, and I will not deny that I have tried to bear it. But Love has overcome me, a god well-known in the upper world, but whether here or not I do not know; and yet I surmise that he is known here as well, and if the story of that old-time ravishment is not false, you, too, were joined by Love. By these fearsome places, by this huge void and these vast and silent realms, I beg of you, unravel the fates of my Eurydice, too quickly run. We are in all things due to you, and though we tarry on earth a little while, slow or swift we speed to one abode. Hither we all make our way; this is our final home; yours is the longest sway over the human race. She also shall be yours to rule when of ripe age she shall have lived out her allotted years. I ask the enjoyment of her as a boon; but if the fates deny this privilege for my wife, I am resolved not to return. Rejoice in the death of two.'

As he spoke thus, accompanying his words with the music of his lyre, the bloodless spirits wept; Tantalus did not catch at the fleeing wave; Ixion's wheel stopped in wonder; the vultures did not pluck at the liver; the Belides rested from their urns, and thou, O Sisyphus, didst sit upon thy stone. Then first, tradition says, conquered by the song, the cheeks of the Eumenides were wet with tears; nor could the queen nor he who rules the lower world refuse the suppliant. They called Eurydice. She was among the new shades and came with steps halting from her wound. Orpheus, the Thracian, then received his wife and with her this condition, that he should not turn his eyes backward until he had gone forth from the valley of Avernus, or else the gift would be in vain. They took the up-sloping path through places of utter silence, a steep path, indistinct and clouded in pitchy darkness. And now they were nearing the margin of the upper earth, when he, afraid that she might fail him, eager for sight of her, turned back his longing eyes; and instantly she slipped into the depths. He stretched out his arms, eager to catch her or to feel her clasp; but, unhappy one, he clasped nothing but the yielding air. And now, dying a second time, she made no complaint against her husband; for of what could she complain save that she was beloved? She spake one last 'farewell' which scarcely reached her husband's ears, and fell back again to the place whence she had come.

Ovid, Metamorphoses, trans. Frank Justus Miller, 1951

They walked quickly, Leamas glancing over his shoulder from time to time to make sure she was following. As he reached the end of the alley, he stopped, drew into the shadow of a doorway and looked at his watch.

'Two minutes,' he whispered.

She said nothing. She was staring straight ahead towards the wall, and the black ruins rising behind it.

'Two minutes,' Leamas repeated.

Before them was a strip of thirty yards. It followed the wall in both directions. Perhaps seventy yards to their right was a watch tower; the beam of its searchlight played along the strip. The thin rain hung in the air, so that the light from the arclamps was sallow and chalky, screening the world beyond. There was no one to be seen; not a sound. An empty stage.

The watch tower's searchlight began feeling its way along the wall towards them, hesitant; each time it rested they could see the separate bricks and the careless lines of mortar hastily put on. As they watched the beam stopped immediately in front of them. Leamas looked at his watch.

'Ready?' he asked.

She nodded.

Taking her arm he began walking deliberately across the strip. Liz wanted to run, but he held her so tightly that she could not. They were half-way towards the wall now, the brilliant semicircle of light drawing them forward, the beam directly above them. Leamas was determined to keep Liz very close to him, as if he were afraid that Mundt would not keep his word and somehow snatch her away at the last moment.

They were almost at the wall when the beam darted to the North leaving them momentarily in total darkness. Still holding Liz's arm, Leamas guided her forward blindly, his left hand reaching ahead of him until suddenly he felt the coarse, sharp contact of the cinder brick. Now he could discern the wall and, looking upwards, the triple strand of wire and the cruel hooks which held it. Metal wedges, like climbers' pitons, had been driven into the brick. Seizing the highest one, Leamas pulled himself quickly upwards until he had reached the top of the wall. He tugged sharply at the lower strand of wire and it came towards him, already cut.

'Come on,' he whispered urgently, 'start climbing.'

Laying himself flat he reached down, grasped her upstretched hand and began drawing her slowly upwards as her foot found the first metal rung.

Suddenly the whole world seemed to break into flame; from everywhere, from above and beside them, massive lights converged, bursting upon them with savage accuracy.

Leamas was blinded, he turned his head away, wrenching wildly at Liz's arm. Now she was swinging free; he thought she had slipped and he called frantically, still drawing her upwards. He could see nothing – only a mad confusion of colour dancing in his eyes.

Then came the hysterical wail of sirens, orders frantically shouted. Half kneeling astride the wall he grasped both her arms in his, and began dragging her to him inch by inch, himself on the verge of falling.

Then they fired – single rounds, three or four and he felt her shudder. Her thin arms slipped from his hands. He heard a voice in English from the Western side of the wall:

'Jump, Alec! Jump, man!'

Now everyone was shouting, English, French and German mixed; he heard Smiley's voice from quite close:

'The girl, where's the girl?'

Shielding his eyes he looked down at the foot of the wall and at last he managed to see her, lying still. For a moment he hesitated, then quite slowly he climbed back down the same rungs, until he was standing beside her. She was dead; her face was turned away, her black hair drawn across her cheek as if to protect her from the rain.

They seemed to hesitate before firing again; someone shouted an order, and still no one fired. Finally they shot him, two or three shots. He stood glaring round him like a blinded bull in the arena. As he fell, Leamas saw a small car smashed between great lorries, and the children waving cheerfully through the window.

John Le Carré, *The Spy Who Came in from the Cold*, 1963

EIGHT

'I do feel sometimes like nothing on earth'

Leaps over walls – especially when taken late in life – can be extremely perilous. To leap successfully, you need a sense of humour, the spirit of adventure and an unshakeable conviction that what you are leaping over is an obstacle upon which you would otherwise fall down.

My own leap was taken on October 26, 1941.

On that day I left the convent, where for twenty-eight years I had lived in the strictest possible enclosure, and came out again into the world.

In reality, it was not necessary to do any leaping, either of walls or of anything else. As soon as the customary formalities were ended, the doors were opened and I simply walked out.

The story of what led me to do this might be interesting: this, however, is not the place for it. This book deals with what happened after the convent doors were closed behind me and I stepped out into a world that was just beginning its third year of a new and particularly devilish kind of war.

Naturally, everyone whom I consulted assured me that I could not have chosen a more unsuitable moment for my exodus. What with clothes coupons, food rationing, travelling restrictions and the appalling rise in the cost of living, how on earth – they asked – did I imagine I should ever be able to cope?

I looked at all this, however, from another angle. Just because the world appeared to be in such a crazy turmoil, I felt that it was exactly the background that I required. Everybody was rushing round doing unprecedented things. Old standards had already been swept away. How easy it would be to plunge into the seething waters of the war deluge and splash about unnoticed, listening, looking about, experimenting, learning about things, till the floods died down! Afterwards – always provided that anything of the universe still remained to be lived in, which just then seemed unlikely – one might perhaps start trying to construct a life.

In my opinion, it would have been far more difficult to adjust oneself to the comparatively ordered rhythm of the pre-war world.

My sister Freda came to fetch me away, rather appropriately, on a cold and frosty morning. She brought with her an atmosphere of faint disapproval and a suitcase containing the clothes into which I was to change before finally going forth into the world.

The crescendo of shocks which awaited me began abruptly with my first introduction to up-to-date underwear. Frankly, I was appalled.

The garments to which I was accustomed had been contrived by thoroughgoing ascetics in the fourteenth century, who considered that a nice, thick, long-sleeved 'shift' of rough, scratchy serge was the right thing to wear next your skin. My shifts, when new, had reached almost to my ankles. However, hard washing and much indiscriminate patching soon stiffened and shrank them until they all but stood up by themselves. Stays, shoulder-strapped and severely boned, concealed one's outline; over them, two long serge petticoats were lashed securely round one's waist. Last came the ample habit-coat of heavy cloth, topped by a linen rochet and a stiffly starched *barbette* of cambric, folded into a score of tiny tucks and pleats at the neck.

So, when my sister handed me a wisp of gossamer, about the size and substance of a spider's web, I was startled.

She said, 'Here's your foundation garment. Actually, most people only wear pants and a brassière, but it's cold today so I thought we'd better start you with a vest.'

I examined the object, remembering 1914. In those days, a 'nice' girl 'started' with long, woolly combinations, neck-high and elbow-sleeved, decorated with a row of neat pearl buttons down the front . . .

Next came the modern version of the corset. It was the merest strip of elastic brocade from which suspenders, in a surprising number, dangled. I thought it a great improvement on the fourteenth-century idea. The only drawback was that you had to insert your person into it serpent-fashion, as it had no fastenings.

What bothered me most were the stockings. The kind I was used to were enormous things, far thicker than those men wear for tramping the moors and shrunk by repeated boiling to the shape and consistency of a Wellington boot. The pair with which Freda had provided me were of silk, skin-coloured and so transparent that I wondered why anyone bothered to wear the things at all.

I said firmly, 'Freda, I can't possibly go out in these. They make my legs look naked.'

She smiled patiently.

'Nonsense,' she said. 'Everyone wears them. If you went about in anything else you'd collect a crowd.'

By this time it had become clear to me that the generation which affected the transparencies in which I now was shivering must long ago have scrapped the kind of garments I had worn as a girl. I wondered what they had done about the neck-high camisoles with their fussy trimmings of lace and insertion and those incredibly ample, long-legged white cotton drawers.

The answer turned out to be an airy nothing called 'cami-knickers', made, apparently, of cobweb. I felt my teeth beginning to chatter as I put it – or should one say 'them'? – on.

One further shock awaited me.

An object was handed to me which I can only describe as a very realistically modelled bust-bodice. That its purpose was to emphasize contours which, in my girlhood, were always decorously concealed was but too evident.

'This,' said my sister cheerfully, 'is a brassière. And it's no use looking so horrified, because fashions today go out of their way to stress that part of one's anatomy. These things are supposed to fix one's chest at the classic angle. Like this –' she adjusted the object with expert fingers. 'There – you see the idea?'

The worst problem was my hair.

For twenty-eight years it had been cropped convict-wise beneath the incredible system of headgear exacted by the Order to which I belonged. As a foundation, a 'snood', or long narrow strip of linen, was wound two or three times round the head. Over this, a close-fitting cap – rather like those worn by bathers – was pulled down to the ears. A piece of fine cambric, called a 'tip', was then bound tightly across the forehead and tied at the back with strings. Next came the 'head' – a kind of wimple – which covered the head and ears. It was gathered in closely at the neck and then frilled out as far as the shoulders beneath the starched *barbette*. Over this was pinned an erection of black cashmere which fell, gable-wise, on either side of the head to just above the elbows. Between this and its lining of starched white linen was a double cardboard stiffening with strips of cotton, fortified with yet more starch. Finally, the veil proper – of thin, black material, rather like ninon – was mounted on the underveil and firmly secured with pins. Eight thicknesses in all! In summer it was apt to give one a headache. The wonder, of course, was that, having worn it for so many years, I had any hair left at all.

For about two months before my exodus, however, I had allowed my hair to grow. The result was that my head now resembled that of a moth-eaten golliwog. My sister, foreseeing this dilemma, had been inspired to bring me an admirable hat. Though neither toque, beret nor képi, it combined the advantages of all three. I drew it on now, a little apprehensively. Perhaps the effect may have been a trifle raffish; however, it concealed my elf-locks very satisfactorily.

Now we were on the threshold.

As I crossed it, two thoughts occurred to me. One was that the door which at that instant was being locked behind me was not a door but a guillotine. And it had just chopped off from me, utterly and irrevocably, every single thing which, for twenty-eight years, had made up my life. Henceforward I was a being without a background. And no one who has not actually experienced that sensation can know how grim it is.

The other thought flashed in upon me with the urgency of a commandment:

Thou shalt not look back!

And I knew instinctively that, if I wanted to keep my balance on the tight-rope stretched before me, I must slam the door behind me and keep on looking straight ahead. Otherwise I should have to pay the penalty.

I crossed the courtyard and went out into the pale October sunshine.

For good or ill, I had leapt over the wall.

Monica Baldwin, *I Leap Over the Wall*, 1949

THE DUTCH BOY

Now I come to relate the manner of my Escape from the Corsairs.

You must note, I would have put it in practice sooner than I did, but I had all the while a little Dutch Boy in my Company, that came out of England with me in the Arcana Galley, and my Resolution was to have liv'd and dy'd there, had I not got the Boy away as well as my self: Which at last I did effect at Noonday. For lying at Anteparis with a Prize, I got ashoar, and lighting on a small Greek Boat, I made him carry me to Melo, where I could be safe; but there not being able to subsist without money, I set on a new Project, and having got another small Boat for ourselves, I was resolv'd to sail for Smyrna: But herein I was frustrated again, for under Cherso, meeting with five half galleys belonging to Stanou, it appeared worse and worse for us: For now we thought we should be sold to Matfa Mama at Rhodes: yet it fell out better than we expected, the Turks proving very kind, and never fettered us: So we went for Samos, from whence having been now five Days in their Custody, I, with the Boy on my Back, committed my self to the Mercy of the Sea in the Night and got ashore. But there being many of the Turks, I was afraid to stir, and so lay in the Crevisses of a Rock 6 Days and Nights together, not daring to move, for fear of being retaken; and all the Sustenance we had there, was three Dew Snails, and some roots of wild Weeds. But at length we saw the half Galleys go away, though by this time the Youngster was almost dead, and my self little better: However, I could stand and go a little, but the Boy was not able to budge. We were remote from any Village, yet I would fain have carried the Lad to that which was next, but we fell sometimes both together: then I dragg'd him a little way, but was so faint that I was quickly forc'd to rest my self. Yet at length meeting with a poor Greek, with one Ass laden with Wood, and another unladen; after having some Discourse with him, (telling him who we were, and how we came thither) he took pitty on us, and put the Boy upon one Ass, and Me on the other, leaving his Wood behind him, and brought us to the Monastery at Samos. There for 12 days the Friars took great care of us, and saw us safely sent for Smyrna, by a French ship: Where, God be thanked, I thought my self in Paradise to be at Liberty.

Mr Roberts His Voyage to the Levant, with an Account of his Sufferings
amongst the Corsairs, their Villainous Way of Living and
his Descriptions of the Archipelago islands, 1699

BUTTERFLY HUNTING

In the Crimson Barrack of the incorrigibles in the disciplinary quarters on Royale, a new man was assigned to the space next to mine – a man I had not met before, Pierrot Josse. He was intelligent and had travelled far over the world as a sailor. We struck up a friendship and talked together a great deal. Brought up on sailing ships, Pierrot had later joined the Navy, but he was unruly and was sent to a disciplinary battalion in French Africa. From there he had been sent to Guiana in 1923, condemned to eight years for a theft he had committed while he was a soldier. He was handsome, and also young. Furthermore, although I spent time with him only because of his keen mind, and I was attracted to him merely by intellectual ideas which we shared in common, he was a pervert. He had many admirers among the older men but he knew how to make himself more respected than the usual perverts of the prison colony and chose his intimates carefully, without being intimidated by either force or persuasion.

There is a story connected with Pierrot: a great tale of a romance such as can only exist among the condemned men in the exile colony of Guiana.

The year after Pierrot come to Guiana, there arrived a young convict who was only seventeen years old. His name was Roger Pecquet. He had been given seven years for robbery, and for firing on the police who arrested him. At Saint Martin de Ré, the island concentration port of France, Pecquet had distinguished himself by his bad conduct: ungovernable and temperamental, he was always having to be put in a cell, and it seemed that dry bread and irons meant little to him! He had drawn to himself the admiration of the *forts-à-bras*, and these had shown him respect in spite of his youth and effeminate look. A few months after he arrived in Guiana, he had earned a total of three hundred and twenty days of cell and was classed as incorrigible. And so it was that in August of 1924, Pierrot who was in detention for attempted escape, came to know Roger Pecquet, who was also in the Saint Laurent blockhouse en route to Royale.

Roger slept alone in a cell, while Pierrot slept among others in one of the blockhouses; but Pierrot had noticed him when they walked in the court, and he had been attracted by his youth and manner.

One day he placed himself behind him when they were walking in the court for exercise, and said: 'Go to your cell, for I want to see you. I must talk to you!'

Roger turned on him, red in the face. He thought Pierrot was about to make him another proposition – like those solicitations which had been made to him so often by older men. Pierrot perceived this, and reassured him quickly, saying, 'No, it's not at all what you're thinking about! I want to talk with you!'

So Roger went to his cell. In a few moments Pierrot joined him. And, very openly and without shame, Pierrot admitted his homosexual habits and asked Roger point blank if he would let him become his *môme*.

Roger who had expected the other type of proposal, such as had been made to him by other convicts, was taken off guard by this sudden and open proposal, and did not know exactly what to say. It was already time for the cells to be locked, so he merely said: 'I'll let you know tomorrow.' But Pierrot was a handsome youth, and Roger's vanity was flattered . . .

When he had been at Kourou six days, Pierrot escaped with four other convicts and headed in the direction of the Nouveau camp to find Roger and organise an escape by sea. But on the second day after they left Kourou he and his companions were caught in the vicinity of Sinnamarie. Pierrot, alone, escaped in the night. He continued on his way by himself, following the cut made for telephone wires through the wild jungle. At the end of ten days he was at the edge of Camp Nouveau, and got word to Roger that he was hiding near at hand in the jungle.

Now, again, these two men were once more united. In a hut which Pierrot built a short distance from the camp, they saw each other almost every day. Roger, as though hunting butterflies, would visit him in the afternoon. Again, life was bliss to them. Roger brought Pierrot tobacco and food. Alone, there, in the deep solitude of the jungle they found together the kind of happiness they both desired.

Then, they started getting ready for the escape. Pierrot soon found a good dugout down the river, and brought it back into a creek. In the meantime, several convicts at the camp to whom Roger had talked had decided to go with them. One of these convicts was Big Marcel – the same convict who accompanied me on my bloody second escape. On a clear night they left, eight men altogether, with as much food as they could buy or steal.

Pierrot was at the helm. Roger sat next to him. They gained the mouth of the river. The sea was calm and Pierrot was an excellent sailor. Nine days later they were entering the Orinoco. They were in Venezuela; they were, they thought, at last *free*!

A few months earlier they would have had their freedom, but now the authorities of Venezuela, which had always been a land of liberty to men fleeing from the death and starvation in French Guiana, had begun rounding up and arresting all the escaped French convicts in the country. And these eight, who had come thinking they had sailed to freedom, walked right into prison!

Arrested by the Venezuela police, they were thrown into the citadel of Puerto Cabello. Soon they were taken to work on the highway between Ciudad Bolivar and Caracas – a highway which for many years has been constructed almost entirely by the labour of men who escaped from the French Guiana. Life, labouring on that highway, was trying; bad food, hard work, and rough treatment. All that after they had risked their lives and thought they would be free! It was not long before Roger, with his rebellious nature, had his temper and patience at the cracking point. One day, when one of the guards struck him across the back with the flat of a machete, Roger leaped at his throat. That cost him his life, for he was brought to the ground riddled with bullets! Pierrot had witnessed the murder of his friend. Maddened by grief, a few days later, he attempted to stab one of Roger's murderers. And Pierrot fell, in his turn, under a volley of bullets. Big Marcel, finally brought back to the Isle Royale, told me of Pierrot's and Roger's last adventure and of the end of these two inseparables.

René Belbenoit, *Dry Guillotine*, 1938

THE BROTHER IN THE BATH-CHAIR

When I finished my row and went to get another one Sullivan, the screw, put me on Ken's row and told me to finish it.

He stood looking at me and asked me, 'Did you know Jones was going to scarper, Paddy?'

I looked him straight in the face and said, 'As true as God, Mr Sullivan, I did not.'

He smiled and nodded his head. 'I believe you, Paddy, lad,' and repeated reassuringly, 'I believe you.' Then he walked back to the top of the field.

At one o'clock he came down to me and told me to take the other fork with me to the tool-house along with my own.

On the way to the tool-house Charlie marched beside me, and said he was sorry for having been so leery in the morning. 'You knew he was scarpering, Paddy, didn't you?'

'Of course I knew,' said I. 'But I couldn't tell you that and the screw only a few yards from us.'

'You were dead right. I wouldn't like to grass on a bloke, neither.'

At lunch Joe was very interested in Ken scarpering off our party.

I could just see him myself, maybe lying down in the car while his brother flashed his officer's papers, or maybe he was in his uniform, and the cops would just salute and let him pass, without even stopping him, but then how were they to know that a commissioned officer would be helping a Borstal boy to escape?

Joe told us about his own party that morning, the navvy gang. Ickey Baldock rose a shovel to Tessie O'Shea, the screw.

Tessie O'Shea was six foot and weighed seventeen stone. Ickey was about five foot three and weighed about seven stone, even if he was all muscle. I personally thought him a little ballocks, but I pretended to be impressed by the story, but Joe wasn't.

Joe wasn't. 'Bloody little short-arsed—t. Old Tessie just looked down at 'im and pisses 'imself laughing.'

Then they discussed Ken's chances of getting to the Smoke and stopping out for a few weeks. I thought it would be evens that he was in London at that moment. A fast car could do it in two hours, what with the brother being the sort of young officer driver I could just imagine. But I decided not to tell them anything about it till later. Joe and Charlie and poor old Chewlips were OK, but you never know how these things get out, and even when Ken was safely delivered to wherever he would be hiding out it would certainly mean a court-martial for the brother if it came out.

'I suppose he goes to that bleedin' Sherwood Forest if they get him,' said Charlie.

'No,' said Joe, 'not 'im. I 'eard them talking about it on the navvy gang. He'd be sent to Chelmsford. He's doing HMP.'

'He's doing what?' said I. 'He's in for screwing.'

'He's not, you know,' said Joe, 'he's doing HMP. One of the lucky ones. The judge said he'd have 'ad 'im topped only for 'is age. Most brutal murder and all that lot. He pushed his crippled brother's bath-chair over a cliff. With the brother in it. Paralysed he was or something, from birth.'

'Well, how many brothers had he?' I asked Joe.

' 'Ow the 'ell do I know? Only the one I reckon, but I didn't know the family. Shouldn't fughing want to, neither.'

I was just as glad that I hadn't said anything about the brother being an officer and about the fast car.

In the afternoon we saw two station wagons go down the road. Some of the fellows at the three o'clock break said he would be caught before nightfall.

Charlie asked me my opinion and I said I didn't know because I didn't know the country well enough to give an opinion.

He wasn't caught that night. God help him, I thought, maybe it would be better for him if he was. I never saw such a night for rain. As I lay, warm and dry in bed, I thought of poor Ken, alone with himself and the torment of his thoughts out in that bloody miserable-looking bog.

Charlie whispered across in the dark, as the rain pelted off the windows, 'I wonder how old Jonesy is making out, Pad?'

'I'd sooner it was him than me, kid.'

'Maybe he'd go in a barn.'

'No, these old swede-bashers sit up all night with shotguns looking for scarperers. So I heard one of the blokes say.'

'Shower of sods.' . . .

Joe and Jock and I rambled round, and we were talking and stopping every now and then to roll a fresh rake-up or to get a light and smoking like lords' bastards on the buckshee half-ounce, when who should I see out of the corner of my left eye but Ken Jones, the scarperer, and two other blokes.

I went over to him and said, 'Well, Lamb of Jasus, if it's not yourself.'

He shook hands with me and said, 'Hello, Paddy, it's nice to see you again.'

'The dead arose and appeared to many. Where did you drop out of, at all?'

'I was up in chokey all the time. Our punishment cells were upstairs. I got two months PCTFO for scarpering, and I've been up there all the time. You never saw us because we exercised at the back of the buildings when you were all out at work. We were looking from our cell windows, and one of these chaps' – indicating the two fellows beside him – 'shouted from his window that there was a sports or something going on. I could only hear the cheering and, Christ, it felt awful to be stuck up there, on our own, and all you blokes out in the sun, enjoying yourselves. Then about an hour ago, they brought up a smashing tea, and I said to myself that we haven't been forgotten with the scoff anyway, and just as I was finishing mine the Governor had our doors unlocked and came in to each of us in our turn. He gave each of us half-ounce of snout and a packet of papers and told us to get to hell out of it, and come down here quickly or we'd miss the concert and he said we were to keep out of his way for the rest of our time here, or we'd stop in chokey till our hair fell out.'

'Well, glory be to the old Squire,' said I. 'I saw him going off quietly and I thought it was into his house for a bevy he was gone.'

'Well,' said Joe, ' 'e's a bloody old toff.'

'He's all that,' said Jock. 'What were these other blokes sent up for?'

One was a fair kid of about sixteen and the other was a tall dark lad, and a year or so older.

Ken glanced at them to see if they were listening and said quickly, in a low tone, 'Ring.' Then he said in a louder tone, 'Will I walk round a bit with you fellows?'

'Sure,' said I, 'come on.'

'See you later,' said Ken to the two other ex-chokey blokes and we moved off.

'Oh, I heard about them two,' said Jock. 'The night-watchman caught them kipped in together.'

'That's right,' said Joe, 'they fell asleep on the job.'

'By the same token,' said I, 'how did you make out that night, Ken?'

'Well, I went off that time when I fell out and I hid behind some bushes, as if I was going to have a crap. Then I wheeled around and went up to a ditch and hid in it until dark. I heard them calling me in the distance, and I thought that he would be down asking you where I was gone.'

'He did, too.'

'But I knew you'd say nothing.'

'Oh, the divil a fear of me.'

'I knew that, Paddy. I waited in this old ditch till dark and then made towards the place I told you about, where I had the overalls and the scoff parked. I'd to cross the road to do it and I nearly ran into the screws. Later that night I wished to Christ I had, for it pissed rain. I lay there soaked and shivering till coming on to morning. Then I started moving south or south-west across the fields and I must have covered about fifteen miles that way by the time it was bright. Then I lay down and had a sleep for a while. I was out all that day, and ate my scoff and I pinched some leeks out of a field – it was the only thing I could find, and was out again that night. I passed the night some way and staggered on and thought what a bloody fool I'd been, not to be safe and sound in my warm bed like everyone else. But I cheered up in the morning and thought that I'd shaken them off my tracks and that I'd be OK when I got to London. I waited along till I came to a bus stop and waited there, till the first bus came along and I got on that. I thought that with the overalls on me, and the big boots, the conductor would have taken me for a farm labourer.'

Ah, sure, God give you sense, says I, in my own mind, is it for anyone to take you for a farm labourer – there'd be as much chance of them taking me for the Marquis of Salisbury.

'I looked along the list of fares and picked a place that was marked a shilling. It was called Berry – Berry – something. I've forgotten the name of the sodding place.'

'That doesn't matter,' says Jock, 'we wouldn't know it, anyway.' Joe and I shook our heads too.

'Then the conductor came along and told me the fare had been increased since they printed that notice, and I didn't know what to say,

so I just gave him the shilling and told him to take me wherever that
would bring me. So he brought me to the cop-shop.'

'He had you tumbled all the time,' said Joe, 'it was on the nine
o'clock news.'

Brendan Behan, Borstal Boy, 1958

RECOGNITION

The Korff Berline, fairly ahead of all this riding Avalanche, reached the
little paltry Village of Varennes about eleven o'clock; hopeful, in spite
of that hoarse-whispering Unknown. Do not all Towns now lie behind
us; Verdun avoided, on our right? Within wind of Bouillé himself, in a
manner; and the darkest of midsummer nights favouring us! And so we
halt on the hill-top at the South end of the Village; expecting our relay;
which young Bouillé, Bouillé's own son, with his Escort of Hussars,
was to have ready; for in this Village is no Post. Distracting to think of:
neither horse nor Hussar is here! Ah, and stout horses, a proper relay
belonging to Duke Choiseul, do stand at hay, but in the Upper Village
over the Bridge; and we know not of them. Hussars likewise do wait,
but drinking in the taverns. For indeed it is six hours beyond the time;
young Bouillé, silly stripling, thinking the matter over for this night,
has retired to bed. And so our yellow Couriers, inexperienced, must
rove, groping, bungling, through a Village mostly asleep: Postilons will
not, for any money, go on with the tired horses; not at least without
refreshment; not they, let the Valet in round hat argue as he likes.

Miserable! 'For five-and-thirty minutes' by the King's watch, the
Berline is at a dead stand: Round-hat arguing with Churn-boots; tired
horses slobbering their meal-and-water; yellow Couriers groping,
bungling; – young Bouillé asleep, all the while, in the Upper Village,
and Choiseul's fine team standing there at hay. No help for it; not with
a King's ransom; the horses deliberately slobber, Round-hat argues,
Bouillé sleeps. And mark now, in the thick night, do not two
Horsemen, with jaded trot, come clank-clanking; and start with half-
pause, if one noticed them, at sight of this dim mass of a Berline, and its
dull slobbering and arguing; then prick off faster, into the Village? It is
Drouet, he and Clerk Guillaume! Still ahead, they two, of the whole,
riding hurlyburly; unshot, though some brag of having chased them.

[197]

Perilous is Drouet's errand also; but he is an Old-Dragoon, with his wits shaken thoroughly awake.

The Village of Varennes lies dark and slumberous; a most unlevel Village, of inverse saddle-shape, as men write. It sleeps; the rushing of the River Aire singing lullaby to it. Nevertheless from the Golden Arm, *Bras d'Or* Tavern, across that sloping Marketplace, there still comes shine of social light; comes voice of rude drovers, or the like, who have not yet taken the stirrup-cup; Boniface Le Blanc, in white apron, serving them: cheerful to behold. To this *Bras d'Or*, Drouet enters, alacrity looking through his eyes; he nudges Boniface, in all privacy, '*Camarade, es-tu bon Patriote*, Art thou a good Patriot?' – '*Si, je suis!*' answers Boniface. – 'In that case,' eagerly whispers Drouet – what whisper is needful, heard of Boniface alone.

And now see Boniface Le Blanc bustling, as he never did for the jolliest toper. See Drouet and Guillaume, dexterous Old Dragoons, instantly down blocking the Bridge, with a 'furniture-wagon they find there,' with whatever wagons, tumbrils, barrels, barrows their hands can lay hold of; – till no carriage can pass. Then swiftly, the Bridge once blocked, see them take station hard by, under Varennes Archway: joined by Le Blanc; Le Blanc's Brother, and one or two alert Patriots he has roused. Some half-dozen in all, with National muskets, they stand close, waiting under the Archway, till that same Korff Berline rumble up.

It rumbles up: *Alte là*! lanterns flash out from under coat-skirts, bridles chuck in strong fists, two National muskets level themselves fore and aft through the two Coach-doors: 'Mesdames, your Pass-ports?' – Alas, alas! Sieur Sausse, Procureur of the Township, Tallow-chandler also and Grocer, is there, with official grocer-politeness; Drouet with fierce logic and ready wit: – The respected Travelling Party, be it Baroness de Korff's, or persons of still higher consequence, will perhaps please to rest itself in M. Sausse's till the dawn strike up!

O Louis; O hapless Marie-Antoinette, fated to pass thy life with such men! Phlegmatic Louis, art thou but lazy semi-animate phlegm then, to the centre of thee? King, Captain-General, Sovereign Frank! if thy heart ever formed, since it began beating under the name of heart, any resolution at all, be it now then, or never in this world: – 'Violent nocturnal individuals, and if it were persons of high consequence? And if it were the King himself? Has the King not the power, which all beggars have, of travelling unmolested on his own Highway? Yes: it is the King; and tremble ye to know it! The King has said, in this one small matter; and in France, or under God's Throne, is no power that shall gainsay. Not the King shall ye stop here under this your miserable Archway; but his dead body only, and answer it to Heaven and Earth. To me, Bodyguards; Postilions, *en avant!*' – One fancies in that case the pale paralysis of these two Le Blanc musketeers; the drooping of Drouet's underjaw; and how Procureur Sausse had melted like tallow in furnace-heat: Louis faring on; in some few steps awakening Young Bouillé, awakening relays and Hussars; triumphant entry, with cavalcading high-brandishing Escort, and Escorts into Montmédi; and the whole course of French History different!

Alas, it was not *in* the poor phlegmatic man. Had it been in him, French History had never come under this Varennes Archway to decide itself. – He steps out; all step out. Procureur Sausse gives his grocer-arms to the Queen and Sister Elizabeth; Majesty taking the two children by the hand. And thus they walk, coolly back, over the Marketplace, to Procureur Sausse's; mount into his small upper story; where straightway his Majesty 'demands refreshments'. Demands refreshments, as is written; gets bread-and-cheese with a bottle of Burgundy; and remarks, that it is the best Burgundy he ever drank!

Thomas Carlyle, *The French Revolution*, 1837

MILK AND BISCUITS

The wood paling could scarcely be called an impediment; and listening attentively for a moment, and hearing nothing to alarm, I silently cut a part out, and crept through on my hands and knees as far and as quick as I could. I was interrupted by no one, and the sentinels were undoubtedly sheltered in their boxes. My success so far inspired me with great confidence. I knew that I had passed the first line of the guards, and that there were no more obstacles on the inside of the wall. If anything at this moment, the hurricane blew with tenfold violence; and justly thinking that no soldier would face it, but seek shelter, I jerked the hook, with the line attached, on the top of the wall, which, fortunately for me, caught the first time, and with but little noise to alarm. I, however, listened for a moment in great agitation; but all appeared quiet. I then tried the rope with my strength, and it proving safe, I made the desperate venture; and desperate indeed it was; but what will not a man attempt for his liberty?

With great difficulty I got to the top, and gently and by degrees peeped my head over. I listened most attentively, but could hear nothing; and had just got my knee upon the wall in the attitude of ascent, when a door opened close by me, and a soldier passed along. In a moment I threw myself flat upon my face on the wall, and very plainly heard his footsteps directly beneath me. I continued in this posture for some minutes, and had almost given myself up to despair, when, after passing and repassing several times – for I could hear him, though not see him – he again retired to his box, and I heard the door close after him. I seized the favourable moment, and pulling up the rope, descended in safety on the other side. I then took off my shoes, and softly walked on tiptoe across the beat of the sentinel, till I had got to some distance, when I threw myself on the wet grass, and stopped to take breath. My greatest difficulties were now surmounted; but as no time was to be lost, I soon started off again, and had nearly approached some of the lamps, which I was obliged to pass, when I plainly saw a picket or patrol of five or six men across my very path. It was astonishing they did not see me; but my good star predominated, and I remained unnoticed. The lamps were now, indeed, in my favour, as they shewed me what to avoid, whilst I was myself shrouded in darkness. Choosing the most obscure places, and proceeding step by step with the utmost precaution, I at last reached, unmolested, the boundary ditch, which I soon cleared; and in a moment after found myself free of the prison and on a high-road, with nothing further to obstruct my progress.

Scarcely crediting my good fortune in succeeding thus far, I put on my shoes, and set off in a northerly direction, running with all my speed, notwithstanding the wind and rain continued for about an hour, when I came to a house situated at a point where four roads meet. Lights were in the windows, and a stage-coach with lamps, and the words 'London and York', which I well remember, painted on it, was standing at the door. Shunning observation by keeping under the hedge, I took the left-hand road, though totally ignorant to what part I was going. Continuing my flight, I proceeded for two hours more, when my apprehensions of immediate pursuit being somewhat abated, and also beginning to feel fatigued, I slackened my pace. I had passed through two or three villages, but had met with nothing to interrupt me, or indeed to notice. I kept on thus some short time longer, when I came to a toll-gate, situated at the foot of an extraordinary long bridge, which led to Oundle, a town of considerable size. The chimes of the church clock were just playing the hour of three as I seated myself for a moment on the steps of the footgate. I was at first in doubt whether or not I should proceed straight on, or seek a by-road, one of which adjoined the bridge on the left hand. I determined, however, on the former, and continued my journey through dark, long, and dirty streets, without stopping or seeing any one, when I came to another bridge, at the farther extremity of the place, almost as long as the one I had before passed, so that the town appeared to be situated on an island. The moon had now got up a little, and afforded me light enough to discern, in a field just beyond the bridge, on the left hand, a small shed or hovel. I was now exceedingly fatigued, and I determined to rest here a short time at least, till I could collect my scattered senses, which had been so long in continual agitation.

The door of the hovel was luckily open, and it afforded me an excellent shelter. I cannot express my mingled feelings of fear and joy, hope and thankfulness, as I now stretched myself on the straw with which the ground was covered. No longer cooped up in what I may call a dungeon, where life itself almost ceased to be worth caring for, I now had before me a fair prospect of succeeding in my enterprise; and my energies being thus brought into action, I became a new man, and felt renovated accordingly: my mind, as it were, expanding and adapting itself to the occasion, called forth all its powers.

In the hovel, tied to a manger, was a cow, and her calf was placed in a pen just by her. At first the cow gave tokens of alarm and uneasiness; but humouring her by degrees, and treating her gently, she suffered me to approach her more familiarly, which I took advantage of, by milking her in the crown of my cap. The milk, with part of a biscuit, afforded me a delicious meal. I had taken off my shoes and wet stockings; and putting on the dry ones which I had in my pocket, I felt inexpressibly refreshed, though my wet clothes and fear of pursuit prevented my sleeping. Indeed it would not have been prudent to have slept, for it was evident the owner of the cow would be there in the morning to milk her; so, contenting myself with the good berth I had obtained, for it still continued raining, I waited very patiently for the first dawn of day, when I intended to start again. Of course I had not yet been able to examine my map, which, being enclosed in a case, was quite dry; but I thought that of little consequence, as, whether the road I had taken was right or not, a few hours would make up the difference.

As the day broke, the weather cleared up a little, so far as to cease raining, but the road was very wet and dirty; however, there was no alternative, and leaving with regret the hovel which had so kindly sheltered me for the night, I continued my journey. My wet clothes made me feel extremely cold and uncomfortable at first, and I kept up a pretty good pace for some time, in order to warm me. It was not my intention to go far, and seeing a haystack in a retired part of a field some distance off on my left, I quitted the high-road, and proceeded to it. It was farther than I expected; but it appeared to be the very spot I should have chosen for concealment, there being no public path or road leading to it. Part of the stack had been cut, so that I easily gathered enough of the hay to make me a soft and dry bed; and here I determined to stop and examine my map, and devise a plan for my future proceedings.

After I had rested some time, the sun, to my infinite delight, suddenly broke forth, and gave sign of a fine day; and though February sun in England is very different from a February sun in the south of France, yet the warmth I derived from it gave me great comfort, and refreshed me exceedingly; so much so, that, after several vain attempts to keep my eyes open, I sank into a sound sleep, which must have lasted for some hours, as the height of the sun on my awakening showed it to be past noon. Having risen and looked around, and finding nothing to interrupt me, I took out my map to see whereabout I was. This I accomplished with great ease; for the names of the places I had passed being painted on the milestones and direction-posts, as I observed when I started in the morning, and corresponding with those on my map, I soon found out that I had come diametrically opposite to the road I had intended to have taken. But this was of no great moment; and I now determined to pursue a direct easterly course, in as straight a line as I could, and to make for the coast in that direction. I may as well mention here, that, through the whole of my route afterwards, I could at any time find out the exact spot I was in by observing the names of the towns or villages painted on the milestones and direction-posts. This I found of great service to me, as I seldom wandered far from my way, and never had occasion to ask the road, even had I been able or inclined to do so. But to proceed. The clock of a neighbouring church was just striking one when I started again, in high spirits, my clothes being now quite dry, eating my last piece of biscuit as I went. How I was to get a fresh supply of provisions did certainly now and then strike me; but it made no very deep impression, my chief object being to get on as fast and as far as I could, not doubting but I should make the coast in two or three days more at farthest; but in that I was woefully out of my reckoning.

A Shocking Sight!

The day continued fine, and I walked on at a pretty round pace, in as straight a line as I could, over hedge and ditch, carefully avoiding any house or person passing, for about two or three hours; and I was congratulating myself on the progress I had made, when, suddenly casting up my eyes, and looking around me, to my utter horror and dismay I saw, but a few fields off, and in the exact path I was taking, the very prison I had left!

I could not be mistaken; its red tiles and striking appearance, with the numerous holes cut in its wooden walls for air by its unfortunate inmates, were too deeply imprinted on my memory to be forgotten. In short, not having any guide across the open fields, and there being no milestones to direct me, I had wandered back again to within half a mile or less of my former prison. I cannot express what I felt at that moment; I seemed to have lost the very power of perception; and, instead of turning back immediately, I absolutely continued for a little time walking on in the same direction – like the squirrel fascinated to its own destruction by the eyes of the rattlesnake.

Fortunately for me, going thus without heed, I tripped and fell, which brought me suddenly to myself, when, turning round, I took to my heels, as if pursued by a whole legion of devils, and never stopped till I once more found myself in the very hovel, near the long bridge I have spoken of at Oundle, where I had before found shelter, and which remained in the same state as I had left it, with the exception that the cow and calf had been removed.

Chambers Miscellany VI, 1845 (events of 1809)

ROYAL PICNICS

So we rode through a town short of Woolverhampton, betwixt that and Worcester, and went through, there lying a troop of the enemies there that night. We rode very quietly through the town, they having nobody to watch, nor they suspecting us no more than we did them, which I learned afterwards from a country fellow.

We went that night about twenty miles, to a place called White Ladys, hard by Tong Castle, by the advice of Mr Giffard, where we stopped, and got some little refreshment of bread and cheese, such as we could get, it being just beginning to be day. This White Ladys was a private house that Mr Giffard, who was a Staffordshire man, had told me belonged to honest people that lived thereabouts.

And just as we came thither, there came in a country fellow, that told us, there were three thousand of our horse just hard by Tong Castle, upon the heath, all in disorder, under David Leslie, and some other of the general officers: upon which there were some of the people of quality that were with me, who were very earnest that I should go to him and endeavour to go into Scotland; which I thought was absolutely impossible, knowing very well that the country would all rise upon us, and that men who had deserted me when they were in good order, would never stand to me when they have been beaten.

This made me take the resolution of putting myself into a disguise, and endeavouring to get a-foot to London, in a country fellow's habit, with a pair of ordinary grey cloth breeches, a leathern doublet, and a green jerkin, which I took in the house of White Ladys. I also cut my hair very short, and flung my clothes into a privy-house, that nobody might see that anybody had been stripping themselves. I acquainting none with my resolution of going to London but my Lord Wilmot, they all desiring me not to acquaint them with what I intended to do, because they knew not what they might be forced to confess; on which consideration, they, with one voice, begged of me not to tell them what I intended to do . . .

As soon as I was disguised I took with me a country fellow, whose name was Richard Penderell, whom Mr Giffard had undertaken to answer for, to be an honest man. He was a Roman Catholic, and I chose to trust them, because I knew they had hiding-holes for priests, that I thought I might make use of in case of need.

I was no sooner gone (being the next morning after the battle, and then broad day) out of the house with this country fellow, but, being in a great wood, I set myself at the edge of the wood, near the highway that was there, the better to see who came after us, and whether they made any search after the runaways, and I immediately saw a troop of horse coming by, which I conceived to be the same troop that beat our three thousand horse; but it did not look like a troop of the army's, but of the militia, for the fellow before it did not look at all like a soldier.

In this wood I staid all day, without meat or drink; and by great good fortune it rained all the time, which hindered them, as I believe, from coming into the wood to search for men that might be fled thither. And one thing is remarkable enough, that those with whom I have since spoken, of them that joined with the horse upon the heath, did say, that it rained little or nothing with them all the day, but only in the wood where I was, this contributing to my safety.

As I was in the wood, I talked with the fellow about getting towards London, and asking him many questions about what gentlemen he knew; I did not find that he knew any man of quality in the way towards London. And the truth is, my mind changed as I lay in the wood, and I resolved of another way of making my escape; which was, to get over the Severn into Wales, and so to get either to Swansea or some other of the sea-towns that I knew had commerce with France, to the end I might get over that way, as being a way that I thought none would suspect my taking; besides that, I remembered several honest gentlemen that were of my acquaintance in Wales.

So that night, as soon as it was dark, Richard Penderell and I took our journey on foot towards the Severn, intending to pass over a ferry, half-way between Bridgenorth and Shrewsbury. But as we were going in the night, we came by a mill where I heard some people talking (Memorandum, that I had got some bread and cheese the night before at one of the Penderells' houses, I not going in), and as we conceived, it was about twelve or one o'clock at night, and the country fellow desired me not to answer if anybody should ask me any questions, because I had not the accent of the country.

Just as we came to the mill, we could see the miller, as I believed, sitting at the mill door, he being in white clothes, it being a very dark night. He called out, 'Who goes there?' Upon which Richard Penderell answered, 'Neighbours going home,' or some such like words. Whereupon the miller cried out, 'If you be neighbours, stand, or I will knock you down.' Upon which, we believing there was company in the house, the fellow bade me follow him close; and he ran to a gate that went up a dirty lane, up a hill, and opening the gate, the miller cried out, 'Rogues, rogues!' And thereupon some men came out of the mill after us, which I believed was soldiers: so we fell a-running, both of us, up the lane, as long as we could run, it being very deep, and very dirty, till at last I bade him leap over a hedge, and lie still to hear if anybody followed us; which we did, and continued lying down upon the ground about half an hour, when, hearing nobody come, we continued our way on to the village upon the Severn; where the fellow told me there was an honest gentleman, one Mr Woolfe that lived in that town, where I might be with great safety; for that he had hiding-holes for priests. But I would not go in till I knew a little of his mind, whether he would receive so dangerous a guest as me, and therefore staid in a field, under a hedge by a great tree, commanding him not to say it was I; but only to ask Mr Woolfe, whether he would receive an English gentleman, a person of quality, to hide him the next day, till we could travel again by night, for I durst not go but by night.

Mr Woolfe, when the country fellow told him that it was one that had escaped from the battle of Worcester, said, that for his part, it was so dangerous a thing to harbour anybody that was known, that he would not venture his neck for any man, unless it were the king himself. Upon which Richard Penderell very indiscreetly, and without any leave, told him that it was I. Upon which Mr Woolfe replied, that he should be very ready to venture all he had in the world to secure me. Upon which Richard Penderell came and told me what he had done. At which I was a little troubled, but then there was no remedy, the day being just coming on, and I must either venture that, or run some greater danger.

So I came into the house a back way, where I found Mr Woolfe, an old gentleman, who told me he was very sorry to see me there; because there was two companies of the militia foot, at that time, in arms in the town, and kept a guard at the ferry, to examine everybody that came that way, in expectation of catching some that might be making their escape that way; and that he durst not put me into any of the hiding-holes of his house, because they had been discovered, and, consequently, if any search should be made, they would certainly repair to these holes; and that therefore I had no other way of security but to go into his barn, and there lie behind his corn and hay. So after he had given us some cold meat, that was ready, we, without making any bustle in the house, went and lay in the barn all the next day; when towards evening, his son, who had been prisoner at Shrewsbury, an honest man, was released, and came home to his father's house. And as soon as ever it began to be a little darkish, Mr Woolfe and his son brought us meat into the barn; and there we discoursed with them, whether we might safely get over the Severn into Wales; which they advised me by no means to adventure upon, because of the strict guards that were kept all along the Severn, where any passage could be found, for preventing anybody's escaping that way into Wales.

Upon this I took resolution of going that night the very same way back again to Penderell's house, where I knew I should hear some news, what was become of my Lord Wilmot, and resolved again upon going for London.

So we set out as soon as it was dark. But, as we came by the mill again, we had no mind to be questioned a second time there; and therefore, asking Richard Penderell whether he could swim or no, and how deep the river was, he told me it was a scurvy river, not easy to be passed in all places, and that he could not swim. So I told him, that the river being but a little one, I would undertake to help him over. Upon which we went over some closes to the river side, and I entering the river first, to see whether I could myself go over, who knew how to swim, found it was but a little above my middle; and thereupon taking Richard Penderell by the hand I helped him over.

Which being done, we went on our way to one of Penderell's brothers (his house being not far from White Ladys), who had been guide to my Lord Wilmot, and we believed might, by that time, be come back again; for my Lord Wilmot intended to go to London upon his own horse. When I came to this house, I inquired where my Lord Wilmot was; it being now towards morning, and having travelled these two nights on foot, Penderell's brother told me that he had conducted him to a very honest gentleman's house, one Mr Pitchcroft, not far from Woolverhampton, a Roman Catholic. I asked him what news? He told me that there was one Major Careless in the house that was that countryman; whom I knowing, he having been a major in our army, and made his escape thither, a Roman Catholic also, I sent for him into the room where I was, and consulting with him what we should do the next day, he told me that it would be very dangerous for me either to stay in that house, or to go into the wood, there being a great wood hard by Boscobel; that he knew but one way how to pass the next day, and that was, to get up into a great oak, in a pretty plain place, where we might see round about us; for the enemy would certainly search at the wood for people that had made their escape. Of which proposition of his I approving, we (that is to say, Careless and I) went, and carried up with us some victuals for the whole day, viz, bread, cheese, small beer, and nothing else, and got up into a great oak, that had been lopped some three or four years before, and being grown out again, very bushy and thick, could not be seen through, and here we staid all the day. I having, in the meantime, sent Penderell's brother to Mr Pitchcroft's to know whether my Lord Wilmot was there or no; and had word brought me by him, at night, that my lord was there; that there was a very secure hiding-hole in Mr Pitchcroft's house, and that he desired me to come thither to him.

Memorandum – That while we were in this tree we see soldiers going up and down, in the thicket of the wood, searching for persons escaped, we seeing them, now and then, peeping out of the wood.

An Account of the Preservation of Charles II after the Battle of Worcester,
Drawn up by Himself, 1766

10 *September*

The other night I had to fetch in two Americans, Hank and Martin.

Hank hails from Chicago but is far from looking like a gangster. Mart comes from Ohio.

Martin still bears the marks of the heavy burns he sustained when he jumped out of his plane in full daylight. All his clothes were on fire. Everything he had on was burning except his parachute.

The two Americans landed near a river, which Hank helped Mart to cross by swimming beside him. He then took him to shelter amongst the bulrushes. Meanwhile, the Germans had seen the men come down and were searching the countryside for them, so they hid in this swamp for nine hours. At night they were helped out of their uncomfortable hiding-place by members of the Belgian underground movement who, in a boat rowed by the young son of the local farmer, brought a doctor and a nurse with them to give Mart morphia and attend to his burns before taking them both off to the nearby farm.

After staying in the district until Martin's burns were healed the two men came to Brussels. There was then the usual procedure first, at Mr P's house, where it was decided that as it was late Martin should stay the night but that I would take Hank to stay at my house.

It is now dark, and as we walk part of the way home we stumble, for we can't see very much. The Brussels streets have cobbles which date back to the sixteenth century, or at least they feel as if they do. I know the way pretty well, as I have done this journey often in the heavy black-out, but Hank, poor man, I pity him.

Hank, however, has given me some good advice. At least, he *says* it's good, or rather, good for the eyesight. 'Eat as many raw carrots as you can,' he says. 'They are good for night vision.'

Well, I'm not fond of carrots, either cooked or raw, but as they are about the only thing the Germans are leaving us I shall have a go at eating them raw, as he advises. But oh for a nice juicy steak!

Half-way home we took a tram and it so happened that the two carriages were filled with Germans. I jumped in first and saw Hank hesitate, just for a second. Then he got on after me. We were the only civilians in this tram. Hank's face was most expressive.

There was no hesitation, however, when I went to get off. Hank jumped up double quick and followed me at once. He heaved a sigh of relief, and as a matter of fact, so did I. If those Germans had only known what a bundle of medals they were missing.

The following day I took Hank down town again to have his photo taken for his French identity card.

12 *September*

This journey passed off without incident but on another one that night I really found myself in a tight corner. Two more Americans having arrived, I went off to fetch them in, and as we got on the tram one of the men took out his cigarette-case and offered cigarettes around.

Now, since the Germans have tumbled to a habit the Belgians have of burning soldiers' uniforms with their lighted cigarettes, smoking on trams is forbidden, although of course the Belgians soon found another way of annoying their oppressors. (Now they pour a few drops of acid on the uniforms instead, and then get off the tram.)

However, this was not the time to tell this story, so before the men had time to light up their cigarettes I gave them the wink and hastily got off the tram. They looked surprised to have to leave the car after so short a journey, but were even more surprised when I told them how nearly they had given themselves away. Of course, it is my fault, for I should have thought of warning them about this before. Funny how these small and quite innocent daily habits may lead us all to face a firing squad.

Arriving about half past nine at Mlle C's house I have a funny feeling, though I don't know why, that the house is not safe any more. So I ask the boys to stand by and watch. 'If I flash my torch,' I tell them, 'everything is in order. But if I walk into the house without signalling, walk to the top of the street and wait for me there.'

Then I walk up alone to the house and ring the bell. There is a short wait, then Mlle C comes to the door and opens it. Everything was all right, after all.

We go in, and there they are all congregated, all laughing and joking. With those in there already, there are now twelve of them, and it is good to see them, and to hear them talk and make fun of their foreign civilian clothes. The Americans don't like the long-tailed shirts that men wear in Belgium; it's a lot of wasted material, they say. The British don't like the style of men's hats. As for the Canadians, they don't seem to care: all they long for is a good, strong drink. One tall American has wider interests – he wants to know if the use of peroxide is unknown in Belgium, for he has not seen a nice young blonde since he came here.

I returned home with the last tram to find Julien getting anxious. I suppose it is worse for those who are waiting at home for those who are out on the road. But I could not resist staying with the boys to listen to all the latest news from England. All are anxious to get back to take part in the big invasion, but after their description of the amount of planes and bombs they are accumulating on the other side of the Channel in preparation for this, I felt more like running away.

It's no use pretending otherwise, I do feel sometimes like nothing on earth. This continuous strain is geting me down. Yet I must keep on. I know that by now the Allies are counting on us. Again and again I remind myself that each man we send back is a man of experience, and that the mere fact they do go back is good for the morale of those who, day after day, night after night, go out into the skies to face and meet death. And what a death! Burned alive or machine-gunned as they come down by parachute. Yes, we must keep on.

Word has come through to expect three more Americans. One is badly wounded, with a bullet in the leg. This happened ten days ago and he cannot be moved from where he is because the Germans have encircled the village and are patrolling all the roads. The wounded man is hiding at a priest's house and as soon as all is clear will be brought into Brussels, where Mlle C will take him in, for he must be sheltered where there are no children. Our doctor friend has been warned, for he will be needed. And so we are all standing by. Meanwhile, the wounded man is being nursed by a Belgian nurse who belongs to the underground movement in the district where the man is hiding.

This week Julien took Hank to visit the bombed area. As Julien is in the ARP he has a special pass and arm-band which enables him to enter the forbidden zone, so he got an extra arm-band for Hank and off they went.

When they came back Hank was speechless. It is one thing to be in a plane and drop bombs; quite another to be the target. Hank says he does not want to be in Belgium when the invasion starts (after seeing this). This sounds joyful to us. It looks as if we are going to have a tough time. Well, let it come. The sooner the better.

Hank has left. I took him down town at 8 p.m. He will stay one night with Mart and then leave for Paris. Thrilled at the idea of seeing 'gay Paree' he has made up his mind to buy some perfume for his wife – 'Soir de Paris' he wants.

In their place I have four more men to fetch. I shall get two in the morning and two in the afternoon. If these airmen keep coming in at the rate they are doing now we shall soon see them walk down the streets four abreast.

Rendez-vous 127: The Diary of Madame Brusselmans, MBE
September 1940–September 1944, 1954

NINE

'The strength to hope for success'

I rowed all night. Finally my hands were so sore I could hardly close them over the oars. We were nearly smashed up on the shore several times. I kept fairly close to the shore because I was afraid of getting lost on the lake and losing time. Sometimes we were so close we could see a row of trees and the road along the shore with the mountains behind. The rain stopped and the wind drove the clouds so that the moon shone through and looking back I could see the long dark point of Castagnola and the lake with white-caps and beyond, the moon on the high snow mountains. Then the clouds came over the moon again and the mountains and the lake were gone, but it was much lighter than it had been before and we could see the shore. I could see it too clearly and pulled out where they would not see the boat if there were customs guards along the Pallanza road. When the moon came out again we could see white villas on the shore on the slopes of the mountain and the white road where it showed through the trees. All the time I was rowing.

The lake widened and across it on the shore at the foot of the mountains on the other side we saw a few lights that should be Luino. I saw a wedgelike gap between the mountains on the other shore and I thought that must be Luino. If it was we were making good time. I pulled in the oars and lay back on the seat. I was very, very tired of rowing. My arms and shoulders and back ached and my hands were sore.

'I could hold the umbrella,' Catherine said. 'We could sail with that with the wind.'

'Can you steer?'

'I think so.'

'You take this oar and hold it under your arm close to the side of the boat and steer and I'll hold the umbrella.' I went back to the stern and showed her how to hold the oar. I took the big umbrella the porter had given me and sat facing the bow and opened it. It opened with a clap. I held it on both sides, sitting astride the handle hooked over the seat. The wind was full in it and I felt the boat suck forward while I held as hard as I could to the two edges. It pulled hard. The boat was moving fast.

'We're going beautifully,' Catherine said. All I could see was umbrella ribs. The umbrella strained and pulled and I felt us driving along with it. I braced my feet and held back on it, then suddenly, it buckled; I felt a rib snap on my forehead, I tried to grab the top that was bending with the wind and the whole thing buckled and went inside out and I was astride the handle of an inside-out, ripped umbrella, where I had been holding a wind-filled pulling sail. I unhooked the handle from the seat, laid the umbrella in the bow and went back to Catherine for the oar. She was laughing. She took my hand and kept on laughing.

'What's the matter?' I took the oar.

'You looked so funny holding that thing.'

'I suppose so.'

'Don't be cross, darling. It was awfully funny. You looked about twenty feet broad and very affectionate holding the umbrella by the edges—' she choked.

'I'll row.'

'Take a rest and a drink. It's a grand night and we've come a long way.'

'I have to keep the boat out of the trough of the waves.'

'I'll get you a drink. Then rest a little while, darling.'

I held the oars up and we sailed with them. Catherine was opening the bag. She handed me the brandy bottle. I pulled the cork with my pocket-knife and took a long drink. It was smooth and hot and the heat went all through me and I felt warmed and cheerful. 'It's lovely brandy,' I said. The moon was under again but I could see the shore. There seemed to be another point going out a long way ahead into the lake.

'Are you warm enough, Cat?'

'I'm splendid. I'm a little stiff.'

'Bail out that water and you can put your feet down.'

Then I rowed and listened to the oarlocks and the dip and scrape of the bailing tin under the stern seat.

'Would you give me the bailer?' I said. 'I want a drink.'

'It's awfully dirty.'

'That's all right. I'll rinse it.'

I heard Catherine rinsing it over the side. Then she handed it to me dipped full of water. I was thirsty after the brandy and the water was icy cold, so cold it made my teeth ache. I looked toward the shore. We were closer to the long point. There were lights in the bay ahead.

'Thanks,' I said and handed back the tin pail.

'You're ever so welcome,' Catherine said. 'There's much more if you want it.'

'Don't you want to eat something?'

'No. I'll be hungry in a little while. We'll save it till then.'

'All right.'

What looked like a point ahead was a long high headland. I went further out in the lake to pass it. The lake was much narrower now. The moon was out again and the *guardia di Finanza* could have seen our boat black on the water if they had been watching.

'How are you, Cat?' I asked.

'I'm all right. Where are we?'

'I don't think we have more than about eight miles more.'

'That's a long way to row, you poor sweet. Aren't you dead?'

'No. I'm all right. My hands are sore is all.'

We went on up the lake. There was a break in the mountains on the right bank, a flattening-out with a low shore line that I thought must be Cannobio. I stayed a long way out because it was from now on that we ran the most danger of meeting *guardia*. There was a high dome-capped mountain on the other shore a way ahead. I was tired. It was no great distance to row but when you were out of condition it had been a long way. I knew I had to pass that mountain and go up the lake at least five miles further before we would be in Swiss water. The moon was almost down now but before it went down the sky clouded over again and it was very dark. I stayed well out in the lake, rowing awhile, then resting and holding the oars so that the wind struck the blades.

'Let me row awhile,' Catherine said.

'I don't think you ought to.'

'Nonsense. It would be good for me. It would keep me from being too stiff.'

'I don't think you should, Cat.'

'Nonsense. Rowing in moderation is very good for the pregnant lady.'

'All right, you row a little moderately. I'll go back, then you come up. Hold on to both gunwales when you come up.'

I sat in the stern with my coat on and the collar turned up and watched Catherine row. She rowed very well but the oars were too long and bothered her. I opened the bag and ate a couple of sandwiches and took a drink of the brandy. It made everything much better and I took another drink.

'Tell me when you're tired,' I said. Then a little later, 'watch out the oar doesn't pop you in the tummy.'

'If it did' – Catherine said between strokes – 'life might be much simpler.'

I took another drink of the brandy.

'How are you going?'

'All right.'

'Tell me when you want to stop.'

'All right.'

I took another drink of the brandy, then took hold of the two gunwales of the boat and moved forward.

'No. I'm going beautifully.'

'Go on back to the stern. I've had a grand rest.'

For a while, with the brandy, I rowed easily and steadily. Then I began to catch crabs and soon I was just chopping along again with a thin brown taste of bile from having rowed too hard after the brandy.

'Give me a drink of water, will you?' I said.

'That's easy,' Catherine said.

Before daylight it started to drizzle. The wind was down or we were protected by mountains that bounded the curve the lake had made. When I knew daylight was coming I settled down and rowed hard. I did not know where we were and I wanted to get into the Swiss part of the lake. When it was beginning to be daylight we were quite close to the shore. I could see the rocky shore and the trees.

'What's that?' Catherine said. I rested on the oars and listened. It was a motor boat chugging out on the lake. I pulled close up to the shore and lay quiet. The chugging came closer; then we saw the motor boat in the rain a little astern of us. There were four *guardia di finanza* in the stern, their *alpini* hats pulled down, their cape collars turned up and their carbines slung across their backs. They all looked sleepy so early in the morning. I could see the yellow on their hats and the yellow marks on their cape collars. The motor boat chugged on and out of sight in the rain.

I pulled out into the lake. If we were that close to the border I did not want to be hailed by a sentry along the road. I stayed out where I could just see the shore and rowed on for three quarters of an hour in the rain. We heard a motor boat once more but I kept quiet until the noise of the engine went away across the lake.

'I think we're in Switzerland, Cat,' I said.

'Really?'

'There's no way to know until we see Swiss troops.'

'Or the Swiss navy.'

'The Swiss navy's no joke for us. That last motor boat we heard was probably the Swiss navy.'

'If we're in Switzerland let's have a big breakfast. They have wonderful rolls and butter and jam in Switzerland.'

Ernest Hemingway, *A Farewell to Arms*, 1929

We were up early. As we walked to and fro, all four together, before breakfast, I deemed it right to recount what I had seen. Again our charge was the least anxious of the party. It was very likely that the men belonged to the Custom House, he said quietly, and that they had no thought of us. I tried to persuade myself that it was so – as, indeed, it might easily be. However, I proposed that he and I should walk away together to a distant point we could see, and that the boat should take us aboard there, or as near there as might prove feasible, at about noon. This being considered a good precaution, soon after breakfast he and I set forth, without saying anything at the tavern.

He smoked his pipe as we went along, and sometimes stopped to clap me on the shoulder. One would have supposed that it was I who was in danger, not he, and that he was reassuring me. We spoke very little. As we approached the point, I begged him to remain in a sheltered place, while I went on to reconnoitre; for it was towards it that the men had passed in the night. He complied, and I went on alone. There was no boat off the point, nor any boat drawn up anywhere near it, nor were there any signs of the men having embarked there. But, to be sure, the tide was high, and there might have been some footprints under water.

When he looked out from his shelter in the distance, and saw that I waved my hat to him to come up, he rejoined me, and there we waited; sometimes lying on the bank wrapped in our coats, and sometimes moving about to warm ourselves: until we saw our boat coming round. We got aboard easily, and rowed out into the track of the steamer. By that time it wanted but ten minutes of one o'clock, and we began to look out for her smoke.

But it was half-past one before we saw her smoke, and soon after we saw behind it the smoke of another steamer. As they were coming on at full speed, we got the two bags ready, and took that opportunity of saying good-bye to Herbert and Startop. We had all shaken hands cordially, and neither Herbert's eyes nor mine were quite dry, when I saw a four-oared galley shoot out from under the bank but a little way ahead of us, and row out into the same track.

A stretch of shore had been as yet between us and the steamer's smoke, by reason of the bend and wind of the river; but now she was visible coming head on. I called to Herbert and Startop to keep before the tide, that she might see us lying by for her, and adjured Provis to sit quite still, wrapped in his cloak. He answered cheerily, 'Trust to me, dear boy,' and sat like a statue. Meanwhile the galley, which was skilfully handled, had crossed us, let us come up with her, and fallen alongside. Leaving just room enough for the play of the oars, she kept alongside, drifting when we drifted, and pulling a stroke or two when we pulled. Of the two sitters, one held the rudder lines, and looked at us attentively – as did all the rowers, the other sitter was wrapped up, much as Provis was, and seemed to shrink, and whisper some instruction to the steerer as he looked at us. Not a word was spoken in either boat.

Startop could make out, after a few minutes, which steamer was first, and gave me the word 'Hamburg,' in a low voice as we sat face to face. She was nearing us very fast, and the beating of her paddles grew louder and louder. I felt as if her shadow were absolutely upon us, when the galley hailed us. I answered.

'You have a returned transport there,' said the man who held the lines. 'That's the man, wrapped in the cloak. His name is Abel Magwitch, otherwise Provis. I apprehend that man, and call upon him to surrender, and you to assist.'

At the same moment, without giving any audible direction to his crew, he ran the galley aboard of us. They had pulled one sudden stroke ahead, had got their oars in, had run athwart us, and were holding on to our gunwale, before we knew what they were doing. This caused great confusion on board of the steamer, and I heard them calling to us, and heard the order given to stop the paddles, and heard them stop, but felt her driving down upon us irresistibly. In the same moment, I saw the steersman of the galley lay his hand on his prisoner's shoulder, and saw that both boats were swinging round with the force of the tide, and saw that all hands on board the steamer were running forward quite frantically. Still in the same moment, I saw the prisoner start up, lean across his captor, and pull the cloak from the neck of the shrinking sitter in the galley. Still in the same moment, I saw that the face disclosed was the face of the other convict of long ago. Still in the same moment, I saw the face tilt backward with a white terror on it that I shall never forget, and heard a great cry on board the steamer and a loud splash in the water, and felt the boat sink from under me.

It was but for an instant that I seemed to struggle with a thousand mill-weirs and a thousand flashes of light; that instant past, I was taken on board the galley. Herbert was there, and Startop was there; but our boat was gone, and the two convicts were gone.

Charles Dickens, *Great Expectations*, 1860–1

'I WANT TO SMELL YOU'

Two weeks later I was transferred with eleven other convicts to Campbell County chain gang. Prior to our arrival at this camp, the County Warden, Sam Parkins, would only accept 'niggers', and there had been no white convicts there for several years.

Conditions here were almost the same as at Fulton County, with these exceptions: Our sleeping-quarters were worse. Twelve men slept in a 'pie wagon' (a steel-barred wagon on wheels, four tiers of three bunks each), and we barely had room to turn around. The mess hall was simply a shed built inside a barbed wire stockade, and there was no wash-room at all – we washed in the open from a bucket.

The nightly whippings took place in the yard – the convict being laid on a semicircular piece of corrugated iron.

The 'pie wagon' and bedding were lousy, full of vermin, and were old and decayed, and had a foul odour.

We did not work on a squad chain as at Fulton County, here we worked on the roads and were spread out a little more. We also worked with the negroes.

Here, then, was a chance to run, if you could run with twenty pounds of chain or if you could remove the chain.

Bloodhounds were taken to the road each day and the guards were increased, two guards to each twelve convicts. For six weeks I racked my brain for a method of removing those chains. Two others of the twelve convicts in my group were also willing to take desperate measures to escape. One tried cutting the steel rivets in his shackles with an improvised saw made from a safety-razor blade.

But as our chains and shackles were thoroughly examined once a day, he was discovered and received several terrific beatings. Besides, at night we were so fatigued and exhausted that it was impossible to use any skill or strength for such delicate tasks.

At night, as we filed in through the entrance to the mess hall, blacks on one side, whites on the other, came a voice:

'Come by me – I want to smell you. Come by me – I want to smell you.'

Meaning that the speaker wanted to smell the perspiration on each convict so as to be sure the convicts had 'put out' a day of strenuous and fatiguing toil. If he didn't smell you, you got the leather.

From a thorough study of conditions I had also arrived at this conclusion: any escape would have to be made on a Monday morning, for that would be the only time in the week that one would have the strength to hope for success. The rest on Sunday would refresh and quicken the brain, but by Tuesday morning this would vanish, and for the balance of the week the convict would go through his daily labours in almost a semi-conscious state, so great was the exhaustion and fatigue from the heat and long hours of toil.

That was the first fact I planted in my brain – *Monday morning when I was fresh*; some Monday morning – when? But Monday morning it must be! No other time would I try.

The next problem was the chains. How to get these off – when and where I wanted them off. Finally this idea struck me. The shackles around my ankles were circular in shape. I knew that if they could be bent into an elliptical shape perhaps I could slip them over my heel after removing my shoes. But how to bend them? That was a difficulty, for they were made of steel as thick as a man's finger.

Day in and day out, every conscious moment I studied, planned and discarded, planned anew, discarded again – plans – plans; but all seemed idle dreams. And thousands of convicts the whole world over are all dreaming the same dream: a successful escape from the tortures and obsolete treatment modern society deals out to its weaker element . . .

One day I noticed a certain negro in my group swing a twelve-pound sledgehammer. He had been in the gang so long and had used a sledge so much that he had become an expert. Claimed he could hit a pin on the head with his eyes closed.

Suddenly, like a flash, an idea came to me. I might try to get that negro to hit my shackles and bend them into an elliptical shape, if I could put my leg against something to take up the shock and hold the shackle against it. I determined to think this over.

Of course, if I were discovered, many brutal beatings were in store for me.

A week later we were tearing up an old railroad, ties, rails and all. And there was my answer – I could place my foot against the end of a railroad tie that was still embedded in the road ballast. This would give the support needed. The negro could hit the shackle and perhaps it would bend. If he missed the shackle, it would mean perhaps the loss of a foot. Not pleasant thoughts, but life-or-death problems call for both daring and courage.

I manoeuvred things so that I worked near this negro at all times, waiting for a chance to speak to him.

One day in June, when the heat was terrific and the guards were half asleep from the humidity, I spoke to this nigger.

'Sam,' I said, 'would you do me a favour?'

'Boss, if I can, I sho' will,' he replies.

'Sam, I got six years; that's a long time, and I'm going to try to "hang it on the limb", and I need a little help. Will you help me?' I asked.

'Boss, it sho' is pretty rough, and I ain't much for hunting trouble, but if I's can help you, I sho' will,' he answered.

'Well, Sam, here's the idea: if I put my leg against this tie, do you think you could hit my shackles hard enough to bend it and still not break my ankle?' I asked.

'Boss, if you can keep the shackle from turning, I can hit it right plump,' he answered.

I looked up at the two guards; all was quiet and serene. I put my right foot against the tie (by spreading my legs the connecting chain became taut), one side of the shackle against the tie. I looked at Sam. He grinned. I looked at the guards. All was as it should be. I took a deep breath, closed my eyes, and said to Sam, 'Shoot Sam.' Sam shot. Bang went the sledge. I felt a sharp quick pain in my shins. One side of the shackle was embedded in the end of the tie. I looked at the shackle, but couldn't see much difference in the shape. Another look at the guards. All was well. 'Again, Sam,' I whispered. Another bull's-eye by Sam. 'Again, Sam,' I said. And again the sledge fell right on the shackle. Then the left foot. Three solid whacks of the sledge on the left shackle.

'Thanks, Sam,' I said. 'If they won't come off now we'll try again.'

Night could not come quick enough. Would the shackles come off? Would the guard discover the change from circular to elliptical when examining the chains when we returned for the night?

The day was over at last, supper finished, and we were lined up single file in front of the 'pie wagon' to be searched and our chains inspected. My heart was beating hard and fast. My turn came, I was searched, the chains were examined, I counted off and passed on. What a relief!

Ten minutes later, lying on my bunk, I tried to pass the shackle over my heel. What a thrill! *It would come off!* A little tight, but it would come off. Wet it with a little saliva and it would come off. This was

Wednesday night. Monday was the day! Four days to lay my plans –
four days till Monday. Monday was my day!

Robert E. Burns, *I Am a Fugitive*, 1932

LOST HAT

A nobleman, named M. de Chateaubrun, having been condemned to
death by the revolutionary tribunal, had been placed on the fatal
tumbril and taken to the Place de la Revolution, to be put to death.
After the 'Terror' he was met by a friend, who gave a cry of surprise;
and, scarcely able to believe the evidence of his senses, asked De
Chateaubrun, to explain the mystery of his appearance. The explanation was given, and I heard it from his friend.

He was taken away with twenty other unhappy victims. 'After
twelve or fifteen executions,' he said, 'one part of the horrible
instrument broke, and a workman was sent for to mend it. M. De
Chateaubrun was, with the other victims, near the scaffold, with his
hands tied behind his back. The repairing took a long time. The day
began to darken; the great crowd of spectators were far more intent on
watching the repairing of the guillotine than on looking at the victims
who were to die; and all, even the gendarmes themselves, had their eyes
fixed on the scaffold. Resigned, but very weak, the condemned man
leant, without meaning it, on those behind him; and they, pressed by
the weight of his body, mechanically made way for him, till gradually,
and by no effort of his own, he came to the last ranks of the crowd. The
instrument once repaired, the executions began again, and they hurried
to the end. A dark night concealed both executioners and spectators.
Led on by the crowd, De Chateaubrun was at first amazed at his
situation, but soon conceived the hope of escaping. He went to the
Champs Elysées, and there, addressing a man who looked like a
workman, he told him, laughingly, that some comrades with whom he
had been joking had tied his hands behind his back, and taken his hat,
telling him to go and look for it. He begged the man to cut the cords,
and the workman pulled out a knife and did so, laughing all the while
at the joke. M. de Chateaubrun then proposed going into one of the
small wineshops in the Champs Elysées. During a slight repast he
seemed to be expecting his comrades to bring back his hat; and seeing

nothing of them, he begged his guest to carry a note to some friend, whom he knew would lend him one, for he could not go bareheaded through the streets. He added that his friend would bring him some money, for his comrades, in fun, had taken away his purse. The poor man believed every word M. de Chateaubrun told him, took the note, and returned in half an hour, accompanied by the friend, who embraced Chateaubrun, and gave him all the help he required.'

Viennot de Vaublanc, *Memoirs*, English trans. 1870

THE MISTRAL

The door opened, and a dim light reached Dantès' eyes through the coarse sack that covered him, he saw two shadows approach his bed, a third remaining at the door with a torch in his hand. Each of these two men, approaching the ends of the bed, took the sack by its extremities.

'He's heavy though for an old and thin man,' said one, as he raised the head.

'They say every year adds half a pound to the weight of the bones,' said another, lifting the feet.

'Have you tied the knot?' inquired the first speaker.

'What would be the use of carrying so much more weight?' was the reply; 'I can do that when we get there.'

'Yes, you're right,' replied the companion.

'What's the knot for?' thought Dantès.

They deposited the supposed corpse on the bier. Edmond stiffened himself in order to play his part of a dead man, and then the party lighted by the man with the torch who went first, ascended the stairs.

Suddenly he felt the fresh and sharp night air, and Dantès recognised the *Mistral*. It was a sudden sensation, at the same time replete with delight and agony.

The bearers advanced twenty paces, then stopped, putting their bier down on the ground.

One of them went away, and Dantès heard his shoes on the pavement.

'Where am I then?' he asked himself.

'Really, he is by no means a light load!' said the other bearer, sitting on the edge of the hand-barrow.

Dantès' first impulse was to escape, but fortunately he did not attempt it.

'Light me, you sir,' said the other bearer, 'or I shall not find what I am looking for.'

The man with the torch complied, although not asked in the most polite terms.

'What can he be looking for?' thought Edmond. 'The spade, perhaps.'

An exclamation of satisfaction indicated that the grave-digger had found the object of his search.

'Here it is at last,' he said, 'not without some trouble though.'

'Yes,' was the answer, 'but it has lost nothing by waiting.'

As he said this the man came towards Edmond, who heard a heavy and sounding substance laid down beside him, and at the same moment a cord was fastened round his feet with sudden and painful violence.

'Well, have you tied the knot?' inquired the grave-digger, who was looking on.

'Yes and pretty tight, too, I can tell you,' was the answer.

'Move on, then.'

And the bier was lifted once more, and they proceeded.

They advanced fifty paces farther, and then stopped to open a door, then went forward again. The noise of the waves dashing against the rocks, on which the Château is built, reached Dantès' ear distinctly as they progressed.

'Bad weather!' observed one of the bearers; 'not a pleasant night for a dip in the sea.'

'Why, yes, the abbé runs a chance of being wet,' said the other; and then there was a burst of brutal laughter.

Dantès did not comprehend the jest, but his hair stood erect on his head.

'Well, here we are at last,' said one of them. 'A little farther – a little farther,' said the other. 'You know very well that the last was stopped on his way, dashed on the rocks, and the governor told us next day that we were careless fellows.'

They ascended five or six more steps, and then Dantès felt that they took him one by the head and the other by the heels, and swung him to and fro.

'One!' said the grave-diggers. 'Two! Three and away!'

And at the same instant Dantès felt himself flung into the air like a wounded bird falling, falling with a rapidity that made his blood curdle. Although drawn downwards by the same heavy weight which hastened his rapid descent, it seemed to him as if the time were a century. At last, with a terrific dash, he entered the ice-cold water, and as he did so he uttered a shrill cry, stifled in a moment by his immersion beneath the waves.

Dantès had been flung into the sea, into whose depths he was dragged by a thirty-six pound shot tied to his feet.

The sea is the Cemetery of Château d'If.

Alexandre Dumas, *The Count of Monte-Cristo*, English trans. 1846

UNWANTED BREAKFAST

He said very quietly:

'There was one of us in the party today who did not give a parole.'

'Who? – the Padre? – yes, he did,' I said, a little at a loss.

'No, not the Padre.' He paused. 'What about W—— in his coffin? Did he give a parole? Eh?'

He stood back and let the full significance of this take effect. I saw it all in a flash.

'Of course not!' I cried. 'And had he been alive he would be free in Athens now. And the Germans would never know that he was around – never look for him!'

I stopped to give 'Skipper' an excited hug. 'Old man, dear old Methuselah, you have hit on an idea in a million. We can die off one by one, or somehow take the place of patients who die, and the rest will be easy. If things go anything like today we will only have to get out of that shallow hole and drink *ouzo* with the priests until the guard takes all the mourners back.'

'Yes. It's not bad, is it?' 'Skipper' beamed his pleasure. 'The coffin could be loosely lidded with a few airholes for comfort. A chap could stow all his escape kit in easily. It is a really de-luxe way of going.'

'I expect every case of death is the same. What I mean is, do they let our doctors make out the certificate?'

'Well, I've known of three officers dying here, and in each case the Germans left it entirely to our own doctors.'

'That seems OK. But what about putting the corpse into the coffin? Is that a British fatigue or a German?'

'You can be sure that any dirty work such as that is left to our own orderlies. No, if the doctors will play, the scheme is foolproof.'

'Now what about details at the cemetery? Suppose some dumb-cluck of a gravedigger buried one of us just to be a bit different?'

'That's not so difficult. We would have to take Padre —— along with us: he speaks good Greek. He could get hold of the two priests and they would fix it. The only dirt that need go on the coffin would be the stuff they throw during the "ashes to ashes, and dust to dust" part of the ceremony.'

In the morning we approached the doctors. They were vastly tickled with the orginality of the plot, but were rather hard to pin down for co-operation. We had to appreciate, they pointed out, that failure would bring a large measure of blame on the doctor concerned. The Germans were particularly harsh in punishment of any abuse of the privileges accorded to protected people.

However, a young New Zealand doctor, Ron Granger, was willing. We drew lots to decide who should have first turn, and I won.

In half an hour I was in bed and it was generally known around the ward, and later round the hospital, that I had a temperature of a hundred and four.

For a whole week the chart over my bed showed alarming temperatures, and people started talking in low whispers about my condition. Some of the medical orderlies who were not in the know became really worried, and helped to create the atmosphere we wanted. The Padre became a constant visitor.

At three o'clock in the morning of Friday, 14th September 1944, I died peacefully in my bed from pneumonia. Friday was a good day to die, because on that day Lieutenant Bruning left early for Athens and did not get back until night – so it gave a man a decent twelve hours to be buried in.

As dawn crept into the ward a group of mournful figures could be seen standing around my bed. Their voices were respectfully lowered and probably only I from under my shroud could tell that their sympathetic whispering consisted mostly of derogatory remarks about me. As it grew lighter I could see that I would have trouble to prevent the sheet over my head from rippling up and down as I breathed.

Ron had come up at three. I heard him now saying that the German sergeant had been very sympathetic and was arranging for a later afternoon funeral. That sounded very satisfactory. 'Skipper' Shannon was heard saying in sepulchral tones that he thought it would be difficult to get a Greek coffin long enough for me, and in the event of it being too short, did Captain Granger think he could take off the feet, or perhaps the head? Ron thought that would be easy enough. After a pause he sent off one of the orderlies to bring a padre. I cursed them all. It was difficult enough not to giggle as it was.

An hour dragged slowly past. Breakfast arrived and, hungry as I was, I had the infuriating experience of hearing the orderly say with an unmistakable sniff and almost a break in his voice:

'Here you are, Goodwin' – sniff – 'you'd better have poor Mr Thomas's breakfast this morning. He' – sniff – 'won't be wanting it.'

I was snoozing complacently about ten o'clock, when I heard the orderly whispering urgently as he scrubbed the top of a dresser near my bed. I could not make out all he said, but his message came through like this . . . '. . . worried . . . German doctor . . . grey hair . . . maybe coincidence, but . . . ' and then he was interrupted by a shout from the far end of the ward.

I immediately thought of the portly, grey-haired doctor who had dressed my wound in Corinth and later showed a kindly interest in me. What if he should choose today of all days to visit the hospital!

There was a commotion at the end of the ward and, oh horrors, someone was coming towards me speaking German. I froze stiff – I was not acting; it was sheer panic. As they came nearer someone said to someone else in a very German accent, *'Parlez-vous français?'* and I knew that my worst fears were realised. It was my doctor friend. The party clattered to a halt at the foot of my bed.

Someone said, *'Et si jeune, il n'a pas vingt-deux ans.'*

Someone moved quietly down to the head of my bed and stood there a moment. I could hear him breathing. Then, very gently, the sheet was raised from above my head, drawn reverently back and down my face. I could stand that. Then though I had my eyes closed I felt a hand coming near my face. It was too much. I gave a snort and a giggle and looked up into the startled blue eyes of the German doctor.

W. B. Thomas, *Dare to be Free* 1951

'BRED EN BAWN IN A BRIER-PATCH'

'Uncle Remus,' said the little boy one evening, when he had found the old man with little or nothing to do, 'did the fox kill and eat the rabbit when he caught him with the Tar-Baby?'

'Law, honey, ain't I tell you 'bout dat?' replied the old darkey, chuckling slyly. 'I clar ter grashus I ought er tole you dat, but ole man Nod wuz ridin' on my eyeleds 'twel a leetle mon'n I'd a dis'member'd my own name, en den on to dat here come yo' mammy hollerin' atter you.

'W'at I tell you w'en I fus' begin? I tole you Brer Rabbit wuz a monstus soon beas'; leas'ways dat's w'at I laid out fer ter tell you. Well, den, honey, don't you go en make no udder kalkalashuns, kaze in dem days Brer Rabbit en his fambly wuz at de head er de gang w'en enny racket wuz on han', en dar dey stayed. 'Fo' you begins fer ter wipe yo' eyes 'bout Brer Rabbit, you wait en see whar'bouts Brer Rabbit gwineter fetch up at. But dat's needer yer ner dar.

'W'en Brer Fox fine Brer Rabbit mixt up wid de Tar-Baby, he feel mighty good, en he roll on de groun' en laff. Bimeby, he up'n say, sezee:

' "Well, I speck I got you dis time, Brer Rabbit," sezee; "maybe I ain't, but I speck I is. You been runnin' roun' here sassin' atter me a mighty long time, but I speck you done come ter de een' er de row. You bin cuttin' up yo' capers en bouncin' 'roun' in dis naberhood ontwel you come ter b'leeve yo'se'f de boss er de whole gang. En den youer allers some'rs whar you got no bizness," sez Brer Fox, sezee. "Who ax you fer ter come en strike up a 'quaintence wid dish yer Tar-Baby? En who stuck you up dar whar you iz? Nobody in de roun' worril. You des tuck en jam yo'se'f on dat Tar-baby widout waitin' fer enny invite," sez Brer Fox, sezee, "en dar you is, en dar you'll stay twell I fixes up a bresh-pile and fires her up, kaze I'm gwineter bobbycue you dis day, sho," sez Brer Fox, sezee.

'Den Brer Rabbit talk mighty 'umble.

' "I don't keer w'at you do wid me, Brer Fox," sezee, "so you don't fling me in dat brier-patch. Roas' me, Brer Fox," sezee, "but don't fling me in dat brier-patch," sezee.

' "Hit's so much trouble fer ter kindle a fier," sez Brer Fox, sezee, "dat I speck I'll hatter hang you," sezee.

' "Hang me des ez high as you please, Brer Fox," sez Brer Rabbit, sezee, "but do fer de Lord's sake don't fling me in dat brier-patch," sezee.

' "I ain't got no string," sez Brer Fox, sezee, "en now I speck I'll hatter drown you," sezee.

' "Drown me des ez deep ez you please, Brer Fox," sez Brer Rabbit, sezee, "but do do'nt fling me in dat brier-patch," sezee.

' "Dey ain't no water nigh," sez Brer Fox, sezee, "en now I spec I'll hatter skin you," sezee.

' "Skin me, Brer Fox," sez Brer Rabbit, sezee, "snatch out my eyeballs, t'ar out my years by de roots, en cut off my legs," sezee, "but do please, Brer Fox, don't fling me in dat brier-patch," sezee.

'Co'se Brer Fox wanter hurt Brer Rabbit bad ez he kin, so he cotch 'im by de behime legs en slung 'im right in de middle er de brier-patch. Dar wuz a considerbul flutter whar Brer Rabbit struck de bushes, en Brer Fox sorter hang 'roun' for ter see w'at wuz gwineter happen. Bimeby he hear somebody call 'im, en way up de hill he see Brer Rabbit settin' cross-legged on a chinkapin log koamin' de pitch outen his har wid a chip. Den Brer Fox know dat he bin swop off mighty bad. Brer Rabbit wuz bleedzed for ter fling back some er his sass, en he holler out:

' "Bred en bawn in a brier-patch, Brer Fox – bred en bawn in a brier-patch!" en wid dat he skip out des ez lively ez a cricket in de embers.'

Joel Chandler Harris, *Uncle Remus*, 1881

MAKING A NOISE

This sely wydwe and eek hir doghtres two
Herden thise hennes crie and maken wo,
And out at dores stirten they anon,
And syen the fox toward the grove gon,
And bar upon his bak the cok away,
And cryden, 'Out! harrow! and weyl away!
Ha! ha! the fox!' and after hym they ran,
And eek with staves many another man.
Ran Colle oure dogge, and Talbot and Gerland,
And Malkyn, with a dystaf in hir hand;
Ran cow and calf, and eek the verray hogges,
So fered for the berkyng of the dogges
And shoutyng of the men and wommen eeke,
They ronne so hem thoughte hir herte breeke.
They yolleden as feendes doon in helle;
The dokes cryden as men wolde hem quelle;
The gees for feere flowen over the trees;
Out of the hyve cam the swarm of bees.

So hydous was the noyse, a, *benedicitee!*
Certes, he Jakke Straw and his meynee
Ne made nevere shoutes half so shrille
Whan that they wolden any Flemyng kille,
As thilke day was maad upon the fox.
Of bras they broghten bemes, and of box,
Of horn, of boon, in whiche they blewe and powped,
And therwithal they skriked and they howped.
It semed as that hevene sholde falle.
    Now, goode men, I prey yow herkeneth alle:
Lo, how Fortune turneth sodeynly
The hope and pryde eek of hir enemy!
This cok, that lay upon the foxes bak,
In al his drede unto the fox he spak,
And seyde, 'Sire, if that I were as ye,
Yet sholde I seyn, as wys God helpe me,
"Turneth agayn, ye proude cherles alle!
A verray pestilence upon your falle!
Now am I come unto the wodes syde;
Maugree youre heed, the cok shal heere abyde.
I wol hym ete, in feith, and that anon!" '
    The fox answerde, 'In feith, it shal be don.'
And as he spak that word, al sodeynly
This cok brak from his mouth delyverly,
And heighe upn a tree he fleigh anon.
And whan the fox saugh that the cok was gon,
    'Allas!' quod he, 'O Chauntecleer, allas!
I have to yow,' quod he, 'ydoon trespas,
In as muche as I maked yow aferd
Whan I yow hente and broghte out of the yerd.
But, sire, I dide it in no wikke entente.
Com doun, and I shal telle yow what I mente;
I shal seye sooth to yow, God help me so!'
    'Nay thanne,' quod he, 'I shrewe us bothe two.
And first I shrewe myself, bothe blood and bones,
If thou bigyle me ofter than ones.
Thou shalt namoore, thurgh thy flaterye,
Do me to synge and wynke with myn ye;
For he that wynketh, when he sholde see,
Al wilfully, God lat him nevere thee!'

[231]

'Nay,' quod the fox, 'but God yeve hym meschaunce,
That is so undiscreet of governaunce
That jangleth whan he sholde holde his pees.'

Geoffrey Chaucer, *The Nun's Priest's Tale*, c.1387

A PRIEST ON MY LAP

A few days after, one of the keepers told Béchard that it was seriously spoken of discharging me, because I was found dangerous. The gaoler insisted strongly on my removal, because he thought that sooner or later the confounded madman would kill somebody, for he had the strength of two horses instead of that of one man.

Béchard informed me of the fact. I of course, commenced a general row, and in the afternoon the stove took a fancy to fall on one side.

The gaoler came up this time in a fury with ropes, threatening to tie me up. Instead of flying in a passion as usual, I took the cords, passed them round my wrists and placed the ends into his hands to make the knots. This disarmed him, and he unfastened the cords, saying: 'This poor fellow must positively leave this place.'

On the following day, Messrs Delisle and Leclerc came to the prison and examined me. They left me fully persuaded that I was totally bereft of my reason, and that it was impossible to make anything out of me.

Two days later, on a Saturday, a priest conducted by one of the keepers approached me.

—Here, sir, is the madman and the greatest one I have seen yet, most assuredly. Do not irritate him, for in his state of insanity, your cloth would not be respected for any length of time; I have already passed through his clutches, and it is no joke.

Such a visit appeared to me suspicious, it struck me that they were laying a trap for me, and that the priest was only sent to see how I would behave towards him. He addressed me a few friendly words, and I conversed with him for some time, taking care to drop here and there in the midst of the conversation, some absurd piece of nonsense to bewilder him. I then took a chair to sit down and took him on my knees rather unceremoniously. When I held him there, I spoke such absurd nonsense that after leaving me, he was convinced, as well as the others, that my poor head was completely and for ever deranged.

Messrs Leclerc and Delisle had been so pressing upon the Governor, that they had obtained an order for my release. They came to me on the

Monday (what a date!) to inform me that I could be off. I was struck with the idea that if I left at once, something might be suspected, and that it would be better to be on my guard.

I therefore answered that it was not my intention to leave at all, because the Queen would be dissatisfied if I left her service without due warning.

These gentlemen assured me that I could go away at once and that they would be answerable for all that might happen.

I positively refused.

My baggage was brought down and they attempted to turn me out. It was about nine in the morning. They tried with three, four, and even five men, but I made a most desperate resistance. I held fast to everything, and when I laid hold of something with my hands, it was impossible to move me one inch. Several of the soldiers on guard were sent for without success. I slipped through their fingers like an eel, and after several fruitless attempts they determined to draw off my attention during one hour or two. I waited and walked about the passages of the gaol, and after a few hours I was conducted to the door and invited to take a walk outside. I refused a second time, intimating that I would not quit Her Majesty's service. Suddenly five men seized me and pushed me forward as far as the door. As soon as I arrived there, I placed my hands against the frame and drove them back most furiously.

—What a devil of a man! exclaimed the gaoler.

They tried it again, but I pretended to become furious and they made no further attempts.

The sensible men were beginning to be more embarrassed than the madman.

It was getting late and I was still in gaol. Several means of taking me by surprise were resorted to, but all failed. At last, towards four in the afternoon, Mr Leclerc, if I mistake not, had the idea of showing me a bottle of brandy, promising me a glass if I would go out. I went out immediately and had one glass. But I was still in the court, and whenever they induced me to go towards the door, I offered resistance. Somebody therefore went outside of the door of the court and showed me the bottle. I made no further resistance and walked out of the court. The door was closed immediately. I made a dash at it, but I was told through the wicket: 'Ah! you may be off, we have had enough of you.'

I therefore found myself in St Mary street at liberty, and with my pardon in my pocket, Mr Delisle having pinned it inside in the morning. I thought that my heart would burst with joy.

·Felix Poutré, *Escape from the Gallows: Souvenirs of a Canadian State Prisoner in 1838–1885*

ARGUING

We worked all morning, grading on the railroad embankment. At noon we knocked off for soup and a rest. We were on the edge of a large wood. Some of the men flung themselves on the bank. Others went to see if the soup was ready. A few went into the wood. The solitary guard was elsewhere. We said good-bye to the few who knew of our plans. They bade us God-speed, and then we, too, faded into the recesses of the wood.

We had no sooner set foot in it than I noticed a curious change come over my companion. He said that it was a bad time, a bad place, found fault with everything, and said that we should not do it that day. However, we continued, half-heartedly on his part, to shove our way on into the wood. Occasionally he glanced fearfully over his shoulder and voiced querulous protests. I did not answer him. A little further on and he stopped. A dog was barking.

'There's too many dogs about, Edwards. And just look at all those houses!' He pointed to where a village showed through the trees.

'Sure thing, there'll be houses thick like that all the way. It's our job to keep clear of them.'

'Yes, but look at the people. There's bound to be lots of them where there's so many houses.'

'Of course there are,' I replied. 'Germany's full of houses and people. That's no news. Come on.'

'Oh, they'll see us sure, Edwards – and telegraph ahead all over the country. We haven't got any more show than a rabbit.'

With that I lost patience and gave him a piece of my mind. We stood there arguing it back and forth.

It was no use. He fell prey to his own fears. He saw certain capture and a dreadful punishment. He conjured up all the dangers that an active imagination could envisage. Every bush was a German, every sound the occasion of a fresh alarm. He was like to ruin my own nerves with his petty panics.

It was in vain that I pleaded with him. He could not face the dangers that he saw ahead. The laager seemed to him by comparison a haven of safety. When all else failed I appealed to his pride. He had none. I warned him that we would meet with nothing but scorn from our comrades excepting laughter, which was worse. I begged and pleaded with him to go on with me. No use. All his courage was foam and had settled back into dregs.

And so we returned. I was heartbroken.

George Eustace Pearson, *The Escape of a Princess Pat, Being the Full Account of the Capture and Fifteenth Months' Imprisonment of Corporal Edwards, of The Princess Patricia's Canadian Light Infantry*, 1918

WHISTLES AND WALKIE-TALKIES

Joe started to climb up, and Wally was already underneath him as he got through the hole in the roof next to the library window. He made a terrible racket. I saw Wally wince. He started to go up as I finished dressing. He went up carrying the rope dangling round his waist and afterwards I followed. Neither Wally nor I made any noise on the plastic sheeting. As I came out Joe was balancing on the office roof, backing towards the section of wall we wanted to make for. I started to crawl towards him, but he waved me back with his hand and then started to come back himself. As he got near he said:

'There's a screw with a dog looking towards us. He must have heard us on the plastic. We'll have to go the other way.'

This was across the plastic roof and past our wing and the remand section which abutted onto it, and then round the end of the wing towards the front gate; though we didn't know if there was any place where we could get over. I knew that the first way was all right, because I had seen it when I'd been over to the main prison. But we had no choice.

Joe picked up the rope and Wally went off across the roof. I followed him, with Joe behind me. It made a bastard of a noise, and guys were getting up at their windows in the remand wing, their figures silhouetted by their cell lights. Then I heard Charlie shouting from the wing:

'Bastards! You bastards!'

'Hear that cunt?' said Wally, as we reached the end of the roof.

'Yeah,' I said; 'I hear him.'

We dropped down, and the wall was only about forty feet from us, but this section had a continuous reel of barbed wire attached to the top by brackets. The ground was damp and cold, with a few patches of grass; we went a few steps to the end of the wing, and then to our left. Here the wall ran into a high building, perhaps thirty-five feet at its highest, but the nearest part was only one storey. We ran towards it. Wally stopped and put his foot on the window-sill and got up on the flat roof. That led to a higher part of the building and looked easy to climb. I got up and turned to take the rope from Joe, but before he could move a screw came round the far corner of the wing and grabbed Joe from behind.

'All right,' the screw said, 'I've got you. Don't move.'

'I'm sorry, Joe,' I said. He looked exhausted and nodded his head in resignation.

'Can you give me the rope,' I said. He fumbled at his side, but the screw smothered him, and other screws were arriving by now.

'See you, Joe,' I said, and ran towards Wally. He was in the far corner of the roof, looking up at the next obstacle. The roof ended at the wall, which was only about ten feet here, but it still had barbed wire at the top. On the left, however, the next section of the wall rose about ten feet but about six feet from the top a line of foot-long spikes jutted out horizontally. I pushed Wally up and he grabbed the spikes and heaved himself over. I took my pullover off and threw it over the spikes and pulled myself up, but the pullover kept tearing.

'Wally,' I said, 'double it up.' He was leaning over but every time he heard a whistle go or a walkie-talkie coming (and there were plenty of both by now) his head would turn aside. I thought for a moment he was going to leave me. He twisted the pullover and leaned over, holding it out to me. I grabbed it, scrambled up, got hold of a spike in one hand and let go of the pullover, but I couldn't seem to lever myself over the spikes. Wally had moved away.

'Wally,' I called. He looked round.

'Come on, John.'

I laughed. 'It's the fucking spikes.'

He grabbed my shoulders and pulled me over. I followed Wally along the edge of this roof. It had a concrete drainage system and led straight at the wall; on my left there was another group of rising tiled roofs. We reached another small flat roof, which the last section of the wall ran into; standing on this, we were only nine feet below the top of the wall. We both looked over; a road ran round the wall of the nick, and beyond it a patch of open common. We were about twenty-eight feet up in the air, and below there were about twenty screws scattered around, and even though we instantly drew back one of them spotted us and shouted, 'There's one of them!'

We couldn't drop down from that height.

'What do you think, Wally?'

'Don't know.'

Everything was turning to ashes in my mouth. I turned back towards the roofs. I said to Wally: 'I'm going this way.' I found a way between the tiled roofs which hid me from the screws on both sides. After going about ten yards I looked back and Wally wasn't there. He'd gone his own way. I went on for about seventy yards and gradually the roofs became lower. I knew that by now I wasn't any longer in the nick.

John McVicar, *McVicar By Himself*, 1974

TEN

'The right place at the right time'

Shortly after this, orders were given to prepare ourselves, as we were to be transported to America in three days. Some one said to us: 'When you get to a little distance from the shore you will be made to pass along a narrow plank, off which you will be thrown into the sea, so that the whole race of Huguenots may be extirpated.' I answered: 'What difference does it make whether my body be consumed by fishes or by worms? for the day will come when the sea must deliver up its dead.'

As soon as we were alone Susanne de Montélimard said: 'Had we not better break these bars, and make our escape through the window?' I said: 'We are so very high above the ground, that we must either be killed or maimed in getting down, and then we should be retaken, and treated even worse than now. If that were to happen, and I were to be scourged again, I should not survive it. I prefer going to America, and trusting to God to deliver us, as He has delivered us from La Rapine.' She said: 'If they had done to me what they have done to you, I should be dead by this time. But the fact is they are now starving us to death; and it seems to me as if we were despising the means of escape which God has put before us; for I am sure that we could get through this window. I am for trying it.'

So we cut up a sheet into strips, which we knotted and sewed together. Then the height of the window from the ground was measured by tying a stone to the end of a cord, and we managed to open the padlock which fastened the grating. We were on the fourth storey, so that the rope was much too short, and we were obliged to tear up two more sheets to add to it. Then I went to the window, and when I saw how high up we were, I said to my dear sisters: 'Alas! we shall be killed; for it is quite fearful to look down.'

At about ten o'clock at night the great bell of the hospital rang for half an hour, which was not at all usual. We asked the meaning of it, and were told that robbers had got into the kitchen through the garden. But others said: 'The hospital is on fire; they want to burn us all.' Then a Papist came up with the same news, and there was running backwards and forwards, some going to Monsieur Genest's room, and some to waken the servants. Presently a Huguenot came to us and said: 'It is all over for this evening: but some night, when we are in our first sleep, we shall be surprised in our beds, and burnt alive.'

As soon as our guards had gone to sleep we arose quietly, and crept over to the window on our bare feet: for we feared that the priest who slept in a room underneath might hear us moving. The first to get out was Susanne of Montélimard, in Dauphiny; then Mademoiselle Terrasson of Diè, in Dauphiny; I followed; and last came Mademoiselle Anne Dumasse of La Salle, in Languedoc. When I had got outside the window, and had just taken hold of the sheet, my strength failed me, and I heard the bones of my arms cracking. Besides this, my dress had caught on a nail, so that I was obliged to hold on to the rope with one hand while with the other I freed my dress. I felt all my strength and courage going, and crying 'Lord Jesus, receive my spirit!' I seized the sheet between my teeth, and then grasping it with both hands, let myself down. I fell with violence on some building stones beneath the window. My dear sisters, who were waiting for me, lifted me up, and asked where I was hurt. I answered: 'I am hurt all over, and I have broken or dislocated my thigh. It is God's will. Help me to bind it up with my apron.' So we moved on, my two companions supporting me, for my wounded leg was quite useless; and after sixty or seventy paces we arrived at the gate of the Faubourg de Valence, where we were obliged to stop, finding it locked. I was helped up to the top of the wall; but when I looked down on the other side, and saw how high it was, I exclaimed, 'This is a second precipice, and I have not the courage to face it. Leave me, and do you go on.' They let me down from the wall at the side from which we had come, and then with great difficulty themselves descended at the other side.

Mademoiselle Dumasse called out to me: 'We are going, and are very sorry to leave you. God bless you, and save you from the hands of your enemies. Give me your blessing.'

I answered: 'What am I that I should bless you? but I pray that God may bless and prosper and guide you in all your ways. I beg of you to go as quickly as possible; one is quite enough to be retaken.'

Blanche Gamond: A Heroine of the Faith, 1869 (events of 1688)

SOFT LANDING

I put on my coat and was just preparing to go out when the door opened and the night nurse came in. There was a little group round me and I sat down on one of the beds. She walked straight to one of the lads in bed and gave him a sleeping draught. He drank quickly and she took the glass and walked out without even glancing in my direction. I started to breathe again and moved quickly to the door. It was now or never.

David Blair hobbled with me and presented me with a cloth cap he had made from odd bits of cloth. It would be very useful and I accepted it with gratitude. Albert Moore also insisted on coming to the outside door with me. The three of us crept out of the ward and across the courtyard in the bright moonlight. On the far side we entered the other wing of the hospital and went downstairs to a side door near the nurses' quarters. It led out to a spot near the wall, and was not locked. I opened it quietly and looked out. There was the wall, about ten yards away, with the main wall some twenty yards further on. The moon was shining and the sentry stood at the gate about thirty yards away. He was looking straight ahead, with his rifle slung on his shoulder.

Something told me to have no fear but to walk across quite naturally. I set off. My two companions watched breathlessly as I advanced across the ash-covered roadway, my boots crunching firmly. The sentry made no move. I walked on and stepped on to the top of my wall. I was silhouetted against the moon as I went along it, and my boots seemed to make a frightful noise on the stone. I expected to be shot any moment. But the sentry continued to gaze passively ahead of him although I was only about twenty degrees off his line of sight.

It seemed an age, but I reached the main wall at last. On my left was the dentist's building. I heard voices coming from an open window. Inside, some German soldiers were playing cards. They were so close that I could have spat on them. Fortunately, no one looked up to where I stood, silhouetted in the moonlight above them.

The main wall now barred my path. It came up to my waist and was covered with broken glass. I swung my leg up to try to stride it, and my boot crashed loudly on the stonework. I was unable to get it over. I stood with bated breath for a moment – surely the sentry behind me must have heard the noise. But neither he nor the soldiers below appeared to have noticed it.

I tried again, quietly this time, but it was clear that the wall was too high for my leg to cross. I stood there, utterly confounded, expecting discovery at any moment.

In despair, I prayed to be shown what to do next. Should I go back? Or try elsewhere? What had I done wrong? With that my fear left me. I was no longer worried about the sentry or the other soldiers. At the same time, I was strangely reassured – I had done as I had been directed up till then. I was at the right place at the right time. There must be a way.

Suddenly I realised that I could get over the wall without depending on my arms if I lay face downwards over it and wriggled my body round until I lay along it. Then I could drop off on the outside, feet first.

I quickly pulled out the woollen things in my pocket, my socks and helmet, and also my mosquito net, and put them over the broken glass. Then I lent over them. The other side of the wall was dark in the shadow of some trees and houses. I could not see the ground or how far I should have to fall. I hoped it was not more than I had judged it previously – about nine feet. I started to wriggle my body round to lie along the wall rather than across it. My arms were useless and I kicked my legs in the air in the effort to get round. This made me lose my precarious balance and I fell head first over the wall into the darkness.

I found myself standing on the ground. I had fallen on my feet and was not even conscious of any jar to my arms as I landed. As I stood there, the padding which I had put over the broken glass fell into my hands. I did not even have to stoop to pick it up.

The miracle of it all astounded me. I listened carefully for sounds of pursuit, but all was quiet. I was filled with an overwhelming sense of gratitude. I had ventured and not been let down. I knew that the venture was just beginning, but I knew that, wherever it led, it was life. I had escaped to live.

Wing-Commander Edward Howell, *Escape to Live*, 1947

SIR HENRY'S CHILDREN

So we all sat down once more against our chests of useless diamonds in that dreadful inaction, which was one of the hardest circumstances of our fate; and I am bound to say that, for my part, I gave way in despair. Laying my head against Sir Henry's broad shoulder I burst into tears; and I think I heard Good gulping away on the other side, and swearing hoarsely at himself for doing so.

Ah, how good and brave that great man was! Had we been two frightened children, and he our nurse, he could not have treated us more tenderly. Forgetting his own share of miseries, he did all he could to soothe our broken nerves, telling stories of men who had been in somewhat similar circumstances, and miraculously escaped; and when these failed to cheer us, pointing out how, after all, it was only anticipating an end that must come to us all, that it would soon be over, and that death from exhaustion was a merciful one (which is not true). Then, in a diffident sort of a way, as I had once before heard him do, he suggested that we should throw ourselves on the mercy of a higher Power, which for my part I did with great vigour.

His is a beautiful character, very quiet, but very strong.

And so somehow the day went as the night had gone (if, indeed, one can use the terms where all was densest night), and when I lit a match to see the time it was seven o'clock.

Once more we ate and drank, and as we did so an idea occurred to me.

'How is it,' said I, 'that the air in this place keeps fresh? It is thick and heavy, but it is perfectly fresh.'

'Great heavens!' said Good, starting up, 'I never thought of that. It can't come through the stone door, for it is air-tight, if ever a door was. It must come from somewhere. If there were no current of air in the place we should have been stifled when we first came in. Let us have a look.'

It was wonderful what a change this mere spark of hope wrought in us. In a moment we were all three groping about the place on our hands and knees, feeling for the slightest indication of a draught. Presently my ardour received a check. I put my hand on something cold. It was poor Foulata's dead face.

For an hour or more we went on feeling about, till at last Sir Henry and I gave it up in despair, having got considerably hurt by constantly knocking our heads against tusks, chests, and the sides of the chamber. But Good still persevered, saying, with an approach to cheerfulness, that it was better than doing nothing.

'I say, you fellows,' he said, presently, in a constrained sort of voice, 'come here.'

Needless to say we scrambled over towards him quick enough.

'Quatermain, put your hand here where mine is. Now, do you feel anything?'

'I *think* I feel air coming up.

'Now, listen.' He rose and stamped upon the place, and a flame of hope shot up in our hearts. *It rang hollow.*

With trembling hands I lit a match. I had only three left, and we saw that we were in the angle of the far corner of the chamber, a fact that accounted for our not having noticed the hollow ring of the place during our former exhaustive examination. As the match burnt we scrutinised the spot. There was a join in the solid rock floor, and, great heavens! there, let in level with the rock, was a stone ring. We said no word, we were too excited, and our hearts beat too wildly with hope to allow us to speak. Good had a knife, at the back of which was one of those hooks that are made to extract stones from horses' hoofs. He opened it, and scratched away at the ring with it. Finally he got it under, and levered away gently for fear of breaking the hook. The ring began to move. Being of stone, it had not got set fast in all the centuries it had lain there, as would have been the case had it been of iron. Presently it was upright. Then he got his hands into it and tugged with all his force, but nothing budged.

'Let me try,' I said, impatiently, for the situation of the stone, right in the angle of the corner, was such that it was impossible for two to pull at once. I got hold and strained away, but with no results.

Then Sir Henry tried and failed.

Taking the hook again, Good scratched all round the crack where we felt the air coming up.

'Now, Curtis,' he said, 'tackle on, and put your back into it; you are as strong as two. Stop,' and he took off a stout black silk handerchief, which, true to his habits of neatness, he still wore, and ran it through the ring. 'Quatermain, get Curtis round the middle and pull for dear life when I give the word. *Now*.'

Sir Henry put out all his enormous strength, and Good and I did the same, with such power as nature had given us.

'Heave! heave! it's giving,' gasped Sir Henry; and I heard the muscles of his great back cracking. Suddenly there came a parting sound, then a rush of air, and we were all on our backs on the floor with a great flag-stone on the top of us. Sir Henry's strength had done it, and never did muscular power stand a man in better stead.

'Light a match, Quatermain,' he said, as soon as we had picked ourselves up and got our breath; 'carefully, now.'

I did so, and there before us was, God be praised! the *first step of a stone stair.*

'Now what is to be done?' asked Good.

'Follow the stair, of course, and trust to Providence.'

H. Rider Haggard, *King Solomon's Mines*, 1885

Now while we were together that day, I – though nothing was less in my thoughts when I came over than any idea of escape (for I sought only our true deliverer Jesus Christ, as He was prefigured in the little ash-baked loaf of Elias, that I might with more strength and courage travel the rest of my way even to the mount of God) – seeing how close this part of the Tower was to the moat by which it was surrounded, began to think with myself that it were a possible thing for a man to descend by a rope from the top of the building to the other side of the moat. I asked my companion therefore what he thought about it, and whether it seemed possible to him.

'Certainly,' said he, 'it could be done, if a man had some true and real friends to assist him, who would not shrink from exposing themselves to danger to rescue one they loved.'

'There is no want of such friends,' I replied, 'if only the thing is feasible, and worth while trying.'

'For my part,' said he, 'I should only be too glad to make the attempt; since it would be far better for me to live even in hiding, where I could enjoy the Sacraments and the company of good men, than to spend my life here in solitude between four walls.'

'Well then,' I answered, 'let us commend the matter to God in prayer; in the meanwhile I will write to my Superior, and what he thinks best we will do.'

I returned that night to my cell; and wrote a letter to Father Garnett by John Lilly, putting all the circumstances before him. He answered me that the thing should be attempted by all means, if I thought it could be done without danger to my life in the descent.

Upon this I wrote to my former host, telling him that an escape in this way could be managed, but that the matter must be communicated to as few as possible, lest it should get noised abroad and stopped. I appointed moreover John Lilly and Richard Fulwood, the latter of whom was at that time serving Father Garnett, if they were willing to expose themselves to the peril, to come on such a night to the outer bank of the moat opposite the little tower in which my friend was kept, and near the place where Master Page was apprehended, as I described before. They were to bring with them a rope, one end of which they were to tie to a stake; then we from the leads on the top of the tower would throw over to them a ball of lead with a stout string attached, such as men use for sewing up bales of goods. This they would find in the dark by the noise it would make in falling, and would attach the string to the free end of their rope, so that we who retained one end of the string would thus be able to pull the rope up. I ordered moreover that they should have on their breasts a white paper or handkerchief, that we might recognise them as friends before throwing out our string, and that they should come provided with a boat in which we might quickly make our escape . . .

When the appointed night came, I prevailed on the gaoler by entreaties and bribes to allow me to visit my friend. So he locked us both in together with bolts and bars of iron as usual, and departed. But as he had also locked the inside door that led to the roof, we had to loosen the stone, into which the bolt shot, with our knives, or otherwise we could not get out. This we succeeded in doing at length, and mounted the leads softly and without a light, for a sentinel was placed in the garden every night, so that we durst not even speak to each other but in a very low whisper.

About midnight we saw the boat coming with our friends, namely, John Lilly, Richard Fulwood, and another who had been my gaoler in the former prison, through whom they procured the boat, and who steered the boat himself. They neared the shore; but just as they were about to land, some one came out of one of the poor cottages thereabouts to do somewhat, and seeing their boat making for the shore, hailed them, taking them for fishermen, The man indeed returned to his bed without suspecting anything, but our boatman durst not venture to land till they thought the man had gone to sleep again. They paddled about so long however that the time slipped away, and it became impossible to accomplish anything that night; so they returned by London Bridge. But the tide was now flowing so strongly that their boat was forced against some piles there fixed to break the force of the water, so that they could neither get on nor get back. Meanwhile the tide was still rising, and now came so violently on the boat that it seemed as if it would be upset at every wave. Being in these straits they commended themselves to God by prayers, and called for help from men by their cries. All this while we on the top of the tower heard them shouting, and saw men coming out on the bank of the river with candles, running up and getting into their boats to rescue those in danger. Many boats approached them but none durst go up to them, fearing the force of the current. So they stood there in a sort of circle round them, spectators of their peril, but not daring to assist. I recognised Richard Fulwood's voice in the shouts, and said, 'I know it is our friends who are in danger.' My companion indeed did not believe I could distinguish any one's voice at that great distance; but I knew it well, and groaned inwardly to think that such devoted men were in peril of their lives for my sake. We prayed fervently therefore for them, for we saw that they were not yet saved, though many had gone to assist them. Then we saw a light let down from the bridge, and a sort of basket attached to a rope, by which they might be drawn up, if they could reach it. This it seems they were not able to do. But God had regard to the peril of His servants, and at last there came a strong sea boat with six sailors, who worked bravely, and bringing their boat up to the one in danger, took out Lilly and Fulwood. Immediately they had got out, the boat they had left capsized before the third could be rescued, as if it had only kept right for the sake of the two who were Catholics. However by God's mercy the one who was thrown into the river caught a rope that was let down from the bridge, and was so dragged up and saved. So they were all rescued and got back to their homes.

On the following day John Lilly wrote me by the gaoler as usual. What could I expect him to say but this: 'We see, and have proved it by our peril, that it is not God's will we should proceed any further in this business.' But I found him saying just the contrary. For he began his letter as follows:– 'It was not the will of God that we should accomplish our desire last night, still He rescued us from a great danger, that we might succeed better the next time. What is put off is not cut off: so we mean to come again tonight with God's help.'

My companion on seeing such constancy joined with such strong and at the same time pious affection, was greatly consoled and did not doubt success. But I had great ado to obtain leave from the gaoler to remain another night out of my cell; and had misgivings that he would discover the loosening of the stone when he locked the door again. He however remarked nothing of it . . .

At the proper hour we mounted again on the leads. The boat arrived and put to shore without any interruption. The schismatic, my former gaoler at the Clink, remained with the boat, and the two Catholics came with the rope. It was a new rope, for they had lost the former one in the river on occasion of their disaster. They fastened the rope to a stake, as I had told them; they found the leaden ball which we threw, and tied the string to the rope. We had great difficulty however in pulling up the rope, for it was of considerable thickness, and double too. In fact Father Garnett ordered this arrangement, fearing lest otherwise the rope might break by the weight of my body. But now another element of danger showed itself, which we had not reckoned on: for the distance was so great between the tower and the stake to which the rope was attached, that it seemed to stretch horizontally rather than slopingly; so that we could not get along it merely by our weight, but would have to propel ourselves by some exertion of our own. We proved this first by a bundle which we had made of books and some other things wrapped up in my cloak. This bundle we placed on the double rope to see if it would slide down of itself, but it stuck at once. And it was well it did; for if it had gone out of our reach before it stuck, we should never have got down ourselves. So we took the bundle back and left it behind.

My companion, who had before spoken of the descent as a thing of the greatest ease, now changed his mind, and confessed it to be a thing very difficult and full of danger. 'However,' said he, 'I shall most certainly be hung if I remain now, for we cannot throw the rope back without its falling into the water, and so betraying both us and our friends. I will therefore descend, please God, preferring to expose myself to danger with the hope of freedom, rather than to remain here with good certainty of being hung.' So he said a prayer, and took to the rope. He descended fairly enough, for he was strong and vigorous, and the rope was then taut; his weight however slackened it considerably, which made the danger for me greater, and though I did not then notice this, yet I found it out afterwards when I came to make the trial.

So commending myself to God, to our Lord Jesus, to the Blessed Virgin, to my Guardian Angel, and all my Patrons, particularly Father Southwell, who had been imprisoned near this place for nearly three years before his martyrdom, and Father Walpole, I took the rope in my right hand and held it also with my left arm; then I twisted my legs about it, to prevent falling, in such a way that the rope passed between my shins. I descended some three or four yards face downwards, when suddenly my body swung round by its own weight and hung under the rope. The shock was so great that I nearly lost my hold, for I was still but weak, especially in the hands and arms. In fact, with the rope so slack and my body hanging beneath it, I could hardly get on at all. At length I made a shift to get on as far as the middle of the rope, and there I stuck, my breath and my strength failing me, neither of which were very copious to begin with. After a little time, the Saints assisting me, and my good friends below drawing me to them by their prayers, I got on a little further and stuck again, thinking I should never be able to accomplish it. Yet I was loth to drop into the water as long as I could possibly hold on. After another rest therefore I summoned what remained of my strength, and helping myself with legs and arms as well as I could, I got as far as the wall on the other side of the moat. But my feet only touched the top of the wall, and my whole body hung horizontally, my head being no higher than my feet, so slack was the rope. In such a position, and so exhausted as I was, it was hopeless to expect to get over the wall by my own unaided strength. So John Lilly got on to the wall somehow or other (for, as he afterwards asserted, he never knew how he got there), took hold of my feet, and by them pulled me to him, and got me over the wall on to *terra firma*. But I was quite unable to stand, so they gave me some cordial waters and restoratives, which they had brought on purpose. By the help of these I managed to walk to the boat, into which we all entered. They had however before leaving the wall untied the rope from the stake and cut off a part of it, so that it hung down the wall of the tower. We had previously indeed determined to pull it away altogether, and had with this object passed it round a great gun on the tower without knotting it. But God so willed it that we were not able by any exertion to get it away; and if we had succeeded it would certainly have made a loud splash in the water, and perhaps have brought us into a worse danger.

During the Persecution: Autobiography of Father John Gerard,
trans. G. R. Kingdon, 1886 (events of 1597)

SIXTEEN GUARDS

Now about that time Herod the king stretched forth *his* hands to vex certain of the church.

2 And he killed James the brother of John with the sword.

3 And because he saw it pleased the Jews, he proceeded further to take Peter also. (Then were the days of unleavened bread.)

4 And when he had apprehended him, he put *him* in prison, and delivered *him* to four quaternions of soldiers to keep him; intending after Easter to bring him forth to the people.

5 Peter therefore was kept in prison: but prayer was made without ceasing of the church unto God for him.

6 And when Herod would have brought him forth, the same night Peter was sleeping between two soldiers, bound with two chains: and the keepers before the door kept the prison.

7 And, behold, the angel of the Lord came upon *him*, and a light shined in the prison: and he smote Peter on the side, and raised him up, saying, Arise up quickly. And his chains fell off from *his* hands.

8 And the angel said unto him, Gird thyself, and bind on thy sandals.

And so he did. And he saith unto him, Cast thy garment about thee, and follow me.

9 And he went out, and followed him; and wist not that it was true which was done by the angel; but thought he saw a vision.

10 When they were past the first and the second ward, they came unto the iron gate that leadeth unto the city; which opened to them of his own accord: and they went out, and passed on through one street; and forthwith the angel departed from him.

11 And when Peter was come to himself, he said, Now I know of a surety, that the Lord hath sent his angel, and hath delivered me out of the hand of Herod, and *from* all the expectation of the people of the Jews.

Acts 12: 1–11

THE SPIDER'S WEB

In fact, by the time the murderers arrived before the dwelling of Mahomet, he was apprised of the impending danger. As usual, the warning is attributed to the angel Gabriel, but it is probable it was given by some Koreishite, less bloody-minded than his confederates. It came just in time to save Mahomet from the hands of his enemies. They paused at his door, but hesitated to enter. Looking through a crevice they beheld, as they thought, Mahomet wrapped in his green mantle, and lying asleep on his couch. They waited for a while, consulting whether to fall on him while sleeping, or wait until he should go forth. At length they burst open the door and rushed towards the couch. The sleeper started up; but, instead of Mahomet, Ali stood before them. Amazed and confounded, they demanded, 'Where is Mahomet?' 'I know not,' replied Ali, sternly, and walked forth; nor did any one venture to molest him. Enraged at the escape of their victim, however, the Koreishites proclaimed a reward of a hundred camels to any one who should bring them Mahomet alive or dead.

Divers accounts are given of the mode in which Mahomet made his escape from the house after the faithful Ali had wrapped himself in his mantle and taken his place upon the couch. The most miraculous account is, that he opened the door silently, as the Koreishites stood before it, and, scattering a handful of dust in the air, cast such blindness upon them, that he walked through the midst of them without being perceived. This, it is added, is confirmed by the verse of the 30th chapter of the Koran: 'We have thrown blindness upon them, that they shall not see.'

The most probable account is that he clambered over the wall in the rear of the house, by the help of a servant, who bent his back for him to step upon it.

He repaired immediately to the house of Abu Beker, and they arranged for instant flight. It was agreed that they should take refuge in a cave in Mount Thor, about an hour's distance from Mecca, and wait there until they could proceed safely to Medina: and in the meantime the children of Abu Beker should secretly bring them food. They left Mecca while it was yet dark, making their way on foot by the light of the stars, and the day dawned as they found themselves at the foot of Mount Thor. Scarce were they within the cave, when they heard the sound of pursuit. Abu Beker, though a brave man, quaked with fear. 'Our pursuers,' said he, 'are many, and we are but two.' 'Nay,' replied Mahomet, 'there is a third; God is with us!' And here the Moslem writers relate a miracle, dear to the minds of all true believers. By the time, say they, that the Koreishites reached the mouth of the cavern, an acacia tree had sprung up before it, in the spreading branches of which a pigeon had made its nest, and laid its eggs, and over the whole a spider had woven its web. When the Koreishites beheld these signs of undisturbed quiet, they concluded that no one could recently have entered the cavern; so they turned away, and pursued their search in another direction.

Whether protected by miracle or not, the fugitives remained for three days undiscovered in the cave, and Asama, the daughter of Abu Beker, brought them food in the dusk of the evenings.

On the fourth day, when they presumed the ardour of pursuit had abated, the fugitives ventured forth, and set out for Medina, on camels which a servant of Abu Beker had brought in the night for them. Avoiding the main road usually taken by the caravans, they bent their course nearer to the coast of the Red Sea. They had not proceeded far, however, before they were overtaken by a troop of horse, headed by Soraka Ibn Malec. Abu Beker was again dismayed by the number of their pursuers; but Mahomet repeated the assurance, 'Be not troubled; Allah is with us.' Soraka was a grim warrior, with shagged iron-grey locks, and naked sinewy arms rough with hair. As he overtook Mahomet, his horse reared and fell with him. His superstitious mind was struck with it as an evil sign. Mahomet perceived the state of his feelings, and by an eloquent appeal wrought upon him to such a degree, that Soraka, filled with awe, entreated his forgiveness; and turning back with his troop, suffered him to proceed on his way unmolested.

The fugitives continued their journey without further interruption, until they arrived at Koba, a hill about two miles from Medina. It was a favourite resort of the inhabitants of the city, and a place to which they sent their sick and infirm, for the air was pure and salubrious. Hence, too, the city was supplied with fruit; the hill and its environs being covered with vineyards, and with groves of the date and lotus; with gardens producing citrons, oranges, pomegranates, figs, peaches, and apricots; and being irrigated with limpid streams.

On arriving at this fruitful spot, Al Kaswa, the camel of Mahomet, crouched on her knees, and would go no further. The prophet interpreted it as a favourable sign, and determined to remain at Koba, and prepare for entering the city.

Washington Irving, *Lives of Mahomet and his Successors*, 1850

DRAIN IMPROVEMENTS

At last everything was ready and we arranged to make the attempt on September 25th. Early that morning I had my hair cropped, and then all our kit was brought out from various hiding-places up in the roof of our building. Just as we were beginning to change our clothes an orderly came in to say that one of the German officers wanted to see me. We were much perturbed and I wondered if rumours of our plans had somehow got round to the Germans. I dressed again and went down to the office, where I was told that I was on the list of prisoners to be inoculated against cholera and typhoid that morning. Fortunately the camp doctor had not yet arrived and I managed to get away almost at once, although of course my German-looking hair-cut was noticed. I heard afterwards that the German officer in question remarked to one of his subordinates, that he wondered why my hair had been clipped and that he felt sure I was going to try to escape. Luckily he took no steps to prevent us.

We hurried on with our dressing and by ten o'clock we were ready, with our khaki overcoats and half-trousers over the German kit. We looked remarkably stout, but, as it was a cold, misty morning and every one was wearing thick clothes and heavy overcoats, we were not very noticeable. Our three assistants preceded us to the *Kommandantur* carrying our German caps hidden under raincoats. Then, as soon as they signalled that the camp was more or less clear of Germans, we sallied forth one by one. Each of us went through the gardens by a different path and entered the *Kommandantur* enclosure at short intervals. There were a few prisoners going in or coming out of the building and the usual sentry on the gate, but otherwise there were no Germans about and everything seemed favourable.

We walked in up the steps and turned into the dark passage. Campbell and the other two at once took our overcoats, wrenched off the half-trousers and gave us our German caps. We made a hurried examination of each other's kit to see that everything was still correct and walked out of the sheltering passage.

As we reached the steps, I seemed to realise for the first time the utter absurdity of our position. Here we were, British prisoners of war, dressed in ill-fitting German uniform, about to demand an exit from the camp in broad daylight. Now that it was too late to turn back, the whole scheme seemed ridiculous. We were certain to be caught and made to look thoroughly foolish; possibly we might even be shot at. Why on earth had we ever thought of anything so stupid?

I went on walking more or less mechanically, and we went down the steps and turned to the right out of the building. I was positively trembling with nervousness, when just at that moment several British officers passed us. They glanced up, obviously without recognising us, saluted and went on. This steadied me a bit and I fancied the other two felt the same. The gate was twenty yards off and the sentry on duty was talking to a NCO, while a third man was only a few yards away. We walked quite slowly towards them and, as arranged, I began talking loudly to my brother in German. I talked about various alterations to camp buildings and improvements to the drains, while my brother took down my observations in a notebook and occasionally murmured 'Ja wohl, Herr Leutnant!' – generally at the wrong moment.

Our progress was a veritable triumph. The Germans near the gate sprang to attention; the man in charge jumped for the key, rattled it in the lock and threw open the gate. Some workmen doing a job on the *Kommandantur* building stood up and took off their caps. I nodded and answered the salutes, still talking nonsense to my brother, and we strolled on with Fairweather just behind us. The gap in the barbed-wire fence was reached; the sentries, still standing stiffly to attention, were passed and the next moment we were outside. At that very instant I heard a strange gurgling noise coming from my brother and I looked round in alarm, thinking he might be on the verge of collapse. To my surprise I found that he was merely shaking with laughter! I was glad somebody could see the joke; personally I felt extremely uncomfortable and by no means safe.

Duncan Grinnell-Milne, An Escaper's Log, 1926

THE SS AMONG THE FIRST

I was spared the labour commandos because I couldn't see. But for the unfit like me, they had another system, the Invalids' Block. Since they were no longer sure of winning the war, mercy had become official with the Nazis. A year earlier being unfit for physical work in the service of the Greater German Reich would have condemned you to death in three days.

The Invalids' Block was a barracks like the others. The only difference was that they had crowded in 1500 men instead of 300 – 300 was the average for the other blocks – and they had cut the food ration in half. At the Invalids' you had the one-legged, the one-armed, the trepanned, the deaf, the deaf-mute, the blind, the legless – even they were there, I knew three of them – the aphasic, the ataxic, the epileptic, the gangrenous, the scrofulous, the tubercular, the cancerous, the syphilitic, the old men over seventy, the boys under sixteen, the klepto maniacs, the tramps, the perverts, and last of all the flock of madmen. They were the only ones who didn't seem unhappy.

No one at the Invalids' was whole, since that was the condition of entrance. As a result people were dying there at a pace which made it impossible to make any count of the block. It was a greater surprise to fall over the living than the dead. And it was from the living that danger came.

The stench was so terrible that only the smell of the crematory, which sent up smoke around the clock, managed to cover it up on days when the wind drove the smoke our way. For days and nights on end, I didn't walk around, I crawled. I made an opening for myself in the mass of flesh. My hands travelled from the stump of a leg to a dead body, from a body to a wound. I could no longer hear anything for the groaning around me.

Towards the end of the month all of a sudden it became too much for me and I grew sick, very sick. I think it was pleurisy. They said several doctors, prisoners like me and friends of mine, came to listen to my chest. It seems they gave me up. What else could they do? There was no medicine at all at Buchenwald, not even aspirin.

Very soon dysentery was added to pleurisy, then an infection in both ears which made me completely deaf for two weeks, then erysipelas, turning my face into a swollen pulp, with complications which threatened to bring on blood poisoning. More than fifty fellow prisoners told me all this later. I don't remember any of it myself. I had taken advantage of the first days of sickness to leave Buchenwald.

Two young boys I was very fond of, a Frenchman with one leg, and a Russian with one arm, told me that one morning in April they carried me to the hospital on a stretcher. The hospital was not a place where they took care of people, but simply a place to lay them down until they died or got well. My friends, Pavel and Louis, didn't understand what happened. Later they kept telling me that I was 'a case'. A year afterwards Louis was still amazed: 'The day we carried you, you had a fever of 104 or more, but you were not delirious. You looked quite serene, and every now and then you would tell us not to put ourselves out on your account.' I would gladly have explained it to Louis and Pavel, but the whole affair was beyond words and still is.

Sickness had rescued me from fear, it had even rescued me from death. Let me say to you simply that without it I never would have survived. From the first moments of sickness I had gone off into another world, quite consciously. I was not delirious. Louis was right, I still had the look of tranquillity, more so than ever. That was the miracle.

I watched the stages of my own illness quite clearly. I saw the organs of my body blocked up losing control one after the other, first my lungs, then my intestines, then my ears, all my muscles, and last of all my heart, which was functioning badly and filled me with a vast, unusual sound. I knew exactly what it was, this thing I was watching: my body in the act of leaving this world, not wanting to leave it right away, not even wanting to leave it at all. I could tell by the pain my body was causing me, twisting and turning in every direction like snakes that have been cut in pieces.

Have I said that death was already there? If I have I was wrong. Sickness and pain, yes, but not death. Quite the opposite, life, and that was the unbelievable thing that had taken possession of me. I had never lived so fully before.

Life had become a substance within me. It broke into my cage, pushed by a force a thousand times stronger than I. It was certainly not made of flesh and blood, not even of ideas. It came towards me like a shimmering wave, like the caress of light. I could see it beyond my eyes and my forehead and above my head. It touched me and filled me to overflowing. I let myself float upon it.

There were names which I mumbled from the depths of my astonishment. No doubt my lips did not speak them, but they had their own song: 'Providence, the Guardian Angel, Jesus Christ, God.' I didn't try to turn it over in my mind. It was not just the time for metaphysics. I drew my strength from the spring. I kept on drinking and drinking still more. I was not going to leave that celestial stream. For that matter it was not strange to me, having come to me right after my old accident when I found I was blind. Here was the same thing all over again, the Life which sustained the life in me.

The Lord took pity on the poor mortal who was so helpless before him. It is true I was quite unable to help myself. All of us are incapable of helping ourselves. Now I knew it, and knew that it was true of the SS among the first. That was something to make one smile.

But there was one thing left which I could do: not refuse God's help, the breath he was blowing upon me. That was the one battle I had to fight, hard and wonderful all at once: not to let my body be taken by the fear. For fear kills, and joy maintains life.

Slowly I came back from the dead, and when, one morning, one of my neighbours – I found out later he was an atheist and thought he was doing the right thing – shouted in my ear that I didn't have a chance in the world of getting through it, so I had better prepare myself, he got my answer full in the face, a burst of laughter. He didn't understand that laugh, but he never forgot it.

On 8 May, I left the hospital on my two feet. I was nothing but skin and bones, but I had recovered. The fact was I was so happy that now Buchenwald seemed to me a place which if not welcome was at least possible. If they didn't give me any bread to eat, I would feed on hope.

It was the truth. I still had eleven months ahead of me in the camp. But today I have not a single evil memory of those three hundred and thirty days of extreme wretchedness. I was carried by a hand. I was covered by a wing. One doesn't call such living emotions by their names. I hardly needed to look out for myself, and such concern would have seemed to me ridiculous. I knew it was dangerous and it was forbidden. I was free now to help the others; not always, not much, but in my own way I could help.

Jacques Lusseyran, *And There Was Light*, 1963

SANCTUARY

ESCAPED!

*(The boiler-house whistle is blown 'wildcat' when
a prisoner makes a 'getaway')*

A man has fled . . .! We clutch the bars and wait;
The corridors are empty, tense and still;
The guards have gathered at the prison gate.
Then suddenly the 'wildcat' blares its hate
Like some mad Moloch screaming for the kill,
Shattering the air with terror loud and shrill,
The dim, grey walls become articulate.

Freedom, you say? Behold her altar here!
In those far cities men can only find
A vaster prison and a redder hell.
O'ershadowed by new wings of greater fear.
Brave fool, for such a world to leave behind
The iron sanctuary of a cell!

From *Bars and Shadows: The Prison Poems of Ralph Chaplin*, 1922

GODS AND ANGELS

I

When Love with unconfined wings
    Hovers within my Gates;
And my divine *Althea* brings
    To whisper at the Grates;
When I lye tangled in her haire,
    And fetterd to her eye;
The *Gods* that wanton in the Aire,
    Know no such Liberty.

II

When flowing Cups run swiftly round
    With no allaying *Thames*,

Our carelesse heads with Roses bound,
  Our hearts with Loyall Flames;
When thirsty griefe in Wine we steepe,
  When Healths and draughts go free,
Fishes that tipple in the Deepe,
  Know no such Libertie.

III

When (like committed Linnets) I
  With shriller throat shall sing
The sweetness, Mercy, Majesty,
  And glories of my KING;
When I shall voyce aloud, how Good
  He is, how Great should be;
    Inlarged Winds that curle the Flood,
    Know no such Liberty.

IV

Stone Walls doe not a Prison make,
  Nor I'ron bars a Cage;
Mindes innocent and quiet take
  That for an Hermitage;
If I have freedome in my Love,
  And in my soule am free;
Angels alone that sore above,
  Injoy such Liberty.

Richard Lovelace, 'To Althea, from Prison,' 1649

A MORE LITERARY STYLE

In a previous chapter I have alluded to a man, Edward Morrell, who had been tortured in St Quentin Prison, California, and through his tortures had gained certain psychic powers recorded by Jack London in his *Jacket* or *Star-Rover*. I have seen more of him now, and he is certainly one of the strangest personalities I have encountered in this country. He is snappy, with a click to all he does or says, like the cock of a pistol; but behind it all is a well-poised brain and a steady purpose, as his clear eyes and firm mouth can testify. Picture him the clean-cut, deadly-earnest man, leaning forward eagerly in his chair, and then read this, our dialogue.

'How came you into prison, Mr Morrell?'

'It was really a small civil war, sir – a feud between squatters and a great railroad company who tried to do them out of their holdings. They had the whole force of the State, police, judges, and everything, at their back. They could do what they liked. We had only our guns. So they proclaimed us bandits and treated us as such when taken. If they killed us, no more said; if we killed them, it was sure murder.'

'So they jailed you.'

'Yes, sir, and I was little more than a boy. And I could not stand for the way they treated us, and so I got it the harder. At last they had me in the black cell, and there were five years of my life during which I could only see my own hand at certain hours in the day when a ray of light came through a hole. Five years, sir, and I never left that cell except the days I was tortured. My beard was over my chest in front and my hair was down to my waist behind.'

'Tell me about the tortures?'

'It was mostly the jacket. They lace it up until they squeeze the very heart out of you. And there I came upon this way of getting your soul out of your body. It was self-hypnotising, I suppose. I could not have done it if I had not been so weak, anyhow. I used to lie there and watch a light over the door. Then I felt it coming on. I cursed the keepers to make them strap tighter. I knew it was either death that time, or else I would get my result. I got their goat. It didn't take much to do that. There were three of them with their knees in the small of my back pulling on a half-inch rope. Then they left me. And it came just as I expected. I felt it easing till it was no more than a great-coat, and then it vanished, and I was out of the body. I had forty-eight hours on end, and I laughed when they came for me, and I got forty-eight more hours for that. But it was worth it.'

'What were these visions you saw?'

'They were bits out of my own previous lives.'

'How do you know they were not bits out of your readings?'

'You've read them, have you not?'

'Yes.'

'Well, how could they be things I had read when I was only a boy that knew nothing and had read nothing when I was jailed?'

It was true. I recalled the wonderful series of pictures of the life of a primitive man, of a Norse pirate, of a mediæval knight, of all sorts of people which are given in Jack London's *Jacket* and which I recognised when I read them as being different, a finer, and a more literary style than his own.

'Yes, sir, I dictated them to Jack with a stenographer taking every word. I did 10,000 words at a stretch once. It was all branded in my brain. Every word was as I had it. I was like a man possessed. When I got waving a stick, Jack cried "Stop! You put fear into me!" '

'Then you think that under self-hypnotism you went back along the line of your vanished lives, and that when these brutes thought that you were under torture you were really living the outstanding scenes over again?'

'Yes, sir, that was so.'

'If the prisoners were misused, as you say, how came it that there were no inquests and inquiries?'

'There was at that time no law for prisoners. It was just a hole in the hill-side and no more said.'

Arthur Conan Doyle, *Our American Adventure*, 1923

INSOMNIA

While in St John's I met a Dr Steeves, who then was in charge of a large insane asylum, and received an invitation from him to visit his institution, which I accepted. After showing me the various wards, he eventually showed me the padded cells, in one of which, through the small bars of the cell door, I saw a maniac struggling on the canvas-padded floor, rolling about and straining each and every muscle in a vain attempt to get his hands over his head and striving in every conceivable manner to free himself from his canvas restraint, which I later on learned was called a strait-jacket.

Entranced, I watched the efforts of this man, whose struggles caused the beads of perspiration to roll off from him, and from where I stood, I noted that were he able to dislocate his arms at the shoulder joint, he would have been able to cause his restraint to become slack in certain parts, and so allow him to free his arms. But as the straps were drawn tight, the more he struggled the tighter his restraint encircled him, and eventually he lay exhausted, panting, and powerless to move.

Previous to this incident I had seen and used various restraints, such as insane restraint muffs, belts, bed-straps, etc., but this was the first time I saw a strait-jacket, and it left so vivid an impression on my mind that I hardly slept that night, and in such moments as I slept I saw nothing but strait-jackets, maniacs, and padded cells! In the wakeful part of the night I wondered what the effect would be to an audience to have them see a man placed in a strait-jacket and watch him force himself free therefrom.

The very next morning I obtained permission to try to escape from one, and during one entire week I practised steadily and then presented it on the stage, and made my escape therefrom behind a curtain. I pursued this method for some time, but as it was so often repeated to me that people seeing me emerge from the cabinet after my release with hair dishevelled, countenance covered with perspiration, trousers covered with dust, and ofttimes even my clothes being torn, remarked, 'Oh, he is faking, it did not take all that effort to make his escape,' eventually I determined to show to the audience exactly what means I resorted to to effect my release, and so did the strait-jacket release in full view of everybody.

Harry Houdini, Handcuff Secrets, 1910

ELEVEN

'Full of the joys of spring'

As it turned out E-day was a typical English summer day. The forecast was rain!

When my cell was unlocked soon after 1.30 p.m. the screw found me doubled up in agony, gasping for medical attention. To say it must have been something I ate wasn't that far-fetched in Wandsworth! Two screws were summoned to escort me to the sick bay. The quack had seen it all before and, as I had expected, prescribed a good dose of 'white mixture'. Miracle of miracles, it worked and by 2.30 p.m. I was fully recovered and back in the mailbag workshop, sewing away.

Eric was smiling after having spent the last half-hour with his loved ones, while Brian was looking relieved after a similar length of time on the crapper. Wee Jock also looked confident as he emerged from the storeroom.

At 3 p.m., as expected, the call went up to put our work away and line up for exercise. Before five past three we were in the yard and, conforming to regulations, were walking around the footpath in pairs, Eric and I together, Brian and Jock a few yards ahead. The wall was almost within touching distance.

Dark clouds lowered above us and it began to drizzle.

Fuck!

The discipline officer – the screw in charge of the exercise – gave a signal to the other three screws to take us back into the prison wing for 'indoor exercise'. I protested, pointing out that it was only raining lightly, but as I was speaking the heavens opened and it started to piss down. Eric and I exchanged dejected looks.

At the very same moment the escape team was trundling towards the prison in their converted furniture van. But when Paul saw the rain he knew from experience that we would be taken off the yard. Given Britain's inclement weather we had foreseen the situation and it had been decided that should rain 'stop play' we would carry out the same procedure the following day.

Happily nothing we or the escape team had done had attracted any attention, so the escape was very much on. But there was still the frustration of knowing that we had nearly done it and would have to do it all over again. We would all have to be missing from our place of work the next day when the screws chose the cons for the first exercise period. Whether it meant having a crap, sharpening our scissors, going special sick or whatever, not one of the four of us could afford to be in the workshop until well after 2 p.m.

The delay had given Paul some extra time and he decided to tour the phone boxes in the direct vicinity of the escape and disconnect the mouthpieces to stop people telephoning our getaway to the police or reporting a suspicious-looking van. We only discovered later that not even a prison of the size and importance of Wandsworth had a direct line to the police. When I did go over the top the screws had to call 999 like everyone else and this meant a twenty-minute delay until the cops arrived.

Thursday 8 July, one year and eleven months to the day since the robbery, the sun rose brightly over London and I sensed that this was going to be the day. Charmian, who must have been fed up of traipsing off to museums with the kids as an alibi, set off for Whipsnade Zoo in Bedfordshire. She also thought that after the disappointment of Wednesday this would be the day.

Never had the exercise yard looked so good. I felt like peeing with pleasure, so we headed for the toilets, where – surprise, surprise – Brian and Jack were to be found just shaking the drops off as Eric and I arrived.

'Tell me, do you boys hang around here all the time?' I said. With his back to the screw, who was watching closely to make sure that no one was having a crafty smoke, Eric checked the time by his watch and gave a nod. The four of us joined the other cons on exercise.

As we drew level with the wall I heard the sound of a heavy vehicle on the other side. I stopped to tie my shoelace, looking up at the wall. Suddenly, a head in a nylon stocking appeared. A split second later the first of the rope ladders came snaking down the wall. As Eric and I made for them the screws came running, blowing their whistles. Brian and Jock went into action.

As I cocked my leg over the wall, Paul, the man in the nylon mask, greeted me.

'Hello, you big ugly bastard!' I gave him a slap on the back and looked down at the mêlée in the prison yard. My boys were hanging on to the screws as if they loved them.

'You're too late,' Brian shouted gleefully, 'Biggsy's away.'

The truck was parked close to the wall, something that would be unthinkable today, so it was an easy matter to drop on to the roof. A large rectangular opening had been cut in the van to allow a five-foot hinged platform to be pushed up through the roof, giving Paul those vital extra feet needed to reach the top of the wall and throw the rope ladders down. On the floor of the van were a number of old mattresses for us to jump down on to. A getaway car was parked nearby with Paul's trusty friend, Ronnie Leslie, at the wheel. Two other cons seized the opportunity to follow us over the wall and because of this Paul never got to burn the truck as he had planned.

Besides Ronnie Leslie, a motor mechanic who had worked on converting the van, there was a third member of the escape team, Ronnie Black, a Ron I had had my doubts about.

Ronnie Black had spent time with me in Wandsworth where he had proved to be a bit of a hothead. The last thing I wanted was to have any kind of violence. No guns and no violence was a strict rule and Paul had grudgingly agreed to go along with this. I was pissed off, therefore, when I heard that there had been a shotgun involved. But Paul just offered to put me back inside. There is also a story that before we got over the wall Blackie had locked some screw's child in an outside toilet after he had emerged suddenly from a house.

As Eric and I scrambled into the car with Paul and the two Ronnies, the other two Special Watch cons came racing to the car looking for a lift.

'Let 'em in,' I shouted. They piled in and we zoomed off, full of the joys of being sprung.

We had made it!

We had done it!

We had fucking escaped from Wandsworth!

Ronald Biggs, *Odd Man Out*, 1994

'HE COUDE NAT PYSSE WITHOUT THEIR KNOWLEDGE'

Thus the erle of Flaunders was long in danger amonge the Flemmynges in cortoyse prison, and it greatly anoyed hym. Then at last he sayde he wolde byleve their counsayle, for he knewe well, he sayde, that he shulde have more profet there than in any other contrey. These wordes rejoysed greatly the Flemmynges; then they toke hym out of prison and suffred hym to go a haukyng to the ryver, the which sport the erle loved well; but ever ther was good watche layde on hym, that he shulde nat steale away fro theym, and they were charged on their lyves to take good hede to hym, and also they were suche as were favourable to the kyng of England: they watched hym so nere, that he coude nat pysse without their knowledge. This endured so longe that at last the erle sayd that he wolde gladly have to his wyfe the kyng of Englandes doughter. Than the Flemmynges sende worde therof to the kynge and to the quene, and poynted a day that they shuld come to Bergus in the abbey, and to bringe their doughter wit theym, and they wolde bring thyder their lorde the erle of Flanders, and there to conclude up the maryage. The kyng and the quene were gladde therof, and sayde that the Flemmynges were good men; so to Bergus bytwene Newport and Gravelynge, came the moost saddest men of the gode townes in Flaunders, and brought with them the erle their lorde in great estate. The kyng of Englande and the quene were ther redy: the erle curtesly inclyned to the kyng and to the quene; the kyng toke the erle by the ryght hande right swetely, and ledde hym forthe, sayeng, As for the dethe of the erle your father, as God helpe me, the day of the batayle of Cressey, nor the nexte day after I never herde worde of hym that he shulde be there. The yong erle by semblant made as thoughe he had ben content with the kynges excuse. Than they fyll in communycacyon of the maryage: there were certayne artycles agreed unto by the kyng of Englande and the erle Loyes of Flaunders, and great amyties ther was sworne bytwene them to be holden; and there the erle fyaunced Isabell the kyng of Englandes doughter, and promysed to wedde her. So that journey brake of, and a newe day to be apoynted at more leaser: the Flemmynges retourned into Flaunders with their lorde, and the kynge of Englande with the quene went agayne to the siege of Calays. Thus the mater stode a certayne tyme, and the kynge and the quene prepayred greatly agayne the maryage for jewelles and other thynges to gyve away, accordyng to their behavyours. The erle of Flanders dayly past the tyme at the ryver, and made semblant that this maryage pleased him greatly: so the Flemmynges thought that they were than sure ynough of hym, so that there was nat so great watch made on hym as was before. But they knewe nat well the condycion of their lorde, for whatsover countenance he made outwarde, his inwarde courage was all Frenche. So on a day he went forthe with his hawkes, the same weke the maryage shulde have ben finysshed; his fauconer cast of a faukon to an hearon, and therle cast of another. So these two faukons chased the hearon, and the erle rode after, as to folowe his faucon; and when he was a gode way of and had the advantage of the feldes, he dasshed his spurres to his horse and galoped forth in suche wyse, that his kepars lost hym: styll he goloped forthright, tyll he came into Arthoyes, and ther he was in suretie: and so than he rode into Fraunce to kyng Philyp and shewed hym all his adventure.

Jean Froissart, *Chronicles*, trans. Lord Berners, 1523 (events of 1347)

Rob-Roy, in the mean time, was employing his thoughts about forming a Scheme to regain his Liberty; and, having resolv'd upon one that carry'd an air of Success, it was presently put in execution.

He gain'd the Hearts of his Guard, by frequently calling for large Quantities of Brandy, and other strong Liquors; of which he had been accustom'd to drink so heartily, that not a little would disorder him. The Glass was handed about a-pace, the Soldiers drank freely, and so did Rob-Roy himself to their thinking: but he generally deceiv'd 'em, by letting the Liquor run thro' his Beard; which, the Reader may remember, was of an extraordinary length. He was so far from appearing discontented at his present Circumstances, that he was almost continually diverting the Company with comical old Songs, and pleasant Stories of his own Adventures; not forgetting at proper intervals to insinuate that he had a profound Respect for the Duke their Master; and that his Grace had no indifferent Regard for him.

These Artifices, corroborated by the Charge that the Duke had before given them, to treat him with Civility beyond the condition of a common Prisoner, produc'd the Effect that Mac-gregor desir'd. They vainly thought that both his Will and Interest were so united with his Grace's Pleasure, that there was not the least Danger of his Escape. This made them so incurious in observing his Management, that he found an Opportunity of bribing a Servant, to be ready next Morning in a neighbouring Wood, with an able Horse, and what else was necessary for his intended Flight.

The night was wasted in drinking, swearing, roaring, and all that a Sot calls pleasure: but when morning appear'd, Rob-Roy told his Guards that he had a favour to beg of them. They were eager to know what it was, and swore (as intelligibly as the Fumes of the Brandy would let them) that they should think themselves the most ungrateful Dogs in nature, if they deny'd any thing that was reasonable, to a Gentleman that had shew'd himself so generous. He thank'd 'em for their Civility; and added, that he had reason to believe, his great Strength and the Preservation of his Health, were chiefly owing to a constant practice of Bathing himself every morning; and therefore hop'd, that they would not deny him the liberty of continuing a Custom which he had been us'd to from his Infancy; and especially since the Omission of it might be of ill consequence to him. They, without the least Scruple, comply'd with his Request, and readily attended him to a River, that ran along by the side of the Wood, in which he had given orders for a Horse to be ready. He plung'd into the Water, and, bathing himself as usual, came out, seeing no sign of the Horse, and return'd with his Guard to the Prison.

They were no sooner got in, but, as a Gratuity for the Favour they had granted him, he gives orders for a Bowl of Punch; which, being brought before 'em, they welcom'd it with loud Acclamations of Joy, and the cup ran merrily round, with 'a Health to the Duke, and Captain Mac-gregor.' But, in the height of their carousing, Rob-Roy puts his Hand in his Pocket, and, in a seeming Consternation, tells them he had lost his Pocket-book since he went out last; that there were Notes in it of great value; besides, some particular Memorandums, that nearly concern'd the Duke. They (as drunk as they were) express'd a great concern for his loss, and unanimously offer'd their Service to go with him, and look for it. He thank'd them, and, accepting their Kindness, led them toward the River, where, while they were diligently searching the Grass, he suddenly call'd to them, and bid them give over. They look'd up, and were surpriz'd, to see him well mounted. 'My humble Service to the Duke, your Master, (says he) and pray assure his Grace, that I shall take all opportunities of returning the Favours he has oblig'd me with.' He spoke, and setting Spurs to his Horse, they were left in the utmost Confusion, cursing one another, and damning the Blood of the Pocket-book.

The Highland Rogue: Or, The Memorable Actions of the Celebrated Robert Mac-Gregor, Commonly Called Rob-Roy, 1723

SMOKING IN EARNEST

As I began to regain my composure I was filled with wild regrets at the prospect of no longer taking a hand in what seemed to me the making of history and the wildly exciting game of occupying the Caucasus and creating a belt of states from the Black Sea to the Pamirs. In those days such undreamt-of things were materialising. The world was in flux and everything was possible. My first attempt at escape had failed, but I was already considering the possibility of another, impelled by the thought that I was still close to the outside world, whereas in a short time I should doubtless find myself on the way to, God knows what, jungle seclusion.

My captors meanwhile had placidly settled down to smoke their opium pipes. At first I was too busy thinking of escape to notice them, and then suddenly the thought came to me that if I could keep them at it they might become so doped by the drug that they would let me escape. After a pipe or two, however, they sank into the pleasant self-satisfied condition which opium induces, so different from the boisterous exhilaration of alcohol. I felt that something had to be done to keep them to it. Their supply of opium seemed limited, but to offer them money to buy more would be too blatant.

During years spent in Persia, especially during the war, I had found that opium helped me in my work. The persons with whom I smoked became expansive under its influence, and this in its turn led to confidences. I remembered this, and also the curious fact that a habitué will open his heart to a novice. When, therefore, I asked for a pipe my captors were galvanised with interest and astonishment. They took my money quite naturally, and we got down to smoking in earnest. I began to hope that my plans would work, but at the same time I feared that I might myself be reduced to a state in which I would be incapable of taking advantage of the condition of my guards who were as keen on making me smoke as on smoking themselves. I had to pretend to cough and to have reached what the opium-smoker knows as 'kaif', which might be translated by the word 'lift'.

Opium is a wonderful comforter. It has been described in the East as the soldier's emergency ration, the muleteer's tonic, the solace of the starveling, the easer of the pain of thousands of sick and injured men who cannot hope for medical assistance.

As I smoked I began to feel the effects of the drug. My determination to escape began to weaken. I postponed from minute to minute the decision to act. I realised that if I made some excuse to go out to relieve nature I should probably be allowed to go without an escort, and still I delayed.

As I procrastinated a Jungali official with an escort entered the room. My guards shuffled sheepishly to their feet. The official rebuked them sharply and ordered me to collect my belongings and follow him to a boat. A few minutes later we were out in the open sea and my chances of escape were gone.

Lieutenant-Colonel E. Noel, 'A Prisoner Among the Jungali Bolsheviks',
in *On the Run*, ed. H. C. Armstrong, 1934

Nov. 22. [1864] – And now my turn has come, and I get off with the next load going today. My trunk is packed and baggage duly checked; shall try and get a 'lay-over' ticket, and rusticate on the road. Will see the conductor about it. A nice cool day with sun shining brightly – a fit one for an adventure and I am just the boy to have one. Coverlid folded up and thrown across my shoulder, lower end tied as only a soldier knows how. My three large books of written matter on the inside of my thick rebel jacket, and fastened in. Have a small book which I keep at hand to write in now. My old hat has been exchanged for a red zouave cap, and I look like a red-headed woodpecker. Leg behaving beautifully. My latest comrades are James Ready and Bill Somebody. We have decided to go and keep together on the cars. One of them has an apology for a blanket and the two acting in conjunction keep all three warm nights. LATER. – On the cars, in vicinity of Savannah en route for Blackshear, which is pretty well south and not far from the Florida line. Are very crowded in a close box car and fearfully warm. Try to get away tonight.

IN THE WOODS NEAR DOCTORTOWN STATION. No. 5, Ga., *Nov. 23.* – A change has come over the spirit of my dreams. During the night the cars ran very slow, and sometimes stopped for hours on side tracks. A very long, tedious night, and all suffered a great deal with just about standing room only. Impossible to get any sleep. Two guards at each side door, which are open about a foot. Guards were passably decent, although strict. Managed to get near the door, and during the night talked considerable with the two guards on the south side of the car. At about three o'clock this a.m. and after going over a long bridge which spanned the Altamaha River and in sight of Doctortown, I went through the open door like a flash and rolled down a high embankment. Almost broke my neck, but not quite. Guard fired a shot at me, but as the cars were going, though not very fast, did not hit me. Expected the cars to stop but they did not, and I had the inexpressible joy of seeing them move off out of sight. Then crossed the railroad track going north, went through a large open field and gained the woods, and am now sitting on the ground leaning up against a big pine tree *and out from under rebel guard!* The sun is beginning to show itself in the east and it promises to be a fine day. Hardly know what to do with myself. If those on the train notified Doctortown people of my escape they will be after me. Think it was at so early an hour that they might have gone right through without telling any one of the jump off. Am happy and hungry and considerably bruised and scratched up from the escape. The happiness of being here, however, overbalances everything else. If I had George Hendryx with me now would have a jolly time, and mean to have as it is. Sun is now up and it is warmer; birds chippering around, and chipmunks looking at me with curiosity. Can hear hallooing off a mile or so, which sounds like farmers calling cattle or hogs or something. All nature smiles – why should not I? – and I do.

John L. Ransom, *Andersonville Diary*, 1881

'ORR DID IT'

'I'm going to run away,' Yossarian announced in an exuberant, clear voice, already tearing open the buttons of his pajama tops.

'Oh, no,' Major Danby groaned, and began patting his perspiring face rapidly with the bare palms of both hands. 'You can't run away. Where can you run to? Where can you go?'

'To Sweden.'

'To Sweden?' Major Danby exclaimed in astonishment. 'You're going to run to Sweden? Are you crazy?'

'Orr did it.'

'Oh, no, no, no, no, no,' Major Danby pleaded. 'No, Yossarian, you'll never get there. You can't run away to Sweden. You can't even row.'

'But I can get to Rome if you'll keep your mouth shut when you leave here and give me a chance to catch a ride. Will you do it?'

'But they'll find you,' Major Danby argued desperately, 'and bring you back and punish you even more severely.'

'They'll have to try like hell to catch me this time.'

'They will try like hell. And even if they don't find you, what kind of way is that to live? You'll always be alone. No one will ever be on your side, and you'll always live in danger of betrayal.'

'I live that way now.'

'But you can't just turn your back on all your responsibilities and run away from them,' Major Danby insisted. 'It's such a negative move. It's escapist.'

[272]

Yossarian laughed with buoyant scorn and shook his head. 'I'm not running away from my responsibilities. I'm running to them. There's nothing negative about running away to save my life. You know who the escapists are, don't you, Danby? Not me and Orr.'

'Chaplain, please talk to him, will you? He's deserting. He wants to run away to Sweden.'

'Wonderful!' cheered the Chaplain, proudly throwing on the bed a pillowcase full of Yossarian's clothing. 'Run away to Sweden, Yossarian. And I'll stay here and persevere. Yes, I'll persevere. I'll nag and badger Colonel Cathcart and Colonel Korn every time I see them. I'm not afraid. I'll even pick on General Dreedle.'

'General Dreedle's out,' Yossarian reminded, pulling on his trousers and hastily stuffing the tails of his shirt inside. 'It's General Peckem now.'

The chaplain's babbling confidence did not falter for an instant. 'Then I'll pick on General Peckem, and even on General Scheisskopf. And do you know what else I'm going to do? I'm going to punch Captain Black in the nose the very next time I see him. Yes, I'm going to punch him in the nose. I'll do it when lots of people are around so that he may not have a chance to hit me back.'

'Have you both gone crazy?' Major Danby protested, his bulging eyes straining in their sockets with tortured awe and exasperation. 'Have you both taken leave of your senses? Yossarian, listen—'

'It's a miracle, I tell you,' the chaplain proclaimed, seizing Major Danby about the waist and dancing him around with his elbows extended for a waltz. 'A real miracle. If Orr could row to Sweden, then I can triumph over Colonel Cathcart and Colonel Korn, if I only persevere.'

'Chaplain, will you please shut up?' Major Danby entreated politely, pulling free and patting his perspiring brow with a fluttering motion. He bent toward Yossarian, who was reaching for his shoes. 'What about Colonel—'

'I couldn't care less.'

'But this may actua—'

'To hell with them both!'

'This may actually help them,' Major Danby persisted stubbornly. 'Have you thought of that?'

'Let the bastards thrive, for all I care, since I can't do a thing to stop them but embarrass them by running away. I've got responsibilites of my own now, Danby. I've got to get to Sweden.'

'You'll never make it. It's impossible. It's almost a geographical impossibility to get there from here.'

'Hell, Danby, I know that. But at least I'll be trying. There's a young kid in Rome whose life I'd like to save if I can find her. I'll take her to Sweden with me if I can find her, so it isn't all selfish, is it?'

'It's absolutely insane. Your conscience will never let you rest.'

'God bless it.' Yossarian laughed. 'I wouldn't want to live without strong misgivings. Right, Chaplain?'

'I'm going to punch Captain Black right in the nose the next time I see him,' gloried the chaplain, throwing two left jabs in the air and then a clumsy haymaker. 'Just like that.'

'What about the disgrace?' demanded Major Danby.

'What disgrace? I'm more in disgrace now.' Yossarian tied a hard knot in the second shoelace and sprang to his feet. 'Well, Danby, I'm ready. What do you say? Will you keep your mouth shut and let me catch a ride?'

Major Danby regarded Yossarian in silence, with a strange, sad smile. He had stopped sweating and seemed absolutely calm. 'What would you do if I did try to stop you?' he asked with rueful mockery. 'Beat me up?'

Yossarian reacted to the question with hurt surprise. 'No, of course not. Why do you say that?'

'I will beat you up,' boasted the chaplain, dancing up very close to Major Danby and shadowboxing. 'You and Captain Black, and maybe even Corporal Whitcomb. Wouldn't it be wonderful if I found I didn't have to be afraid of Corporal Whitcomb any more?'

'Are you going to stop me?' Yossarian asked Major Danby, and gazed at him steadily.

Major Danby skipped away from the chaplain and hesitated a moment longer. 'No, of course not!' he blurted out, and suddenly was waving both arms toward the door in a gesture of exuberant urgency. 'Of course I won't stop you. Go, for God sakes, and hurry! Do you need any money?'

'I have some money.'

'Well, here's some more.' With fervent, excited enthusiasm, Major Danby pressed a thick wad of Italian currency upon Yossarian and clasped his hand in both his own, as much to still his own trembling fingers as to give encouragement to Yossarian. 'It must be nice to be in Sweden now,' he observed yearningly. 'The girls are so sweet. And the people are so advanced.'

'Goodbye, Yossarian,' the chaplain called. 'And good luck. I'll stay here and persevere, and we'll meet again when the fighting stops.'

'So long, Chaplain. Thanks, Danby.'

'How do you feel, Yossarian?'

'Fine. No, I'm very frightened.'

'That's good,' said Major Danby. 'It proves you're still alive. It won't be fun.'

Yossarian started out. 'Yes it will.'

'I mean it, Yossarian. You'll have to keep on your toes every minute of every day. They'll bend heaven and earth to catch you.'

'I'll keep on my toes every minute.'

'You'll have to jump.'

'I'll jump.'

'Jump!' Major Danby cried.

Yossarian jumped. Nately's whore was hiding just outside the door. The knife came down, missing him by inches, and he took off.

Joseph Heller, Catch-22, 1962

SCROOGING OUT

The Mole had been working very hard all the morning, spring-cleaning his little home. First with brooms, then with dusters; then on ladders and steps and chairs, with a brush and a pail of whitewash; till he had dust in his throat and eyes, and splashes of whitewash all over his black fur, and an aching back and weary arms. Spring was moving in the air above and in the earth below and around him, penetrating even his dark and lowly little house with its spirit of divine discontent and longing. It was small wonder, then, that he suddenly flung down his brush on the floor, said 'Bother!' and 'O blow!' and also 'Hang spring-cleaning!' and bolted out of the house without even waiting to put on his coat. Something up above was calling him imperiously, and he made for the steep little tunnel which answered in his case to the gravelled carriage-drive owned by animals whose residences are nearer to the sun and air. So he scraped and scratched and scrabbled and scrooged, and then he scrooged again and scrabbled and scratched and scraped, working busily with his little paws and muttering to himself, 'Up we go! Up we go!' till at last, pop! his snout came out into the sunlight, and he found himself rolling in the warm grass of a great meadow.

'This is fine!' he said to himself. 'This is better than whitewashing!' The sunshine struck hot on his fur, soft breezes caressed his heated brow, and after the seclusion of the cellarage he had lived in so long the carol of happy birds fell on his dulled hearing almost like a shout. Jumping off all his four legs at once, in the joy of living and the delight of spring without its cleaning, he pursued his way across the meadow till he reached the hedge on the further side.

'Hold up!' said an elderly rabbit at the gap. 'Sixpence for the privilege of passing by the private road!' He was bowled over in an instant by the impatient and contemptuous Mole, who trotted along the side of the hedge chaffing the other rabbits as they peeped hurriedly from their holes to see what the row was about. 'Onion-sauce! Onion-sauce!' he remarked jeeringly, and was gone before they could think of a thoroughly satisfactory reply.

Kenneth Grahame, *The Wind in the Willows*, 1908

PILLOWTALK

Now *Giant Despair* had a Wife, and her name was *Diffidence*: so when he was gone to bed, he told his Wife what he had done, to wit, that he had taken a couple of Prisoners, and cast them into his *Dungeon*, for trespassing on his grounds. Then he asked her also what he had best to do further to them. So she asked him what they were, whence they came, and whither they were bound; and he told her; Then she counselled him, that when he arose in the morning he should beat them without any mercy: So when he arose, he getteth him a grievous Crab-tree Cudgel, and goes down into the *Dungeon* to them; and there, first falls to rateing of them as if they were dogs, although they gave him never a word of distaste; then he falls upon them, and beats them fearfully, in such sort, that they were not able to help themselves, or to turn them upon the floor. This done, he withdraws and leaves them, there to condole their misery, and to mourn under their distress: so all that day they spent the time in nothing but sighs and bitter lamentations. The next night she talking with her Husband about them further, and understanding that they were yet alive, did advise him to counsel them, to make away themselves: So when morning was come, he goes to them in a surly manner, as before, and perceiving them to be very sore with the stripes that he had given them the day before; he told them, that since they were never like to come out of that place, their only way would be, forthwith to make an end of themselves, either with Knife, Halter or Poison: For why, said he, should you chuse life, seeing it is attended with so much bitterness. But they desired him to let them go; with that he looked ugly upon them, and rushing to them, had doubtless made an end of them himself, but that he fell into one of his fits; (for he sometimes in Sun-shine weather fell into fits) and lost (for a time) the use of his hand: wherefore he withdrew, and left them, (as before) to consider what to do. Then did the Prisoners consult between themselves, whether 'twas best to take his counsel or no: and thus they began to discourse.

Chr. Brother, said *Christian*, what shall we do? the life that we now live is miserable: for my part, I know not whether is best, to live thus, or to die out of hand? *My soul chuseth strangling rather than life*; and the Grave is more easie for me than this Dungeon: Shall we be ruled by the Giant?

Hope. *Indeed our present condition is dreadful, and death would be far more welcome to me than thus for ever to abide: but yet let us consider, the Lord of the Country to which we are going, hath said, Thou shalt do no murther, no not to another man's person; much more then are we forbidden to take his counsel to kill our selves. Besides, he that kills another, can but commit murder upon his body; but for one to kill himself, is to kill body and soul at once. And moreover, my Brother, thou talkest of ease in the Grave; but hast thou forgotten the Hell whither, for certain, the murderers go? for no murderer hath eternal life, &c. And, let us consider again, that all the Law is not in the hand of* Giant Despair: *Others, so far as I can understand, have bene taken by him, as well as we; and yet have escaped out of his hand: Who knows, but that God that made the world, may cause that* Giant Despair *may die; or that, at some time or other he may forget to lock us in; or, but he may in short time have another of his fits before us, and may lose the use of his limbs; and if ever that should come to pass again, for my part, I am resolved to pluck up the heart of a man, and to try my utmost to get from under his hand. I was a fool that I did not try to do it before, but however, my Brother, let's be patient, and endure a while; the time may come that may give us a happy release: but let us not be our own murderers.* With these words, Hopeful, *at present did moderate the mind of his Brother; so they continued together (in the dark) that day, in their sad and doleful condition.*

Well, towards evening the Giant goes down into the Dungeon again, to see if his Prisoners had taken his counsel; but when he came there, he found them alive, and truly, alive was all: for now, what for want of Bread and Water, and by reason of the Wounds they received when he beat them, they could do little but breath: But, I say, he found them alive, at which he fell into a grievous rage, and told them, that seeing they had disobeyed his counsel, it should be worse with them, than if they had never been born.

At this they trembled greatly, and I think that *Christian* fell into a Swound; but coming a little to himself again, they renewed their discourse about the *Giants* counsel; and whether yet they had best to take it or no. Now *Christian* again seemed to be for doing it, but *Hopeful* made his second reply as followeth.

Hope. *My Brother, said he, remembrest thou not how valiant thou hast been heretofore; Apollyon could not crush thee, nor could all that thou didst hear or see, or feel in the Valley of the Shadow of Death; what hardship, terror, and amazement hast thou already gone through, and art thou now nothing but fear? Thou seest that I am in the Dungeon with thee, a far weaker man by nature than thou art: Also this Giant has wounded me as well as thee; and hath also cut off the Bread and Water from my mouth; and with thee I mourn without the light: but let's exercise a little more patience. Remember how thou playedst the man at* Vanity-Fair, *and wast neither afraid of the Chain nor Cage; nor yet of bloody Death: wherefore let us (at least to avoid the shame, that becomes not a Christian to be found in) bear up with patience as well as we can.*

Now night being come again, and the *Giant* and his Wife being in bed, she asked him concerning the Prisoners, and if they had taken his counsel: To which he replied, They are sturdy Rogues, they chuse rather to bear all hardship, than to make away themselves. Then said she, Take them into the Castle-yard to morrow, and shew them the *Bones* and *Skulls* of those that thou hast already dispatch'd; and make them believe, e're a week comes to an end, thou also wilt tear them in pieces as thou hast done their fellows before them.

So when the morning was come, the *Giant* goes to them again, and takes them into the Castle-yard, and shews them, as his Wife had bidden him. These, said he, were Pilgrims as you are, once, and they trespassed in my grounds, as you have done; and when I thought fit, I tore them in pieces; and so within ten days I will do you. Go get you down to your Den again; and with that he beat them all the way thither: they lay therefore all day on *Saturday* in a lamentable case, as before. Now when night was come, and when Mrs *Diffidence*, and her Husband, the *Giant*, were got to bed, they began to renew their discourse of their Prisoners: and withal, the old *Giant* wondered, that he could neither by his blows, nor counsel, bring them to an end. And with that his Wife replied, I fear, said she, that they live in hope that some will come to relieve them, or that they have pick-locks about them; by the means of which they hope to escape. And, sayest thou so, my dear, said the *Giant*, I will therefore search them in the morning.

Well, on *Saturday* about midnight they began to *pray*, and continued in Prayer till almost break of day.

Now a little before it was day, good *Christian*, as one half amazed, brake out in this passionate speech, *What a fool, quoth he, am I, thus to lie in a stinking Dungeon, when I may as well walk at liberty?* I have a *Key* in my bosom, called *Promise*, that will, (I am perswaded) open any Lock in *Doubting-Castle*. Then said *Hopeful*, That's good news; good Brother pluck it out of thy bosom, and try: Then *Christian* pulled it out of his bosom, and began to try it at the Dungeon door, whose bolt (as he turned the Key) gave back, and the door flew open with ease, and *Christian* and *Hopeful* both came out. Then he went to the outward door, that leads into the *Castle yard*, and with his Key opened the door also. After he went to the *Iron* Gate, for that must be opened too, but that Lock went *damnable* hard, yet the Key did open it; then they thrust open the Gate to make their escape with speed; but that Gate, as it opened, made such a creaking, that it waked *Giant Despair*, who hastily rising to pursue his Prisoners, felt his Limbs to fail, for his fits took him again, so that he could by no means go after them. Then they went on, and came to the Kings high way again, and so were safe, because they were out of his Jurisdiction.

John Bunyan, *The Pilgrim's Progress*, 1678

QUEEN'S VISIT

I got into the boat and was again detected – was called on the quarter-deck and was stripped naked. I was again ironed and put into the black hole, and was kept there fourteen days and nights upon a pound of bread a day and plenty of water. Seven of these days I did not see daylight, but the other seven days I was allowed to exercise an hour in the day. After the expiration of these fourteen days, I was brought out of the black hole, and when I got on deck I for the first time of my life *fainted*. The irons were kept on me; I was then under the doctor's care for about three weeks. After this I went to work as usual with about twenty pounds' weight of iron upon me for full three months. During this time, my wife came to see me. I was cut to my heart on account of her great distress of mind. She wept bitterly when she saw the heavy irons upon me, and told me that both her and the children were almost in a state of starvation, as the parish would not allow sufficient to support them. I thought to myself when I saw her, I will try again to make my escape for her sake and for the sake of my dear children. I could not rest night nor day on their account. After having seen her, I became more determined and desperate than ever. I was again set to work in the dock-yard with light irons. I considered a plan one night when in my hammock, and which I was resolved to try the next day, although I had several guards to pass, and a very long way to swim. I prayed that God would assist me through it for my family's sake. Consequently on the following night when we had left off work to go into the small boat, which always took us from our work to the ship, the *York*, which was on 25th of November; instead of going into the boat, I ran up to the piles under the jetty, up to my middle in water, where I remained for about an hour and a half. When the boat was pushed off to return to the hulks I heard the guard say where is D.? I heard one of them say 'He has done us at last, for he is not here.' When they came on shore they were over my head and again exclaimed he has done us. They asked one of the soldiers whether he had seen one of their men, he answered *No!* All this time I was in the water. I was afraid to use my file to take off my irons lest the soldier above me should hear me; presently the *drum* on board the *Victory* was beaten, as is usual; I then began to use my file and got my irons off. As soon as it became dusk, it was very foggy, I began to strip. I uttered up a few words in prayer and cast myself into the water. The tide was coming in very strongly. I went at a rapid rate and had to pass by a guard, on board the *Illustrious*; and several other guards higher up the harbour. After I had been in the water about a quarter of an hour, I heard a gun shot; after this several more had been fired. I thought they were all coming to me. I then thought it is all up with me. I was alarmed. But I believe it was only in consequence of the Queen having visited Portsmouth that day; and they were taking down the standard. I was so much terrified at this shooting, that when I passed by the King George's Yacht, I fastened myself to one of the buoys. It was however, so very cold, that I was obliged to let go, and plunge again into the great deep. I ultimately landed at Polchester Castle, a distance of about five miles from the dock-yard. When I got out of the water, I was almost exhausted, and was forced to lie down for a considerable time, as I had nearly lost the use of my arms. I then started off naked; I think it must have been about nine o'clock; and travelled on some distance, when I heard footsteps of some one; and it struck me it was one of the guards on Portdown-bridge, where a file of soldiers are always kept. I returned back again, and went over a small hill, at the bottom of which was a small river, about as wide as the Dee. I swam across this river, which I found much more cold than the Sea. I went over hedges and ditches, quite naked, until it came on daylight. I got into a pig-sty, and covered myself over with straw, and remained there till night, without food or drink, and several thorns in my feet, I then started off again, and travelled all night, until I got to a farm-house, and made way into one of the stables, where I found an old smock-frock, which I gladly put on. Here I remained all day. This was the third day I had had no food. I started off again; and going over Epsom Race-course, I saw a policeman; I turned down a lane before he could see me, and got into a cottage, where I found an old woman. I begged for mercy and pardon. She took me to the fire; she gave me a pair of stockings, a cap, and an old pair of shoes. I travelled on; but was so much fatigued, that I was obliged to go to a house, and beg for a bit of bread. I got some, with some cheese. On my way onwards, I saw a man with some cattle, going to London. I helped him to drive the cattle; and he gave me fourpence-halfpenny, being all he had. I wanted a night's rest, and went to a lodging-house on the road. I asked the woman how much my lodgings would be. She said fourpence. I had only then one halfpenny left; with this I bought some apples. I went to bed, and had a good night's rest, and started off early next morning, for London. When within a mile of the town, I stopped at some common, and there was a load of coals brought to a house. I got the coals in for them, and received sixpence and something to eat. I then went into London; and found out a man, whose brother was a convict. He gave me clothing; plenty to eat; and ten shillings to start me off. I started off the day after, and went by the way of the canal, until I reached Oxford. I stayed one night on the road. I travelled on to Banbury; and from there I went to Warwick. Here I got two shillings for taking care of some cattle in the Fair. Next day I got three shillings and sixpence, to take some cattle to Birmingham. I had now seven shillings and sixpence, and laid it all out in steel pens. I wrote to my wife, and informed her where I was: I then went out hawking my pens, and cleared three shillings the first day. I travelled on towards Wolverhampton, and earned four shillings more, and got rid of all my pens. I wrote to my wife to meet me at Wolverhampton. In the meantime I bought three umbrellas; I sold them, and was able to purchase five more the next day. At night, my wife not having arrived, I became very unhappy, and almost mad, as I found I was as badly off as ever. The following day, I went out again in the Newport Road, and there met my wife coming to me from C. It was indeed a happy meeting. We then travelled on together to Newport, where I carried on my hawking umbrellas. My wife soon returned to C. She contrived to get my children sent off by the parish, at B., but did not succeed. I received a letter to that effect from her. I then left the town; when, I understand, about half an hour afterwards Mr H., Superintendent of Police, arrived there in search of me. Eager to get my poor children, I got nearer and nearer to C., within 20 miles, at W., where I again met with my wife. Soon after we had got our supper, two policemen came into the house; one through the front door, and the other through the back. I saw them both. They took hold of my wife. I heard her shout out, 'Let me alone, what have I done?' At this I leaped over the garden wall, and went off to Wem.

'The Life of P. D.' in *Memoirs of Convicted Prisoners,* ed. Rev. H. S. Joseph, 1853

TWELVE

'Do *the worst you can*'

On April 22nd, 1796, men were crying in the streets of Paris the victory of Montenotte, gained by the General-in-chief of the army of Italy, whom the message of the Directory to the Five Hundred of 2 Floréal, an IV., calls Buona-Parte; and on the same day a heavy gang was put in chains at Bicetre, and Jean Valjean formed part of the chain. An exgaoler of the prison, who is now nearly ninety years of age, perfectly remembers the wretched man, who was chained at the end of the fourth cordon, in the north angle of the court-yard. He was seated on the ground like the rest, and seemed not at all to understand his position, except that it was horrible. It is probable that he also saw something excessive through the vague ideas of an utterly ignorant man. While the bolt of his iron collar was being riveted with heavy hammer blows behind his head, he wept, tears choked him, and prevented him from speaking, and he could only manage to say from time to time: 'I was a wood-cutter at Faverolles.' Then, while still continuing to sob, he raised his right hand, and lowered it gradually seven times, as if touching seven uneven heads in turn, and from this gesture it could be guessed that whatever the crime he had committed, he had done it to feed and clothe seven children.

He started for Toulon, and arrived there after a journey of twenty-seven days in a cart, with the chain on his neck. At Toulon he was dressed in the red jacket. All that had hitherto been his life, even to his name, was effaced. He was no longer Jean Valjean, but No. 24,601. What became of his sister, what became of the seven children? Who troubles himself about that? What becomes of the spray of leaves when the stem of the young tree has been cut at the foot? It is always the same story. These poor living beings, these creatures of God, henceforth without support, guide, or shelter, went off hap-hazard, and gradually buried themselves in that cold fog in which solitary destinies are swallowed up, that mournful gloom in which so many unfortunates disappear during the sullen progress of the human race. They left their country; what had once been their steeple forgot them; what had once been their hedge-row forgot them; and after a few years' stay in the bagne, Jean Valjean himself forgot them. In that heart where there had once been a wound there was now a scar: that was all. He only heard about his sister once during the whole time he spent at Toulon; it was, I believe, toward the end of the fourth year of his captivity, though I have forgotten in what way the information reached him. She was in Paris, living in the Rue du Geindre, a poor street, near Saint-Sulpice, and had only one child with her, the youngest, a boy. Where were the other six? perhaps she did not know herself. Every morning she went to a printing-office, No. 3, Rue du Sabot, where she was a folder and stitcher; she had to be there at six in the morning, long before day-light in winter. In the same house as the printing-office there was a day-school, to which she took the little boy, who was seven years of age, but as she went to work at six and the school did not open till seven o'clock, the boy was compelled to wait in the yard for an hour, in winter, – an hour of night in the open air. The boy was not allowed to enter the printing-office, because it was said that he would be in the way. The workmen as they passed in the morning saw the poor little fellow seated on the pavement, and often sleeping in the darkness, with his head on his satchel. When it rained, an old woman, the portress, took pity on him; she invited him into her den, where there were only a bed, a spinning-wheel, and two chairs, when the little fellow fell asleep in a corner, clinging to the cat, to keep him warm. This is what Jean Valjean was told; it was a momentary flash, as it were a window suddenly opened in the destiny of the beings he had loved, and then all was closed again; he never heard about them more. Nothing reached him from them; he never saw them again, never met them, and we shall not come across them in the course of this melancholy narrative.

Toward the end of this fourth year, Jean Valjean's turn to escape arrived, and his comrades aided him as they always do in this sorrowful place. He escaped and wandered about the fields at liberty for two days: if it is liberty to be hunted down; to turn one's head at every moment; to start at the slightest sound: to be afraid of everything, of a chimney that smokes, a man who passes, a barking dog, a galloping horse, the striking of the hour, of day because people see, of night because they do not see, of the highway, the path, the thicket, and even sleep. On the evening of the second day he was recaptured; he had not eaten or slept for six-and-thirty hours. The maritime tribunal added three years to his sentence for his crime, which made it eight years. In the sixth year, it was again his turn to escape; he tried, but could not succeed. He was missing at roll call, the gun was fired, and at night the watchman found him hidden under the keel of a ship that was building, and he resisted the *garde chiourme*, who seized him. Escape and rebellion: this fact, foreseen by the special code, was punished by an addition of five years, of which two would be spent in double chains. Thirteen years. In his tenth year his turn came again, and he took advantage of it, but succeeded no better: three years for this new attempt, or sixteen years in all. Finally, I think it was during his thirteenth year that he made a last attempt, and only succeeded so far as to be recaptured in four hours: three years for these four hours, and a total of nineteen years. In October, 1815, he was liberated; he had gone in in 1796 for breaking a window and stealing a loaf.

Victor Hugo, *Les Misérables*, trans. F. C. L. Wraxall, 1862

CRYING MEN

This camp had been but recently established, and there was not many prisoners here. They yelled to us to 'grab your pocket-books,' as we came in sight. This referred to the strict search to which all new comers were subjected, in which everything, even to a few Confederate dollars, was taken from you. It was labelled and put away, to be returned to you when you were leaving; but the valuables were never returned, as they could not be found. We were now regularly initiated as prisoners of war, and began to feel all the rigours and severities of such. We were divided into companies of one hundred men each, and were allowed for some time to draw and cook our own rations, each company sergeant being supplied with the necessary utensils. Soon, however, large numbers of prisoners began to arrive, most of them from Fort Delaware. They were in a most destitute and deplorable condition – many of them not having sufficient clothing to clothe them, and all were without blankets. The severity of a winter on this barren place can only be imagined by those who have been there, and our prospects were now gloomy indeed. Our camp had formerly been a corn-field, and consisted of about fifty acres. The Federal authorities conceived the plan of fencing in the camp, and erecting cook-houses, a commissary, &c., and for this purpose secured the services of several good carpenters. They employed about two hundred prisoners to assist, paying them in extra rations and tobacco. When these were erected the camp was thoroughly reorganised. The men were divided into divisions of one thousand men each – each under a Yankee sergeant – and the division into companies of one hundred men each, under a Confederate sergeant. We were compelled to keep the camp clean, well drained, &c., and for this purpose carts and barrows were furnished. Each company street was well drained, and made as hard and firm as pebble and sand could make it. Each drain ran into the main drain, which ran through the centre of the camp, and from which all the refuse water was thrown into the bay. Our tents were miserable affairs, being full of holes, and very rotten. They were of the 'Sibley pattern', and into each one of these sixteen men were crowded. In order to lie down at night, the men were compelled to lie so close together as to exclude sleep. The winter of 1803 was now approaching, and gloom, privation and starvation were staring us in the face. On the 9th of November, snow fell and there was not a stick of wood in camp. The day was bitter cold, most of us were but poorly clad, and very few of us had shoes of any description. We were compelled to stand in our damp tents, and 'mark time' to keep from freezing. This scarcely seems possible, yet it can be attested by hundreds who were there. Previous to this time – November, 1863 – we had no reason to complain of our rations, but now we began to feel the pangs of hunger. Shortly after the cook-houses were finished, a detail of ten or twelve men, under a sergeant, was assigned to each house, whose duty it was to cook the rations and issue them. Each house was furnished with three huge boilers – holding perhaps, forty gallons apiece – thus enabling them to feed about five hundred men at once. Our rations were now reduced as follows: for breakfast, half-pint coffee, or, rather, slop water; for dinner, half-pint greasy water (called soup for etiquette), also a small piece of meat, perhaps three or four ounces. For bread we were allowed eight ounces per day; this you could press together in your hand and take at a mouthful. Our water was of such a character that we could scarcely use it, being so highly tinctured with sulphur and iron as to render it almost unbearable. Clothes which were washed in it were turned black and yellow. To our suffering from the cold and the want of pure water was now added that of hunger. To those who have never suffered in this respect, it is almost impossible to describe the sensations. The writer has known large, stout men to lie in their tents at night and cry like little babies from hunger and cold. We were not allowed to walk about, but were compelled to retire to our tents at 'taps', which was sounded quite early. Even the poor privilege of keeping ourselves warm by walking up and down in front of our tents was denied us, and we were compelled to lie in the cold. The supply of blankets was very scant, and 'bunks' were unknown. The cold ground was our bed, and pillows we had none. To add to our discomforts, the tide from the bay occasionally backed into the camp, and compelled those whose tents had been flooded to stand all night. Midwinter was now upon us, and the intense cold we suffered may be judged when it is stated that the Chesapeake bay was frozen hard full twenty feet from the bank.

Point Lookout is situated in Saint Mary's county, Maryland. The Department was commanded by General Barnes, United States army. Major Patterson was provost-marshal and had charge of the prisoners. The Second, Fifth and Twelfth New Hampshire constituted the guard, with two batteries of artillery and a squadron of cavalry. These troops were housed in comfortable tents, and as we saw the smoke rising from the innumerable stove-pipes projecting from their tents, we could not but indulge in bitter thoughts of their cruelty. If this man Patterson still lives his conscience must burn him. He was the impersonation of cruel malignity, hatred and revenge, and he never let an opportunity pass in which he could show his disposition in this respect. Of the guards we could not complain, as they acted under orders and were not responsible for any of the cruelties to which we were subjected. As might be inferred, our Christmas was a dull one, and we passed the day in thinking of 'Dixie' and the loved ones at home. About the 10th of January, our suffering had grown so intense that a party formed a plan to escape. It was a bold one in conception, and required men of determination and courage to undertake it. Sergeant Shears, a man of about sixty years of age and a member of a Virginia cavalry regiment, was placed in command. A tunnel was to be dug from the rear of Company A, first division, to the fence, a distance of about twenty feet, and was commenced in a small tent. This work was extremely dangerous, and had to be carried on with great caution. It was large enough for a man to crawl through. It was worked by detail, and as the dirt was dug out of it, it was drawn to the mouth of the tunnel in an old haversack, and distributed over the bottom of the tent. At last it was completed, and the party was divided into squads of ten each. The squads were to make their exit on separate nights. After getting beyond the enclosure, each party was to choose its own mode of proceeding. The first party made the attempt. They were betrayed by a sentinel, whom some of them had most foolishly bribed, as there was no necessity for it. The alarm was given, and the prisoners who had succeeded in getting out had taken refuge behind the protecting banks of sand on the beach. As soon as the officers reached the spot, they called upon the prisoners to surrender, saying they would not be harmed. Major Patterson (the Provost-Marshal) stood at the gate, and as each prisoner came up, he deliberately shot at him. One was shot in the head, from which he never recovered, and the last account we had of him he was in a lunatic asylum. Another was shot in the shoulder, and another in the abdomen, from the effects of which he died. The remaining seven managed to get into the camp again, without being hurt, for which they could thank the darkness of the night. The tunnel was fired into several times, but no one was in it. The next day it was filled up, and the men in whose tent the opening had been made were confined in the guard house, on bread and water, for ten days. The shooting of these men was without any excuse whatever, as they had expressed a willingness to surrender, and were proceeding to do so; besides, it is a recognised principle that a prisoner of war has a right to escape if he can, and the capturing party has no right to punish, but simply to remand to proper custody. This event stopped all idea of escape for awhile, and we became resigned to our fate.

James T. Wells, 'Prison Experience', *Southern Historical Society Papers*, January 1879

'STARK-NAKED, HEAD-SHAVED-AND-BLISTERED'

In the early spring of 1884 I was transferred into an association dormitory of twelve beds – these being about four feet apart. In the bed next to mine was a prison genius named Heep, who was one of the most singular characters I ever met. As I shall have occasion to speak of him frequently up to the time of my release, I may as well give here a sketch of his life as related to me by himself. He was born in the town of Macclesfield, near Manchester, in 1852, of respectable mechanics, or trades-people as they are called in England. His father died when Heep was about five years of age, and after a time his mother married a carpenter and joiner of the place.

Young Heep was a lively child, up to all sorts of tricks, and does not remember the time since he could walk that he was not in some mischief, and, as he remarked, 'took to all sorts of deviltry as naturally as a duck to water.' As long as his own father lived there was not much check on his mischievous propensities, but his step-father proved to be a severe and stern judge, and brought him to book for every irregularity, thrashing him most unmercifully for each offence. His mother could not have filled her maternal duty very judiciously, judging from the fact that before he was twelve years old she set him to follow and watch his step-father to the house of a woman of whom she was jealous. The boy possessed great natural abilities, and in good hands would have turned out something different than a life-long prison drudge. He was handsome, genteel in appearance, an apt scholar, though very self-willed and headstrong, and as he grew up his naturally hot temper became uncontrollable. At an early age he had discovered that by threats of self-injury he could bend his parents to his wishes, but found in his step-father one who would put up with no nonsense: even when he cut himself so as to bleed freely, instead of the coveted indulgence it only procured him an additional thrashing.

At fifteen he had become ungovernable at home, and his father had him put in the county insane asylum, where he remained a year and a half. While there he caused so much trouble that the attendants were only too glad when he escaped and went to Liverpool. Here he succeeded in getting a situation with a dealer in bric-à-brac, rare books, and antiquities. In a short time the proprietor placed so much confidence in his integrity that he gave him the charge of his place during his own absences, and young Heep was not long in taking advantage of his position to rob his employer by taking a book or other article which he sold to some one of his master's customers. This went on for some time until on one occasion he took a book to a shop kept by a woman to whom he had previously sold several articles and offered it for a sovereign. She examined it and found that it was an ancient, illuminated Greek manuscript, worthy fifty times more than the price young Heep asked for it, and, suspecting something wrong, she told him to come again for the money the next evening. At the appointed time he entered the place and was confronted by his master, who contented himself with upbraiding him for his perfidy, and discharging him from his service.

At this period of his career he had contracted vicious habits, the most pernicious for him being that of drink, for when sober he was in his right mind, but the moment the drink was in – like Edgar A. Poe – his common sense departed, and he became a raving maniac, ready to fight or perpetrate any other act of folly.

Up to this time he had never associated with thieves, and had been tempted to steal only in order to supply means for improper indulgences.

Not long after being discharged from his situation he was found by the police acting in so insane a manner under the influence of drink, that the magistrate before whom he was taken had him sent to the Raynell lunatic asylum. Here, being perfectly reckless, he carried on all sorts of games which made him obnoxious, although making himself very useful in work which he liked, such as gardening, etc. He also took up fancy painting and soon became a skilful copyist of prints of any description, enlarging or reducing, and painting them in oil or water colours. He also became a good decorator and scene-painter, besides devoting time to various studies, including music.

At last he found means to effect his escape and lay in hiding until night, then as he had on the asylum clothes, which would betray him, he went back and got in through the window of the tailors' shop, which was in an isolated building, and exchanged the clothes he had on for a suit belonging to one of the attendants. Thinking himself now safe from recognition he started off across the country, but had not gone more than twenty miles when, in passing through a small town, a policeman who had just heard of the escape from Raynell, arrested him on suspicion.

The Raynell authorities sent some one to identify him; he was taken back, tried on the charge of stealing the attendant's suit of clothes, which he still had on, was convicted by the usual 'intelligent' jury and sentenced to five years penal servitude.

Let the reader mark this and what follows, then compare it with the fact that *no person certified by the doctors to be of unsound mind can according to English law be tried for any offence whatever*. He finished his term of imprisonment at Chatham and instead of being set at liberty was sent under guard back to the asylum!

According to English law, if a person confined in a lunatic asylum escapes and keeps away fourteen days he cannot after that be arrested, until he commits fresh acts of insanity.

After several futile attempts he at last made good his escape and obtained work with a farmer, where he remained safe for thirteen days, and was congratulating himself that in less than another day he would be free, when his thoughts were broken off by the appearance of two attendants who seized and carried him back to the asylum.

The events above narrated had driven him into a state of desperation at what he felt to be gross injustice, and he carried on in such a way that the doctor ordered his head to be shaved and blistered as a punishment, the strait-jacket and all other coersive measures having been of no avail. The night watchmen had orders to watch him closely, but he kept so sharp an eye on the watchman that he caught him asleep, and creeping to the closet window, which he had previously tampered with, crept out, and after climbing the low wall found himself on a raw November night, with the rain falling in torrents, a stark-naked, head-shaved-and-blistered, but once more a free man. In this condition he wandered on throughout the night, and just before daylight he entered a cemetery to find that refuge among the dead of which he thought himself so cruelly deprived by the living.

Beneath the entrance to the church there was a passage which led to some family vaults in the basement, and he crept down the passage to seek some shelter for his nude body from the driving rain, which had chilled him through. While groping about in the dark his hand rested on something soft, which, to his unbounded delight, proved to be an old coat which had probably been left there by the sexton, and forgotten. He remained hidden all day, and travelled through the fields all night, during which he found a scarecrow, from which he transferred to his own person its old hat and trousers.

He said that although so hungry, he never had felt so happy as he did at finding himself once more 'dressed up'. After proceeding a few miles farther, he ventured into a labourer's cottage in quest of food, which was given him, and with it a pair of old boots. As dilapidated, ragged, vagabond-looking, honest people are common in England, no questions were asked, and he proceeded on his way, rejoicing in that freedom of which he had been deprived for ten years or more.

George Bidwell, *Forging his Chains*, 1888

WHISKEY AND URINE

The next day, our dinner was no sooner served than we put together our great rope ladder; we afterwards hid it under our beds, that the turnkey might not perceive it when he brought us our supper. (An officer had searched us in the morning.) We then arranged our wooden ladder, and made every thing else up into little packages, quite certain that nobody would come to visit us before five o'clock, according to custom. The two iron bars which were necessary to us were taken out and put into their cases, that in moving them we might make no noise, and use them more conveniently. We had taken care to have a bottle of usquebaugh to warm and refresh us in case of being obliged to work in the water. This succour became very necessary, for without it we should never have been able to remain in ice-water up to the neck during six hours.

The dangerous moment now arrived. – As soon as our supper was served, notwithstanding the rheumatism which I had in my left arm, I climbed the chimney and it was with the greatest difficulty I got to the top: I was near being stifled with soot; for I was not aware of the precaution used by chimney-sweepers of covering their elbows, girding their loins, and putting something over their heads, to guarantee them from the dust of chimnies. Therefore all the skin of my elbows and knees was rubbed off: the blood from elbows ran down to my hands, and that from my knees down to my ancles. At length I arrived at the chimney top; I set myself astride it and let down a ball of packthread which I had in my pocket, at the end of which it was agreed that my comrade should tie the strongest cord which was attached to my portmanteau: by this means I drew it up to me and let it down upon the platform. I let down the cord again to my companion who tied it to the wooden ladder. I afterwards drew up in the same manner the two iron bars, and all the other things of which we were in need. After this I let down my cord again, to get up the rope ladder: I left my comrade enough of it to get up the chimney more commodiously than I had done. I kept the ladder steady whilst he ascended, and he got to me easily enough; we drew up the rest of the ladder, and that part of it which my comrade had just made use of, on being thrown across the chimney, served to let us both down at once upon the platform, serving as a counter-poise to each other.

Two horses would not have been able to carry all our apparatus: we began to roll up our rope ladder, which made a volume of five feet high, and a foot thick: we rolled it upon that tower of the treasury which we judged most favourable to our descent. We fixed this ladder to a piece of canon, and afterwards let it gently down into the fosse. We fixed our pully also; and ran through it our rope of three hundred and sixty feet long. After having brought all our packages to this side, I tied my self fast by the thigh to the end of the pulley cord: I got upon the ladder; and, as I descended from round to round, my comrade let go the rope. Notwithstanding this precaution, at every motion my body seemed like a paper-kite in the air; and, to such a degree, that if a like adventure had happened in the day time amongst a thousand persons, who would have seen me float in the air, I firmly believe that not one of them would have refused to offer up prayers to heaven for my safety. At length I arrived safe in the fosse. My companion immediately let down my portmanteau, the iron bars, the wooden ladder, and all our equipage, which I placed, in the dry, upon a little eminence which commanded the water in the fosse about the tower. Dalégre then tied himself by the knee to the other end of the pulley-cord; and, when he had made me the signal of his being upon the ladder, I made below the same manœuvre which he had made above to support me in the air, in case I had lost hold of the ladder. I took care even to put the two last rounds between my thighs, and thus seating myself, I spared him the floating which I had experienced. He arrived safe; and, during all this time, the centinel was not more than ten fathoms length from us, and, as it did not rain, walking upon the Corridor – This would have prevented us from getting up to it to go into the garden, as we had at first designed to do; we therefore found ourselves obliged to make use of our iron bars: I took one upon my shoulder with the wimble, and my companion took the other. I did not forget to put the bottle of usquebaugh into my pocket, and we went straight to the wall which separates the fosse of the Bastille, from that of the gate Saint Antoine, between the garden and the Governor's house. In this place there had formerly been a little fosse, a fathom wide, and one or two feet deep: here the water was up to our arm-pits.

The moment I began with the wimble to make a hole between two stones, to introduce our levers, the Round Major passed by with his great lantern, at the distance of ten or twelve feet over our heads. To prevent our being discovered, we sunk up to our chins in the water. As soon as the Major had passed, I made two or three little holes with my wimble, and we took out the great stone we had begun with. From this moment I assured Dalégre of our success: I drank some usquebaugh, and made him do the same: we attacked a second stone, and afterwards a third. A second Round came by, and we sunk down again until the water was up to our chins. We were obliged to repeat this ceremony every half hour when the Round came by, and always at the same distance.

Before midnight, we had pulled out upwards of ten cart-loads of stone. The reader may perhaps believe, that what I am going to relate is on purpose to make him laugh; but it is, however, strictly true. Having heard the centinel walk over our heads, the rubbish which we had drawn round the hole obliged us to sink down into the water a little behind it: the centinel stopped short: we thought he had heard or seen something, and that we were undone; but an instant afterwards he made water precisely upon my head. When he was gone, I told my companion what had happened; adding, that had he performed another ceremony upon my nose, he would not have made me break silence. We then drank some usquebaugh to recover us from our fear. Finally, in less than six hours we had pierced this wall, which, according to the Major's account, is more than four feet and an half thick. The moment after we had made the hole quite through, I told Dalégre to go out and wait for me on the other side; and that, if unhappily anything happened to me in going to fetch the portmanteau, to make off upon hearing the least noise: no accident, however, befel me: I brought the portmanteau; he drew it through the hole, and I got out, abandoning everything else without regret.

Both of us being in the great fosse of the gate Saint Antoine, we thought ourselves out of danger: Dalégre held one end of my portmanteau, and I the other, to get into the road to Bercy. Scarcely had we made fifty steps before we fell into an aqueduct which is in the middle of the great fosse: we had, at least, six feet water above our heads. My companion, instead of reaching the other side (the aqueduct is but six feet wide) quitted the portmanteau to get hold of me. Finding myself entangled, I gave a great kick, and made him let go his hold; at the same time I grappled the other side; and, putting my arm into the water, I caught his hair, and drew him to me, and afterwards my portmanteau, which had swam. This is the last place wherein we were in danger; and here finished this terrible night.

Memoirs of Henry Masers de Latude, during a Confinement of Thirty-five Years in the State Prisons of France, English trans. 1787

A BROKEN KNIFE

I immediately made the trial if it was possible to rid myself of my irons, and luckily broke the iron off the right hand, although the blood ran under my nails; but could not get off that from my left; yet with some pieces of the brick of my seat I hammered so fortunately against the peg of my handcuff, which was but negligently fastened, that I got it out, and thus freed both my arms.

To the ring round my body there was only one hasp, fastened to the chain of my arm-bar. I opposed my foot to the wall, and found I could bend it. There now remained the principal chain between the wall and my feet; nature had given me strength; I twisted it across, sprang with force back from the wall, and two links instantly gave way.

Free from chains, I fancied myself already happy, went to the door, felt for the points of the nails with which the lock was fastened on the outside, and found that I had not a great deal of wood to cut out. I immediately took my knife, made a small hole through, discovered that the oak boards were only one inch thick, and that there was a possibility of opening all the four doors in the space of one day. Full of hope, I returned to put on my irons; but what difficulty had I here to surmount!

The broken links I found after a long search, and threw them into my night-stool; fortunately for me that nobody visited it, not even until the day of my attempt, because they suspected nothing. With a piece of my hair ribbon I bound the chain together; but when I wanted to put the irons on my hands, they were so swelled that every attempt was in vain; I worked the whole night, but to no purpose.

Twelve o'clock, the visiting hour, approached; necessity and danger urged me on; fresh attempts were made, with incredible torments; and when my keepers entered everything was in proper order.

I found it impossible to get my tortured hand out again for some time.

On the fourth of July, as soon as the doors were shut, all my fetters were laid off, and with my knife I commenced this Herculean labour.

In less than an hour the first door was opened; but, O heavens, what hardships did I meet with in the second! The lock was soon cut round, but as the bar was fastened to it, and it opened on the outside, there was no other method than by cutting through the door above the bar. This, with great labour, I likewise accomplished, but found it the more difficult as everything was to be done by groping in the dark. My fingers were all wounds, the sweat streamed on the ground, and the raw flesh hung bleeding to my hands.

I now found daylight, and climbed over the half door. In the antechamber was a small window; I got up, and saw that my prison was in the main ditch. I perceived the entry to it, and the guard about fifty yards from me; likewise the high palisades which were in front of my jail, and which I must climb over before I could gain the rampart. My hopes increased, and my labour was doubled when I arrived at the third door, which was similar to the first, and only required the lock to be cut round. The sun was setting when I had finished this. The fourth was to be operated upon like the second; my strength had almost failed me, and the lacerated state of my hands banished all my hopes.

After I had rested awhile I made another attack, and the aperture was finished within a foot, when my knife broke, and the blade fell to the ground.

Was there ever any creature more justifiable in despair than myself at this moment? The moon shone bright; I looked steadfastly towards heaven, fell upon my weary knees, sought new courage and comfort, but found none either in religion or philosophy.

Without accusing Providence – without the smallest fear for my defeat, or for the justice of a God who is the disposer of our fate, and who had given me but manly strength in circumstances which far surpassed this strength, I recommended myself to the Judge of Death, seized the broken piece of my knife, and cut the veins of my left arm and foot, sat down quietly in a corner of my jail, and suffered my blood to flow.

Memoirs of Frederick Baron Trenck, English trans. 1881

DISGUST

In my cell, it was without any sense of triumph that I realised I had again survived a Gestapo beating. Lying on the pallet, everything that my body touched contributed to the throbbing pain that spread from head to foot. Running my tongue across my bleeding gums, I felt, without any emotion, that four of my teeth had been knocked out. My face felt inhuman, an ugly, bloody, distorted mask. I realised that another beating would probably kill me and I burned with humiliation and impotent rage.

I knew that I had arrived at the end. That I should never be free again, that I should not survive another beating, and that in order to escape the degradation of betraying my friends while I was half-conscious, the only thing for me to do was to use the razor blade and to take my own life.

I had often wondered what people had in mind when they died for an ideal. I was certain that they were absorbed by great, soaring thoughts about the cause for which they were about to die. I was frankly surprised when I discovered it was not so. I felt only overwhelming hatred and disgust which surpassed even my physical pain.

And I thought of my mother. My childhood, my career, my hopes. I felt a bottomless sorrow that I had to die a wretched, inglorious death, like a crushed insect, miserable and anonymous. Neither my family nor my friends would ever learn what had happened to me and where my body would lie. I had assumed so many aliases that even if the Nazis wished to inform anyone of my death they probably could not track down my real identity.

I lay down on the pallet, awaiting the hour when the Slovak would complete his rounds. Till then my purpose seemed to have formed itself. I had hardly reasoned or reflected, merely acted on the promptings of pain and the desire to escape, to die. I thought of my religious convictions and the undeniable guilt which would be mine. But the memory of the last beating was too vivid. One phrase dominated my mind. I am disgusted, I am disgusted.

The guard had finished his rounds. I took out the razor and cut into my right wrist. The pain was not great. Obviously, I hadn't hurt the vein. I tried again, this time lower, this time cutting back and forth as hard as I could. Suddenly the blood streamed like a fountain. I knew I had got it this time. Then, clutching the razor in my bleeding right hand, I cut the vein on the left wrist. This time it was easier. I lay on my bed with my arms outstretched at my sides. The blood spurted out evenly, forming pools beside my legs. In a few minutes I felt I was getting weaker. In a haze I realised that the blood had stopped flowing and that I was still alive. In fear of being unsuccessful, I flung my arms about to make them bleed again. The blood flowed in thick streams. I felt as though I were suffocating and tried to draw breath through my mouth. I became nauseous, retched, and vomited. Then I lost consciousness.

Jan Karski, *Story of a Secret State*, 1944

'MORE FIERY THAN WHEN HE WAS IN HEALTH'

The castellan, meanwhile, ill and afflicted as he was, had himself transported to my prison, and exclaimed: 'You see that I have recaptured you!' 'Yes,' said I, 'but you see that I escaped, as I told you I would. And if I had not been sold by a Venetian cardinal, under Papal guarantee, for the price of a bishopric, the Pope a Roman and a Farnese (and both of them have scratched with impious hands the face of the most sacred laws), you would not have recovered me. But now that they have opened this vile way of dealing, do you the worst you can in your turn; I care for nothing in the world.' The wretched man began shouting at the top of his voice: 'Ah, woe is me! woe is me! It is all the same to this fellow whether he lives or dies, and behold, he is more fiery than when he was in health. Put him down there below the garden, and do not speak to me of him again, for he is the destined cause of my death.'

So I was taken into a gloomy dungeon below the level of a garden, which swam with water, and was full of big spiders and many venomous worms. They flung me a wretched mattress of coarse hemp, gave me no supper, and locked four doors upon me. In that condition I abode until the nineteenth hour of the following day. Then I received food, and I requested my jailers to give me some of my books to read. None of them spoke a word, but they referred my prayer to the unfortunate castellan, who had made inquiries concerning what I said. Next morning they brought me an Italian Bible which belonged to me, and a copy of the Chronicles of Giovanni Villani. When I asked for certain other of my books, I was told that I could have no more, and that I had got too many already.

Thus, then, I continued to exist in misery upon that rotten mattress, which in three days soaked up water like a sponge. I could hardly stir because of my broken leg; and when I had to get out of bed to obey a call of nature, I crawled on all fours with extreme distress, in order not to foul the place I slept in. For one hour and a half each day I got a little glimmering of light, which penetrated that unhappy cavern through a very narrow aperture. Only for so short a space of time could I read; the rest of the day and night I abode in darkness, enduring my lot, nor ever without meditations upon God and on our human frailty. I thought it certain that a few more days would put an end to my unlucky life in that sad place and in that miserable manner. Nevertheless, as well as I was able, I comforted my soul by calling to mind how much more painful it would have been, on passing from this life, to have suffered that unimaginable horror of the hangman's knife. Now, being as I was, I should depart with the anodyne of sleepiness, which robbed death of half its former terrors. Little by little I felt my vital forces waning, until at last my vigorous temperament had become adapted to that purgatory. When I felt it quite acclimatised, I resolved to put up with all those indescribable discomforts so long as it held out.

I began the Bible from the commencement, reading and reflecting on it so devoutly, and finding in it such deep treasures of delight, that, if I had been able, I should have done naught else but study it. However, light was wanting; and the thought of all my troubles kept recurring and gnawing at me in the darkness, until I often made my mind up to put an end somehow to my own life. They did not allow me a knife, however, and so it was no easy matter to commit suicide. Once, notwithstanding, I took and propped a wooden pole I found there, in position like a trap. I meant to make it topple over on my head, and it would certainly have dashed my brains out; but when I had arranged the whole machine, and was approaching to put it in motion, just at the moment of my setting my hand to it, I was seized by an invisible power and flung four cubits from the spot, in such a terror that I lay half dead. Like that I remained from dawn until the nineteenth hour, when they brought my food. The jailers must have visited my cell several times without my taking notice of them; for when at last I heard them, Captain Sandrino Monaldi had entered, and I heard him saying: 'Ah, unhappy man! behold the end to which so rare a genius has come!' Roused by these words, I opened my eyes, and caught sight of priests with long gowns on their backs, who were saying: 'Oh, you told us he was dead!' Bozza replied: 'Dead I found him, and therefore I told you so.' Then they lifted me from where I lay, and after shaking up the mattress, which was now as soppy as a dish of macaroni, they flung it outside the dungeon. The castellan, when these things were reported to him, sent me another mattress. Thereafter, when I searched my memory to find what could have diverted me from the design of suicide, I came to the conclusion that it must have been some power divine and my good guardian angel.

The Life of Benvenuto Cellini, trans. John Addington Symonds, 1888

THIRTEEN

'The love of life prevailed'

There, in the sheep-pen, I remained for the night, an object lesson to my fellow-prisoners of what they might expect, should they, in their turn, attempt to escape. Perhaps I could not do better now than state how deplorable my condition *appeared* to them. I quote from *The Black Hole of the Desert*, a book published by Messrs Hodder and Stoughton, and written from the diary of Allen, my Yeoman of Signals. I will begin from the beginning, as it gives a good idea of what had occurred at Bir Hakkim during my absence:

At about 6.30 p.m., on Saturday night, February 20th, just before the moon came up, our Captain made his escape. He got clear away without being detected. Some few of us knew that he was going and fully understood the perils he would have to encounter. We prayed earnestly to our Heavenly Father to protect and guide his footsteps. The distance, we believed, was by the quickest route seventy-five miles. The next day our captors were unaware what had happened, and we had hopes that our Captain would not fail. Unfortunately, the following day our interpreter became ill with an ulcer on the back, which caused him to keep his tent. The man in charge of the wells (Holy Joe), wishing to speak to him, entered the officers' tent at 8.30 a.m., and, on looking round, missed the face of the 'Captain'. He at once told Salem Affendi (Selim), who visited each tent on the pretext of seeing the sick. It was the first time any of our captors had troubled their heads about them. All of us were fallen in and counted, and soldiers were sent off in all directions to search for the Captain. There was great excitement, and extra sentries were put on, even some of the women strutting about with rifles in their hands. At midnight on the 23rd, Salem Affendi hurried away. [*Note:* he did not arrive at Gweider until the afternoon of the 27th, so probably he did some searching of his own on the way], and we were told by the Sergeant left in charge that he had gone to bring our Captain back, as he had been captured near the Italian frontier. [*Note:* An obvious lie, but the Senoussi probably thought that I had made for Tobruk, which was nearer than Sollum.] We did not believe it, and anxiously watched the sky for the signal of the searchlights . . .

On February 26th, four days after his escape, there was still no news of him. Meanwhile our food was reduced to four ounces of rice per man, and three days later there was no rice at all. In desperation we all fell in to see the Sergeant in charge, and ask for more food. The movement was made too suddenly for the guard. The whole lot of them took alarm, and, rushing out of their tents, opened fire on us with their rifles. Fortunately their aim was very bad, and no one was hit.

We appealed to the Sergeant, who promised us that on Monday, two days later, he would march us to a place where there was some food. Monday arrived, but there was no march, no food, and no news from the Captain . . .

The next day all our slender hopes came crashing down. At three o'clock in the afternoon we heard a series of rifle shots to the north. The guard were fallen in and marched off in that direction. A few minutes later there appeared over the brow of a small hill some men and camels, and there, walking apart from the rest, was our brave Captain. We were now witnesses of one of the most degrading spectacles it has been my lot to see. When the guard of the Senoussi reached our Captain they punched with their fists until his face was streaming with blood. He was struck with their rifles until he was nearly unconscious. The man in charge of the well lashed him with an elephant-thong whip. Soon afterwards up came the black women with large stones. They ran close up to him and hurled them in his face. Of course, we were powerless to interfere. They made him sleep in the sheep-pen that night, with a guard standing over him . . .

This, no doubt, to the reader, will all sound terrible enough, and the spectacle no doubt succeeded for the time being in effecting the purpose it was intended to have, namely, to discount future rash attempts to escape. But, as a matter of hard fact, my public punishment did not *really* amount to much. After my two-hundred mile walk, and the days of agony from blistered and bleeding feet, one hardly noticed a little thing like a whip. The blood seen streaming from my face was, I fancy, mostly sweat, and the black ladies' stones were as ill-aimed as they were ill-intentioned; and after the tragedy, as always, came the comedy!

For all that the other prisoners' eyes could see, I passed that night in the sheep-pen, bruised, hungry, and half naked; but as soon as it was fully dark, so that prying eyes could no longer observe what happened, my clothes and bernous were restored to me, two mats were placed at my disposal, one to lie upon and the other with which to form a roof, and, what was more important still, I was given water and a liberal supply of dates!

With a thankful heart, and a mouth still full of date-stones, I was fast asleep in a few minutes.

In an hour or so's time I was wakened by Mahmoud, the black-faced, bright-eyed, merry little nine-year-old body-servant of Selim. The sentry had kindled a bright fire to warm me, and I saw by its light that in his hand Mahmoud held out a huge bowl of rice. He was, for the time being, my black fairy god-mother, and he watched delightedly while I ate, obviously taking as much interest in the proceedings as I myself did. This rice was, in fact, Selim's own supper, and so liberal was my helping, that, for the first and last time as a prisoner, I was unable to consume it all. Such affluence amazed me, and like a fool, I left some of the rice in the bottom of the bowl, instead of putting it in my pocket, an omission of which I was often to think regretfully in still hungrier days.

Before I finally closed my eyes, the sentry who had so ostentatiously loaded his rifle, gave me one of his own rare cigarettes to smoke. Such is the Arab character!

Captain R. S. Gwatkin-Williams, *Prisoners of the Red Desert*, 1919

CHILDREN'S BONES

4 ¶ Then the presidents and princes sought to find occasion against Daniel concerning the kingdom; but they could find none occasion nor fault; forasmuch as he *was* faithful, neither was there any error or fault found in him.

5 Then said these men, We shall not find any occasion against this Daniel, except we find *it* against him concerning the law of his God.

6 Then these presidents and princes assembled together to the king, and said thus unto him, King Darius, live for ever.

7 All the presidents of the kingdom, the governors, and the princes, the counsellers, and the captains, have consulted together to establish a royal statute, and to make a firm decree, that whosoever shall ask a petition of any God or man for thirty days, save of thee, O king, he shall be cast into the den of lions.

8 Now, O king, establish the decree, and sign the writing, that it be not changed, according to the law of the Medes and Persians, which altereth not.

9 Wherefore king Darius signed the writing and the decree.

10 ¶ Now when Daniel knew that the writing was signed, he went into his house; and his windows being open in his chamber toward Jerusalem, he kneeled upon his knees three times a day, and prayed, and gave thanks before his God, as he did aforetime.

11 Then these men assembled, and found Daniel praying and making supplication before his God.

12 Then they came near, and spake before the king concerning the king's decree; Hast thou not signed a decree, that every man that shall ask *a petition* of any God or man within thirty days, save of thee, O king, shall be cast into the den of lions? The king answered and said,

[304]

The thing *is* true, according to the law of the Medes and Persians, which altereth not.

13 Then answered they and said before the king, That Daniel, which *is* of the children of the captivity of Judah, regardeth not thee, O king, nor the decree that thou hast signed, but maketh his petition three times a day.

14 Then the king, when he heard *these* words, was sore displeased with himself, and set *his* heart on Daniel to deliver him: and he laboured till the going down of the sun to deliver him.

15 Then these men assembled unto the king, and said unto the king, Know, O king, that the law of the Medes and Persians *is*, That no decree nor statute which the king establisheth may be changed.

16 Then the king commanded, and they brought Daniel, and cast *him* into the den of lions. *Now* the king spake and said unto Daniel, Thy God whom thou servest continually, he will deliver thee.

17 And a stone was brought, and laid upon the mouth of the den; and the king sealed it with his own signet, and with the signet of his lords; that the purpose might not be changed concerning Daniel.

18 ¶ Then the king went to his palace, and passed the night fasting: neither were instruments of musick brought before him: and his sleep went from him.

19 Then the king arose very early in the morning, and went in haste unto the den of lions.

20 And when he came to the den, he cried with a lamentable voice unto Daniel: *and* the king spake and said to Daniel, O Daniel, servant of the living God, is thy God, whom thou servest continually, able to deliver thee from the lions?

21 Then said Daniel unto the king, O king, live for ever.

22 My God hath sent his angel, and hath shut the lions' mouths, that they have not hurt me: forasmuch as before him innocency was found in me: and also before thee, O king, have I done no hurt.

23 Then was the king exceeding glad for him, and commanded that they should take Daniel up out of the den. So Daniel was taken up out of the den, and no manner of hurt was found upon him, because he believed in his God.

24 ¶ And the king commanded, and they brought those men which had accused Daniel, and they cast *them* into the den of lions, them, their children, and their wives; and the lions had the mastery of them, and brake all their bones in pieces or ever they came at the bottom of the den.

Daniel 6: 4–24

Apion, who was called Plistonices, was a man widely versed in letters, and possessing an extensive and varied knowledge of things Greek. In his works, which are recognised as of no little repute, is contained an account of almost all the remarkable things which are to be seen and heard in Egypt. Now, in his account of what he professes either to have heard or read he is perhaps too verbose through a reprehensible love of display – for he is a great self-advertiser in parading his learning; but this incident, which he describes in the fifth book of his *Wonders of Egypt* he declares that he neither heard nor read, but saw himself with his own eyes in the city of Rome.

'In the Great Circus,' he says, 'a battle with wild beasts on a grand scale was being exhibited to the people. Of that spectacle, since I chanced to be in Rome, I was,' he says, 'an eye-witness. There were many savage wild beasts, brutes remarkable for their huge size, and all of uncommon appearance or unusual ferocity. But beyond all others,' says he, 'did the vast size of the lions excite wonder, and one of these in particular surpassed all the rest. This one lion had drawn to himself the attention and eyes of all because of the activity and huge size of his body, his terrific and deep roar, the development of his muscles, and the mane streaming over his shoulders. There was brought in, among many others who had been condemned to fight with the wild beasts, the slave of an ex-consul; the slave's name was Androclus. When that lion saw him from a distance,' says Apion, 'he stopped short as if in amazement, and then approached the man slowly and quietly, as if he recognised him. Then, wagging his tail in a mild and caressing way, after the manner and fashion of fawning dogs, he came close to the man, who was now half dead from fright, and gently licked his feet and hands. The man Androclus, while submitting to the caresses of so fierce a beast, regained his lost courage and gradually turned his eyes to look at the lion. Then,' says Apion, 'you might have seen man and lion exchange joyful greetings, as if they had recognised each other.'

He says that at this sight, so truly astonishing, the people broke out into mighty shouts; and Gaius Caesar called Androclus to him and inquired the reason why that fiercest of lions had spared him alone. Then Androclus related a strange and surprising story, 'My master,' said he, 'was governing Africa with proconsular authority. While there, I was forced by his undeserved and daily floggings to run away, and that my hiding-places might be safer from my master, the ruler of that country, I took refuge in lonely plains and deserts, intending, if food should fail me, to seek death in some form. Then,' said he, 'when the midday sun was fierce and scorching, finding a remote and secluded cavern, I entered it, and hid myself. Not long afterwards this lion came to the same cave with one paw lame and bleeding, making known by groans and moans the torturing pain of his wound.' And then, at the first sight of the approaching lion, Androclus said that his mind was overwhelmed with fear and dread. 'But when the lion,' said he, 'had entered what was evidently his own lair, and saw me cowering at a distance, he approached me mildly and gently, and lifting up his foot, was evidently showing it to me and holding it out as if to ask for help. Then,' said he, 'I drew out a huge splinter that was embedded in the sole of the foot, squeezed out the pus that had formed in the interior of the wound, wiped away the blood, and dried it thoroughly, being now free from any great feeling of fear. Then, relieved by that attention and treatment of mine, the lion, putting his paw in my hand, lay down and went to sleep, and for three whole years from that day the lion and I lived in the same cave, and on the same food as well. For he used to bring for me to the cave the choicest parts of the game which he took in hunting, which I, having no means of making a fire, dried in the noonday sun and ate. But,' said he, 'after I had finally grown tired of that wild life, I left the cave when the lion had gone off to hunt, and after travelling nearly three days, I was seen and caught by some soldiers and taken from Africa to Rome to my master. He at once had me condemned to death by being thrown to the wild beasts. But,' said he, 'I perceive that this lion was also captured, after I left him, and that he is now requiting me for my kindness and my cure of him.'

Apion records that Androclus told this story and that when it had been made known to the people by being written out in full on a tablet and carried about the Circus, at the request of all Androclus was freed, acquitted and presented with the lion by vote of the people. 'Afterwards,' said he, 'we used to see Androclus with the lion, attached to a slender leash, making the rounds of the shops throughout the city; Androclus was given money, the lion was sprinkled with flowers, and everyone who met them anywhere exclaimed: "This is the lion that was a man's friend, this is the man who was physician to a lion." '

Aulus Gellius, *Attic Nights*, trans. John C. Rolfe, 1961

'Can that winch handle him?' said Brody.

'Seems to be. It'd never haul him out of the water, but I bet it'll bring him up to us.' The winch was turning slowly, humming, taking a full turn every three or four seconds. The rope quivered under the strain, scattering drops of water on Quint's shirt.

Suddenly the rope started coming too fast. It fouled on the winch, coiling in snarls. The boat snapped upright.

'Rope break?' said Brody.

'Shit no!' said Quint, and now Brody saw fear in his face. 'The sonofabitch is coming up!' He dashed to the controls and threw the engine into forward. But it was too late.

The fish broke water right beside the boat, with a great rushing whoosh of noise. It rose vertically, and in an instant of horror Brody gasped at the size of the body. Towering overhead, it blocked out the light. The pectoral fins hovered like wings, stiff and straight, and as the fish fell forward, they seemed to be reaching out to Brody.

The fish landed on the stern of the boat with a shattering crash, driving the boat beneath the waves. Water poured in over the transom. In seconds, Quint and Brody were standing in water up to their hips.

The fish lay there, its jaw not three feet from Brody's chest. The body twitched, and in the black eye, as big as a baseball, Brody thought he saw his own image reflected.

'God damn your black soul!' screamed Quint. 'You sunk my boat!' A barrel floated into the cockpit, the rope writhing like a gathering of worms. Quint grabbed the harpoon dart at the end of the rope and, with his hand, plunged it into the soft white belly of the fish. Blood poured from the wound and bathed Quint's hands.

The boat was sinking. The stern was completely submerged, and the bow was rising.

The fish rolled off the stern and slid beneath the waves. The rope, attached to the dart Quint had stuck into the fish, followed.

Suddenly, Quint lost his footing and fell backward into the water. 'The knife!' he cried, lifting his left leg above the surface, and Brody saw the rope coiled around Quint's foot.

Brody looked to the starboard gunwale. The knife was there, embedded in the wood. He lunged for it, wrenched it free, and turned back, struggling to run in the deepening water. He could not move fast enough. He watched in helpless terror as Quint, reaching towards him

with grasping fingers, eyes wide and pleading, was pulled sl●
into the dark water.

For a moment there was silence, except for the sucking sound of ●
boat slipping gradually down. The water was up to Brody's shoulders,
and he clung desperately to the gin pole. A seat cushion popped to the
surface next to him, and Brody grabbed it. ('They'd hold you up all
right,' Brody remembered Hendricks saying, 'if you were an eight-year-
old boy.')

Brody saw the tail and dorsal fin break the surface twenty yards
away. The tail waved once left, once right, and the dorsal fin moved
closer. 'Get away, damn you!' Brody yelled.

The fish kept coming, barely moving, closing in. The barrels and
skeins of rope trailed behind.

The gin pole went under, and Brody let go of it. He tried to kick over
to the bow of the boat, which was almost vertical now. Before he could
reach it, the bow raised even higher, then quickly and soundlessly slid
beneath the surface.

Brody clutched the cushion, and he found that by holding it in front
of him, his forearms across it, and by kicking constantly, he could stay
afloat without exhausting himself.

The fish came closer. It was only a few feet away, and Brody could
see the conical snout. He screamed, an ejaculation of hopelessness, and
closed his eyes, waiting for an agony he could not imagine.

Nothing happened. He opened his eyes. The fish was nearly touching
him, only a foot or two away, but it had stopped. And then, as Brody
watched, the steel-grey body began to recede downward into the
gloom. It seemed to fall away, an apparition evanescing into darkness.

Brody put his face into the water and opened his eyes. Through the
stinging saltwater mist he saw the fish sink in a slow and graceful spiral,
trailing behind it the body of Quint – arms out to the sides, head
thrown back, mouth open in mute protest.

The fish faded from view. But, kept from sinking into the deep by the
bobbing barrels, it stopped somewhere beyond the reach of light, and
Quint's body hung suspended, a shadow twirling slowly in the
twilight.

Brody watched until his lungs ached for air. He raised his head,
cleared his eyes, and sighted in the distance the black point of the water
tower. Then he began to kick towards shore.

Peter Benchley, *Jaws*, 1974

e 10th. Wind ESE. Fresh gales and fair weather,
)f much sea, which, by breaking almost constantly
e us miserably wet, and we had much cold to endure

I suffered great sickness from the oily nature of part
of the ___ of the fish, which had fallen to my share at dinner. At
sun-set I served an allowance of bread and water for supper. In the
morning, after a very bad night, I could see an alteration for the worse
in more than half my people. The usual allowance was served for
breakfast and dinner. At noon I found our situation to be in latitude
9°16'S; longitude from the north part of New Holland 12°1'W; course
since yesterday noon W ½ S, distance 111 miles.

Thursday, June the 11th. Fresh gales and fair weather. Wind SE and
SSE.

Birds and rock-weed showed that we were not far from land; but I
expected such signs must be here, as there are many islands between the
east part of Timor and New Guinea. I however hoped to fall in with
Timor every hour, for I had great apprehensions that some of my
people could not hold out. An extreme weakness, swelled legs, hollow
and ghastly countenances, great propensity to sleep, with an apparent
debility of understanding, seemed to me melancholy presages of their
approaching dissolution. The surgeon and Lebogue, in particular,
were most miserable objects. I occasionally gave them a few tea-
spoonfuls of wine, out of the little I had saved for this dreadful stage,
which no doubt greatly helped to support them.

For my own part, a great share of spirits, with the hopes of being able
to accomplish the voyage, seemed to be my principal support; but the
boatswain very innocently told me, that he really thought I looked
worse than any one in the boat. The simplicity with which he uttered
such an opinion diverted me, and I had good humour enough to return
him a better compliment.

Every one received his 25th of a pound of bread, and quarter of a
pint of water, at evening, morning, and noon, and an extra allowance
of water was given to those who desired it.

At noon I observed in latitude 9°41'S; course S 77° W; distance 109
miles; longitude made 13° 49' W. I had little doubt of having now
passed the meridian of the eastern part of Timor, which is laid down in
128° E. This diffused universal joy and satisfaction.

Friday, June the 12th. Fresh breezes and fine weather, but very hazy. Wind from E to SE.

All the afternoon we had several gannets, and many other birds, about us, that indicated we were near land, and at sun-set we kept a very anxious look-out. In the evening we caught a booby, which I reserved for our dinner the next day.

At three in the morning, with an excess of joy, we discovered Timor bearing from WSW to WNW, and I hauled on a wind to the NNE till day-light, when the land bore from SW by S about two leagues to NE by N seven leagues.

It is not possible for me to describe the pleasure which the blessing of the sight of land diffused among us. It appeared scarce credible, that in an open boat, and so poorly provided, we should have been able to reach the coast of Timor in forty-one days after leaving Tofoa, having in that time run, by our log, a distance of 3618 miles, and that, notwithstanding our extreme distress, no one should have perished in the voyage.

Lieutenant William Bligh, *A Narrative of the Mutiny on Board his Majesty's Ship 'Bounty'*, 1790

ONE MORE NIGHT

That day and the following day passed for us in a sort of nightmare. Our mouths were dry and our tongues were swollen. The wind was still strong and the heavy sea forced us to navigate carefully, but any thought of our peril from the waves was buried beneath the consciousness of our raging thirst. The bright moments were those when we each received our one mug of hot milk during the long, bitter watches of the night. Things were bad for us in those days, but the end was coming. The morning of May 8 broke thick and stormy, with squalls from the north-west. We searched the waters ahead for a sign of land, and though we could see nothing more than had met our eyes for many days, we were cheered by a sense that the goal was near at hand. About ten o'clock that morning we passed a little bit of kelp, a glad signal of the proximity of land. An hour later we saw two shags sitting on a big mass of kelp, and knew then that we must be within ten or fifteen miles of the shore. These birds are as sure an indication of the proximity of land as a lighthouse is, for they never venture far to sea. We gazed ahead with increasing eagerness, and at 12.30 p.m., through a rift in the clouds, McCarthy caught a glimpse of the black cliffs of South Georgia, just fourteen days after our departure from Elephant Island. It was a glad moment. Thirst-ridden, chilled, and weak as we were, happiness irradiated us. The job was nearly done.

We stood in towards the shore to look for a landing-place, and presently we could see the green tussock-grass on the ledges above the surf-beaten rocks. Ahead of us and to the south, blind rollers showed the presence of uncharted reefs along the coast. Here and there the hungry rocks were close to the surface, and over them the great waves broke, swirling viciously and spouting thirty and forty feet into the air. The rocky coast appeared to descend sheer to the sea. Our need of water and rest was wellnigh desperate, but to have attempted a landing at that time would have been suicidal. Night was drawing near, and the weather indications were not favourable. There was nothing for it but to haul off till the following morning so we stood away on the starboard tack until we had made what appeared to be a safe offing. Then we hove to in the high westerly swell. The hours passed slowly as we waited the dawn, which would herald, we fondly hoped, the last stage of our journey. Our thirst was a torment and we could scarcely touch our food; the cold seemed to strike right through our weakened bodies. At 5 a.m. the wind shifted to the north-west and quickly increased to one of the worst hurricanes any of us had ever experienced. A great cross-sea was running, and the wind simply shrieked as it tore the tops off the waves and converted the whole seascape into a haze of driving spray. Down into valleys, up to tossing heights, straining until her seams opened, swung our little boat, brave still but labouring heavily. We knew that the wind and set of the sea was driving us ashore, but we could do nothing. The dawn showed us a storm-torn ocean, and the morning passed without bringing us a sight of the land; but at 1 p.m., through a rift in the flying mists, we got a glimpse of the huge crags of the island and realised that our position had become desperate. We were on a dead lee shore, and we could gauge our approach to the unseen cliffs by the roar of the breakers against the sheer walls of rock. I ordered the double-reefed mainsail to be set in the hope that we might claw off, and this attempt increased the strain upon the boat. The *James Caird* was bumping heavily, and the water was pouring in everywhere. Our thirst was forgotten in the realisation of our imminent danger, as we baled unceasingly, and adjusted our weights from time to time; occasional glimpses showed that the shore was nearer. I knew that Annewkow Island lay to the south of us, but our small and badly marked chart showed uncertain reefs in the passage between the island and the mainland, and I dared not trust it, though as a last resort we could try to lie under the lee of the island. The afternoon wore away as we edged down the coast, with the thunder of the breakers in our ears. The approach of evening found us still some distance from Annewkow Island, and, dimly in the twilight, we could see a snow-capped mountain looming above us. The chance of surviving the night, with the driving gale and the implacable sea forcing us on to the lee shore, seemed small. I think most of us had a feeling that the end was very near. Just after 6 p.m., in the dark, as the boat was in the yeasty backwash from the seas flung from this iron-bound coast, then, just when things looked their worst, they changed for the best. I have marvelled often at the thin line that divides success from failure and the sudden turn that leads from apparently certain disaster to comparative safety. The wind suddenly shifted, and we were free once more to make an offing. Almost as soon as the gale ceased, the pin that locked the mast to the thwart fell out. It must have been on the point of doing this throughout the hurricane, and if it had gone nothing could have saved us; the mast would have snapped like a carrot. Our backstays had carried away once before when iced up and were not too strongly fastened now. We were thankful indeed for the mercy that had held that pin in its place throughout the hurricane.

We stood off shore again, tired almost to the point of apathy. Our water had long been finished. The last was about a pint of hairy liquid, which we strained through a bit of gauze from the medicine-chest. The pangs of thirst attacked us with redoubled intensity, and I felt that we must make a landing on the following day at almost any hazard. The night wore on. We were very tired. We longed for day. When at last the dawn came on the morning of May 10 there was practically no wind, but a high cross-sea was running. We made slow progress towards the shore. About 8 a.m. the wind backed to the north-west and threatened another blow. We had sighted in the meantime a big indentation which I thought must be King Haakon Bay, and I decided that we must land there. We set the bows of the boat towards the bay and ran before the freshening gale. Soon we had angry reefs on either side. Great glaciers came down to the sea and offered no landing-place. The sea spouted on the reefs and thundered against the shore. About noon we sighted a line of jagged reef, like blackened teeth, that seemed to bar the entrance to the bay. Inside, comparatively smooth water stretched eight or nine miles to the head of the bay. A gap in the reef appeared, and we made for it. But the fates had another rebuff for us. The wind shifted and blew from the east right out of the bay. We could see the way through the reef, but we could not approach it directly. That afternoon we bore up, tacking five times in the strong wind. The last tack enabled us to get through, and at last we were in the wide mouth of the bay. Dusk was approaching. A small cove, with a boulder-strewn beach guarded by a reef, made a break in the cliffs on the south side of the bay, and we turned in that direction. I stood in the bows directing the steering as we ran through the kelp and made the passage of the reef. The entrance was so narrow that we had to take in the oars, and the swell was piling itself right over the reef into the cove; but in a minute or two we were inside, and in the gathering darkness the *James Caird* ran in on a swell and touched the beach. I sprang ashore with the short painter and held on when the boat went out with the backward surge. When the *James Caird* came in again three of the men got ashore, and they held the painter while I climbed some rocks with another line. A slip on the wet rocks twenty feet up nearly closed my part of the story just at the moment when we were achieving safety. A jagged piece of rock held me and at the same time bruised me sorely. However, I made fast the line, and in a few minutes we were all safe on the beach, with the boat floating in the surging water just off the shore. We heard a gurgling sound that was sweet music in our ears, and, peering around, found a stream of fresh water almost at our feet. A moment later we were down on our knees drinking the pure, ice-cold water in long draughts that put new life into us. It was a splendid moment.

Sir Ernest Shackleton, *South: The Story of Shackleton's 1914–1917 Expedition*, 1921

SATISFACTORY PEOPLE

In the afternoon the weather again threatened, and in squalls blew strong; the sea ran high, and one of the boats, the Yawl, stove alongside and sunk. As the evening approached, the ship appeared little more than suspended in water. There was no certainty that she would swim from one minute to another; and the love of life, which I believe never shewed itself later in the approach to death, began now to level all distinctions. It was impossible indeed for any man to deceive himself with a hope of being saved upon a raft in such a sea; besides, that the ship in sinking, it was probable, would carry every thing down with her in a vortex, to a certain distance.

It was near five o'clock, when coming from my cabin I observed a number of people looking very anxiously over the side; and looking myself, I saw that several men had forced the pinnace, and that more were attempting to get in. I had immediate thoughts of securing this boat before she might be sunk by numbers. There appeared not more than a moment for consideration; to remain and perish with the ship's company, whom I could not be any longer of use to, or seize the opportunity which seemed the only way of escaping, and leave the people who I had been so well satisfied with on a variety of occasions, that I thought I could give my life to preserve them. – This indeed was a painful conflict, and which I believe no man can describe, nor any man have a just idea of, who has not been in a similar situation.

The love of life prevailed – I called to Mr Rainy, the Master, the only officer upon deck, desired him to follow me, and immediately descended into the boat, at the after-part of the chains, but not without great difficulty got the boat clear from the ship, twice the number that the boat would carry pushing to get in, and many jumping into the water. Mr Baylis, a young gentleman fifteen years of age, leaped from the chains after the boat had got off, and was taken in. The boat falling astern, became exposed to the sea, and we endeavoured to pull her bow round to keep her to the break of the sea, and to pass to windward of the ship; but in the attempt she was nearly filled; the sea ran too high, and the only probability of living was keeping her before the wind.

It was then that I became sensible how little, if any thing, better our condition was, than that of those who remained in the ship; at best, it appeared to be only a prolongation of a miserable existence. We were altogether twelve in number, in a leaky boat, with one of the gunwhales stove, in nearly the middle of the Western Ocean, without compass, without quadrant, without sail, without great coat or cloak; all very thinly cloathed, in a gale of wind, with a great sea running! – It was now five o'clock in the evening, and in half an hour we lost sight of the ship. Before it was dark, a blanket was discovered in the boat. This was immediately bent to one of the stretchers, and under it as a sail we scudded all night, in expectation of being swallowed up by every wave, it being with great difficulty that we could sometimes clear the boat of the water before the return of the next great sea; all of us half drowned, and sitting, except those who bailed at the bottom of the boat: and without having really perished, I am sure no people ever endured more. In the morning the weather grew moderate, the wind having shifted to the southward, as we discovered by the sun. Having survived the night, we began to recollect ourselves, and think of our future preservation.

Capt. Inglefield's Narrative, Concerning the Loss of His Majesty's Ship, The Centaur, 1783

'BELOVED RAM'

Soon we were within the cave, to find its owner absent, grazing his goodly flocks in their pastures. So we explored the cave, staring round-eyed at cheese racks loaded with cheeses, and crowded pens of lambs and kids, each sort properly apart, the spring-younglings in this, mid-yearlings there, and the last born to one side. There were pails, buckets and tubs all brimming with whey: well-made vessels too, these milk-vessels of his. My men's first petition was that they might lay hold of the cheeses and make off with them, to return at a run and drive kids and lambs from the pens to the ship, in which we should then put hastily to sea. This advice, in the issue, would have profited us: but now I would not heed it, so set was I on seeing the master and getting (if he would give it) the guest's present from him. Yet was his coming to prove disastrous to my party.

We built up a fire, made a burnt offering, helped ourselves to cheese and ate as we sat there inside the cavern waiting for our man to come home from the pastures. He brought with him an immense burden of dried wood, kindling for his supper fire, and flung it upon the cave's floor with a crash that sent us scurrying in terror to its far corners. Then he drove under the arch his splendid flock, or rather those of them that were in milk. The rest, rams and he-goats, he left in the broad yard before the entry. Next he lifted into place and fixed in the cave's mouth a huge tall slab of stone, gigantic like himself. Two and twenty stout four-wheeled waggons would not have shifted it along the ground. So huge was it, this rock he used to block his door. Then he sat down to milk his ewes and bleating goats, all orderly, later putting her young lamb or kid beneath each mother-animal. One half of this white milk he curdled and put to press in the wicker cheese-baskets. The other half he left standing in the buckets as provision against his supper-time when he would drink it and satisfy himself.

So far he had been wholly engaged in work, but now he rebuilt the fire and looked around and saw us. 'Why, strangers,' said he, 'who are you and where have you come from across the water? Are you traders? or pirates, those venturers who sea-prowl at hazard, robbing all corners for a livelihood?' So he asked, and our confidence cracked at the giant's dread booming voice and his hugeness. Yet I made shift to speak out firmly, saying, 'We are waifs of the Achaeans from Troy, intending homeward, but driven off our course haphazard across the boundless ocean gulfs by adverse winds from heaven; it may be by the will and decree of Zeus. We can vaunt ourselves companions of Atrides, Agamemnon's men, whose is now the widest fame under heaven for having sacked earth's greatest city and brought such multitudes to death. Here therefore we find ourselves suppliant at your knees, in hope of the guesting-fee or other rich gift such as is the meed of strangers. Have regard for the Gods, Magnificent! We are your suppliants: and Zeus who fares with deserving strangers along their road is the champion of suppliants, their protector and patron-God.'

Thus far I got: but the reply came from his pitiless heart. 'Sir Stranger, you are either simple or very outlandish if you bid me fear the Gods and avoid crossing them. We are the Cyclopes and being so much the bigger we listen not at all to aegis-bearing Zeus or any blessed God: so if I should spare your life and your friends' it would not be to shun the wrath of Zeus, but because my heart counselled me mercy. Now tell me where you moored the stout ship when you came. On the far shore was it, or the near? I want to know.' With these words he laid a crafty snare for me, but to my subtlety all his deceits were plain. So I spoke back, meeting fraud with fraud: 'My ship was broken by Poseidon the Earthshaker, who swept her towards the cape at the very end of your land, and cast her against the reefs: the wind drifted us in from the high sea. Only myself with these few escaped.' So I said.

His savagery disdained me one word in reply. He leapt to his feet, lunged with his hands among my fellows, snatched up two of them like whelps and rapped their heads against the ground. The brains burst out from their skulls and were spattered over the cave's floor, while he broke them up, limb from limb, and supped off them to the last shred, eating ravenously like a mountain lion, everything – bowels and flesh and bones, even to the marrow in the bones. We wept and raised our hands to Zeus in horror at this crime committed before our eyes: yet there was nothing we could do. Wherefore the Cyclops, unhindered, filled his great gut with the human flesh, and washed it down with raw milk. Afterwards he stretched himself out across the cavern, among the flocks, and slept.

I was wondering in my bold heart whether I should now steal in, snatch the keen sword hanging on my hip, and stab him in the body; after making sure with my fingers where was that vital place in the midriff, below the heart and above the liver. Yet my second thoughts put me off this stroke, for by it I should finally seal our own doom: not enough strength lay in our hands to roll back the huge block with which he had closed the cave. So we sighed there night-long with misery, awaiting Dawn: upon whose shining the giant awoke, relit his fire, milked his flock in due order and put each youngling under its dam. After his busy work was done, he seized two more of us, who furnished his day-meal. Then he drove his sleek beasts out of the cave, easily pulling aside the great door-block and putting it back, as one of us might snap its lid upon a quiver. With loud halloos to the flock the Cyclops led them into the hills, leaving me imprisoned there to plot evil against him in the depths of my mind, wherein I sought means to pay him back, would but Athene grant me the opportunity for which I prayed.

Of what came to me this seemed best. There lay in the sheep-pens a great cudgel belonging to Cyclops, or rather a limb of green olive wood from which he meant to make himself a staff when it had seasoned. In our estimation we likened it to the mast of a twenty-oared black ship, some broad-beamed merchantman of the high-seas – it looked so long and thick. I straddled it and cut off about a fathom's length which I took to my fellows, bidding them taper it down. They made it quite even while I lent a hand to sharpen its tip. Then I took it and revolved it in the blazing flame till the point was charred to hardness. Thereafter we hid it under the sheep-droppings which were largely heaped up throughout the cave. Lastly I made the others draw lots, to see who would have the desperate task of helping me lift up our spike and grind it into his eye when heavy sleep had downed him. The luck of the draw gave me just the four men I would have chosen with my eyes open. I appointed myself the fifth of the party.

Cyclops came back at evening shepherding his fleecy flocks and straightway drove them into the wide-vaulted cave, the whole fat mass of them, leaving no single one in the outer yard. Something on his mind, was it, or did some God move him? Then he lifted up the great door-stone and propped it into place before he sat down to his milking, dealing in turn with every ewe and noisy milch-goat and later setting their young beneath them. Briskly he attacked his household work; only after it to snatch up two more of us and dine off them. Then I went up to the giant with an ivy-cup of my dark wine in hand and invited him, saying, 'Cyclops, come now and on top of your meal of man's flesh try this wine, to see how tasty a drink was hidden in our ship. I brought it for you, hoping you would have compassion on me and help me homeward: but your wisdom is far beyond all comprehending. O sinful one, how dare you expect any other man from the great world to visit you, after you have behaved towards us so unconscionably?' I spoke: he took and drank. A savage gladness woke in him at the sweetness of the liquor and he demanded a second cup, saying, 'Give me another hearty helping and then quickly tell me your name, for me to confer on you a guest-gift that will warm your heart. It is true our rich soil grows good vines for us Cyclopes, and the moisture of heaven multiplies their yield: but this vintage is a drop of the real nectar and ambrosia.' Thus he declared and at once I poured him a second cup of the glowing wine: and then one more, for in his folly he tossed off three bowls of it. The fumes were going to his Cyclopean wits as I began to play with him in honeyed phrase:– 'Cyclops, you ask me for my public name: I will confess it to you aloud, and do you then give me my guest-gift, as you have promised. My name is No-man: so they have always called me, my mother and father and all my friends.'

I spoke, and he answered from his cruel heart, 'I will eat No-man finally, after all his friends. The others first – that shall be your benefit.' He sprawled full-length, belly up, on the ground, lolling his fat neck aside; and sleep that conquers all men conquered him. Heavily he vomited out all his load of drink, and gobbets of human flesh swimming in wine spurted gurgling from his throat. Forthwith I thrust our spike into the deep embers of the fire to get it burning hot: and cheered my fellows with brave words lest any of them hang back through fear. Soon the stake of olive wood despite its greenness was almost trembling into flame with a terrible glowing incandescence. I snatched it from the fire, my men helping. Some power from on high breathed into us all a mad courage, by whose strength they charged with the great spear and stabbed its sharp point right into his eye. I flung my weight upon it from above so that it bored home. As a ship-builder's bit drills its timbers, steadily twirling by reason of the drag from the hide thong which his mates underneath pull to and fro alternately, so we held the burning pointed stake in his eye and spun it, till the boiling blood bubbled about its pillar of fire. Eyebrows with eyelids shrivelled and stank in the blast of his consuming eyeball: yea the very roots of the eye crackled into flame.

Just as a smith plunges into cold water some great axe-head or adze and it hisses angrily – for that is the treatment, and the strength of iron lies in its temper – just so his eye sizzled about the olive-spike. He let out a wild howl which rang round the cavern's walls and drove us hither and thither in terror. He wrenched the spike of wood from his eye and it came out clotted and thick with blood. The maddening pain made him fling it from his hands, and then he began to bellow to the other Cyclopes living about him in their dens among the windy hills. They had heard his screaming and now drew towards the closed cave, calling to know his trouble: 'What so ails you, Polyphemus, that you roar across the heavenly night and keep us from sleep? Do not pretend that any mortal is driving your flocks from you by force, or is killing you by sheer might or trickery.' Big Polyphemus yelled back to them from within his cave, 'My friends, No-man is killing me by sleight. There is no force about it.' Wherefore they retorted cuttingly, 'If you are alone and no one assaults you, but your pain is some unavoidable malady from Zeus, why then, make appeal to your father King Poseidon.'

They turned away and my dear heart laughed because the excellent cunning trick of that false name had completely taken them in. Cyclops was groaning in his extremity of torment. He groped with his hands until he had found and taken the stone from the entrance. Then he sat himself in the cave's mouth with his fingers extended across it, to catch anyone who tried to steal through with the sheep. In his heart he judged me such a fool as that: while I was thinking my very hardest to contrive a way out for myself and my fellows from destruction, we being truly in the jaws of death. Many notions and devices I conceived thus for dear life, and the best of them seemed finally as follows. Some rams there were of big stock, fleecy great splendid beasts with wool almost purple in its depth of colour. I took them by threes silently and bound them abreast with the pliant bark-trips from which the wicked monster's bed was plaited. The middle beast could then take a man and the one on either side protect him from discovery. That meant three rams for each shipmate: while for myself there remained the prize ram of all the flock. I took hold of him, tucked myself under his shaggy belly and hung there so, with steadfast courage: clinging face upwards with my hands twisted into his enormous fleece. Thus we waited in great trepidation for the dawn.

At its first redness the rams rushed out towards their pasture: but the ewes hung about their pens unmilked, bleating distressfully with bursting udders. The lord, distraught with his terrible pains, felt the back of each sheep as it stood up to march straight past him. The dullard suspected not that there were men bound beneath their fleecy ribs. Last of all the prime ram came to go out, walking stiffly with the weight of his wool and me the deep plotter. Strong Polyphemus stroked him and said, 'Beloved ram, why are you the last of all my flock to quit the cave? Never before have you let yourself lag behind the others; but have been always the first to stride freely into the hill-streams to drink: while at evening, which was homing time, you would be ever the first that wanted to turn back. And now you come last! Are you feeling the loss of your lord's sight, blinded by that villain with his knavish crew after he had made me helpless with wine? That No-man, who I swear has not yet got away from death. If only you could feel like me and had the gift of speech to tell where he skulks from my wrath. How I would dash his brains out against the ground and spill them over the cave, to lighten my heart of the pains which this worthless No-man has inflicted!'

He pushed the ram gently from him through the doorway. When we were a little space from the cave and its surrounding yard I loosed myself and then set free my men. Often turning head to look back we drove the leggy flock, the fat ripe beasts, down to the ship where the sight of us gladdened the others at thought of the death we had escaped. They would have stayed to lament the fallen: but I would not have it. Sternly I bent my brows and checked each man's weeping: and set them instead by sharp gestures to tumbling the glossy-fleeced animals into the ship and launching out for the open sea. At once they were aboard and on their benches. Smartly they sat and gave way, so that the sea paled beneath their oar-strokes: but when we were just as far from the land as a man's shout might carry, then I hailed the Cyclops in malignant derision. 'So, Cyclops, you were unlucky and did not quite have the strength to eat all the followers of this puny man within your cave? Instead the luck returned your wickedness upon yourself in fit punishment for the impiety that had dared eat the guests in your house. Zeus has repaid you, the other Gods agreeing.'

My cry stung his heart more terribly yet. He tore the crest from a great mountain and flung it at the black-prowed ship, but overcast by a hair's breadth. The rock nearly scraped the end of the tiller. The sea heaped up above its plunging, and the backthrust, like a tidal wave from the deep, washed us landward again very swiftly, almost to shore. I snatched a long pole and used it as a quaint, while I signed with my head to the crew how they must lay to it over the oar-looms if we were to avoid disaster. They put their backs into it and rowed till we were twice our former distance from the coast. Then I would have taunted Cyclops once more, but my followers, each in his vein sought with gentle words to restrain me, protesting, 'Hothead, why further provoke this savage creature who with his last deadly shot so nearly brought our ship to shore that we did already judge ourselves dead? Had he caught but a whisper or sound from us just now, he would have crushed our heads and our ship's timbers flat beneath some jagged stone, the marvellous thrower that he is.' Thus ran their plea, but my pride was not to be dissuaded. Wherefore once again I spilled my heart's malice over him: 'Cyclops, if any human being asks of you how your eye was so hideously put out, say that Odysseus, despoiler of cities, did it; even the son of Laertes, whose home is in Ithaca.'

Homer, *The Odyssey*, trans. T. E. Lawrence, 1932

CANDLELIGHT

In the year 1598, or in that next before it, Mr Darell's house in Sussex, about forty-six miles distant from London, was twice searched, Father Blount at each time being in the house, where for the space of seven or eight years from his coming into England he had resided. The first search was by two Justices of the Peace, with a pursuivant and such as they brought with them to watch and beset the house: who, at their first coming, sent Mr Darell to London prisoner, his wife to one of the Justices' houses, and most of the servants to the county gaol; suffering in the house one maid to stay with the little children, and the searchers having the house.

This during about the space of a week, Father Blount was in a secret place under a stair, having one man with him, with very small provision; and when it seemed they could subsist no longer, Father Blount sent out his man, who offered himself to the searchers, feigning that he came out of another hole which he showed them, and was carried away for a Priest, and the other escaped.

About one year after, a household servant, or one employed in husbandry, a Protestant, plotted to betray the house, and three Justices of the Peace, with a pursuivant and their retinue, beset the house in the dead of the night about Christmas, and got into the house; which being perceived, Father Blount was awaked by the noise, and, putting on nothing but his breeches, with the same man got into another secret place, digged in a thick stone wall, carrying with him some church stuff and books, some of which things were afterwards a hindrance to his saving himself by swimming.

At that time Mr Darell was from home, and Mrs Darell was shut up in one room over the gate with her children, and the searchers had possession and liberty of the whole house for the space of ten days; Father Blount and the man having no other sustenance but a little bottle of wine and a little loaf of bread, and no other clothes but their breeches and a Priest's cassock. During this time they searched and found nothing.

About the end of this time Mrs Darell found means to go sometimes out of her chamber; and at the last got to the door of the place, where finding the end of a girdle used at Mass to be shut out, hanging on the outside of the door of the hiding-place (strange Providence!), she cut it off, but yet not so close but that some remained, which she thought might betray them, whereupon she called to them within, 'Pull in the string,' which presently they did. Those that, it seems, watched her came presently to her and asked her to whom she spake, and of what string. She answered that the door by which she meant to pass being shut, she heard somebody in the next room and called to them to open the door, which was done by pulling the string of the latch.

This answer not satisfying them, they fell to search about the place, which was a little court with stone buildings about it, beating with a beetle upon the stones; and many times on the door of the place, which was a stone in show not differing from the rest. With many great blows, the hinges of the door began to yield, at which they within set their backs to the door to support it against the blows what they could, but it was so much moved as that they saw the candlelight of the searchers, and could hear all they said.

It grew late in the evening, and it rained extremely fast, and the gutters poured down on the searchers; and one of the company that dwelt at the next town, a man very forward and a director of the rest, came to the searchers and persuaded them to desist, saying, if there were anything, they might better find it the next morning by daylight. They presently left off and made a good fire in the hall, and there sat drying themselves and drinking. And soon after the Justices went to bed, and most of the rest sat by the fire drinking.

Father Blount (who, without this act of God's Providence, which seemed accidental, by all likelihood had died in the place, as resolving so rather than to put himself into the hands of the searchers, which had overthrown the house), taking the opportunity of the stormy and dark night, first sent out his man and soon followed himself. Barefoot, they got over two walls about ten feet high, and so to a broken tower about sixteen feet above the water of the moat, which was there about eighty feet broad, and so deep as could not be waded. From thence the Father leaped into the moat, by his courage out-leaping certain piles which stood near the tower and were covered with water and not known to him.

William Darell, 'Mr Blunt's Escape out of his Father's House', 1598

FOURTEEN

'He confused the public mind'

PREGNANCY

The next morning I could not go to the Tower, having so many things upon my hands to put in readiness; but in the evening, when all was ready, I sent for Mrs Mills with whom I lodged, and acquainted her with my design of attempting my lord's escape, as there was no prospect of his being pardoned, and that this was the last night before the execution. I told her that I had every thing in readiness, and that I trusted she would not refuse to accompany me, that my lord might pass for her. I pressed her to come immediately as we had no time to lose. At the same time I sent to Mrs Morgan, then usually known by the name of Hilton, to whose acquaintance my dear Evans had introduced me, which I look upon as a very singular happiness. I immediately communicated my resolutions to her. She was of a very tall slender make, so I begged her to put under her own riding-hood one that I had prepared for Mrs Mills, as she was to lend hers to my lord, that in coming out he might be taken for her. Mrs Mills was then with child, so that she was not only of the same height, but nearly of the same size as my lord. When we were in the coach, I never ceased talking, that they might have no leisure to reflect. Their surprise and astonishment when I first opened my design to them had made them consent, without ever thinking of the consequences. On our arrival at the Tower, the first I introduced was Mrs Morgan (for I was only allowed to take in one at a time), she brought in the cloaths that were to serve Mrs Mills when she left her own behind her. When Mrs Morgan had taken off what she had brought for my purpose, I conducted her back to the staircase, and in going, I begged her to send me my maid to dress me, that I was afraid of being too late to present my last petition that night if she did not come immediately. I dispatched her safe, and went partly down stairs to meet Mrs Mills, who had the precaution to hold her handkerchief to her face, as is natural for a woman to do, when she is going to take her last farewell of a friend on the eve of his execution. I had, indeed, desired her to do so, that my lord might go out in the same manner. Her eyebrows were rather inclined to be sandy, and my lord's were very dark and very thick; however, I had prepared some paint of the colour of her's to disguise his with; I also brought an artificial head-dress of the same coloured hair as hers, and I painted his face with white and his cheeks with rouge, to hide his long beard which he had not time to shave. All this provision I had before left in the Tower. The poor guards, whom my slight liberality the day before had endeared me to, let me go quietly out with my company, and were not so strictly on the watch as they usually had been and the more so, as they were persuaded, from what I had told them the day before, that the prisoners would obtain their pardon. I made Mrs Mills take off her own hood and put on that which I had brought for her; I then took her by the hand and led her out of my lord's chamber, and in passing through the next room, in which were several people, with all concern imaginable, I said, 'My dear Mrs Catharine, go in all haste and send me my waiting-maid, she certainly cannot reflect how late it is; I am to present my petition to-night, and if I let slip this opportunity I am undone, for tomorrow will be too late; hasten her as much as possible, for I shall be on thorns till she comes.' Every body in the room, who were chiefly the guards' wives and daughters, seemed to compassionate me exceedingly, and the centinel officiously opened me the door. When I had seen her safe out I returned to my lord, and finished dressing him. I had taken care that Mrs Mills did not go out crying, as she came in, that my lord might better pass for the lady who came in crying and afflicted, and the more so, because he had the same dress which she wore. When I had almost finished dressing my lord in all my petticoats except one, I perceived it was growing dark, and was afraid that the light of the candles might betray us, so I resolved to set off. I went out leading him by the hand, whilst he held his handkerchief to his eyes. I spoke to him in the most piteous and afflicted tone of voice, bewailing bitterly the negligence of Evans, who had ruined me by her delay. Then said I, 'My dear Mrs Betty, for the love of God run quickly, and bring her with you; you know my lodging, and if you ever made dispatch in your life, do it at present; I am almost distracted with this disappointment.' The guards opened the door, and I went down stairs with him, still conjuring him to make all possible dispatch. As soon as he had cleared the door I made him walk before me, for fear the centinel should take notice of his walk; but I still continued to press him to make all the dispatch he possibly could. At the bottom of the stairs I met my dear Evans, into whose hands I confided him. I had before engaged Mrs Mills to be in readiness before the Tower, to conduct him to some place of safety, in case we succeeded. He looked upon the affair as so very improbable to succeed, that his astonishment when he saw us, threw him into such a consternation that he was almost out of himself; which Evans perceiving, with the greatest presence of mind, without telling him any thing lest he should mistrust them, conducted him to some of her own friends on whom she could rely, and so secured him, without which, we should have been undone. When she had conducted him and left him with them, she returned to Mr Mills, who by this time had recovered himself from his astonishment. They went home together, and having found a place of security they conducted him to it. In the mean time, as I had pretended to have sent the young lady on a message, I was obliged to return up stairs, and go back to my lord's room in the same feigned anxiety of being too late, so that every body seemed sincerely to sympathise in my distress. When I was in the room, I talked as if he had been really present: I answered my own questions in my lord's voice as nearly as I could imitate it; I walked up and down as if we were conversing together, till I thought they had time enough thoroughly to clear themselves of the guards. I then thought proper to make off also. I opened the door, and stood half in it that those in the outward chamber might hear what I said, but held it so close that they could not look in. I bade my lord formal farewell for the night, and added, that something more than usual must have happened to make Evans negligent on this important occasion, who had always been so punctual in the smallest trifles; that I saw no other remedy but to go in person: that if the Tower was still open, when I had finished my business, I would return that night; but that he might be assured I would be with him as early in the morning as I could gain admittance into the Tower, and I flattered myself I should bring more favourable news. Then, before I shut the door, I pulled through the string of the latch, so that it could only be opened in the inside. I then shut it with some degree of force, that I might be sure of its being well shut. I said to the servant as I passed by (who was ignorant of the whole transaction) that he need not carry in candles to his master, till my lord sent for them, as he desired to finish some prayers first. I went down stairs and called a coach, as there were several on the stand, and drove home to my own lodgings, where poor Mr McKenzie had been waiting to carry the petition, in case my attempt had failed. I told him there was no need of any petition, as my lord was safe out of the Tower, and out of the hands of his enemies as I supposed, but that I did not know where he was.

A Letter from the Countess of Nithsdale, 1827 (events of 1716)

A NEW PROVERB

Grotius had been above eighteen months shut up in Louvestein, when, on the eleventh of January, 1621, Muys-van-Holi, his declared enemy, who had been one of his judges, informed the States-General, that he had advice from good hands their prisoner was seeking to make his escape: some persons were sent to Louvestein to examine into this matter; but notwithstanding all the enquiry that could be made, they found no reason to believe that Grotius had laid any plot to get out.

His wife however was wholly employed in contriving how to set him at liberty. He had been permitted to borrow books of his friends, and when he had done with them, they were carried back in a chest with his foul linen, which was sent to Gorcum, a town near Louvestein, to be washed. The first year his guards were very exact, in examining the chest when it went from Louvestein; but being used to find in it only books and linen, they grew tired of searching, and did not take the trouble to open it. Grotius's wife observing their negligence, purposed to take advantage of it. She represented to her husband that it was in his power to get out of prison when he pleased, if he would put himself in the chest that carried his books. However, not to endanger his health, she caused holes to be bored opposite to the part where his face was to be, to breathe at; and made him try if he could continue shut up in that confined posture as long as it would require to go from Louvestein to Gorcum. Finding it might be done, she resolved to seize the first favourable opportunity.

It soon offered. The Commandant of Louvestein going to Heusden to raise recruits, Grotius's wife made a visit to his lady, and told her in conversation, that she was desirous of sending away a chest full of books, for her husband was so weak, it gave her great uneasiness to see him study with such application. Having thus prepared the Commandant's wife, she returned to her husband's apartment, and in concert with a valet and a maid, who were in the secret, shut him up in the chest. At the same time, that people might not be surprised at not seeing him, she spread a report of his being ill. Two soldiers carried the chest: one of them, finding it heavier than usual, said, There must be an Arminian in it: this was a kind of proverb that had lately come into use. Grotius's wife, who was present, answered with great coldness, There are indeed Arminian books in it. The chest was brought down on a ladder with great difficulty. The soldier insisted on its being opened, to see what was in it; he even went and informed the Commandant's wife that the weight of the chest gave him reason to think there was something suspicious contained in it, and that it would be proper to have it opened. She would not; whether it was that she was willing to wink at the thing, or through negligence; she told him that Grotius's wife had assured her there was nothing but books in it; and that they might carry it to the boat. It is affirmed that a soldier's wife who was present, said there was more than one example of prisoners making their escape in boxes. The chest however was put into the boat, and Grotius's maid, who was in the secret, had orders to go with it to Gorcum, and put it into a house there. When it came to Gorcum, they wanted to put it on a sledge; but the maid telling the boatman there were some brittle things in it, and begging of him to take care how it was carried, it was put on a horse, and brought by two chairmen to David Dazelaer's, a friend of Grotius, and brother-in-law to Erpenius, having married his sister. When everybody was gone, the maid opened the chest. Grotius had felt no inconvenience in it, though its length was not above three feet and a half. He got out, dressed himself like a mason, with a rule and a trowel, and went by Dazelaer's back-door, through the market-place to the gate that leads to the river, and stept into a boat which carried him to Valvic in Brabant. At this place he made himself known to some Arminians; and hired a carriage to Antwerp, taking the necessary precautions not to be known by the way: it was not the Spaniards he feared, for there was then a truce between them and the United Provinces. He alighted at Antwerp at the house of Nicholas Grevincovius, who had been formerly a Minister at Amsterdam; and made himself known to no body but him. It was on the 22d of March 1621, that Grotius thus recovered his liberty.

In the mean time it was believed at Louvestein that he was ill; and to give him time to get off, his wife gave out that his illness was dangerous; but as soon as she learnt by the maid's return that he was in Brabant, and consequently in safety, she told the guards, the bird was flown. They informed the Commandant, by this time returned from Heusden, who hastened to Grotius's wife, and asked her where she had hid her husband? She answered he might search for him: but being much pressed and even threatened, she confessed that she had caused him to be carried to Gorcum in the book chest: and that she had done no more than kept her word to him, to take the first opportunity of setting her husband at liberty. The Commandant in a rage went immediately to Gorcum, and acquainting the Magistrate with his prisoner's escape, both came to Dazelaer's, where they found the empty chest. On his return to Louvestein the Commandant confined Grotius's wife more closely: but presenting a petition to the States-General, April 5, 1621, praying that she might be discharged, and Prince Maurice, to whom it was communicated, making no opposition, the majority were for setting her at liberty. Some indeed voted for detaining her a prisoner; but they were looked on as very barbarous, to want to punish a woman for an heroic action. Two days after presenting the petition, she was discharged, and suffered to carry away everything that belonged to her in Louvestein. Grotius continued some time at Antwerp. March 30, he wrote to the States-General that in procuring his liberty he had employed neither violence nor corruption with his keepers; that he had nothing to reproach himself with in what he had done; that he gave those counsels which he thought best for appeasing the troubles that had arisen before he was concerned in public business; that he only obeyed the Magistrates of Rotterdam his masters, and the States of Holland his sovereigns; and that the persecution he had suffered would never diminish his love to his Country, for whose prosperity he heartily prayed.

Grotius's escape exercised the pens of the most famous poets of that period. Barlæus wrote some very good verses on it: and also celebrated his wife's magnanimity. Rutgersius composed a poem on his imprisonment, in which he places the day of his arrest among the most unfortunate for the Republic. Grotius himself wrote some verses on his happy deliverance, which were translated into Flemish by the famous poet John Van Vondel. He made also some lines on the chest to which he owed his liberty, and in the latter part of his life was at great pains to recover it.

M. de Burigny, *The Life of Grotius*, English trans. 1754

LOSS OF ENERGY

The last occasion on which the author, under strict test conditions, saw Houdini demonstrate his powers of dematerialisation, was before thousands, upon the public stage of the Grand Theatre, Islington, London. Here a small iron tank, filled with water, was deposited upon the stage, and in it Houdini was placed, the water completely covering his body. Over this was placed an iron lid with three hasps and staples, and these were securely locked. The body was then completely dematerialised within this tank within one and a half minutes, while the author stood immediately over it. Without disturbing any of the locks, Houdini was transferred from the tank direct to the back of the stage in a dematerialised state. He was there materialised, and returned to the stage front dripping with water, and attired in the blue jersey suit in which he entered the tank. From the time that he entered it to his appearance on the front of the stage only one and a half minutes had expired. While the author stood adjacent to the tank, during the dematerialisation process, a great loss of physical energy was felt by him, such as is usually experienced by sitters in materialising séances, who have a good stock of vital energy, as in such phenomena a large amount of energy is required. Dematerialisation is performed by methods similar in operation to those in which the psycho-plastic essence is drawn from the medium. The body of the medium may be reduced to half its ordinary weight in the materialising séance room, but in the case of dematerialisation the essence continues to be drawn until the whole physical body vanishes, and the substance composing it is held in suspension within the atmosphere, much in the same way as moisture is held by evaporation. While in this state Houdini was transferred from the stage to the retiring-room behind, and there almost instantaneously materialised. The speed with which this dematerialisation is performed is much more rapid than is possible in the materialising séance room, where time is required for the essence to be crystallised into psycho-plastic matter. Not only was Houdini's body dematerialised, but it was carried through the locked iron tank, thus demonstrating the passage of matter through matter. This startling manifestation of one of nature's profoundest miracles was probably regarded by most of the audience as a very clever trick.

J. Hewat McKenzie, *Spirit Intercourse*, 1916

DROWNED SCEPTICS

Whatever may have been the true source of Houdini's powers – and I am not prepared to be dogmatic about the point – I am very sure that the explanations of his fellow-conjurers do not always meet the case. Thus we have Mr Harry Kellock, to whose book I am indebted for much supplementary information, talking persuasively about the magician's skill with a pick-lock. He had told reporters that his method was to have a small instrument which was concealed by surgeon's plaster upon the sole of his foot. This would certainly seem to be very useful when he was lowered in a coffin to the bottom of the sea!

Of course, I am aware that Houdini really was a very skilful conjurer. All that could be known in that direction he knew. Thus he confused the public mind by mixing up things which were dimly within their comprehension with things which were beyond anyone's comprehension. I am aware also that there is a box trick, and that there is a normal handcuff and bag trick. But these are not in the same class with Houdini's work. I will believe they are when I see one of these other gentlemen thrown in a box off London Bridge. One poor man in America actually believed these explanations, and on the strength of them jumped in a weighted packing-case into a river in the Middle West; and one did so in Germany. They are there yet!

Arthur Conan Doyle, *The Edge of the Unknown*, 1930

WEIGHTS AND ROLLERS

The mystery of the submerged trunk was devised by Houdini in 1909, or before; his complete notations and sketches are dated Croydon, England, September 9, 1909. It is one of those rare escapes that carry a double mystery, and it illustrates Houdini's capability for making a seemingly miraculous effect out of a rather hackneyed trick. For with the submerged trunk, the escape seems unbelievable even after it has been accomplished. The trunk used in the escape is large and solidly made. It possesses no air-holes; on the contrary it must be made air-tight, so that it may be submerged in a tank of water. This tank has a glass front; after the performer is locked in the trunk, the air-tight prison is lifted and lowered into the tank, where it is completely under water. Then the curtain is drawn around the tank.

It is obvious that the performer must escape quickly. The trunk has been hurriedly locked and roped, and the expectant audience realises that no time must be lost, because of the limited supply of air. This adds to the tenseness of the situation. After several minutes have passed, the curtain opens and out steps the performer. He has made the escape, but to the amazement of the audience he is as dry as when he entered the trunk! The cabinet is removed, and everything undergoes the most rigid examination. The trunk is still in the tank, under water. It is lifted from the tank and inspected; the locks are still fastened, and the ropes are intact. The trunk is opened, and the interior is shown to be quite dry.

This bewildering effect is particularly good from the magician's standpoint, for it offers a variety of impractical solutions, all of which, like the trunk, do not hold water. 'An optical illusion' – 'duplicate trunks' – 'the performer is never in the trunk' – 'the tank empties and refills itself' – these are the theories that will occur to members of the committee on the stage; yet they will find no evidence to support any of these pet beliefs. This is indeed an escape that can create amazement. Yet the secret is very simple; in fact, it should be, in an escape of this sort, and the practical ingenuity of the trick is something that will not be noticed.

The tank is unprepared; the trick lies in the trunk, which is nothing more nor less than an escape trunk of the well-known style, operating by means of a secret panel in the end, the panel opening inward. A trunk of this type will stand close examination by any committee, and the trunk used in this particular escape, being water-tight and heavy, is particularly well designed to preserve its secret. In the trunk are two flat metal weights. They may be placed in the trunk beforehand, or they may be inserted just before the performer enters. In either event their purpose is too obvious to excite comment. Without them the trunk would not sink; when they are inside the trunk there is no possibility of their removal while the trunk is under water. The weights are in the bottom of the trunk, rather close to the ends, held in place by hooks or fasteners. On the bottom of the tank are two bars or rollers on which the trunk rests. The apparent purpose of these bars, which are rather close together, is to keep the trunk above the bottom of the tank, so that there is no possibility of exit in that direction, and the audience may see under the trunk when it is submerged.

But the weights and the bars serve a much more important purpose than the spectators suppose. Houdini's method would be to remove the weight, when he was in the trunk, from the end where the secret door was situated, and to transfer it to the other end of the trunk, at the same time moving his body to the end with the weights. The bars in the bottom of the tank, being high, crosswise, and close together, would immediately produce the desired results. The heavy end of the trunk would tip so that the trunk would stand on end, the upper end coming just above the level of the water in the tank! The next step would be for Houdini to open the secret panel and make his escape from the trunk, swinging his body over the edge of the tank and bringing the loose weight along with him. By this system he could replace the loose weight in its proper position at the upper end of the trunk, close the secret opening, and give the upper end of the trunk a push that would immediately cause it to drop back and resume its original position.

In a sketch accompanying the explanation of this mystery, Houdini indicated that the cross-rods should be attached to the bottom of the trunk and not to the tank itself. This was evidently intended to make the return journey of the trunk a positive matter, the bars having a curved bottom to make the tipping easy. This appears to be the final design of the apparatus. The size and depth of the tank are, of course, important. It must be long to allow for the space into which the trunk turns when on end; it must be deep enough to be convincing, yet shallow enough so that the end of the trunk will emerge. Distance from front to back was reduced to a minimum, so that the rear edge of the tank would be within the performer's reach. The use of very heavy weights is justifiable and logical, for the trunk is supposed to be definitely submerged with no chance of floating. Hence the very factors that aid the performer in his escape are accepted by the spectators as obstacles to his success.

W. B. Gibson, Houdini's Escapes, 1931

WATSON IN THE HOTEL

'Holmes!' I cried. 'Is it really you? Can it indeed be that you are alive? Is it possible that you succeeded in climbing out of that awful abyss?'

'Wait a moment,' said he. 'Are you sure that you are really fit to discuss things? I have given you a serious shock by my unnecessarily dramatic reappearance.'

'I am all right, but indeed, Holmes, I can hardly believe my eyes. Good heavens! to think that you – you of all men – should be standing in my study.' Again I gripped him by the sleeve, and felt the thin, sinewy arm beneath it. 'Well, you're not a spirit, anyhow,' said I. 'My dear chap, I'm overjoyed to see you. Sit down, and tell me how you came alive out of that dreadful chasm.'

He sat opposite to me, and lit a cigarette in his old, nonchalant manner. He was dressed in the seedy frockcoat of the book merchant, but the rest of that individual lay in a pile of white hair and old books upon the table. Holmes looked even thinner and keener than of old, but there was a dead-white tinge in his aquiline face which told me that his life recently had not been a healthy one.

'I am glad to stretch myself, Watson', said he. 'It is no joke when a tall man has to take a foot off his stature for several hours on end. Now, my dear fellow, in the matter of these explanations, we have, if I may ask for your co-operation, a hard and dangerous night's work in front of us. Perhaps it would be better if I gave you an account of the whole situation when that work is finished.'

'I am full of curiosity. I should prefer to hear now.'

'You'll come with me tonight?'

'When you like and where you like.'

'This is, indeed, like the old days. We shall have time for a mouthful of dinner before we need go. Well, then, about that chasm. I had no serious difficulty in getting out of it, for the very simple reason that I never was in it.'

'You never were in it?'

'No, Watson, I never was in it. My note to you was absolutely genuine. I had little doubt that I had come to the end of my career when I perceived the somewhat sinister figure of the late Professor Moriarty standing upon the narrow pathway which led to safety. I read an inexorable purpose in his grey eyes. I exchanged some remarks with him, therefore, and obtained his courteous permission to write the short note which you afterwards received. I left it with my cigarette-box and my stick, and I walked along the pathway, Moriarty still at my heels. When I reached the end I stood at bay. He drew no weapon, but he rushed at me and threw his long arms around me. He knew that his own game was up, and was only anxious to revenge himself upon me. We tottered together upon the brink of the fall. I have some knowledge, however, of baritsu, or the Japanese system of wrestling, which has more than once been very useful to me. I slipped through his grip, and he with a horrible scream kicked madly for a few seconds, and clawed the air with both his hands. But for all his efforts he could not get his balance, and over he went. With my face over the brink, I saw him fall for a long way. Then he struck a rock, bounded off, and splashed into the water.'

I listened with amazement to this explanation, which Holmes delivered between the puffs of his cigarette.

'But the tracks!' I cried. 'I saw, with my own eyes, that two went down the path and none returned.'

'It came about in this way. The instant that the Professor had disappeared, it struck me what a really extraordinary lucky chance Fate had placed in my way. I knew that Moriarty was not the only man who had sworn my death. There were at least three others whose desire for vengeance upon me would only be increased by the death of their leader. They were all most dangerous men. One or other would certainly get me. On the other hand, if all the world was convinced that

I was dead they would take liberties, these men, they would soon lay themselves open, and sooner or later I could destroy them. Then it would be time for me to announce that I was still in the land of the living. So rapidly does the brain act that I believe I had thought this all out before Professor Moriarty had reached the bottom of the Reichenbach Fall.

'I stood up and examined the rocky wall behind me. In your picturesque account of the matter, which I read with great interest some months later, you assert that the wall was sheer. That was not literally true. A few small footholes presented themselves, and there was some indication of a ledge. The cliff is so high that to climb it all was an obvious impossibility, and it was equally impossible to make my way along the wet path without leaving some tracks. I might, it is true, have reversed my boots, as I have done on similar occasions, but the sight of three sets of tracks in one direction would certainly have suggested a deception. On the whole, then, it was best that I should risk the climb. It was not a pleasant business, Watson. The fall roared beneath me. I am not a fanciful person, but I give you my word that I seemed to hear Moriarty's voice screaming at me out of the abyss. A mistake would have been fatal. More than once, as tufts of grass came out in my hand or my foot slipped in the wet notches of the rock, I thought that I was gone. But I struggled upward, and at last I reached a ledge several feet deep and covered with soft green moss, where I could lie unseen, in the most perfect comfort. There I was stretched, when you, my dear Watson, and all your following were investigating in the most sympathetic and inefficient manner the circumstances of my death.

'At last, when you had all formed your inevitable and totally erroneous conclusions, you departed for the hotel, and I was left alone. I had imagined that I had reached the end of my adventures, but a very unexpected occurrence showed me that there were surprises still in store for me. A huge rock, falling from above, boomed past me, struck the path and bounded over into the chasm. For an instant I thought that it was an accident, but a moment later, looking up, I saw a man's head against the darkening sky, and another stone struck the very ledge upon which I was stretched, within a foot of my head. Of course, the meaning of this was obvious. Moriarty had not been alone. A confederate – and even that one glance had told me how dangerous a man that confederate was – had kept guard while the Professor had attacked me. From a distance, unseen by me, he had been a witness of his friend's death and of my escape. He had waited, and then making his way round to the top of the cliff, he had endeavoured to succeed where his comrade had failed.

'I did not take long to think about it, Watson. Again I saw that grim face look over the cliff, and I knew that it was the precursor of another stone. I scrambled down on to the path. I don't think I could have done it in cold blood. It was a hundred times more difficult than getting up. But I had no time to think of the danger, for another stone sang past me as I hung by my hands from the edge of the ledge. Halfway down I slipped, but, by the blessing of God, I landed, torn and bleeding, upon the path. I took to my heels, did ten miles over the mountains in the darkness, and a week later I found myself in Florence, with the certainty that no one in the world knew what had become of me.'

Arthur Conan Doyle, *The Return of Sherlock Holmes*, 1903

'I BEAT IT AND HACKED IT CONSIDERABLE'

It was a drift-canoe, sure enough, and I clumb in and paddled her ashore. Thinks I, the old man will be glad when he sees this – she's worth ten dollars. But when I got to shore pap wasn't in sight yet, and as I was running her into a little creek like a gully, all hung over with vines and willows, I struck another idea; I judged I'd hide her good, and then, stead of taking to the woods when I run off, I'd go down the river about fifty mile and camp in one place for good, and not have such a rough time tramping on foot.

It was pretty close to the shanty, and I thought I heard the old man coming, all the time; but I got her hid; then I out and looked around a bunch of willows, and there was the old man down the path apiece just drawing a bead on a bird with his gun. So he hadn't seen anything.

When he got along, I was hard at it taking up a "trot" line. He abused me a little for being so slow, but I told him I fell in the river and that was what made me so long. I knowed he would see I was wet, and then he would be asking questions. We got five cat-fish off of the lines and went home.

While we laid off, after breakfast, to sleep up, both of us being about wore out, I got to thinking that if I could fix up some way to keep pap and the widow from trying to follow me, it would be a certainer thing than trusting to luck to get far enough off before they missed me; you see, all kinds of things might happen. Well, I didn't see no way for a while, but by-and-by pap raised up a minute, to drink another barrel of water, and he says:

'Another time a man comes a-prowling round here, you roust me out, you hear? That man warn't here for no good. I'd a shot him. Next time, you roust me out, you hear?'

Then he dropped down and went to sleep again – but what he had been saying give me the very idea I wanted. I says to myself, I can fix it now so nobody won't think of following me.

About twelve o'clock we turned out and went along up the bank. The river was coming up pretty fast, and lots of driftwood going by on the rise. By-and-by, along comes part of a log raft—nine logs fast together. We went out with the skiff and towed it ashore. Then we had dinner. Anybody but pap would a waited and seen the day through, so as to catch more stuff; but that warn't pap's style. Nine logs was enough for one time; he must shove right over to town and sell. So he locked me in and took the skiff and started off towing the raft about half-past three. I judged he wouldn't come back that night. I waited till I reckoned he had got a good start, then I out with my saw and went to work on that log again. Before he was t'other side of the river I was out of the hole; him and his raft was just a speck on the water away off yonder.

I took the sack of corn meal and took it to where the canoe was hid, and shoved the vines and branches apart and put it in; then I done the same with the side of bacon; then the whisky jug; I took all the coffee and sugar there was, and all the ammunition; I took the wadding; I took the bucket and gourd, I took a dipper and a tin cup, and my old saw and two blankets, and the skillet and the coffee-pot. I took fish-lines and matches, and other things – everything that was worth a cent. I cleaned out the place. I wanted an axe, but there wasn't any, only the one out at the wood pile, and I knowed why I was going to leave that. I fetched out the gun, and now I was done.

I had wore the ground a good deal, crawling out of the hole and dragging out so many things. So I fixed that as good as I could from the outside by scattering dust on the place, which covered up the smoothness and the sawdust. Then I fixed the piece of log back into its place, and put two rocks under it and one against it to hold it there—for it was bent up at that place, and didn't quite touch ground. If you stood four or five feet away and didn't know it was sawed, you wouldn't ever notice it; and besides, this was the back of the cabin and it warn't likely anybody would go fooling around there.

It was all grass clear to the canoe; so I hadn't left a track. I followed around to see. I stood on the bank and looked out over the river. All safe. So I took the gun and went up a piece into the woods and was hunting around for some birds, when I see a wild pig; hogs soon went wild in them bottoms after they had got away from the prairie farms. I shot this fellow and took him into camp.

I took the axe and smashed in the door. I beat it and hacked it considerable, a-doing it. I fetched the pig in and took him back nearly to the table and hacked into his throat with the axe, and laid him down on the ground to bleed – I say ground, because it *was* ground – hard packed, and no boards. Well, next I took an old sack and put a lot of big rocks in it, – all I could drag – and I started it from the pig and dragged it to the door and through the woods down to the river and dumped it in, and down it sunk, out of sight. You could easy see that something had been dragged over the ground. I did wish Tom Sawyer was there, I know he would take an interest in this kind of business, and throw in the fancy touches. Nobody could spread himself like Tom Sawyer in such a thing as that.

Well, last I pulled out some of my hair, and bloodied the axe good, and stuck it on the back side, and slung the axe in the corner. Then I took up the pig and held him to my breast with my jacket (so he couldn't drip) till I got a good piece below the house and then dumped him into the river. Now I thought of something else. So I went and got the bag of meal and my old saw out of the canoe and fetched them to the house. I took the bag to where it used to stand, and ripped a hole in the bottom of it with the saw, for there warn't no knives and forks in the place – pap done everything with his clasp-knife, about the cooking. Then I carried the sack about a hundred yards across the grass and through the willows east of the house, to a shallow lake that was five miles wide and full of rushes – and ducks too, you might say, in the season. There was a slough or a creek leading out of it on the other side, that went miles away, I don't know where, but it didn't go to the river. The meal sifted out and made a little track all the way to the lake. I dropped pap's whetstone there too, so as to look like it had been done by accident. Then I tied up the rip in the meal sack with a string, so it wouldn't leak no more, and took it and my saw to the canoe again.

It was about dark, now; so I dropped the canoe down the river under some willows that hung over the bank, and waited for the moon to rise.

Mark Twain, Huckleberry Finn, 1884

9 And the evil spirit from the LORD was upon Saul, as he sat in his house with his javelin in his hand: and David played with *his* hand.

10 And Saul sought to smite David even to the wall with the javelin; but he slipped away out of Saul's presence, and he smote the javelin into the wall: and David fled, and escaped that night.

11 Saul also sent messengers unto David's house, to watch him, and to slay him in the morning: and Michal David's wife told him, saying, If thou save not thy life to night, to morrow thou shalt be slain.

12 ¶ So Michal let David down through a window: and he went, and fled, and escaped.

13 And Michal took an image, and laid *it* in the bed, and put a pillow of goats *hair* for his bolster, and covered *it* with a cloth.

14 And when Saul sent messengers to take David, she said, He *is* sick.

15 And Saul sent the messengers *again* to see David, saying, Bring him up to me in the bed, that I may slay him.

16 And when the messengers were come in, behold, *there was* an image in the bed, with a pillow of goats' *hair* for his bolster.

17 And Saul said unto Michal, Why hast thou deceived me so, and sent away mine enemy, that he is escaped? And Michal answered Saul, He said unto me, Let me go; why should I kill thee?

18 ¶ So David fled, and escaped, and came to Samuel to Ramah, and told him all that Saul had done to him. And he and Samuel went and dwelt in Naioth.

19 And it was told Saul, saying, Behold, David *is* at Naioth in Ramah.

20 And Saul sent messengers to take David: and when they saw the company of the prophets prophesying, and Samuel standing *as* appointed over them, the Spirits of God was upon the messengers of Saul, and they also prophesied.

21 And when it was told Saul, he sent other messengers, and they prophesied likewise. And Saul sent messengers again the third time, and they prophesied also.

22 Then went he also to Ramah, and came to a great well that *is* in Sechu: and he asked and said, Where *are* Samuel and David? And *one* said, Behold, *they be* at Naioth in Ramah.

23 And he went thither to Naioth in Ramah: and the Spirit of God was upon him also, and he went on, and prophesied, until he came to Naioth in Ramah.

24 And he stripped off his clothes also, and prophesied before Samuel in like manner, and lay down naked all that day and all that night. Wherefore they say, *Is* Saul also among the prophets?

I Samuel, 19:9–24

FIFTEEN

'Knowledge is more than equivalent
to force'

NO MAGIC

Cœlius Secundus Curion, a zealous Lutheran, having had the boldness to convict of falsehood, in open church, at Casal, a monk who had indulged in the most calumnious insinuations against the great leader of the German Reformation, was immediately arrested by order of the inquisitor of Turin. After having been transferred successively to several prisons, he contrived to escape in a manner so skilful and unexpected, that his enemies accused him of having had recourse to magic. As this was an accusation not less dangerous than that of heresy, Curion hastened to exculpate himself by publishing the details of his enterprise in a short Latin dialogue entitled 'Probus'. The following extracts will satisfy the reader's curiosity:

'In my new prison I had been confined for a week, with huge pieces of wood chained to my feet, where I was favoured with a sudden inspiration from Heaven.

'As soon as the young man who acted as my keeper entered my chamber, I begged and prayed of him to release one of my feet from its encumbrances. It would be sufficient security, I said, that I should still by the other foot be fastened to an enormous log. As he was a humane sort of fellow, he consented, and set one foot free. A day, two days passed, during which I applied myself to work. Taking off my shirt, and also the stocking from the leg which was at liberty, I made them up into a dummy resembling a leg, on which I put a shoe. I was in want of something, however, to give it consistency, and was anxiously looking about in all directions, when I caught sight of a canestick lying under a row of seats. Seizing it joyfully, I inserted it into the sham limb, and concealing the true one under my cloak, waited the result of my stratagem. When my young keeper made his appearance next morning, he asked me how I was. "I should do pretty well," I said, "if you would be good enough to put my fetters on the other leg, so that each may have a rest in turn." He assented; and, without perceiving it, attached the log to the dummy.'

At night, when their loud snores informed him that his gaolers were asleep, Curion threw aside the false leg, resumed his shirt and stocking, and opened noiselessly the prison door, which was fastened by a simple bolt. Afterwards, though not without difficulty, he scaled the wall, and got away without interruption.

All The Year Round, 21 September 1889

It was now the third morning since they had left their father's house, and they still walked on; but they only got deeper and deeper into the wood, and Hansel saw that if help did not come very soon they would die of hunger. As soon as it was noon they saw a beautiful snow-white bird sitting upon a bough, which sang so sweetly that they stood still and listened to it. It soon left off, and spreading its wings flew off; and they followed it until it arrived at a cottage, upon the roof of which it perched; and when they went close up to it they saw that the cottage was made of bread and cakes, and the window panes were of clear sugar.

'We will go in there,' said Hansel, 'and have a glorious feast. I will eat a piece of the roof, and you can eat the window. Will they not be sweet?' So Hansel reached up and broke a piece off the roof, in order to see how it tasted; while Grethel stepped up to the window and began to bite it. Then a sweet voice called out in the room, 'Tip-tap, tip-tap, who raps at my door?' and the children answered, 'The wind, the wind, the child of heaven;' and they went on eating without interruption. Hansel thought the roof tasted very nice, and so he tore off a great piece; while Grethel broke a large round pane out of the window, and sat down quite contentedly. Just then the door opened, and a very old woman, walking upon crutches, came out. Hansel and Grethel were so frightened that they let fall what they had in their hands; but the old woman, nodding her head, said, 'Ah, you dear children, what has brought you here? Come in and stop with me, and no harm shall befall you;' and so saying she took them both by the hand, and led them into her cottage. A good meal of milk and pancakes, with sugar, apples, and nuts, was spread on the table, and in the back room were two nice little beds, covered with white, where Hansel and Grethel laid themselves down, and thought themselves in heaven. The old woman had behaved very kindly to them, but in reality she was a wicked witch who waylaid children, and built the bread-house in order to entice them in; but as soon as they were in her power she killed them, cooked and ate them, and made a great festival of the day. Witches have red eyes, and cannot see very far; but they have a fine sense of smelling, like wild beasts, so that they know when children approach them. When Hansel and Grethel came near the witch's house she laughed wickedly, saying, 'Here come two who shall not escape me.' And early in the morning, before they awoke, she went up to them, and saw how lovingly they lay sleeping, with their chubby red cheeks; and she mumbled to herself,

'That will be a good bite.' Then she took up Hansel with her rough hand, and shut him up in a little cage with a lattice-door; and although he screamed loudly it was of no use. Grethel came next, and, shaking her till she awoke, she said, 'Get up, you lazy thing, and fetch some water to cook something good for your brother, who must remain in that stall and get fat; when he is fat enough I shall eat him.' Grethel began to cry, but it was all useless, for the old witch made her do as she wished. So a nice meal was cooked for Hansel, but Grethel got nothing else but a crab's claw.

Every morning the old witch came to the cage and said, 'Hansel, stretch out your finger that I may feel whether you are getting fat.' But Hansel used to stretch out a bone, and the old woman, having very bad sight, thought it was his finger, and wondered very much that he did not get more fat. When four weeks had passed, and Hansel still kept quite lean, she lost all her patience and would not wait any longer. 'Grethel,' she called out in a passion, 'get some water quickly; be Hansel fat or lean, this morning I will kill and cook him.' Oh, how the poor little sister grieved, as she was forced to fetch the water, and how fast the tears ran down her cheeks! 'Dear good God, help us now!' she exclaimed. 'Had we only been eaten by the wild beasts in the wood then we should have died together.' But the old witch called out, 'Leave off that noise; it will not help you a bit.'

So early in the morning Grethel was forced to go out and fill the kettle, and make a fire. 'First we will bake, however,' said the old woman; 'I have already heated the oven and kneaded the dough;' and so saying she pushed poor Grethel up to the oven, out of which the flames were burning fiercely. 'Creep in,' said the witch, 'and see if it is hot enough, and then we will put in the bread;' but she intended when Grethel got in to shut up the oven and let her bake, so that she might eat her as well as Hansel. Grethel perceived what her thoughts were, and said, 'I do not know how to do it; how shall I get in?' 'You stupid goose,' said she, 'the opening is big enough. See, I could even get in myself!' and she got up and put her head into the oven. Then Grethel gave her a push, so that she fell right in, and then shutting the iron door she bolted it. Oh! how horribly she howled; but Grethel ran away, and left the ungodly witch to burn to ashes.

Now she ran to Hansel, and, opening his door, called out, 'Hansel, we are saved; the old witch is dead!' So he sprang out, like a bird out of his cage when the door is opened; and they were so glad that they fell upon each other's neck, and kissed each other over and over again.

Household Stories Collected by the Brothers Grimm, Newly Translated, 1853

[346]

The chief instigator of this mad plot was Ranulf Flambard, bishop of Durham. Rising from low origins, he had been a sycophant of William Rufus and had so pandered to him with his cunning machinations that the king had raised him up above all the magnates of the realm. He became chief manager of the king's wealth and justice, and through his many acts of cruelty made himself hated and feared by most men. He himself grew wealthy with the riches he raked in from all sides and the enlargement of his estates, and in spite of being almost illiterate was promoted to a bishop's chair not because of any piety, but through secular power. However, since no power is long enduring in this mortal life, after his king's death he was imprisoned by the new king as an incorrigible plunderer of the country. For the many injuries he had inflicted on Henry himself and his subjects, poor as well as rich, and the many ways in which he had often impiously oppressed the suffering, by God's will when the wind of fortune changed he was hurled down from the summit of power and given into the charge of William of Mandeville, to be imprisoned in fetters in the tower of London. Truly, as Ovid says in his poem about Daedalus, 'Often misfortunes stir the wit'; the ingenious bishop plotted to escape from close imprisonment and craftily arranged through friends for his flight. He was resourceful and persuasive, and though cruel and quick-tempered was also generous and affable on many occasions, so that numerous people found him acceptable and likeable. He received every day by the king's command two shillings sterling for food, and with this and the help of his friends he made merry in prison, and every day ordered a fine feast to be set before him and his guards. One day a rope was smuggled to him in a flagon of wine, and plentiful provisions for the feast were purchased by the bishop's largesse. The guards feasted with him and grew merry as they drained copious draughts of Falernian wine. When they were thoroughly drunk and safely snoring, the bishop fastened the rope to a mullion in the middle of a window in the tower and, taking his pastoral staff with him, slid down the rope. However, as he had forgotten to protect his hands with gloves, they were torn to the bone by the roughness of the rope, and as it did not reach quite to the ground the portly ecclesiastic suffered a heavy fall, which almost flattened him and made him groan with pain. His loyal friends and tried followers were waiting at the foot of the tower and, though in great trepidation, had good horses ready for him. Mounting, he fled like the wind, and met on his way trusted companions bringing his treasure. With them he sailed swiftly towards Normandy to find Duke Robert. Flambard's mother, who was a sorceress and had often conversed with the devil, losing an eye through this infamous familiarity, was conveyed across the sea to Normandy in another ship with her son's treasure. Her companions in the boat mocked her with crude gestures for her accursed incantations.

In the course of the voyage priates attacked the ship and plundered all the treasure, so that the old witch was deposited, naked and sorrowing, with the mariners and guards on the Norman shore.

Orderic Vitalis, *Ecclesiastical History*, ed. and trans. Marjorie Chibnall, 1975

TREMBLING FINGERS

Meanwhile Daedalus, hating Crete and his long exile, and longing to see his native land, was shut in by the sea. 'Though he may block escape by land and water,' he said, 'yet the sky is open, and by that way will I go. Though Minos rules over all, he does not rule the air.' So saying, he sets his mind at work upon unknown arts, and changes the laws of nature. For he lays feathers in order, beginning at the smallest, short next to long, so that you would think they had grown upon a slope. Just so the old-fashioned rustic pan-pipes with their unequal reeds rise one above another. Then he fastened the feathers together with twine and wax at the middle and bottom; and, thus arranged, he bent them with a gentle curve, so that they looked like real birds' wings. His son, Icarus, was standing by and, little knowing that he was handling his own peril, with gleeful face would now catch at the feathers which some passing breeze had blown about, now mould the yellow wax with his thumb, and by his sport would hinder his father's wondrous task. When now the finishing touches had been put upon the work, the master workman himself balanced his body on two wings and hung poised on the beaten air. He taught his son also and said: 'I warn you, Icarus, to fly in a middle course, lest, if you go too low, the water may weight your wings; if you go too high, the fire may burn them. Fly between the two. And I bid you not to shape your course by Boötes or Helice or the drawn sword of Orion, but fly where I shall lead.' At the same time he tells him the rules of flight and fits the strange wings on his boy's shoulders. While he works and talks the old man's cheeks are wet with tears, and his fatherly hands tremble. He kissed his son, which he was destined never again to do, and rising on his wings, he flew on ahead, fearing for his companion, just like a bird which has led forth her fledglings from the high nest into the unsubstantial air. He encourages the boy to follow, instructs him in the fatal art of flight, himself flapping his wings and looking back on his son. Now some fisherman spies them, angling for fish with his flexible rod, or a shepherd, leaning upon his crook, or a ploughman, on his plough-handles – spies them and stands stupefied, and believes them to be gods that they could fly through the air. And now Juno's sacred Samos had been passed on the left, and Delos and Paros; Lebinthus was on the right and Calymne, rich in honey, when the boy began to rejoice in his bold flight and, deserting his leader, led by a desire for the open sky, directed his course to a greater height. The scorching rays of the nearer sun softened the fragrant wax which held his wings. The wax melted; his arms were bare as he beat them up and down, but, lacking wings, they took no hold on the air. His lips, calling to the last upon his father's name, were drowned in the dark blue sea, which took its name from him. But the unhappy father, now no longer father, called: 'Icarus, Icarus, where are you? In what place shall I seek you? Icarus,' he called again; and then he spied the wings floating on the deep, and cursed his skill. He buried the body in a tomb, and the land was called from the name of the buried boy.

Ovid, Metamorphoses, trans. Frank Justus Miller, 1951

NEW SECONDHAND CLOTHES

16 April: Away! Away!
The spell of arms and voices: the white arms of roads, their promise of close embraces and the black arms of tall ships that stand against the moon, their tale of distant nations. They are held out to say: We are alone. Come. And the voices say with them: We are your kinsmen. And the air is thick with their company as they call to me, their kinsman, making ready to go, shaking the wings of their exultant and terrible youth.

26 April: Mother is putting my new secondhand clothes in order. She prays now, she says, that I may learn in my own life and away from home and friends what the heart is and what it feels. Amen. So be it. Welcome, O life! I go to encounter for the millionth time the reality of experience and to forge in the smithy of my soul the uncreated conscience of my race.

27 April: Old father, old artificer, stand me now and ever in good stead.

Dublin 1904
Trieste 1914

James Joyce, *A Portrait of the Artist as a Young Man,* 1914

A HUMBUG

On the fourth day, to her great joy, Oz sent for her, and when she entered the Throne Room he said, pleasantly:

'Sit down, my dear; I think I have found the way to get you out of this country.'

'And back to Kansas?' she asked, eagerly.

'Well, I'm not sure about Kansas,' said Oz; 'for I haven't the faintest notion which way it lies. But the first thing to do is to cross the desert, and then it should be easy to find your way home.'

'How can I cross the desert?' she inquired.

'Well, I'll tell you what I think,' said the little man. 'You see, when I came to this country it was in a balloon. You also came through the air, being carried by a cyclone. So I believe the best way to get across the desert will be through the air. Now, it is quite beyond my powers to make a cyclone; but I've been thinking the matter over, and I believe I can make a balloon.'

'How?' asked Dorothy.

'A balloon,' said Oz, 'is made of silk, which is coated with glue to keep the gas in it. I have plenty of silk in the Palace, so it will be no trouble to make the balloon. But in all this country there is no gas to fill the balloon with, to make it float.'

'If it won't float,' remarked Dorothy, 'it will be of no use to us.'

'True,' answered Oz. 'But there is another way to make it float, which is to fill it with hot air. Hot air isn't as good as gas, for if the air should get cold the balloon would come down in the desert, and we should be lost.'

'We!' exclaimed the girl; 'are you going with me?'

'Yes, of course,' replied Oz. 'I am tired of being such a humbug. If I should go out of this Palace my people would soon discover I am not a Wizard, and then they would be vexed with me for having deceived them. So I have to stay shut up in these rooms all day, and it gets tiresome. I'd much rather go back to Kansas with you and be in a circus again.'

'I shall be glad to have your company,' said Dorothy.

'Thank you,' he answered. 'Now, if you will help me sew the silk together, we will begin to work on our balloon.'

So Dorothy took a needle and thread, and as fast as Oz cut the strips of silk into proper shape the girl sewed them neatly together. First there was a strip of light green silk, then a strip of dark green and then a strip of emerald green; for Oz had a fancy to make the balloon in different shades of the colour about them. It took three days to sew all the strips together, but when it was finished they had a big bag of green silk more than twenty feet long.

Then Oz painted it on the inside with a coat of thin glue, to make it air-tight, after which he announced that the balloon was ready.

'But we must have a basket to ride in,' he said. So he sent the soldier with the green whiskers for a big clothes basket, which he fastened with many ropes to the bottom of the balloon.

When it was all ready, Oz sent word to his people that he was going to make a visit to a great brother Wizard who lived in the clouds. The news spread rapidly throughout the city and everyone came to see the wonderful sight.

Oz ordered the balloon carried out in front of the Palace, and the people gazed upon it with much curiosity. The Tin Woodman had chopped a big pile of wood, and now he made a fire of it, and Oz held the bottom of the balloon over the fire so that the hot air that arose from it would be caught in the silken bag. Gradually the balloon swelled out and rose into the air, until finally the basket just touched the ground.

Then Oz got into the basket and said to all the people in a loud voice:

'I am now going away to make a visit. While I am gone the Scarecrow will rule over you. I command you to obey him as you would me.'

The balloon was by this time tugging hard at the rope that held it to the ground, for the air within it was hot, and this made it so much lighter in weight than the air without that it pulled hard to rise into the sky.

'Come, Dorothy!' cried the Wizard; 'hurry up, or the balloon will fly away.'

'I can't find Toto anywhere,' replied Dorothy, who did not wish to leave her little dog behind. Toto had run into the crowd to bark at a kitten, and Dorothy at last found him. She picked him up and ran toward the balloon.

She was within a few steps of it, and Oz was holding out his hands to help her into the basket, when, crack! went the ropes, and the balloon rose into the air without her.

'Come back!' she screamed; 'I want to go, too!'

'I can't come back, my dear,' called Oz from the basket. 'Good-bye!'

L. Frank Baum, *The Wizard of Oz*, 1926

A SNUG KINGDOM

In the Interim, they shewed them the City, the Edifices that reach almost as high as the Clouds, the Market-Places embellished with a thousand Columns; Foutains of pure Water, besides others of Rose-water, and the Liquors that are extracted from the Sugar Canes, which played incessantly in the Squares, which were paved with a Kind of precious Stones, that diffused a Fragrance like that of Cloves or Cinnamon. Candidus asking them to shew them one of their Courts of Justice, and their Parliament-house; they told him they had none, and that no one was ever tried there. He then enquired if they had any Prisons, and was told they had not. What afforded them the greatest Surprise and Pleasure, was their Schools for the Sciences, in which he saw a Gallery of two thousand Paces, full of Instruments for making Experiments in Philosophy.

After having gone over about a thousand Part of the City in the Afternoon, they were re-conducted to the Palace. Candidus seated himself at Table with his Majesty, his Man Cacambo, and a great many Ladies. Never was a better Entertainment seen; his Majesty was a very sensible clever Man; Cacambo interpreted the King's Repartees to Candidus, and though they were translated, they appeared Repartees still. A Thing which gave Candidus a very great Pleasure!

They spent a whole Month in this hospitable Manner: During which, Candidus was always saying to Cacambo, 'I must say it again and again, that the Castle I was born in was nothing like this Country where we are now; but yet Miss Cunigonda is not here, and I don't question but you have left a Sweetheart behind you in Europe. If we stay where we are, we shall be looked upon only like other Folks, when, if we return to our own World only with twelve Sheep loaded with the common Stones of Eldorado, we shall be richer than all the Kings put together; we shall have no Need to be afraid of the Inquisitors, and we may easily recover Miss Cunigonda.'

Cacambo relished this Proposal prodigiously; so fond are we of running about, of being thought Somebody of Condition among one's Countrymen, and of making Orations on what one has seen on one's Travels, that these two really happy Men, could they have thought so, were resolved not to be so long, and accordingly began to take their Leave of his Majesty.

'You are guilty of a very great Weakness,' said his Majesty to them. 'I am not ignorant that my Country is a despicable Place; but providing it be but passable, you had better stay in it; I must indeed confess that I have no Right to detain People of another Nation; 'tis a Degree of Tyranny inconsistent with our Customs and Laws; all Men here are free: You may go when you please; but you ought first to be informed that you cannot leave us without some Difficulty. It is impossible to go against the Current up the rapid River, which runs under the Rocks; your Passage hither was a Kind of a Miracle. The Mountains which surround my Kingdom are a thousand Foot high, and as steep as a Wall; they are at least ten Leagues over, and their Descent is nothing but Precipices. However, since you seem determined to leave us, I'll give Orders immediately to the Constructors of my Machines, to contrive one to transport you, with the greatest Ease. When they have conveyed you to the other side of the Mountains, no one must attend you; because my Subjects have made a Vow never to pass beyond them, and they are too wise to break it. There is nothing else you can ask of me, which shall not be granted.' 'We ask your Majesty,' said Cacambo, very eagerly, 'only a few Sheep loaded with Provisions, together with some of the common Stones and Dirt of your Country.'

At this strange Desire, the King laughed very heartily; 'I cannot,' said he, 'account for the Fondness which you Europeans have for our yellow Dust; but you are welcome to take as much of it as you please, and much good may it do you.'

He gave immediate Orders to his Engineers to construct a Machine to hoist up and transport these two extraordinary Persons out of his Kingdom. About three thousand able Mechanicks set to work; and in a Fortnight's Time, the Machine was compleated, which cost no more than twenty Millions Sterling of their Currency.

Candidus and Cacambo were both placed in the Machine, together with two large red Sheep bridled and saddled for them to ride on, when they were got clear of the Mountains; a hundred Sheep of Burden loaded with Provisions, thirty charged with the greatest Curiosities of the Country, by Way of Present, and fifty loaded with gold, precious Stones, and Diamonds. The King took his Leave of our two Vagabonds, with the greatest Marks of Affection.

It was certainly a very fine Sight to see them depart, and the Manner in which they and the Sheep were slung over the Mountains. The Philosophers took their Leave of them, after having got them safe over; and Candidus now thought of nothing else but of going to present his Sheep to Miss Cunigonda. 'We have now got enough to pay for the Ransom of Cunigonda, if the Governor will but part with her,' says he, 'let's march towards Cayenne, there take Shipping, and then we'll look out for some snug Kingdom to make a Purchase of.'

Candidus: or, The Optimist. By Mr De Voltaire, trans. W. Rider, 1759

RABBITS

'My dear Imlac,' said the prince, 'I will open to thee my whole heart. I have long meditated an escape from the happy valley. I have examined the mountains on every side, but find myself insuperably barred: teach me the way to break my prison; thou shalt be the companion of my flight, the guide of my rambles, the partner of my fortune, and my sole director in the *choice of life*.'

'Sir,' answered the poet, 'your escape will be difficult, and, perhaps, you may soon repent your curiosity. The world, which you figure to yourself smooth and quiet as the lake in the valley, you will find a sea foaming with tempests, and boiling with whirlpools: you will be sometimes overwhelmed by the waves of violence, and sometimes dashed against the rocks of treachery. Amidst wrongs and frauds, competitions and anxieties, you will wish a thousand times for these seats of quiet, and willingly quit hope to be free from fear.'

'Do not seek to deter me from my purpose,' said the prince: 'I am impatient to see what thou hast seen; and, since thou art thyself weary of the valley, it is evident, that thy former state was better than this. Whatever be the consequence of my experiment, I am resolved to judge with my own eyes of the various conditions of men, and then to make deliberately my *choice of life*.'

'I am afraid,' said Imlac, 'you are hindered by stronger restraints than my persuasions; yet, if your determination is fixed, I do not counsel you to despair. Few things are impossible to diligence and skill.'

The prince now dismissed his favourite to rest, but the narrative of wonders and novelties filled his mind with perturbation. He revolved all that he had heard, and prepared innumerable questions for the morning.

Much of his uneasiness was now removed. He had a friend to whom he could impart his thoughts, and whose experience could assist him in his designs. His heart was no longer condemned to swell with silent vexation. He thought that even the *happy valley* might be endured with such a companion, and that, if they could range the world together, he should have nothing further to desire.

In a few days the water was discharged, and the ground dried. The prince and Imlac then walked out together to converse without the notice of the rest. The prince, whose thoughts were always on the wing, as he passed by the gate, said, with a countenance of sorrow, 'Why art thou so strong, and why is man so weak?'

'Man is not weak,' answered his companion; 'knowledge is more than equivalent to force. The master of mechanicks laughs at strength. I can burst the gate, but cannot do it secretly. Some other expedient must be tried.'

As they were walking on the side of the mountain, they observed that the conies, which the rain had driven from their burrows, had taken shelter among the bushes, and formed holes behind them, tending upwards in an oblique line. 'It has been the opinion of antiquity,' said Imlac, 'that human reason borrowed many arts from the instinct of animals; let us, therefore, not think ourselves degraded by learning from the coney. We may escape by piercing the mountain in the same direction. We will begin where the summit hangs over the middle part, and labour upward till we shall issue out beyond the prominence.'

The eyes of the prince, when he heard this proposal, sparkled with joy. The execution was easy, and the success certain.

No time was now lost. They hastened early in the morning to chuse a place proper for their mine. They clambered with great fatigue among crags and brambles, and returned without having discovered any part that favoured their design. The second and the third day were spent in the same manner, and with the same frustration. But, on the fourth, they found a small cavern, concealed by a thicket, where they resolved to make their experiment.

Imlac procured instruments proper to hew stone and remove earth, and they fell to their work on the next day with more eagerness than vigour. They were presently exhausted by their efforts, and sat down to pant upon the grass. The prince, for a moment, appeared to be discouraged. 'Sir,' said his companion, 'practice will enable us to continue our labour for a longer time; mark, however, how far we have advanced, and you will find that our toil will some time have an end. Great works are performed, not by strength, but perseverance: yonder palace was raised by single stones, yet you see its height and spaciousness. He that shall walk with vigour three hours a day will pass in seven years a space equal to the circumference of the globe.'

They returned to their work day after day, and, in a short time, found a fissure in the rock, which enabled them to pass far with very little obstruction. This Rasselas considered as a good omen. 'Do not disturb your mind,' said Imlac, 'with other hopes or fears than reason may suggest: if you are pleased with prognosticks of good, you will be terrified likewise with tokens of evil, and your whole life will be a prey to superstition. Whatever facilitates our work is more than an omen, it is a cause of success. This is one of those pleasing surprises which often happen to active resolution. Many things difficult to design prove easy to performance.'

They had now wrought their way to the middle, and solaced their toil with the approach of liberty, when the prince, coming down to refresh himself with air, found his sister Nekayah standing before the mouth of the cavity. He started and stood confused, afraid to tell his design, and yet hopeless to conceal it. A few moments determined him to repose on her fidelity, and secure her secrecy by a declaration without reserve.

'Do not imagine,' said the princess, 'that I came hither as a spy: I had long observed from my window, that you and Imlac directed your walk every day towards the same point, but I did not suppose you had any better reason for the preference than a cooler shade, or more fragrant bank; nor followed you with any other design than to partake of your conversation. Since then not suspicion but fondness has detected you, let me not lose the advantage of my discovery. I am equally weary of confinement with yourself, and not less desirous of knowing what is done or suffered in the world. Permit me to fly with you from this tasteless tranquillity, which will yet grow more loathsome when you have left me. You may deny me to accompany you, but cannot hinder me from following.'

The prince, who loved Nekayah above his other sisters, had no inclination to refuse her request, and grieved that he had lost an opportunity of shewing his confidence by a voluntary communication. It was therefore agreed that she should leave the valley with them; and that, in the mean time, she should watch, lest any other straggler should, by chance or curiosity, follow them to the mountain.

At length their labour was at an end; they saw light beyond the prominence, and, issuing to the top of the mountain, beheld the Nile, yet a narrow current, wandering beneath them.

Samuel Johnson, *Rasselas*, 1759

ONE PARTICULAR PACKAGE

There is a dry bituminous wood upon the plateau – a species of araucaria, according to our botanist – which is always used by the Indians for torches. Each of us picked up a faggot of this, and we made our way up weed-covered steps to the particular cave which was marked in the drawing. It was, as I had said, empty, save for a great number of enormous bats, which flapped round our heads as we advanced into it. As we had no desire to draw the attention of the Indians to our proceedings, we stumbled along in the dark until we had gone round several curves and penetrated a considerable distance into the cavern. Then, at last, we lit our torches. It was a beautiful dry tunnel, with smooth grey walls covered with native symbols, a curved roof which arched over our heads, and white glistening sand beneath our feet. We hurried eagerly along it until, with a deep groan of bitter disappointment, we were brought to a halt. A sheer wall of rock had appeared before us, with no chink through which a mouse could have slipped. There was no escape for us there.

We stood with bitter hearts staring at this unexpected obstacle. It was not the result of any convulsion, as in the case of the ascending tunnel. The end wall was exactly like the side ones. It was, and had always been, a *cul-de-sac*.

'Never mind, my friends,' said the indomitable Challenger. 'You have still my firm promise of a balloon.'

Summerlee groaned.

'Can we be in the wrong cave?' I suggested.

'No use, young fellah,' said Lord John, with his finger on our chart.

'Seventeen from the right and second from the left. This is the cave sure enough.'

I looked at the mark to which his finger pointed, and I gave a sudden cry of joy.

'I believe I have it! Follow me! Follow me!'

'I hurried back along the way we had come, my torch in my hand. 'Here,' said I, pointing to some matches upon the ground, 'is where we lit up.'

'Exactly.'

'Well, it is marked as a forked cave, and in the darkness we passed the fork before the torches were lit. On the right side as we go out we should find the longer arm.'

It was as I had said. We had not gone thirty yards before a great black opening loomed in the wall. We turned into it to find that we were in a much larger passage than before. Along it we hurried in breathless impatience for many hundreds of yards. Then, suddenly, in the black darkness of the arch in front of us we saw a gleam of dark red light. We stared in amazement. A sheet of steady flame seemed to cross the passage and to bar our way. We hastened towards it. No sound, no heat, no movement came from it, but still the great luminous curtain glowed before us, silvering all the cave and turning the sand to powdered jewels, until as we drew closer it discovered a circular edge.

'The moon, by George!' cried Lord John. 'We are through, boys! We are through!'

It was indeed the full moon which shone straight down the aperture which opened upon the cliffs. It was a small rift, not larger than a window, but it was enough for all our purposes. As we craned our necks through it we could see that the descent was not a very difficult one, and that the level ground was no very great way below us. It was no wonder that from below we had not observed the place, as the cliffs curved overhead and an ascent at the spot would have seemed so impossible as to discourage close inspection. We satisfied ourselves that with the help of our rope we could find our way down, and then returned, rejoicing, to our camp to make our preparations for the next evening.

What we did we had to do quickly and secretly, since even at this last hour the Indians might hold us back. Our stores we would leave behind us, save only our guns and cartridges. But Challenger had some unwieldly stuff which he ardently desired to take with him, and one particular package, of which I may not speak, which gave us more labour than any. Slowly the day passed, but when the darkness fell we were ready for our departure. With much labour we got our things up the steps, and then, looking back, took one last long survey of that strange land, soon I fear to be vulgarised, the prey of hunter and prospector, but to each of us a dreamland of glamour and romance, a land where we had dared much, suffered much, and learned much – *our* land, as we shall ever fondly call it. Along upon our left the neighbouring caves each threw out its ruddy cheery firelight into the gloom. From the slope below us rose the voices of the Indians as they laughed and sang. Beyond was the long sweep of the woods, and in the centre, shimmering vaguely through the gloom, was the great lake, the mother of strange monsters. Even as we looked a high whickering cry, the call of some weird animal, rang clear out of the darkness. It was the very voice of Maple White Land bidding us good-bye. We turned and plunged into the cave which led to home.

Arthur Conan Doyle, *The Lost World*, 1912

FALLING WATER

'That soul above, who suffers the worst pain
Judas Iscariot is,' my Master said,
'His head within, he moves his legs without.
Of the two others, with their heads below,
Brutus is he, that from the black face hangs;
Note how he writhes, and utters not a word;
Cassius the other, who so stalwart shows.
But now the night returns, and it is time
For our departure: we have seen the whole.'

On his command, I clasped him round the neck;
He watched the opportunity of time,
And when the wings were opened wide enough,
He threw himself upon the shaggy ribs,
Descending afterwards from fleece to fleece
Between the thick hide and the frozen crust.
When we had come to that part where the thigh
Begins below the swelling of the haunch,
My leader with exertion and with toil,
Brought round his head to where his feet had been,
And grappled with the hide, as one that climbs,

So that I thought we back to Hell returned.

'Observe now well, for by so strange a stair,'
My guide said, panting like a man fatigued,
'From so great evil, we must needs depart.'
Issued he forth then through a hollow rock,
And placed me on the margin sitting wise,
And then towards me wound his cautious steps.
I raised mine eyes and thought that I should see
Lucifer in the posture I had left,
But I saw, that he upwards held his legs.
Perplexed that I on seeing this became
Let those dull people think, who do not note
What that point is, by which I just had passed.

'Raise thyself,' said my Master, 'on thy feet;
The way is long, and dangerous the road,
And now to the half-tierce the sun returns.'
Not smooth was it, like roads to palaces,
Where now we were, but dungeon primitive
With floor uneven, and with scant of light.
'Before I tear myself from the abyss,
Master,' I said, soon as I stood upright,
'To rescue me from error something speak.
Where is the ice? and how comes this one placed
Thus upside down? and how in such brief space
From eve to morn the sun has made his course?'
Then he to me: 'Thou thinkest still thou art
On that side of the centre, where I clutched
That ill worm's skin, who perforates the globe:
While I descended, on that side thou wast;
But when I turned, thou didst then pass the point
Whither from all sides heavy bodies tend:
And thou beneath the hemisphere hast come
Opposed to that, which the expanse of land
Contains, below whose highest point was slain
The Man whose birth and life were without sin:
Thou hast thy feet upon the little sphere
Forming the under surface of Judäica.
Here it is morning, when 'tis evening there:
And he, who made our ladder with his hide,
Remains still planted, as at first he was.

Down to this region he from heaven fell:
The earth which formerly did here extend,
In fear of him, a veil made of the sea,
And came to our hemisphere: and perchance
Flying from him, the space here vacant left
That, which is seen on this side rising up.'

Underneath Belzebub a place is, far
Distant as ever the arched vault extends,
To sight not sensible, but by the sound
Of a small rivulet which that way falls
Through a rock's passage, which itself has worn
With gentle slope along a winding course.
My guide and I, upon this secret path
Entered, returning to the lightsome world:
And without wish for taking any rest
We mounted upwards, he first, second I,
Until I could discern the objects fair
Borne in the sky, through a round aperture:
Thence we came forth once more to see the stars.

From *The Divine Comedy: Inferno* by Dante Alighieri (1265–1321),
English trans. Frederick Pollock, 1854

ACKNOWLEDGEMENTS

The editor and publishers gratefully acknowledge permission to reprint copyright material as follows:

A & C Black Ltd for an excerpt from *Rendez-vous 127: The Diary of Madame Brusselmans*, by Madame Brusselmans (Ernest Benn); Anvil Books Ltd for an excerpt from *On Another Man's Wound* by Ernie O'Malley (Anvil, 1979); Cambridge University Press for an excerpt from *Imprisonment in Medieval England* by Ralph B. Pugh (Cambridge University Press, 1968); Curtis Brown Ltd on behalf of the Estate of Sir Winston S. Churchill for excerpts from *London to Ladysmith* and *Ian Hamilton's March* by Sir Winston S. Churchill (Mandarin, 1990), copyright © the Estate of Sir Winston S. Churchill; André Deutsch Ltd for an excerpt from *Jaws* by Peter Benchley (Deutsch, 1974); Dover Publications Inc for an excerpt from *Houdini on Magic*, compiled and edited by Walter B. Gibson and Morris N. Young (Dover, 1953); Dutton Signet, a division of Penguin Books USA Inc, for an excerpt from *Dry Guillotine: Fifteen Years among the Living Dead*, by René Belbenoit (Jonathan Cape, 1938), copyright © 1938 by E. P. Dutton, renewed 1966 by E. P. Dutton; Educational Company of Ireland for an excerpt from *The Life Story of Eamon De Valera* by Seán O Faoláin (Talbot Press, 1933); HarperCollins Publishers Ltd for excerpts from *Papillon* by Henri Charrière, translated by Patrick O'Brian (Hart-Davis, 1970); HarperCollins Publishers Ltd (Canada) for an excerpt from *Woman on Trial* by Lawrencia Bembenek, copyright © 1994 by Lawrencia Bembenek; A M Heath & Company Ltd for an excerpt from *Catch-22* by Joseph Heller (Jonathan Cape, 1962), copyright © Joseph Heller; David Higham Associates Ltd for an excerpt from *The Spy Who came in from the Cold* by John le Carré (Gollancz, 1963); Houghton Mifflin Company for an excerpt from *Story of a Secret State* by Jan Karski (Houghton Mifflin, 1944), copyright © 1944, © renewed 1972 by Jan Karski; Alfred A. Knopf Inc. for an excerpt from *The Big Sleep* by Raymond Chandler (Pocket Books, 1950), copyright © 1939 by Raymond Chandler and renewed 1967 by Helga Greene, Executrix of the Estate of Raymond Chandler; Needham & Grant (Solicitors) on behalf of Simon Romilly and the Estate of Giles S. B. Romilly for an excerpt from *The Privileged Nightmare* by Giles Romilly and Michael Alexander (Weidenfeld & Nicolson, 1954); Oxford University Press for an excerpt from *The Ecclesiastical History of Orderic Vitalis*, Volume 5, edited and translated by Marjorie Chibnall (Clarendon Press, 1975); Peter Fraser & Dunlop Group Ltd for an excerpt from *And There Was Light* by Jacques Lusseyran, translated by Elizabeth Cameron (Floris/Heinemann, 1964); Laurence Pollinger Ltd for excerpts from *They Fought Back: The Story of the Jewish Resistance in Nazi Europe*, edited and translated

INDEX